Classroom Management

Classroom Management

CREATING A SUCCESSFUL K-12 LEARNING COMMUNITY

Seventh Edition

Paul R. Burden
Kansas State University

JB JOSSEY-BASS™
A Wiley Brand

This seventh edition first published 2020

Edition History
John Wiley & Sons, Inc. (1e, 1995; 2e, 2003; 3e, 2006; 4e, 2010; 5e, 2013; 6e, 2017)

Published by John Wiley & Sons, Inc., Hoboken, New Jersey.

Published simultaneously in Canada.

For general information on our other products and services or for technical support, please contact our Customer Care Department within the United States at (800) 762–2974, outside the United States at (317) 572–3993 or fax (317) 572–4002.

Wiley publishes in a variety of print and electronic formats and by print-on-demand. Some material included with standard print versions of this book may not be included in e-books or in print-on-demand. If this book refers to media such as a CD or DVD that is not included in the version you purchased, you may download this material at http://booksupport.wiley.com. For more information about Wiley products, visit www.wiley.com.

Library of Congress Cataloging-in-Publication Data
Names: Burden, Paul R., author.
Title: Classroom management : creating a successful K-12 learning community
    / Paul R. Burden, Kansas State University.
Description: Seventh edition. | Hoboken : Wiley, [2020] | Includes
    bibliographical references and index.
Identifiers: LCCN 2019057869 (print) | LCCN 2019057870 (ebook) | ISBN
    9781119639985 (paperback) | ISBN 9781119639930 (adobe pdf) | ISBN
    9781119639824 (epub)
Subjects: LCSH: Classroom management—United States. | School
    discipline—United States.
Classification: LCC LB3013 .B873 2020 (print) | LCC LB3013 (ebook) | DDC
    371.102/4—dc23
LC record available at https://lccn.loc.gov/2019057869
LC ebook record available at https://lccn.loc.gov/2019057870

Cover Design: Wiley
Cover Image: © Arthur Tilley/Getty Images

Printed in the United States of America
SKY10036856_101422

Contents

About the Author

Paul R. Burden is an emeritus professor in the College of Education at Kansas State University, Manhattan, where he was an assistant dean. Prior to his administrative service in the college, he supervised student teachers and taught courses on teaching methods, classroom management and discipline, foundations of education, and instructional leadership. Previously, he was a middle-level science teacher in Buffalo, New York, and later earned his doctoral degree at the Ohio State University. He received the College of Education's Outstanding Undergraduate Teaching Award at Kansas State University and the Distinguished Service award from the National Staff Development Council.

His publications include *Methods for Effective Teaching* (Pearson, 2019), *Countdown to the First Day of School* (2006, National Education Association), *Powerful Classroom Management Strategies: Motivating Students to Learn* (2000, Corwin Press), as well as *Establishing Career Ladders in Teaching* (1987, Charles C Thomas Publishers). He served for 11 years as the editor of the *Journal of Staff Development*, a quarterly journal sponsored by the National Staff Development Council, and has presented over 70 papers at regional and national educational conferences in addition to authoring numerous articles and book chapters.

Married with three children, Dr. Burden enjoys traveling with his family and working on genealogy. He can be contacted at burden@ksu.edu.

Preface

This seventh edition of *Classroom Management* has been written to guide teachers and prospective teachers as they create a positive classroom community, with the involvement and cooperation of the students. Fundamental principles of classroom management and discipline are presented, along with ways to involve students in the creation of their learning environment.

The book is a scholarly synthesis of the research base on classroom management and discipline yet is written and formatted in a way that is easy to read, understand, and apply. It carries a practical, realistic view of teaching with the content being organized in a logical, sequential order. The content is applicable for teachers at all levels—elementary, middle level, and high school.

Intended Audience

This book is especially appropriate as the sole book for an undergraduate course on classroom management and discipline or for a seminar on student teaching or professional development. It may be used as a supplementary book to another textbook in educational psychology or teaching methods courses. Additionally, the book may be used in graduate classes, seminars, and staff development programs for in-service teachers. The book may be seen as a handbook for future reference due to its comprehensive coverage of the issues and its use of lists, tables, and figures for recommended practice. The information provides a foundation for decision making.

New to This Edition

A number of significant changes were made in this new edition, including the following:

- Major additions to Chapter 6 on Communication Skills for Teaching

- Major restructuring and updating of Chapter 7 on Knowing and Connecting with Your Students

- New sections in several chapters:

  - Components of Classroom Management (Chapter 1)

  - Designing Classrooms for Students with Diverse Backgrounds (Chapter 3)

  - Relationships in Urban Settings (Chapter 5)

  - Characteristics of Verbal Communication (Chapter 6)

  - Nonverbal Teacher Behaviors (Chapter 6)

  - Student Diversity (Chapter 7)

  - Adverse Conditions and Student Achievement (Chapter 7)

  - Teaching Students Who Are Different from You (Chapter 7)

  - Reports on Bullying (Chapter 9)

- New and expanded content in existing chapter sections:

  - Student and Teacher Perceptions of Classroom Management (Chapter 1)

  - Building Caring Relationships (Chapter 1)

  - Building Positive Teacher–Student Relationships (Chapter 5)

  - Changes and updates in many other chapter sections

- Added 17 "Voices From the Classroom" features, coming to a total of over 50 in the book. This feature includes teacher quotes, many of them from urban districts, with a balance of elementary, middle, and high school teachers

- Updated the "What Would You Decide?" features with content to engage the reader in classroom-related scenarios about the chapter content

- Updated 32 references to new editions

- Added 118 new references to add depth, breadth, and research-based documentation to the content

- Removed 68 old or outdated references

Special Features

Classroom Management: Creating a Successful K–12 Learning Community has several important features that make it both instructor and reader friendly.

- **Standards Tables**. The InTASC Model Core Teaching Standards can be found on the pages after the preface.

- **Objectives**. Each chapter begins with a list of objectives to identify expected reader outcomes.

- **Chapter Outline**. Each chapter begins with an outline of headings and subheadings to serve as an advance organizer for the chapter content.

- **Voices From the Classroom**. Several of these features are included in each chapter to provide descriptions by real elementary, middle school, and high school teachers about ways they deal with particular topics addressed in the chapter. These teachers come from all parts of the country and all different community sizes. There are over 50 "Voices From the Classroom" features, evenly balanced among elementary and middle/high school levels, including many from urban districts.

- **Classroom Case Studies**. Each chapter includes a case study describing a situation that a teacher might encounter. Two or three questions following each case study require the reader to reflect on and apply chapter concepts.

- **What Would You Decide?** Several of these features are placed in each chapter to engage the reader in the content. Each one includes several sentences describing a classroom situation concerning an issue in the chapter, followed by a few questions asking the reader to make decisions about the application of the concepts.

- **Major Concepts**. At the end of each chapter, a list of major concepts serves as a summary of the significant chapter ideas.

- **Discussion/Reflective Questions**. Questions at the end of each chapter promote discussion and reflection in a classroom or seminar in which a number of people are considering the chapter's content.

- *Suggested Activities*. Supplemental activities are suggested at the end of each chapter to enable the reader to investigate and apply issues addressed in the chapter.

- *Further Reading*. An annotated list of recommended readings at the end of each chapter suggests readings for further enrichment.

- *References*. All citations made in the book are included in a reference section at the end of the book to show the source of the research base.

Relating This Book to Standards

Content in this book relates to the professional standards of many agencies. Standards are used to guide the development of new teachers, help in-service teachers improve their performance, and assess both teacher preparation and teacher performance. Many teacher education programs are designed around the Interstate Teacher Assessment and Support Consortium (InTASC) standards. Many states require a passing score on the Principles of Learning and Teaching test (a Praxis Subjects Assessment test) before granting a teaching license. The Praxis Classroom Performance Assessments (which are consistent with Danielson's Framework for Teaching domains) are used to assess and improve the teaching of in-service teachers. A brief description of the standards is provided here, and a table of the InTASC Standards follow the preface.

InTASC Standards

In 1987, the Interstate New Teacher Assessment and Support Consortium (INTASC) was formed as a consortium of state education agencies and national educational organizations dedicated to the reform of the preparation, licensing, and ongoing professional development of teachers. With the 2011 updating of the standards, the Interstate Teacher Assessment and Support Consortium removed the word *new* from its name and made the *n* in its acronym lowercase (now it is InTASC).

InTASC's primary constituency is state education agencies responsible for teacher licensing, program approval, and professional development. Its work is guided by one basic premise: *An effective teacher must be able to integrate content knowledge with the specific strengths and needs of students to ensure that all students learn and perform at high levels.* More information can be found on the Council of Chief State School Officers (CSSCO) website.

Praxis Tests

The Praxis tests have been developed and disseminated by the Educational Testing Service (ETS) for assessing skills and knowledge of each stage of a beginning teacher's career, from entry into teacher education to actual classroom performance. More information about the Praxis tests can be found at the Educational Testing Service (ETS) website. There are several types of Praxis tests:

- **Praxis Core Academic Skills for Educators (CORE)**. These academic skills tests are designed to be taken early in a student's college career to measure reading, writing, and mathematics skills.

- **Praxis Subject Assessments**. There are several Praxis Subject Assessments available, and they measure a teacher candidate's knowledge of the subjects he or she will teach, as well as general and subject-specific pedagogical skills and knowledge. One of these assessments is the

Principles of Learning and Teaching (PLT) test, which many states require teachers to pass for their licensure.

- **Praxis Classroom Performance Assessments**. These assessments are conducted for beginning teachers in classroom settings. Assessment of teaching practice is through direct observation of classroom practice, a review of documentation prepared by the teacher, and semistructured interviews. The framework for knowledge and skills for these assessments consists of 19 assessment criteria organized within four categories: planning and preparation, the classroom environment, instruction, and professional responsibilities. Charlotte Danielson's (2007) *Enhancing Professional Practice: A Framework for Teaching* is based on the categories of the Praxis Classroom Performance Assessments.

This *Classroom Management* book is not intended to address the preprofessional skills of reading, writing, and mathematics in the Praxis CORE. However, it is designed to address the Praxis Subject Assessments test on Principles of Learning and Teaching and the Praxis classroom performance criteria areas, based on Danielson's *Framework for Teaching*.

Acknowledgments

Many people provided support and guidance as I prepared this book. A very special acknowledgment goes to my wife, Jennie, who was understanding during the times I was hidden away at my office working on the revised manuscript. The editors and staff at Wiley facilitated the preparation and refinement of this book. A number of classroom teachers provided descriptions of their professional practice, which are included in the Voices From the Classroom features in each chapter. The experiences that these teachers share help illustrate the issues and bring life to the content.

Standards

InTASC Model Core Teaching Standards

The following table indicates how the 2011 Interstate Teacher Assessment and Support Consortium (InTASC) model core teaching standards are addressed in this book.

THE LEARNER AND LEARNING	Chapter Coverage
1. **Learner Development** Understands how learners grow and develop, recognizing that patterns of learning and development vary individually within and across the cognitive, linguistic, social, emotional, and physical areas, and designs and implements developmentally appropriate and challenging learning experiences.	1, 2, 3, 7, 8
2. **Learning Differences** Uses understanding of individual differences and diverse cultures and communities to ensure inclusive learning environments that enable each learner to meet high standards.	7
3. **Learning Environments** Works with others to create environments that support individual and collaborative learning, and that encourage positive social interaction, active engagement in learning, and self-motivation.	5, 6, 7, 8, 9, 10

CONTENT KNOWLEDGE	
4. **Content Knowledge** Understands the central concepts, tools of inquiry, and structures of the discipline(s) he or she teaches and creates learning experiences that make these aspects of the discipline accessible and meaningful for learners to ensure mastery of the content.	3, 8
5. **Application of Content** Understands how to connect concepts and use differing perspectives to engage learners in critical thinking, creativity, and collaborative problem solving related to authentic local and global issues.	3, 8

INSTRUCTIONAL PRACTICE	
6. **Assessment** Understands and uses multiple methods of assessment to engage learners in their own growth, to monitor learner progress, and to guide the teacher's and learner's decision-making.	3, 7, 8
7. **Planning for Instruction** Plans instruction that supports every student in meeting rigorous learning goals by drawing upon knowledge of content areas, curriculum, cross-disciplinary skills, and pedagogy, as well as knowledge of learners and the community context.	3, 5, 7, 8
8. **Instructional Strategies** Understands and uses a variety of instructional strategies to encourage learners to develop deep understanding of content areas and their connections, and to build skills to apply knowledge in meaningful ways.	2, 8

(continued)

PROFESSIONAL RESPONSIBILITY

9. **Professional Learning and Ethical Practice**   1, 2
   Engages in ongoing professional learning and uses evidence to continually evaluate his/her practice, particularly the effects of his/her choices and actions on others (learners, families, other professionals, and the community), and adapts practice to meet the needs of each learner.

10. **Leadership and Collaboration**   11
   Seeks appropriate leadership roles and opportunities to take responsibility for student learning, to collaborate with learners, families, colleagues, other school professionals, and community members to ensure learner growth, and to advance the profession.

Understanding Management and Discipline in the Classroom

CHAPTER OUTLINE

CHAPTER OBJECTIVES

This chapter provides information that will help you:

- Describe the components of effective classroom management.
- Describe perceptions of classroom management by students and teachers.
- Develop and nurture caring relationships in the classroom.
- Describe the role of classroom management in creating a learning community.
- Identify the areas of responsibility in classroom management and discipline.
- Determine what constitutes order in the classroom.
- Describe the types and causes of student misbehavior.
- Apply principles for working with students to create a positive learning environment.

What do award-winning teachers do that make them so popular and successful? Do they jazz up the curriculum in some way? Do they use especially creative instructional approaches? Do they warm up to the students as if they were their own children? Do they add some magic or sparkle to the classroom experience? The answer is probably a little of each of those things. But it likely goes deeper than that.

Successful teachers are often very effective managers of the classroom environment. They create a positive learning community where students are actively involved in their own learning and in the management of the classroom. They organize the physical environment, manage student behavior, create a respectful environment, facilitate instruction, promote safety and wellness, and interact with others when needed. All of these actions relate to classroom management. The main objective is to create a positive learning community and then to take steps to maintain that positive environment by guiding and correcting student behavior.

What Is Classroom Management?

Classroom management involves teacher actions to create a learning environment that encourages positive social interaction, active engagement in learning, and self-motivation. Many issues come to mind regarding classroom management, such as rules and procedures, guiding and reinforcing appropriate behavior, addressing inappropriate behavior, motivating and engaging students in instruction, teacher–student relationships, and a host of related topics.

To explore some of these issues, this section examines components of classroom management, student and teacher perceptions of classroom management, caring relationships, and areas of responsibility in classroom management.

Components of Classroom Management

Classroom management and discipline has been examined by many educational researchers over the years, and insights can be gained about best practice from these research reports. After examining several comprehensive reviews of the classroom management research, Harlacher (2015) reported that five components of classroom management are identified in the research literature reviews. These components of effective classroom management are further supported by the work of a number of education researchers and theorists, many of whom have championed similar management strategies in the past. The five components are:

1. **Creating and teaching expectations and rules.** Teachers provide explicit, direct instruction about their expectations for students. In doing so, teachers examine the need for expectations and rules, gather input from students, and select the rules. Then they actively teach the rules to students in a very clear and direct manner. (See Chapter 4 for guidelines for selecting and teaching rules.)

2. **Establishing procedures and structure.** Procedures are certain processes that students carry out to successfully complete classroom events. Teachers determine what the procedures will be and then explicitly teach the procedures for certain activities, such as lining up, entering the classroom, turning in homework, transitioning to a new activity, asking to use the restroom, and other events that regularly occur in a classroom. In addition, the physical layout of the classroom contributes to effective structure as a means to facilitate learning and curtail problem behavior. (See Chapter 3 for classroom design and Chapter 4 for procedures.)

3. **Reinforcing expectations.** Once teachers have established expectations, rules, and procedures for their classrooms, they can strengthen their adherence to them by using reinforcement strategies. Student behavior is rewarded when they meet classroom expectations. One type of reinforcement is behavior-specific praise of a particular student (e.g., "Thank you for coming into the classroom quietly and keeping your hands to yourself."). Rewards also can be used that relate to intrinsic and extrinsic motivation. Also, group contingencies can be used to reward all students simultaneously if the whole class reaches a certain goal or meets certain criterion. (See Chapter 5 for reinforcers.)

4. **Actively engaging students**. Teachers ensure that students are engaged in tasks and are academically successful. When students actively respond to tasks or content, they have less time to engage in problem behavior. Teachers also have a chance to correct any errors in the student's thinking and can provide another opportunity to perform the skill correctly. Thus, teachers can increase the level of active engagement by giving students many opportunities to respond. Active student engagement refers to instruction during which students are required to produce a response, such as answering questions verbally or writing responses. (See Chapter 8 for lesson delivery and engagement.)

5. **Managing misbehavior.** Teachers use a continuum of strategies to decrease unwanted, problematic behavior. Effective management involves reinforcing appropriate behavior and using instances of misbehavior as opportunities to teach more appropriate conduct. This continuum of strategies first involves reinforcement of desired behaviors and giving students the opportunity to correct their behaviors when undesired behavior emerges. Next, some type of consequence is delivered to inappropriate behavior. Finally, punishment is administered in which the student receives some type of undesirable outcome. (See Chapter 9 for a three-step plan to address misbehavior.)

Student and Teacher Perceptions of Classroom Management

Many aspects of classroom management have been researched, and it has been reported that the perceptions of students and teachers differ about the types of misbehavior, the nature of classroom management, the role of the teacher, and other factors. We will now examine some of those issues.

Student Perceptions

After reviewing the research on student perceptions of misbehavior and classroom management, Montuoro and Lewis (2015) reported a number of insights and conclusions about how students perceive classroom management. The studies suggest that many students (particularly adolescents) have an inherently different perspective of misbehavior and classroom management compared to their teachers.

1. **Student perceptions of misbehavior.** Students in the studies perceived all forms of misbehavior as being low severity as compared to the teachers' perceptions, which attributed far higher ratings of severity to all forms of student misbehavior.

   In a variety of studies, students reported that misbehavior occurred because the lesson was boring, the student wanted attention, the student didn't believe he or she couldn't do the lesson and so didn't try, had a disconnect in the teacher-student relationship, or had a negative attitude toward school. Some studies indicate that students may be more likely to misbehave when they perceive the misbehavior to be socially acceptable.

2. **Student perceptions of classroom management.** International studies indicate that students are generally dissatisfied with the authoritative approaches that teachers use in dealing with misbehavior. Many of the students indicate that teachers used coercive and autocratic classroom management practices, which made the students feel powerless, oppressed, and disconnected from the learning process.

   A number of studies also indicated that students respond more responsibly to teachers who address misbehavior through discussion and who allow students to find a solution to their misbehavior on their own. Students were willing to take more responsibility for their behavior when the teacher's decision-making process was transparent and democratic. Students with emotional and behavioral difficulties prefer good-quality relationships with their teachers and inclusive classroom management techniques that are underpinned with clarity and fairness.

Teacher Perceptions

The research on teachers' perceptions of classroom management indicates that teachers take a different point of view on classroom management from students (Bullough & Richardson, 2015).

1. **Student characteristics and behavior.** Some studies indicate that teachers want to be pupil-centered to support relationships and to use versatile teaching methods. But the teachers say they cannot teach that way due to student misbehavior, established work conditions requiring teachers to manage large numbers of students, and lack of administrative support. Many teachers believe that different types of students require different approaches to instruction and classroom management.

2. **Teacher personal characteristics.** Teachers tend to be optimistic and hopeful people. This academic optimism is positively correlated with a humanistic management style, student-centered teaching, and an optimistic disposition.

3. **Teacher concerns and perspectives.** Teachers generally define classroom management in terms of rules and behavior management. They hold the belief that the development of student self-control and cooperative skills is critical for school success.

   Teachers indicated that most behavior problems are minor infractions or repeated disruptions rather than major infringements or violent behavior. Teachers generally tend to locate the source of student misbehavior in factors external or internal to the student and outside of the classroom and school.

Practical Implications

The studies of student perceptions of misbehavior and classroom management suggest that students are in search of authentic relationships with their teachers. To bridge the differing perceptions of misbehavior and classroom management, teachers may need to form closer, person-centered relationships with their students. Stronger reliance on relationship-based approaches to classroom management may be more effective. In fact, student reports suggest that teacher coercion has no effect on student misbehavior and that there is no evidence to suggest that tougher school discipline policies and practices deter student misbehavior. Teachers should aim to be supportive and put a priority on developing positive teacher–student relationships and use classroom management techniques that are underpinned with clarity and fairness.

Building Caring Relationships

Schwab and Elias (2015) reviewed the research on social and emotional learning (SEL) and its relationship to classroom management. Their findings confirm the importance of developing caring relationships in the classroom to support instruction and classroom management.

SEL skills include identifying feelings in oneself and others, managing one's emotions, being responsible for one's actions and commitments, showing empathy and respect, communicating effectively, and many other skills for functioning adaptively in classrooms and society. In classrooms, it is helpful to teach SEL skills, build caring relationships, set firm and fair boundaries, and share responsibility with students.

Developing a supportive community in the classroom helps to impart a sense of each student's belonging, alleviate students' social anxieties and frustrations, motivate students to comply with teacher requests, and act prosocially with peers. Consequently, the level of respect for teachers and students increases, negative and aggressive social behaviors are reduced, and students are more likely to comply with the rules. Because of this, building caring relationships is an important step in the promotion of responsible behavior and the prevention of misbehavior (Davis, Summers, & Miller, 2012).

VOICES FROM THE CLASSROOM   What Is Classroom Management?

Claudia Arguello Coca, fifth-grade teacher, Las Cruces, New Mexico

When I began teaching 10 years ago, I thought classroom management meant being the one in control of my class. Control was the number one objective for me, because then I knew that my students would be safe, would receive the best instruction, and would be well behaved (thus making me look good). But every approach I used to control the environment did not work.

Gradually, I learned that children will follow you if you encourage them and take the time to catch them doing great things. Some flexibility is also needed. Students want to impress you and will do anything you ask if you manage your class by focusing on hardworking students and positive behaviors. These lessons have allowed me to have great success with my students.

I always keep in mind that my students are little children. I make a huge effort to treat them like little children, offer them kind words, create a safe and predictable environment, and provide a fun learning stage. I have one rule for myself—always talk to my students as if their parents were standing behind them. When I work with my students, I want us to work together cooperatively. This only happens when my students feel safe and comfortable with me.

There are several aspects when building caring relationships: teacher–student, student–student, the classroom community, and communication.

Teacher–Student Relationships

When students sense that a teacher cares for them, they see the teacher as more credible and as an ally rather than a foe. This increases motivation to follow directions, to adhere to rules, and to put effort into classroom activities and academics. Students want to be respected and supported in the classroom, and they respond best in school environments that they perceive as caring and respectful.

Teachers can express caring and respect for students in many ways, such as by being welcoming, being sensitive to students' concerns, treating students fairly, acting like real people (not just as teachers), sharing responsibility, minimizing the use of external controls, including everyone, searching for students' strengths, communicating effectively, and showing an interest in their students' lives and pursuits.

Student–Student Relationships and the Classroom Community

Peer-to-peer relationships and the classroom community are just as important as teacher–student relationships in maintaining a functional classroom and promoting social and emotional growth. The classroom as a community must teach caring as the bedrock of other values (honesty, courage, responsibility) that are essential for intellectual accomplishment and ethical living. Even though peer relationships do not always directly involve the teacher, teachers can establish the conditions for social interaction and can intervene to help these relationships develop positively in at least three ways.

First, teachers can begin the year by helping students feel comfortable with each other in the classroom. This can be done with group-building activities, creative opportunities to share personal experiences and interests, and establishing an ethic of teamwork and helping one another with everyday tasks and problems. Second, teachers can involve students in deciding what rules should govern social interaction in the classroom and can facilitate conversations on specific ways to show respect and caring. Third, teachers can discuss, teach, and model a problem-solving approach to understanding and resolving personal dilemmas and mistakes to set a personal, supportive tone in the classroom.

Communication

Developing effective communication is a challenging but vital step in building caring, functional relationships throughout the classroom. Effective teacher-to-student communication includes, but is not limited to, clarity and checking for understanding; active listening; facilitative and open-ended questioning; and saying far more positive, complimentary, and encouraging words to all students than negative words.

Classrooms dedicated to integrating SEL and classroom management should have frequent classroom meetings to discuss problems and continually build the classroom community. Such classrooms encourage supportive relationships throughout the classroom, set a positive tone for the classroom, help students process any emotions that they bring to school, and give students an opportunity for input into the daily running of the classroom (Charney, 2002). Providing structured opportunities to share feelings, experiences, and interests makes the classroom the personal and supportive environment that underlies caring relationships.

Areas of Responsibility

An effective classroom manager handles the following seven areas of responsibility in classroom management and discipline:

1. Select a philosophical model of classroom management and discipline.
2. Organize the physical environment.

3. Manage student behavior.

4. Create a respectful, supportive learning environment.

5. Manage and facilitate instruction.

6. Promote classroom safety and wellness.

7. Interact with colleagues, families, and others to achieve classroom management objectives.

Select a philosophical model of classroom management and discipline

A number of educators have proposed certain models of classroom management and discipline, such as teaching with love and logic, cooperative discipline, discipline with dignity, and assertive discipline (see Chapter 2). These models reflect various philosophical views of student development, teaching and learning, and classroom management. Viewing these proposed models on a continuum, they range from low teacher control to high teacher control.

These theoretical models are useful to teachers because they offer a basis for analyzing, understanding, and managing student and teacher behavior. With an understanding of these varied theoretical approaches, you can assess your position on these issues and then select a philosophical model that is consistent with your beliefs. The techniques you use to manage student behavior should be consistent with your beliefs about how students learn and develop.

Organize the physical environment

The way the desks, tables, and other classroom materials are arranged affects instruction and influences order in the classroom (see Chapter 3). To create an effective learning environment, you will need to organize several aspects of the physical space. First, you will need to arrange the floor space by the placement of student desks, the teacher's desk, bookcases, filing cabinets, tables, and activity centers. Second, you will need to decide how to store a number of materials, including textbooks and resource books, frequently used instructional materials, teacher supplies and instructional materials, equipment, and infrequently used materials. Finally, you will need to decide how to use bulletin boards and wall space. Decisions in all of these areas will determine how you will organize the physical environment for teaching and learning.

Manage student behavior

Guidelines are needed to promote order in the classroom and to provide a conducive learning environment (see Chapter 4). Rules and procedures support teaching and learning and provide students with clear expectations and well-defined norms. This, in turn, helps create a safe, secure atmosphere for learning.

Rules are general codes of conduct that are intended to guide individual student behavior in an attempt to promote positive interaction and avoid disruptive behavior. *Procedures* are approved ways to achieve specific tasks in the classroom, such as handing in completed work or sharpening a pencil.

When misbehavior occurs, teachers need to respond in an effort to get the student back on task and to maintain order in the classroom. A three-step response plan is discussed in Chapter 9, including providing assistance to get the student back on task as the first step, followed by the use of mild responses such as nonverbal and verbal signals, and then ending with moderate responses such as withdrawing privileges or changing the seat assignment. Special approaches are often needed to deal with challenging students (see Chapter 10).

To establish order, you must teach, demonstrate, establish, and enforce classroom procedures and routines at the start of the year. Successful classroom managers hover over activities at the beginning of the year and usher them along until students have learned the work system.

Create a respectful, supportive learning environment

There are at least four facets to creating a favorable learning environment, but it is vital for a positive learning community.

1. Teachers can take a number of actions to establish a cooperative, responsible classroom by developing positive teacher–student relationships, promoting students' self-esteem, and building group cohesiveness (see Chapter 5). These actions will help create an environment where students feel valued and comfortable, thus setting the stage for teaching and learning.

2. Teachers can focus student attention on appropriate classroom behavior by helping students assume responsibility for their behavior, by maintaining student attention and involvement, and by reinforcing desired behaviors (see Chapter 5).

3. A comprehensive plan can be developed to motivate students to learn, involving decisions about instructional tasks, feedback and evaluation, and academic and behavioral expectations (see Chapter 8).

4. Teachers can be most effective in creating a respectful, supportive learning environment when they have an understanding of the diverse learners in their classroom and of students with special needs (see Chapter 7).

Manage and facilitate instruction

Certain factors in a lesson have a bearing on classroom order, and teachers need to take these factors into account when planning lessons (see Chapter 8). These include decisions about the degree of structure of the lesson, the type of instructional groups to use, and the means of holding the students academically accountable.

There are also certain actions that teachers often take at the beginning, middle, and end of a lesson that affect the order of the classroom. These include actions such as taking attendance, giving directions, distributing materials, handling transitions, summarizing the lesson, and preparing to leave. Collectively, these instructional management skills help manage and facilitate instruction while also influencing classroom order.

Promote classroom safety and wellness

Students need to feel physically and emotionally safe before they can give their full attention to the instructional tasks. Strategies used to manage student behavior, create a supportive classroom, and manage and facilitate instruction all contribute to classroom safety and wellness. In addition, teachers sometimes need to take actions to solve problems and conflicts that threaten classroom order and the learning environment. For that reason, it is helpful to have a set of tools such as dealing with conflict resolution and anger management to solve problems (see Chapter 10).

Students who are considered difficult or challenging may threaten the sense of safety and wellness in the classroom. Their actions may cause other students to take guarded or even confrontational actions in response to difficult students. For that reason, teachers need to be prepared to deal with challenging students in constructive ways (Chapter 10).

Interact with colleagues, families, and others to achieve classroom management objectives

Working with families is another means to help maintain order in the classroom (see Chapter 11). When families and teachers communicate and get along together, students are more likely to receive the needed guidance and support and will probably have more self-control in the classroom. In addition, teachers may need to consult and interact with colleagues and others when difficulties occur with classroom management and student behavior.

A Community of Learners

Over the years, the way teachers have gone about instruction has changed as more is known about the nature of teaching and learning. In recent years, more emphasis has been placed on building learning communities in the classroom because students appear to be most successful in that environment. Problems with student misbehavior are also minimized in an environment where students are actively involved in their classroom and their instruction.

A learning community is designed to help all students feel safe, respected, and valued in order to learn new skills. Anxiety, discomfort, and fear are incompatible with the learning process and make teaching and learning difficult. Successful classrooms are those in which students feel supported in their learning, are willing to take risks, are challenged to become fully human with one another, and are open to new possibilities.

With the increasing diversity in classrooms, the need to create supportive classroom communities becomes even more important. Teachers must identify community building as a high priority if we are to have classrooms that include diverse students—classrooms that make all students feel welcome, appreciated, and valued members of the classroom environment. Actions can be taken to build an inclusive classroom learning community.

In *Because We Can Change the World*, Sapon-Shevin (2010) identified five characteristics of learning communities:

1. **Security.** A safe, secure community allows for growth and exploration. A nurturing community is a place where it is safe to be yourself, take risks, ask for help and support, and delight in accomplishments. A safe environment helps protect students from distractions and disruptions that interfere with the learning process.

2. **Open communication.** In a cohesive environment, there is open communication. All forms of communication—oral, written, artistic, and nonverbal—are encouraged. In safe, accepting

environments, students' individual differences and needs are openly acknowledged. Students share freely what is happening, what they need, and what they are worried about. Since all students have the right to feel safe, for example, open communication should be encouraged to address the concerns.

3. **Mutual liking.** In supportive classroom communities, students are encouraged to know and like their classmates. Opportunities are provided for students to interact with one another, and students are given many chances and strategies for learning to see and say nice things about classmates.

4. **Shared goals or objectives.** Cooperative communities are those in which students work together to reach a shared goal or objective. This can be achieved with whole-class projects where students work toward a goal while interacting and supporting one another.

5. **Connectedness and trust.** In learning communities, students feel a part of the whole. They know that they are needed, valued members of the group. They know that others are depending on them to put forth their best effort. Trust and connectedness mean sharing the good things as well as any concerns or problems.

To create a learning community, teachers often plan lessons designed to involve students in cooperative learning activities. These activities seem to have three elements that are critical to their success: face-to-face interactions, a feeling of positive interdependence, and a feeling of individual accountability. In addition, it is necessary to teach students social skills and to process group functioning for these learning activities to be successful. Teachers also need to arrange the physical environment for instruction, guide and correct behavior, and create a supportive classroom. All of these responsibilities for creating a learning community relate to classroom management. In *Widening the Circle*, Sapon-Shevin (2007) describes ways to build inclusive classroom communities.

Understanding Misbehavior

Even with an effective management system in place, students may lose interest in the lesson and get off task. You must be prepared to respond with appropriate strategies to restore order. To provide a context for your decision making in this area, you should first understand order in the classroom, misbehavior in context, the types and causes of misbehavior, and the degree of severity that is exhibited.

It is important first to recognize that the best way to deal with discipline problems is to avoid them in the first place. You should develop challenging, interesting, and exciting lessons and treat students with dignity and respect. If misbehavior then occurs, you can consider the guidelines and principles presented in Chapter 9 for dealing with inappropriate behavior.

Order in the Classroom

A learning community needs to have order for students to be successful. *Order* means that students are following the actions necessary for a particular classroom event to be successful; students are focused on the instructional tasks and are not misbehaving. Establishing and maintaining order is an important part of classroom management.

It is useful to distinguish the difference between off-task behavior and misbehavior. *Off-task behavior* includes student actions that are not focused on the instructional activities yet would not be considered to be disruptive or be defined as misbehavior. Off-task behavior includes daydreaming, writing notes or doodling, or not paying attention.

Misbehavior includes behavior that interferes with your teaching, interferes with the rights of others to learn, is psychologically or physically unsafe, or destroys property (Levin & Nolan, 2014). Classroom order is threatened by misbehavior. *Discipline* is the act of responding to misbehaving students in an effort to restore order.

There are four important issues concerning order:

1. **A minimal level of order is necessary for instruction to occur.** Order can be established for instruction by actions such as selecting rules and procedures, encouraging and reinforcing appropriate behavior, reacting to misbehavior, and managing instructional tasks. With many students off task, instruction cannot occur.

2. **Student involvement in learning tasks is affected by order in the classroom.** An effective classroom manager places emphasis on managing the group rather than managing individual students. When there is order in the classroom, then individual students can become engaged in the instructional tasks.

3. **Student cooperation is necessary to establish order.** Order in classrooms is achieved *with* students and depends on their willingness to be part of the sequence of events. Students in a learning community want to cooperate because they see the benefits for them.

4. **Expectations for order are affected by a number of classroom variables.** Teacher expectations for order may vary, depending on factors such as the type of instructional activities, the maturity level of the students, the time of day, the time in the lesson, and the particular students involved. For example, a teacher might not enforce a certain rule at the end of a class period when students are gathering their books and materials in the same way as when a discussion is under way in the middle of the class period.

Misbehavior in Context

Students who are off task are not performing the planned instructional activity. They may be pausing to think about an issue, daydreaming, or doing other things that are nondisruptive but prohibit them from being engaged in the instructional activities. Students who are off task need to be addressed differently than students who are purposely misbehaving and interfering with the academic activities. In such cases, you may need to intervene to stop the misbehavior.

Recognize that your decisions about interventions are complex judgments about the act, the student, and the circumstances at a particular moment in classroom time. Some student actions are clearly misbehavior and require teacher intervention. In many cases, however, the situation is not quite so simple. The key to understanding misbehavior is to view what students do in the context of the classroom structure. Not every infraction of a rule is necessarily misbehavior. For instance, inattention in the last few minutes of a class session will often be tolerated because the lesson is coming to an end. However, you would most likely intervene when inattention is evident earlier in the class.

Misbehavior, then, needs to be seen as "action in context" and requires interpretation based on what the teacher knows about the likely configuration of events. You need to make reliable judgments about the probable consequences of students' actions in different situations. Consistency in your response does not mean that you need to behave in the same way every time, but rather, that your judgments are reliable and consistent.

Types of Misbehavior

Misbehavior includes behavior that interferes with your teaching, interferes with the rights of others to learn, is psychologically or physically unsafe, or destroys property. This misbehavior may show up in the classroom in a number of ways, as indicated in the following categories:

- **Needless talk.** Student talks during instructional time about topics unrelated to the lesson or talks when should be silent.

- **Inappropriate talk.** Student bad-mouths others; swears; uses vulgar or derogatory speech, gestures, or writing.

- **Annoying others.** Student teases, calls names, or bothers others.

- **Moving around the room.** Student moves around the room without permission or goes to areas where not permitted.

- **Noncompliance.** Student does not do what is requested, breaks rules, argues, makes excuses, delays, does the opposite of what is asked.

- **Disruption.** Student talks or laughs inappropriately, hums or makes noises, gets into things, causes "accidents."

- **Aggressive actions.** Student shows hostility toward others, pushes or fights, verbally abuses, is cruel to others, damages property, steals others' property, bullying, and harassment.

- **Defiance of authority or disrespectful behavior.** Student talks back to the teacher, is hostile to comply with the teacher's requests.

VOICES FROM THE CLASSROOM   Hidden Causes of Misbehavior

Kurt Graber, high school science teacher, Dallas, Texas

Some of our students have challenging and even turbulent lives. It can be both emotionally and physiologically difficult for them to achieve a state of readiness to learn when they arrive in our classrooms. We may see the negative classroom behaviors, but we sometimes do not see the causes of their misbehavior. When we are able to identify the cause of the misbehavior, we are sometimes more able to help them.

For example, Johnny was provoking a fight with nearly everyone in class one morning. We didn't know until later that, once again, Johnny had been slapped around in the school parking lot by his stepfather. In class, we only saw his fighting and didn't realize he was in pain and distress.

Sharona came to class nearly every day with a wide array of new and highly fashionable cosmetics—lip gloss, foundation, makeup, eyeliner, and even some lotion for the boys. She had it all. Her show-and-tell in the opening minutes of each day led to some disruption. We later learned that she hails from a small Latin American country and that she is somewhat insecure about herself. She used the cosmetics as a way to gain approval from her peers. For our science fair, I fortunately was able to guide her to do a project about making lipstick, and this earned her quite a bit of admiration and popularity in a constructive way.

Causes of Misbehavior

One way to understand classroom control is to determine why students misbehave. In some cases, the reasons are complex and personal and perhaps beyond your comprehension or control. However, a number of causes of misbehavior can be addressed directly by the teacher.

1. **Health factors.** Student behavior problems may be related to health factors. Lack of sleep, an allergy, illness, or an inadequate diet may greatly affect the student's ability to complete assignments or interact with others. For some children, sugar has an effect on their behavior and may result in hyperactivity. Physical impairments such as a vision or hearing loss, paralysis, or a severe physiological disorder may also contribute to behavior problems.

2. **Neurological conditions.** Some students may have a mental disorder that affects their behavior in some way. For example, attention-deficit/hyperactivity disorder (ADHD) is a mental disorder in which the area of the brain that controls motor activity doesn't work as it should. This is among the most common childhood mental disorders and affects 9% of American children age 13–18 years, according to the National Institute of Mental Health (2017). However, ADHD affected three times as many males (13.0%) as females (4.2%). Such students may be inattentive (are easily distracted, don't follow directions well, shift from one unfinished task to another, and seem not to be listening), hyperactive (are talkative or fidgety), and impulsive (don't wait their turn, blurt out answers, and engage in dangerous activities without considering the consequences).

3. **Medication or drugs.** Medication or drugs, whether legal or illegal, may also be a factor. Over-the-counter medicine for nasal congestion, for example, may cause a student to be less alert than usual. Alcohol or drug abuse also may contribute to unusual behavior at school.

4. **Influences from the home or society.** Conditions in the student's home may be related to behavior problems. Student behavior problems may be associated with a lack of adequate clothing or housing, parental supervision and types of discipline, home routines, or significant events of trauma such as divorce or the death of a friend or relative. Factors in the community or in society also may contribute to student behavior problems. There has been considerable concern and debate over the effects of television and social media on the beliefs and conduct of children. Violence on television is seen by some to influence students to be more aggressive.

5. **The physical environment.** The physical arrangement of the classroom, temperature, noise, and lighting may affect student behavior. Student crowding may also be involved. These factors may contribute to a student's lack of commitment to a lesson and may lead to inattention and misbehavior.

6. **Poor behavior decisions by students.** The classroom is a complex environment for students as well as for teachers. Students are confronted with challenges, temptations, and circumstances that will cause them to make decisions about their own behavior. Their own personalities and habits come into play here. Given all of these factors, students will sometimes make poor decisions that lead to misbehavior.

7. **Other students in the classroom.** Some misbehavior results from students being provoked by other students in the classroom. A student may be drawn into an incident of misbehavior when another student does something inappropriate. In addition, peer pressure from other students may cause individual students to misbehave in ways they would not consider by themselves.

8. **Teacher factors when managing the class.** Teachers sometimes needlessly create disciplinary problems by the way they manage and conduct their classes. Inappropriate teacher behaviors include being overly negative, maintaining an authoritarian climate, overreacting to situations, using mass punishment for all students, blaming students, lacking a clear instructional goal,

repeating or reviewing already learned material, pausing too long during instruction, dealing with one student at length, and lacking recognition of student ability levels. Although few teachers can avoid all of these behaviors all of the time, effective teachers recognize the potentially damaging effects of classroom order and discipline. Being aware of these characteristics is the first step to avoiding them. It is useful to periodically reflect on your own teaching behavior to determine if you are taking actions that are contributing to inattention or misbehavior.

9. **Teacher factors concerning instruction.** Teachers make many decisions about the content and delivery of instruction. Students may lose interest in a lesson if the teacher presents uninteresting lessons, does not plan meaningful activities or engage students in the lessons, is ineffective in instructional delivery, or does not deliberately plan to incorporate motivational elements into the instruction. When students lose interest in a lesson, they are more likely to get off task and misbehave. The proper level of challenge and support is also needed. If the content and expectations are too high, the student may give up in frustration. If it is too easy, the student may become bored.

Degrees of Severity

Misbehavior ranges from mildly to severely disruptive behavior. Severely disruptive behavior and crime in schools may involve violence, vandalism, coercion, robbery, theft, and drug use. These behaviors typically occur outside the classroom in places such as the lunchroom, corridors, or outside the building. Moderate levels of misbehavior involve tardiness, cutting class, talking, calling out answers in class, mild forms of verbal and physical aggression, inattentiveness, and failure to bring supplies and books. Most misbehavior is comparatively mild and is related to attention, crowd control, and getting work accomplished in the classroom.

When selecting an appropriate response to misbehavior, it is important that you take into account the degree of severity of the misbehavior. You can evaluate severity by factors such as appropriateness, magnitude, intent, and extent to which a behavior differs from what is expected in a particular setting. The degree of your response should match the degree of severity of the misbehavior. Teachers often ignore certain minor misbehaviors because their intervention may be more disruptive than the misbehavior.

■ **CLASSROOM CASE STUDY**   Analyzing a Teacher's Classroom Management

Jasmine Nichols is an experienced third-grade teacher in an urban school district. Misbehavior is rare in her classroom because she creates a secure environment that fosters mutual respect. Ms. Nichols and her students generate the classroom rules and their consequences during the first class session of the school year. Each student is asked to sign a copy of the rules and consequences, verifying his or her commitment to them and assuming responsibility for his or her own behavior. The rules and expectations are then posted in the classroom.

Ms. Nichols also gives thought to the classroom arrangement to eliminate distractions for her students. Students' desks are located at a reasonable distance from pencil sharpeners, trash cans, and other such distractions. Infrequently used items are out of the way in a nearby supply closet. Ms. Nichols often moves around the room and monitors her students to be sure they are on task.

At the start of the year, Ms. Nichols plans for activities to help students get to know each other. She becomes aware of the students' interests and needs and takes that information into consideration when planning lessons. She also uses a variety of instructional approaches and always tries to promote active student involvement. She takes steps to monitor student conduct and reinforce appropriate behavior consistent with academic goals. When any student gets off task or misbehaves, however, Ms. Nichols responds promptly with actions that are part of her predetermined discipline plan. Furthermore, she communicates with families regularly about academic and behavioral issues.

Focus Questions

1. Identify the *classroom management* variables that Ms. Nichols addresses to promote and maintain appropriate behavior.

2. Identify the *instructional* variables that Ms. Nichols addresses to promote and academic achievement.

3. What steps did she take to develop a positive classroom community and to promote a caring classroom?

Principles for Working with Students and Preventing Misbehavior

Problem behaviors have a variety of causes, and evidence suggests that some factors are within the school and classroom environment. To promote classrooms that are conducive to learning and to help prevent problem behaviors, teachers must address certain contextual factors within the classroom. The *Handbook of Classroom Management* (Emmer & Sabornie, 2015) reviews research, practice, and contemporary issues and provides considerable guidance for classroom practice. Here are some basic principles for working with students in a manner that establishes a positive, productive classroom in which students learn and have a satisfying educational experience:

1. **Maintain focus on your major task in teaching.** Your major task is to help students be successful in achieving educational objectives, to promote student learning, and to help students develop the knowledge and skills to be successful in your classroom and beyond.

2. **Understand your students' needs and how to meet them.** Know your students' likes and dislikes, what motivates them, their needs and desires, and what influences their lives. Use that information to create an appropriate learning environment.

3. **Understand and respect ethnic or cultural differences.** Teachers are more prepared to facilitate learning and guide behavior when they understand the ethnic or cultural background of their students.

4. **Know what causes misbehavior and how to deal with those causes.** Take steps to reduce or remove the causes of misbehavior.

5. **Provide clear rules and procedures to guide student conduct.** Rules and procedures need to be clearly identified and taught so students understand the behavioral expectations.

6. **Have a specific plan for responding to misbehavior with a hierarchy of interventions.** Have a specific set of strategies to stop the misbehavior, keep students positively on track, and preserve good relations.

7. **Reduce the use of punitive methods of control.** Coercive or punitive environments may promote antisocial behavior. Other techniques that involve the students in creating a positive learning environment are more desirable.

8. **Take actions to establish a cooperative, responsible classroom.** Use techniques to maintain attention and involvement, reinforce desired behaviors, promote student accountability and responsibility, and create a positive learning community.

9. **Involve students meaningfully in making decisions.** Decisions can involve things such as the selection of classroom rules and procedures, instructional activities and assessments, and curriculum materials. Student involvement generates commitment to the learning process and to the classroom environment.

10. **Teach critical social skills and self-regulation.** Many students lack the social skills necessary to relate positively to peers and to do well academically. Teachers who help students develop these social skills help promote learning and successful classroom discipline.

11. **Involve parents and guardians to a reasonable degree.** Communicate with the parents regularly about what you are doing in the classroom and about the progress of their children. Make it clear that you want and need their support.

MAJOR CONCEPTS

1. Classroom management involves teacher actions to create a learning environment that encourages positive social interaction, active engagement in learning, and self-motivation.

2. There are five components of classroom management: creating and teaching expectations and rules, establishing procedures and structure, reinforcing expectations, actively engaging students, and managing misbehavior.

3. Students and teachers have different perceptions about classroom management. Implications for teachers include the need to put effort into creating positive relationships with students, developing reasonable rules and procedures, and recognizing the relationship between classroom management and instruction.

4. Caring relationships in the classroom help support instruction and classroom management. Developing a supportive community in the classroom helps to impart a sense of each student's belonging, alleviate students' social anxieties and frustrations, motivate students to comply with teacher requests, and act prosocially with peers.

5. There are several areas of responsibility in classroom management and discipline.

6. A learning community is designed to help all students feel safe, respected, and valued in order to learn new skills. Characteristics of a learning community include security, open communication, mutual liking, shared goals or objectives, and connectedness and trust.

7. Order means that students are following the actions necessary for a particular classroom event to be successful; students are focused on the instructional tasks and are not misbehaving.

8. Misbehavior includes behaviors that interfere with the act of teaching, interfere with the rights of others to learn, are psychologically or physically unsafe, or destroy property.

9. Off-task behavior includes student actions that are not focused on the instructional activities yet are not considered disruptive or defined as misbehavior.

10. Misbehavior ranges from mildly to severely disruptive behavior.

DISCUSSION/REFLECTIVE QUESTIONS

1. Select one component of classroom management and describe (or give an example) how that would show up in a classroom.

2. Recall your schooling experiences and describe examples where your teacher created caring relationships in the classroom. What did the teacher do to create the caring relationships between the teacher and student, and between students? Also recall negative examples.

3. Of the seven areas of responsibility in classroom management, which are the three most important from your perspective? Why?

4. Give some examples of off-task behaviors and misbehaviors. Clarify the difference.

5. Why is it important to know the cause of the student's misbehavior?

6. What are some benefits of involving students in making decisions about issues such as the selection of rules and procedures, instructional activities and assessments, and curriculum materials? What are the disadvantages?

SUGGESTED ACTIVITIES

1. Select a unit that you might teach. Then describe how you will actively engage students (i.e., one of the five components of classroom management) when teaching the unit.

2. Make a plan of specific activities and other actions that you could take at the start of the school year to help your students feel comfortable with each other in the classroom (e.g., group-building activities, opportunities to share personal experiences and interests, and promoting teamwork).

3. One aspect of a learning community is having shared goals or objectives. Think of a unit you might teach and identify five ways that you could build shared goals into your plans.

4. Talk to several teachers to see what they consider to be mild, moderate, and severe misbehavior. Ask how they respond to the misbehavior at each level. Ask if they have a systematic plan to address misbehavior.

FURTHER READING

Charney, R. S. (2002). *Teaching children to care: Classroom management for ethical and academic growth*, K–8 (Rev. ed.). Turners Falls, MA: Center for Responsive Schools.

Provides substantial ideas for building a learning community, making the community work, using teachers' voices to promote and maintain community, and addressing difficult classroom behaviors.

Lundy, K. G., & Swartz, L. (2011). *Creating caring classrooms: How to encourage students to communicate, create, and be compassionate of others*. Markham, Ontario, Canada: Pembroke Publishers. (Distributed in the U.S. by Stenhouse Publishers.)

Describes ways to build community, communication, collaboration, and compassion in the classroom.

Responsive Classroom (2018b). *Teaching self-discipline: The responsive classroom guide to helping students dream, behave, and achieve in elementary school*. Turners Falls, MA: Center for Responsive Schools.

Provides very useful guidance for creating a safe and predictable learning environment, investing students in the rules, responding to misbehavior, solving behavior problems, and managing challenging situations.

Responsive Classroom (2019). *Seeing the good in students: A guide to classroom discipline in middle school*. Turners Falls, MA: Center for Responsive Schools.

Provides guidance information and techniques for building a foundation for learning, working with the rules, responding to misbehavior, solving ongoing problem behavior, and managing stressful situations.

Sapon-Shevin, M. (2010). *Because we can change the world: A practical guide to building cooperative, inclusive classroom communities* (2nd ed.). Thousand Oaks, CA: Corwin Press.

Discusses techniques to develop a cohesive classroom community in pre-K through middle-school classrooms. Emphasizes creating a caring, supportive classroom.

chapter 2

© Susie Fitzhugh/The Image Works

Models of Discipline

CHAPTER OUTLINE

The Degree of Control

Low Teacher Control Approaches

    Congruent Communication: Haim Ginott

    Discipline as Self-Control: Thomas Gordon

    Teaching with Love and Logic: Jim Fay and David Funk

    Inner Discipline: Barbara Coloroso

    From Discipline to Community: Alfie Kohn

Medium Teacher Control Approaches

    Logical Consequences: Rudolf Dreikurs

    Cooperative Discipline: Linda Albert

    Positive Discipline: Jane Nelsen, Lynn Lott, and Stephen Glenn

    Noncoercive Discipline: William Glasser

    Discipline with Dignity: Richard Curwin, Allen Mendler, and Brian Mendler

    Win–Win Discipline: Spencer Kagan

High Teacher Control Approaches

    Behavior Modification: B. F. Skinner

    Assertive Discipline: Lee and Marlene Canter

CHAPTER OBJECTIVES

This chapter provides information that will help you:

- Identify the features of low-, medium-, and high-control approaches to classroom management and discipline.

- Identify the characteristics of the specific discipline models proposed by educators who are representative of the low-, medium-, and high-control approaches.

- Describe steps to be taken to clarify your own classroom management philosophy and management plan.

Let's say that you want to take your dog out for a walk. You have one of those leashes on which you push a button to control how long or short the cord is on the leash. Would you use a short leash so the dog is by your side, or would you use a longer leash to allow your dog some freedom to walk around and explore? What reasons would you have for using a short or long leash? You see, you determine the degree of freedom the dog has.

In the classroom, you also determine the degree of freedom for your students as a means of creating a successful learning environment. How much freedom or control do you want to establish for your students? What are your purposes for insisting on this degree of control?

As a starting point, it is useful to see how other educators have dealt with this issue of freedom and control in the classroom. Some educators endorse many freedoms for students with limited controls, while other educators endorse stronger controls with limited freedoms. By seeing how other educators view the issue of control and order, you will gain a philosophical perspective about the range of possibilities for decisions that you might make. As you proceed through this book, you can see how the various ideas fit into the continuum of low to high control and then decide on the strategies that you are most comfortable with. No single model is advocated or represented in this book.

This chapter provides a brief orientation to various discipline models, ranging from low to high teacher control. It is not intended to provide extensive information about each model to the point where you would be skilled enough to enact that model. For that purpose, more extensive summaries of these models are available from other sources (e.g., Charles & Cole, 2019; Edwards, 2012; Manning & Bucher, 2013; Wolfgang, 2009). Of course, the original sources mentioned in this chapter for the respective models provide even a fuller description.

The Degree of Control

When deciding how to handle classroom management and discipline, you probably will take into account your views of child development, your educational philosophies, and other factors. These views can be categorized in various ways, but perhaps the most useful organizer is by the degree of control that you exert on the students and the classroom. A continuum showing a range of low to high teacher control can be used to illustrate the various educational views, and the various discipline models can be placed on the continuum. This continuum is based on the organizer that Wolfgang (2009) used when examining models of discipline.

A *model of discipline* is a set of cohesive approaches to deal with establishing, maintaining, and restoring order in the classroom that represent a certain philosophical perspective on a continuum of low to high teacher control. Table 2.1 provides a summary of the characteristics of various discipline models, ranging from low to high teacher control. Table 2.2 identifies representative authors for each of the three discipline models.

Your approach to freedom and control may fall into one particular part of the continuum, but this does not mean that you will follow this approach in every situation. You may branch out and use other strategies as the situation warrants. Now, let's look at the models at each point on the continuum.

▓ TABLE 2.1   Characteristics of Various Discipline Models

Descriptors	The Guiding Model	The Interacting Model	The Intervening Model
Degree of teacher control	Low	Medium	High
Degree of student control	High	Medium	Low
Degree of concern for the students' thoughts, feelings, and preferences	High	Medium	Low
Theoretical basis	Humanistic and psychoanalytic thought	Developmental and social psychology	Behaviorism
View of children	• Children develop primarily from inner forces. • Decision-making enables personal growth. • Students are masters of their destiny.	• Children develop from both internal and external forces.	• Children develop primarily from external forces and conditions. • Children are molded and shaped by influences from their environment.
Main processes used	• Develop caring, self-directed students. • Build teacher–student relationships.	• Confront and contract with students when solving problems. • Counsel students.	• Establish the rules, and deliver the rewards and punishments.
Approaches used by teachers	• Structure the environment to facilitate students' control over their own behavior. • Help students see the problem and guide them into an appropriate decision to solve the problem. • Be an empathic listener. • Allow students to express their feelings.	• Interact with children to clarify and establish boundaries. • Enforce the boundaries. • Formulate mutually acceptable solutions to problems.	• Control the environment. • Select and use appropriate reinforcers and punishments.

■ TABLE 2.2   Proponents of Various Discipline Models

The Guiding Model	The Interacting Model	The Intervening Model
Low-Control Approaches	Medium-Control Approaches	High-Control Approaches
Congruent Communication *Haim Ginott* • Use sane messages. • Invite student cooperation. • Express helpfulness and acceptance.	**Logical Consequences** *Rudolf Dreikurs* • Teach in a democratic manner. • Identify and confront students' mistaken goals. • Use logical consequences.	**Behavior Modification** *B. F. Skinner* • Identify desired behaviors. • Shape behavior through reinforcement. • Use behavior modification systematically.
Discipline as Self-Control (Teacher Effectiveness Training) *Thomas Gordon* • Identify problem ownership. • Maximize communication. • Use the power of influence.	**Cooperative Discipline** *Linda Albert* • Establish a sense of belonging. • Build student self-esteem. • Promote cooperative relationships.	**Assertive Discipline** *Lee and Marlene Canter* • Recognize classroom rights. • Teach desired behavior. • Establish consequences.
Teaching with Love and Logic *Jim Fay and David Funk* • Share control with students. • Maintain student self-concepts. • Balance consequences with empathy.	**Positive Classroom Discipline** *Jane Nelsen, Lynn Lott, and H. Stephen Glenn* • Use classroom meetings. • Exhibit caring attitudes and behaviors. • Use management skills.	**Positive Discipline** *Fredric Jones* • Structure classrooms. • Set limits and promote cooperation. • Have backup systems.
Inner Discipline *Barbara Coloroso* • Enable students to solve problems. • Provide support and structure. • Treat students with dignity and respect.	**Noncoercive Discipline** *(Reality Therapy and Control Theory)* *William Glasser* • Provide quality education. • Help students make good decisions. • Provide support and encouragement.	**Discipline Without Stress** *Marvin Marshall* • Promote responsibility rather than obedience. • Guide and monitor behavior. • Teach the social development and management system.
From Discipline to Community *Alfie Kohn* • Provide an engaging curriculum. • Develop a caring community. • Allow students to make choices.	**Discipline with Dignity** *Richard Curwin, Allen Mendler, and Brian Mendler* • Create a three-dimensional plan. • Establish a social contract. • Teach students to make responsible choices.	
	Win–Win Discipline *Spencer Kagan* • Work with students to solve problems. • Focus on short- and long-term solutions. • Help students make responsible choices.	

Low Teacher Control Approaches

Low-control approaches are based on the philosophical belief that students have primary responsibility for controlling their own behavior and that they have the capability to make these decisions. Children are seen to have an inner potential, and opportunities to make decisions enable personal growth. The child's thoughts, feelings, ideas, and preferences are taken into account when dealing with instruction, classroom management, and discipline.

The teacher has the responsibility for structuring the classroom environment to facilitate the students' control over their own behavior. When determining classroom rules, for example, teachers guide the discussion and help students recognize appropriate behavior and select related rules and consequences. When misbehavior occurs, the teacher helps students see the problem and guides students in making an appropriate decision to resolve the problem. With these nondirective teacher actions, low teacher control approaches fall into the guiding model of discipline.

With this philosophical belief, students have a high degree of autonomy while the teacher exerts a low degree of control. This does not mean that the classroom is a chaotic place for learning. There are standards that the students will help develop, and the teacher is ultimately responsible for enforcing the standards to enable learning to take place in an orderly environment.

Low-control educators might use several types of nondirective approaches to create a supportive learning environment and to guide behavior. To illustrate these nondirective, low teacher control approaches, the discipline models from five representative authors are discussed in the following sections.

Congruent Communication: Haim Ginott

Haim Ginott (1922–1973) was a professor of psychology at New York University and at Adelphi University. Among educators, he is most known for his books that address relationships between adults and children. *Between Parent and Child* (2003) and *Between Parent and Teenager* (1988) offered ideas on how to communicate effectively with children. Ginott focused on how adults can build the self-concepts of children, especially emphasizing that adults should avoid attacks on the child's character and instead focus on the situation or actions. Later, Ginott carried these principles to educators in *Teacher and Child* (1972), proposing that teachers maintain a secure, humanitarian, and productive classroom through the use of congruent communication and appropriate use of praise.

Congruent communication is a harmonious and authentic way of talking in which teacher messages to students match the students' feelings about the situations and about themselves. In this way, teachers can avoid insulting and intimidating their students and instead express an attitude of helpfulness and acceptance while showing increased sensitivity to their needs and desires.

There are several ways that teachers can express congruent communication, all directed at protecting or building students' self-esteem:

- **Deliver sane messages.** Sane messages address situations rather than the students' characters. They acknowledge and accept student feelings. Too often, teachers may use language that blames, orders, admonishes, accuses, ridicules, belittles, or threatens children. This language does not promote children's self-esteem. Instead, Ginott proposes that teachers use language that focuses on the situation and the facts, not threatening that child's self-esteem.

- **Express anger appropriately.** Ginott points out that students can irritate and annoy teachers, making them angry. Anger is a genuine feeling, and teachers should express their anger in reasonable and appropriate ways that do not jeopardize the self-esteem of their students. An effective way is simply to say, "It makes me angry when . . . ," or, "I am appalled when . . . ." In this way, the students hear what is upsetting the teacher without hearing put-down statements such as "You are so irresponsible when you . . . ."

- **Invite cooperation.** Provide opportunities for students to experience independence, thus accepting their capabilities. Give students a choice in matters that affect life in the classroom, including things such as seating arrangements and certain classroom procedures. Avoid long, drawn-out directions, and instead give a brief statement and allow students to decide what their specific course of action should be. By inviting cooperation, you begin to break down students' dependency on yourself.

- **Accept and acknowledge student feelings.** When a problem occurs, listen to students and accept the feelings they are expressing as real. Serve as a sounding board to help students clarify their feelings and let them know that such feelings are common.

- **Avoid labeling the student.** Ginott maintains there is no place for statements such as "You are so irresponsible, unreliable," or "You are such a disgrace to this class, this school, your family." When students hear these statements, they begin to believe them, and then they may start to develop a negative self-image. Avoid labeling, while striving to be helpful and encouraging.

- **Use direction as a means of correction.** Instead of criticizing students when a problem occurs, Ginott proposes that teachers describe the situation to the students and offer guidance about what they should be doing. For example, when a student spills some supplies on the floor, offer some suggestions about ways to do the cleanup rather than criticize the student.

- **Avoid harmful questions.** Ginott points out that an enlightened teacher avoids asking questions and making comments that are likely to incite resentment and invite resistance. For example, don't ask, "Why" questions such as "Why can't you be good for a change?" and "Why do you forget everything I tell you?" Instead, point out that there is a problem and invite the student to discuss ways to solve the problem.

- **Accept students' comments.** Students may ask questions or make statements that seem unrelated to the topic under discussion. Show respect and give the student credit for the question or comment because it may be important to the student in some way.

- **Do not use sarcasm.** While you may use sarcasm as a way to be witty, it may sound clever only to yourself and not to the students receiving the comments. Students may end up with hurt feelings and damaged self-esteem.

- **Avoid hurried help.** When a problem arises, listen to the problem, rephrase it, clarify it, give the students credit for formulating it, and then ask, "What options are open to you?" In this way, you provide students with an opportunity to acquire competence in problem solving and confidence in themselves. Hurried responses to problems are less likely to achieve these purposes.

- **Be brief when dealing with minor mishaps.** Long, logical explanations are not needed when there is a lost paper, a broken pencil, or a forgotten assignment. Brief statements should be solution oriented.

■ WHAT WOULD YOU DECIDE?   Applying Ginott's Low Teacher Control

In your class, you have students working in small groups on a project. Then one of the students begins to talk in an angry way to another group member, stands up, and tosses some papers aside.

1. How would you communicate with that student using Ginott's principles of congruent communication (e.g., to

express sane messages, express anger appropriately, and invite cooperation)?

2. How might you invite the student to discuss ways to solve the problem?

Discipline as Self-Control: Thomas Gordon

Thomas Gordon, a clinical psychologist, is known for his pioneering method of teaching communication skills and conflict resolution to teachers, parents, youth, and business leaders. In education, he is most known for T.E.T.: *Teacher Effectiveness Training* (2003) and *Discipline That Works: Promoting Self-Discipline in Children* (1991). Gordon maintains that effective discipline cannot be achieved through rewards and punishments, but rather, through techniques to promote students' own self-control. He proposed approaches to help students make positive decisions, become more self-reliant, and control their own behavior. To help students make positive decisions, however, teachers must give up their controlling power.

Teachers guide and influence students and also take actions to create an environment where students can make decisions about their behavior. Several principles incorporate the essence of Gordon's concepts.

1. **Identify who owns the problem.** Gordon used a device called a behavior window to determine who owns the problem. The student's behavior may cause a problem for the teacher or for the student, or there may be no problem. The person feeling the negative consequences of the behavior is said to own the problem, and this person is the one to take steps to solve the problem.

2. **Use confrontive skills when teachers own the problem.** Teachers can modify the environment, recognize and respond to student feelings, word statements so they do not trigger the student's coping mechanism, shift gears, and use a no-lose method of conflict resolution. All of these approaches are intended to help guide and influence the students into effective interactions in the classroom.

3. **Use helping skills when the student owns the problem.** When a student owns the problem, the student needs to take steps to solve it. Teachers can provide assistance through the use of helping skills. This can be done by using listening skills and by avoiding communication roadblocks.

4. **Use preventive skills when neither the student nor teacher has a problem with the behavior.** As a means to prevent problems from occurring, teachers can use techniques such as collaboratively setting rules and using participative problem solving and decision making.

Teaching with Love and Logic: Jim Fay and David Funk

In *Teaching with Love and Logic* (1995), Jim Fay and David Funk describe how to create a classroom environment in which students can develop their own self-discipline and independent problem-solving skills. *Love and Logic* is an approach to working with students that teaches students to think for themselves, raises the level of student responsibility, and prepares students to function effectively in society.

There are four basic principles of love and logic: (a) maintain the student's self-concept; (b) share control with the students; (c) balance the consequences with empathy; and (d) share the thinking by asking questions and modeling. With those principles as the foundation for the discipline plan, Fay and Funk selected three basic rules for their love and logic program: (a) use enforceable limits; (b) provide choices within the limits; and (c) apply consequences with empathy.

In describing various types of teaching styles, Fay and Funk (1995, pp. 197–198) describe teachers using the love and logic approach to discipline as *consultants*. Consultant teachers do the following:

1. Set enforceable limits through enforceable statements.

2. Provide messages of personal worth, dignity, and strength through choices.

3. Provide consequences with empathy rather than punishment.

4. Demonstrate how to take good care of themselves and be responsible.

5. Share feelings about their personal performance and responsibilities.

6. Help people solve problems by exploring alternatives while allowing them to make their own decisions.

7. Provide latitude, within reasonable limits, for students to complete responsibilities.

8. Induce thinking through questions.

9. Use more actions than words to convey values.

10. Allow students to experience life's natural consequences, allow time to think through a problem, encourage shared thinking and shared control, and let them be teachers as well as students.

The love and logic approach gives students considerable credit for having the ability to solve their own problems, and teachers create an environment where students have the opportunity to make such decisions.

Inner Discipline: Barbara Coloroso

In *Kids Are Worth It! Giving Your Child the Gift of Inner Discipline* (2002), Barbara Coloroso emphasizes guiding students to make their own decisions and to take responsibility for their choices. To have good discipline, teachers must do three things: (a) treat students with respect and dignity; (b) give them a sense of power in their lives; and (c) give them opportunities to make decisions, take responsibility for their actions, and learn from their successes and mistakes. She believes that dealing with problems and accepting the consequences help students take charge of their lives.

Through these approaches, Coloroso believes that students will develop inner discipline. Her beliefs are humanistic and focused on promoting students' self-worth and dignity. She believes that with guidance from adults, students can grow to like themselves and think for themselves. To enable students to develop inner discipline, teachers need to provide the appropriate degree of structure and support for students.

As a starting point, Coloroso says that teachers need to ask themselves, "What is my goal in teaching?" and "What is my teaching philosophy?" The first question deals with what teachers hope to achieve, and the second with how they will approach the tasks. Because teachers act in accordance with their beliefs, it is important for them to clarify these beliefs concerning the degree of freedom and control they apply to their classrooms. Teachers who want to control students use rewards and punishments, but teachers who want to empower students to make decisions and to resolve their own problems will give students opportunities to think, act, and take responsibility.

■ WHAT WOULD YOU DECIDE?   Applying Low Teacher Control Approaches

Teachers adopting the low teacher control approach—the guiding model—to discipline intentionally exhibit a low degree of control when structuring the classroom environment and responding to misbehavior. They structure the environment to facilitate students' control over their environment and behavior.

1. If you adopted the guiding model, how would you approach the selection of rules and procedures at the start of the school year?

2. If you adopted the guiding model, how might you react to a student who is talking in class, disturbing others, and not getting her work done?

The best way to teach students how to make good decisions is to put them in situations that call for decisions; ask them to make the decision, possibly with guidance from the teacher; and let them experience the results of their decision. Coloroso believes that teachers should not rescue students from bad decisions, but rather guide the student to new decisions that will solve the problem. When students are given ownership of problems and situations, this allows students to take responsibility for their decisions. She describes a six-step problem-solving strategy that students can use to identify and define the problem, list and evaluate possible solutions, and select, implement, and evaluate the preferred option.

From Discipline to Community: Alfie Kohn

Alfie Kohn has written two books related to discipline: *Punished by Rewards* (1999) and *Beyond Discipline: From Compliance to Community* (2006). Kohn challenges traditional thinking by suggesting that our first question about children should not be "How can we make them do what we want?" but rather "What do they require in order to flourish, and how can we provide those things?" After reviewing a number of popular discipline programs, Kohn concludes that all are based on threat, reward, and punishment as the means to obtain student compliance. Kohn even views "consequences" as being punishments. Nothing useful comes from rewards and punishments because they cause students to mistrust their own judgment and stunt their becoming caring and self-reliant.

Instead, Kohn says that teachers should focus on developing caring, supportive classrooms where students participate fully in solving problems, including problems with behavior. He advises teachers to develop a sense of community in their classrooms, where students feel safe and are continually brought into making decisions, expressing their opinions, and working cooperatively toward solutions that benefit the class.

When starting the school year, Kohn doesn't think rules are a good idea. When rules are used, Kohn is critical that students look for loopholes, teachers function as police officers, and punishment is used as a consequence. He maintains that students learn best when they have the opportunity to reflect on the proper way to conduct themselves. In this way, the teacher and students work together to identify how they want their classroom to be and how that can be made to happen. Students help create their own learning environment.

Classroom meetings are seen by Kohn as valuable tools to create a community and to address classroom problems and issues. Classroom meetings bring social and ethical benefits, foster intellectual development, motivate students to be more effective leaders, and greatly cut down on the need to deal with discipline problems. Kohn sees four focal points in these meetings: (a) share—talk about interesting events; (b) decide about issues that affect the class, such as procedures for working on projects; (c) plan for various curricular or instructional issues; and (d) reflect about issues such as what has been learned, what might have worked better, or what changes might improve the class.

Medium Teacher Control Approaches

Medium-control approaches are based on the philosophical belief that development comes from a combination of innate and outer forces. Thus, the control of student behavior is a joint responsibility of the student and teacher. Medium-control teachers accept the student-centered psychology that is reflected in the low-control philosophy, but they also recognize that learning takes place in a group context. Therefore, the teacher promotes individual student control over behavior whenever possible but places the needs of the group as a whole over the needs of individual students. The child's thoughts, feelings, ideas, and preferences are taken into account when dealing with instruction, classroom management, and discipline, but ultimately, the teacher's primary focus is on behavior and meeting the academic needs of the group.

Students are given opportunities to control their behavior in an effort to develop the ability to make appropriate decisions, yet they may not initially recognize that some of their behavior might be a hindrance to their own growth and development. Students need to recognize the consequences of their behavior and make adjustments to reach more favorable results.

The teacher and students often develop rules and procedures jointly. Teachers may begin the discussion of rules by presenting one or two rules that must be followed, or the teacher may hold veto power over the rules that the students select. This represents a higher degree of control than is used by low-control teachers. Medium-control teachers, then, would be responsible for enforcing the rules and helping students recognize the consequences of their decisions and actions. Medium-control educators might use logical consequences, cooperative discipline, non-coercive approaches, or other interactive approaches. These strategies fall into the interacting model of discipline.

Several educators have described cohesive approaches to deal with students that represent the medium-control approach when creating a supportive learning environment and guiding student behavior. The discipline models from several representative authors are discussed in the following sections.

Logical Consequences: Rudolf Dreikurs

Rudolf Dreikurs (Dreikurs, Grunwald, & Pepper, 1998) based his strategies on the belief that students are motivated to get recognition and to belong with others. Students seek social acceptance from conforming to the group and making useful contributions to it. Dreikurs views his approaches as democratic in that teachers and students together decide on the rules and consequences, and they have joint responsibility for maintaining a positive classroom climate. This encourages students to become more responsibly self-governing.

To Dreikurs, discipline is not punishment; it is teaching students to impose limits on themselves. With his approaches, students are responsible for their own actions, have respect for themselves and others, have the responsibility to influence others to behave appropriately, and are responsible for knowing the classroom rules and consequences. Based on Dreikurs's ideas, there are several techniques that you can use to help misbehaving students behave appropriately without reliance on punishment.

■ WHAT WOULD YOU DECIDE?   Applying Medium Teacher Control Approaches

Teachers adopting the medium teacher control approach—the interacting model—to discipline want to involve students to some degree in establishing guidelines in the classroom and in dealing with misbehavior. The teachers may enforce the boundaries and work with the students to determine suitable solutions.

1. How might your selection of rules and consequences be influenced by this philosophical approach?

2. How might this philosophical approach to control also affect your decision-making about aspects of curriculum and instruction, such as your choice of instructional activities and assessment techniques?

3. If two students had a loud verbal disagreement in your classroom, how would you deal with the incident with the use of medium-control approaches?

First, identify the goal of the misbehavior. Examine the key signs of the misbehavior and also consider your feelings and reactions as a means to tentatively identify the goal of the student's misbehavior. The student's goal may be to gain attention, to seek power, to seek revenge, or to display inadequacy. Then disclose this goal to the student in a private session as a means to confirm the goal. This is a positive means of confronting a misbehaving student. Its purpose is to heighten the student's awareness of the motives for the misbehavior.

Second, alter your reactions to the misbehavior. Once the goal of misbehavior has been identified, first control your immediate reaction to misbehavior so that your response does not reinforce the misbehavior. For example, if the student's goal is to seek attention, never give immediate attention, but try to ignore the behavior whenever possible. Then, have a discussion with the student to identify a number of alternatives for changing the behavior.

Third, provide encouragement statements to students. Encouragement consists of words or actions that acknowledge student work and express confidence in the students (Dreikurs, Cassel, & Ferguson, 2004). Encouragement statements help students see what they did to lead to a positive result and also help students feel confident about their own abilities. For example, you might say, "I see that your extra studying for the test paid off, because you did so well." The focus is on what the student did that led to the result obtained.

Most important, use logical consequences. Instead of using punishment, Dreikurs prefers to let students experience the consequences that flow from misbehavior. A *logical consequence* is an event that is arranged by the teacher that is directly and logically related to the misbehavior. For instance, if a student leaves paper on the classroom floor, the student must pick the paper off the floor. If a student breaks the rule of speaking out without raising his or her hand, the teacher ignores the response and calls on a student whose hand is up. If a student makes marks on the desk, the student is required to remove them.

Cooperative Discipline: Linda Albert

Based largely on the philosophy and psychology of Alfred Adler and Rudolf Dreikurs, Linda Albert (2003) developed a classroom management and discipline plan called *cooperative discipline*. Similar to Dreikurs's ideas, cooperative discipline is founded on three concepts of behavior: (a) students choose their behavior; (b) the ultimate goal of student behavior is to fulfill the need to belong; and (c) students misbehave to achieve one of four immediate goals (attention, power, revenge, and avoidance of failure).

Albert's main focus is on helping teachers meet student needs so that students choose to cooperate with the teacher and with each other. Her cooperative discipline includes five action steps: (a) pinpoint and describe the student's behavior, (b) identify the goal of the misbehavior, (c) choose intervention techniques for the moment of misbehavior, (d) select encouragement techniques to build self-esteem, and (e) involve parents as partners.

Albert's cooperative discipline program, therefore, is designed to establish positive classroom control through appropriate interventions and to build self-esteem through encouragement. The building blocks of self-esteem are helping students feel capable, helping students connect (become involved and engaged in the classroom), and helping students contribute. To achieve the goals of cooperative discipline intervention and encouragement strategies, use democratic procedures and policies, implement cooperative learning strategies, conduct classroom guidance activities, and choose appropriate curriculum methods and materials.

Albert offers a number of strategies to implement her cooperative discipline plan. She presents intervention techniques when misbehavior occurs, ways to reinforce desirable behavior, approaches to create a cooperative classroom climate, and ways to avoid and defuse confrontations. Albert also proposes that teachers and students collaboratively develop a classroom code of conduct to involve students and foster their sense of responsibility to the group.

Positive Discipline: Jane Nelsen, Lynn Lott, and Stephen Glenn

Jane Nelsen also has adapted Rudolf Dreikurs's concepts into a program called positive discipline. In *Positive Discipline*, Nelsen (2006) identified kindness, respect, firmness, and encouragement as the main ingredients of this program for parents and teachers. There are several key elements to Nelsen's approach:

- Use natural and logical consequences as a means to inspire a positive atmosphere for winning children over rather than winning over children.

- Understand that children have four goals of misbehavior (attention, power, revenge, and assumed inadequacy).

- Use kindness and firmness at the same time when addressing misbehavior.

- Allow adults and children mutual respect.

- Provide family and class meetings, which can be effectively used to address misbehavior.

- Use encouragement as a means of inspiring self-evaluation and focusing on the actions of the child.

The positive discipline approach to classroom management also can be used to promote social, emotional, and academic success (Nelsen & Gfroerer, 2017).

Nelsen has described how positive discipline principles can be applied to the classroom through the use of classroom meetings. In *Positive Discipline in the Classroom*, Nelsen, Lott, and Glenn (2013) provide detailed descriptions for ways to conduct effective classroom meetings. In addition to eliminating discipline problems, classroom meetings help students develop social, academic, and life skills, and they help students feel that they are personally capable and significant, and that they can influence their own lives.

VOICES FROM THE CLASSROOM   Nonpunitive Responses

Janet Kulbiski, kindergarten teacher, Manhattan, Kansas

After reading Jane Nelsen's book *Positive Discipline in the Classroom* (2013), I changed my attitude about misbehavior and tried some different behavior management strategies in my classroom. I now see misbehavior as an opportunity for teaching appropriate action.

Several of Nelsen's techniques have been very helpful in my classroom. I use natural and logical consequences, allow students choices, and redirect misbehavior. Natural consequences occur without intervention from anyone, such as when a child does not wear his coat and then gets cold. Logical consequences, by contrast, require intervention connected in some logical way to what the child did. If a child draws a picture on the table, a logical consequence would be that the child cleans it up.

It is important to give students choices whenever possible. This gives them a sense of control and worth, but all choices must be acceptable to you. For example, "Please, put the toy on my desk or in your backpack." Redirecting student behavior involves reminding them of the expected behavior. For example, instead of saying, "Don't run," I say, "We always walk." Eliminating "don't" from my vocabulary has helped a lot.

When I deal with misbehavior, I try to always use the situation as an opportunity for the child to learn the expected behavior. My goal is to leave the child feeling good about himself or herself and equipped to handle the situation appropriately next time.

With positive discipline, teachers demonstrate caring by showing personal interest, talking with the students, offering encouragement, and providing opportunities to nurture important life skills. Nelsen and colleagues caution that it is easy to misuse logical consequences because they are often simply punishments. Instead, they maintain that teachers think in terms of solutions rather than consequences. To do so, Nelsen suggests strategies such as involving students in solutions to problems, focusing on the future rather than the present, planning solutions carefully in advance, and making connections among opportunity, responsibility, and consequence.

Noncoercive Discipline: William Glasser

William Glasser, a psychiatrist, received national attention with the publication of *Reality Therapy* (1965), in which he proposed that treating behavioral problems should focus on present circumstances rather than antecedents of the inappropriate behavior. Glasser took his reality therapy message to educators in *Schools Without Failure* (1969). He noted that successful social relationships are basic human needs. Glasser maintained that students have a responsibility for making good choices about their behavior and that they must live with their choices.

When using reality therapy, teachers and students need to jointly establish classroom rules, and the teacher is to enforce the rules consistently without accepting excuses. When misbehavior occurs, the teacher should ask the student, "What are you doing? Is it helping you or the class? What could you do that would help?" The student is asked to make some value judgments about the behavior, and the teacher can suggest suitable alternatives. Together, they create a plan to eliminate the problem behavior. When necessary, the teacher needs to invoke appropriate consequences.

Over time, Glasser expanded his reality therapy concepts. With the development of control theory (1985, 1986), he added the needs of belonging and love, control, freedom, and fun. Without attention to those needs, students are bound to fail. Glasser maintained that discipline problems should be viewed as total behaviors, meaning that the entire context of the situation needs to be examined in an effort to seek a solution. For example, physical inactivity may contribute to student misbehavior, whereas this element might be overlooked if the situation were examined in a more confined way.

With control theory, you must recognize that students want to have their needs met. Students feel pleasure when these needs are met and frustration when they are not. You must create the conditions in which students feel a sense of belonging, have some power and control, have some freedom in the learning and schooling process, and have fun. Thus, students will not be frustrated and discipline problems should be limited.

In *The Quality School* (1998a), Glasser described how to manage students without coercion. Glasser asserts that the nature of school management must be changed in order to meet students' needs and promote effective learning. In fact, he criticizes current school managers for accepting low-quality work. In *The Quality School Teacher* (1998b) and *Every Student Can Succeed* (2000), Glasser offers specific strategies for teachers to move to quality schools.

Discipline with Dignity: Richard Curwin, Allen Mendler, and Brian Mendler

In *Discipline with Dignity* (2018), Richard Curwin, Allen Mendler, and Brian Mendler advocate a discipline model that is highly structured yet extremely flexible. They believe that discipline should focus on teaching and learning rather than retribution or punishment. They stress that all students matter and deserve to be treated in a respectful way, even when they misbehave.

There are eight basic principles of discipline with dignity:

1. Let students know what you need, and then ask what they need from you.

2. Differentiate instruction based on individual strengths.

3. Listen to your students' thoughts and feelings.

4. Use humor.

5. Vary your style of presentation.

6. Offer choices.

7. Use a variety of ways to communicate with students.

8. Realize that being fair does not always mean treating students equally.

Motivated students rarely cause behavior problems. Enthusiastic teachers who present material in stimulating, meaningful ways and treat students with respect and dignity can make any subject come alive, and a teacher who doesn't motivate can make any subject die. They identify four motivating elements in instruction: (a) relevance to students' lives, (b) teacher passion for the subject matter, (c) personal concern for each student, and (d) fun.

Curwin and colleagues identify six things teachers can do to prevent discipline problems:

1. Make connecting with students a top priority.

2. Know yourself, warts and all.

3. Make success a daily goal for each student.

4. Make your classroom a motivating place.

5. Teach responsibility and caring.

6. Establish formal discipline procedures.

Instead of threats, punishments, and rewards to address misbehavior, Curwin and colleagues state that effective consequences should be used instead. These consequences should be the result of students' own choices. Thus, they are logical consequences. Students should be included in developing consequences.

In addition to recommendations for formal discipline rules and procedures, Curwin and colleagues provide guidance for addressing behavioral interruptions, which are minor infractions of the rules. Their low-key recommendations for minor infractions are intended to quickly get the behavior to slow down or stop and to get back to teaching. In addition, *Discipline with Dignity* describes approaches to address chronic misbehavior. Recommendations are provided to deal with special challenges, such as working with students with special needs and difficult parents.

Win–Win Discipline: Spencer Kagan

Spencer Kagan is an educational consultant who specializes in researching and developing discipline strategies and life skills training. Along with Patricia Kyle and Sally Scott, Kagan developed a model of discipline called *Win–Win Discipline* (Kagan, Kyle, & Scott, 2004). The two purposes of this model are to help students meet their needs through responsible, nondisruptive behavior and to develop long-term life skills. To be on the same side in establishing good discipline, teachers and students treat discipline as a joint responsibility.

There are three pillars to win–win discipline:

1. **Same side.** The teacher, students, and parents work together rather than at odds with each other toward building responsible behavior.

2. **Collaboration.** Teachers and students cocreate immediate and long-term solutions to behavior problems.

3. **Learned responsibility.** Teachers help students make responsible choices in how they conduct themselves. Any disruptive behavior that interrupts the learning process can become an important learning opportunity.

Kagan and colleagues identified four types of disruptive behavior—aggression, breaking rules, confrontation, and disengagement. Further, they proposed that disruptive behavior springs from students seeking attention, avoiding failure, being angry, seeking control, and being energetic, bored, or uninformed. Teacher responses are identified for each of these causes. Interventions are designed to help students meet their needs through responsible choices, and the interventions are tailored in accordance to the type of disruption and the reason for the misbehavior.

Heavy emphasis is placed on preventing disruptive behavior through attention to curriculum, instruction, and management. Win–win discipline enables teachers to work with students so that needs that might otherwise prompt disruptive behavior can be identified and satisfied in nondisruptive ways. Students do not often disrupt when engaged in a curriculum that is interesting and adequately challenging.

VOICES FROM THE CLASSROOM   Creating Your Classroom Rules Together

Jennifer Arabolos, third-grade teacher, Guilford, Connecticut

Norms or expectations should focus on fostering a safe learning environment where students feel comfortable taking risks in their learning. To get the biggest bang for your buck when establishing your classroom norms, I highly suggest that you create them with student input. In this way, students have autonomy, feel invested, feel respected and safe, and are more connected to whatever expectations are agreed upon as a class.

Before starting the discussion with your students, especially younger grade levels, you need to brainstorm about the "go to values" that you consider essential for your classroom to run smoothly. For me, I need students to be safe so no one gets hurt physically, be kind so no one gets hurt emotionally, and be willing to take risks in their learning so students can grow! Consider how your classroom rules might align with the school's rules.

Now that you have your list of core values, involve the class. You want to interact with students in this process and get their ideas, but you are still in control by guiding the discussion and influencing the conclusions. For this discussion, you decide how students generate ideas about classroom norms and expectations—whether by identifying ideas verbally or in writing, in partnerships or small groups, after reading a children's text about classroom rules, or some other process.

As I collect student input on chart paper, I list all ideas that are generated so everyone feels they have a voice. Circle or highlight ideas that pop up more than once and seem to be important to your particular group of students. As you circle, find similarities and combine student ideas. Always state the rules in the positive, not the negative. For example, "Don't call out!" can be rephrased as "Take turns."

Once you have created your list of ideas, work as a group to figure out which are most important for learning and growth to occur all year long. Try to limit your list to three to five rules stated in positive language. Once you have your core expectations, explain to your students that this is the contract for the classroom and how we will operate this year.

Spend the next couple weeks demonstrating what each expectation looks like, feels like, and sounds like, and highlight when students are using them. The expectations should be visited often and reviewed throughout the year. They may even be revised as students grow or come back after long breaks and vacations.

High Teacher Control Approaches

High-control approaches are based on the philosophical belief that students' growth and development are the result of external conditions. Children are seen as being molded and shaped by influences from the environment; they are not seen as having an innate potential. Therefore, teachers and adults need to select desired student behaviors, reinforce appropriate behaviors, and take actions to extinguish inappropriate behaviors. Little attention is given to the thoughts, feelings, and preferences of the students since adults are more experienced in instructional matters and have the responsibility for choosing what is best for student development and behavior control.

Teachers using high-control approaches believe that student behavior must be controlled because the students themselves are not able to effectively monitor and control their own behavior. The teachers select the rules and procedures for the classroom, commonly without student input. Teachers then reinforce desired behavior and take actions to have students stop inappropriate, undesired behavior. When misbehavior occurs, teachers take steps to stop the disruption quickly and redirect the student to more positive behavior. Behavior modification, behavioral contracting, and reinforcers are characteristic of high-control approaches. Compared to the previous models, there is more emphasis on managing the behavior of the individuals than the group.

Several educators have described cohesive approaches to deal with students that represent the high teacher control approach to classroom control and order. These approaches are discussed in the following sections.

Behavior Modification: B. F. Skinner

B. F. Skinner (1902–1990) spent most of his academic career at Harvard University, where he conducted experimental studies in learning. In *Beyond Freedom and Dignity* (1971), Skinner challenged traditional views of freedom and dignity and instead claimed that our choices are determined by the environmental conditions under which we live and what has happened to us. The application of these ideas to classroom practice has been called *behavior modification*, a technique that uses reinforcement and punishment to shape behavior.

Behavior modification, as proposed by Skinner and others, has several distinguishing features. Behavior is shaped by its consequences and by what happens to the individual immediately afterward. The systematic use of reinforcers, or rewards, can shape behavior in desired directions. Behavior becomes weaker if it is not followed by reinforcement. Behavior is also weakened by punishment.

Behavior modification is applied in the classroom primarily in two ways: (a) when the teacher rewards the student after a desired act, the student tends to repeat the act and (b) when the student performs an undesired act, the teacher either ignores the act or punishes the student; the misbehaving student then becomes less likely to repeat the act.

■ WHAT WOULD YOU DECIDE?   Your Philosophical Perspective

Some teachers are very teacher centered and prefer to make most of the decisions and direct what goes on in the classroom. Other teachers are student centered and prefer to give some decision-making responsibility to the students and have more student–student interaction. There is a range of these perspectives, from low teacher control to high teacher control.

1. Where do you fall on that continuum of teacher-centered to student-centered perspectives? Why do you place yourself at that point?

2. What are the implications of your philosophical perspective on the selection of rules and procedures, course content, instructional approaches, and assessments?

Several types of reinforcers can be used:

- Edible reinforcers, such as candy, cookies, gum, drinks, nuts, or various other snacks.

- Social reinforcers, such as words, gestures, stickers, certificates, and facial and bodily expressions of approval by the teacher.

- Material or tangible reinforcers, which are real objects that students can earn as rewards for desired behavior.

- Token reinforcers, including stars, points, buttons, or other items that can be accumulated by students for desired behavior and then "cashed in" for other material or tangible reinforcers.

- Activity reinforcers, which include those activities that students prefer in school.

Reinforcers are further discussed in Chapter 5. Behavior modification works best when used in an organized, systematic, and consistent way. The various types of behavior modification systems seem to fit into five categories (Miltenberger, 2016): (a) the "catch them being good" approach, (b) the rules–ignore–praise approach, (c) the rules–reward–punishment approach, (d) the contingency management approach, and (e) the contracting approach.

Assertive Discipline: Lee and Marlene Canter

Lee Canter is an educator who first came into prominence in 1976 with a take-charge approach for teachers to control their classrooms in a firm and positive manner. The revised edition of *Assertive Discipline* (Canter, 2010) goes beyond the initial take-charge approach and includes additional classroom management procedures. The goal of assertive discipline is to teach students to choose responsible behavior, and in doing so, to raise their self-esteem and increase their academic success.

Canter maintains that teachers have the right and responsibility to (a) establish rules and directions that clearly define the limits of acceptable and unacceptable student behavior; (b) teach these rules and directions; and (c) ask for assistance from parents and administrators when support is needed in handling the behavior of students. The manner in which teachers respond to student behavior affects students' self-esteem and success in school. Therefore, teachers must use an assertive response style to state expectations clearly and confidently to students and reinforce these words with actions.

■ CLASSROOM CASE STUDY   A Cooperative Learning Unit Turns Sour

Pedro Ramirez was excited about a new unit he had planned for his high school science students on global climate change. He wanted his students to explore several key aspects: the research evidence, political agreements or disagreements about climate change, the ecological changes, and the influences on people throughout the world. Mr. Ramirez split his class into cooperative learning groups, with each group having responsibility for a separate major aspect. He provided many resources for each group and asked the groups to be ready to report their findings after the groups worked on their topic for several class periods.

Students were on task in their groups at first, but gradually students in each group got off task. They was talking, texting, tossing papers, and walking around the room. By the third class session, only a few students in each group were working on the tasks. Mr. Ramirez was very disappointed and reached a breaking point soon after the start of the fourth class session of group work.

Focus Questions

1. If you were in his shoes, what would you do at that moment?

2. At that moment, what would a teacher with a low teacher control approach do? With a medium-control approach? With a high-control approach? (See Tables 2.1 and 2.2.)

3. What could Mr. Ramirez have done in his planning and preparation to minimize this off-task behavior?

A classroom discipline plan has three parts: (a) rules that students must follow at all times; (b) positive recognition that students will receive for following the rules; and (c) consequences that result when students choose not to follow the rules. Sample rules may be to follow directions, keep hands and feet to oneself, or be in the classroom and seated when the bell rings. Positive recognition may include various forms of praise, positive notes sent home to parents, positive notes to students, or special activities or privileges.

Consequences are delivered systematically with each occurrence of misbehavior. The first time a student breaks a rule, the student receives a warning. The second time, the student may lose a privilege, such as being last in line for lunch or staying in class one minute after the bell. The third time, the student loses additional privileges. The fourth time, the teacher calls the parents. The fifth time, the student is sent to the principal. In cases of severe misbehavior, these preliminary steps may be skipped and the student is sent to the principal.

Another part of Canter's assertive discipline plan is to teach responsible behavior. This includes determining and teaching specific directions (classroom procedures), using positive recognition to motivate students to behave, redirecting nondisruptive off-task behavior, and implementing consequences. Canter further emphasizes that successful teachers need to blend academic and behavior management efforts into a cohesive whole so that classroom management actions are not apparent.

Canter gives special attention to dealing with difficult students, who represent perhaps 5–10% of the students you may encounter. In *Assertive Discipline,* Canter provides recommendations for conducting a one-to-one problem-solving conference with the teacher and the difficult student. The goal of the conference is to help the student gain insight into the problem and ultimately choose more responsible behavior. Parents and administrators can offer additional support when dealing with difficult students. Lee and Marlene Canter have a separate book on this subject: *Succeeding with Difficult Students* (2008). Lee Canter further expanded his concepts in *Classroom Management for Academic Success* (2014).

Positive Discipline: Fredric Jones

Fredric Jones is a psychologist who conducted research on classroom practices and developed training programs for improving teacher effectiveness in behavior management and instruction. In *Positive Classroom Discipline* (1987), Jones emphasized that teachers can help students support their own self-control. His *Tools for Teaching* (2013) extends the discussion of these issues. Jones recommends that teachers use the following five strategies to enact positive discipline.

1. **Structure the classroom.** Teachers need to consider various rules, routines, and standards; seating arrangements; and student–teacher relationships when structuring the classroom. Rules, procedures, routines, and classroom standards need to be taught to students so they understand the standards and expectations in the classroom. Jones points out that the arrangement of the classroom furniture can maximize teacher mobility and allow greater physical proximity to students on a moment-to-moment basis.

2. **Maintain control by using appropriate instructional strategies.** Jones maintains that teachers lose control of their classes when they spend too much time with each student, such as during seatwork. Teachers commonly spend time to find out where a student is having difficulty, to explain further the part the student doesn't understand, and to supply students with additional explanations and examples. Instead, Jones recommends that teachers use the three-step sequence of praise, prompt, and leave.

VOICES FROM THE CLASSROOM   Positive Recognition in Assertive Discipline

Cammie Fulk, fifth-grade teacher, Fulks Run, Virginia

To provide positive recognition in my assertive discipline plan, I post a personal calendar for each student each month. If a student has behaved well and completed all of the work for the day, a stamp is placed on that date. If not, then the reason for not receiving the stamp is written on that date. When a student receives five stamps in a row, a reward is given. For 10 stamps in a row, a free homework pass is provided. At the end of each month, the calendar is sent home to be signed by the parents and then returned to me. This personal calendar has become a strong motivator in my fifth-grade classroom.

In addition to the personal calendars, I have a gem jar on my desk as a reward for the entire class. It is simply a clear coffee cup with three permanent levels marked on the side to indicate 5, 10, and 15 minutes of free time earned. As I observe the entire class on task, I place several gems in the jar. Gems may be marbles, bubble gum, candy corn, jellybeans, or other small items. Gems can be earned for a variety of behaviors such as good hall behavior, the entire class on task, the entire class completing homework, or other valued actions. The sound of the gems hitting the glass cup brings smiles to my fifth graders.

3. **Maintain control with limit-setting techniques.** Jones proposed a series of specific actions that can be taken when a student is *getting off task*. These techniques primarily involve the use of body language to convince the students that the teacher is in control. These steps involve being aware of and monitoring the behavior of all students; terminating instruction when necessary to deal with a student; turning, looking, and saying the student's name; moving to the edge of the student's desk; moving away from the student's desk when the student gets back to work; placing your palms on the desk and giving a short, direct verbal prompt if the student does not get back to work; moving closer over the desk; and finally moving next to the student behind the student's desk.

4. **Build patterns of cooperation.** Jones proposed an incentive system called preferred activity time (PAT) that can be used so students can earn certain benefits if they behave and cooperate. The PAT may be a variety of activities and privileges that are given to the class as a whole at the start of a predetermined time (a week's worth).

5. **Develop appropriate backup systems in the event of misbehavior.** Backups are to be used systematically from lesser sanctions to more serious ones. Low-level sanctions involve issuing a warning; pulling a card with the student's name, address, and telephone number; and then sending a letter to the parents. Mid-level sanctions include time-out, detention, loss of privileges, and a parent conference. High-level sanctions include in-school suspension, Saturday school, delivering the student to a parent at work, asking a parent to accompany the student in school, suspension, police intervention, and expulsion.

Discipline Without Stress: Marvin Marshall

Discipline Without Stress promotes responsibility and learning using an approach that is totally noncoercive, but not permissive. Prior to becoming a staff developer and international speaker, Marvin Marshall was a classroom teacher, guidance counselor, principal, and college instructor. In *Discipline Without Stress, Punishments, or Rewards*, Marshall (2012) described a comprehensive system to guide and monitor student behavior and to promote responsibility and learning.

The following principles are incorporated into the Discipline Without Stress model (pp. 275–276): (a) being positive is a more constructive teacher than being negative, (b) choice empowers, (c) self-evaluation is essential for lasting improvement, (d) people choose their own behaviors, (e) self-correction is the most effective approach to change behavior, (f) acting responsibly is the most satisfying of rewards, and (g) growth is greater when authority is used without punishment. Although many of the program features blend into the interacting model of discipline, Marshall places his system into the intervening model of discipline, since there is a high degree of teacher control in directing the environment.

Marshall stresses the importance of teaching and practicing procedures and not assuming that students automatically know how to do what the teacher desires students to do. He identifies three principles to practice with students in a classroom:

1. **Positivity**. Practice changing negatives into positives ("No running" becomes "We walk in the hallways.").

2. **Choice.** Permit students to choose their responses to a situation so they become more self-controlled, responsible, and empowered.

3. **Reflection.** Ask questions that guide students to reflect and self-evaluate.

Another important aspect of Marshall's program is the Raise Responsibility System (RRS), which has three components: (a) teaching—teaching the hierarchy of social development to students; (b) asking—checking for understanding when students are irresponsible; and (c) eliciting—guiding choices when students continue to misbehave.

The hierarchy of social development has four levels, which Marshall codes with letters:

D for Democracy, where motivation is internal

C for Cooperation/Conformity, where motivation is external

B for Bossing/Bullying, where the student needs to be bossed to behave

A for Anarchy, where there is an absence of order

Only levels C and D are acceptable. When misbehaviors occur, students are led through a process of reflective questions related to the hierarchy, ultimately leading to choices and resolution of the problem. Guided choices stop the disruption by using authority, without being coercive or punitive. A consequence is elicited to help the student prevent repetition of the behaviors that he or she exhibited from level A or B.

Overall, this program is designed to influence students into making responsible decisions about their classroom behavior. *Discipline Without Stress* focuses on promoting responsibility rather than on obedience. When responsibility is promoted, obedience becomes a natural byproduct.

Determining Your Management Plan

How do you develop a philosophy of classroom management and a management plan for your classroom? Bosch (2007) maintains that classroom management must reflect the personality and teaching style of the individual teacher and is a skill that must be learned, practiced, and evaluated, and modified to fit the changing situations in classrooms. Further, teachers must be able to modify and adjust their management strategies as conditions warrant, just as they modify their teaching strategies to match students' needs and learning styles.

≡ **Developing Your Management Plan** Examining Your Philosophical Beliefs

To help form your philosophy of classroom management, answer the following questions to reflect your current beliefs. You may modify your responses over time as you explore more information about classroom management and discipline.

• What is a good teacher, and what is good teaching?

• What should be the goals of a classroom management plan?

• What degree of control do I want to maintain in the classroom? Do I see myself as an autocratic or a democratic teacher, or somewhere in between?

• How do I want my degree of control to be evident in my instructional, management, and disciplinary practices in the classroom?

• Which model of discipline (shown in Table 2.1 and Table 2.2) appeals to me? Why?

Your goals, values, and beliefs about classroom management, discipline, instruction, and child development will affect your management philosophy, and your philosophy, in turn, will affect how you select and enact the particular aspects of your management plan.

Your Management Philosophy

Before you determine your management plan, you must select a philosophical model for classroom management and discipline. This chapter provided a brief orientation to various models of discipline, which went from low to high teacher control, representing a continuum of philosophical perspectives for control in the classroom. This discussion on control is a useful starting point as you consider your philosophical perspective on classroom management and discipline. Adapted from Manning and Bucher (2013), the chapter feature on "Developing Your Management Plan" lists several questions about additional educational issues to prompt your consideration of education, teaching and learning, management, and discipline to help you clarify your philosophical beliefs.

To what degree do you want to exercise control in your classroom? That is the fundamental question when deciding on your approach to classroom management and discipline. To answer that question, you will likely consider a number of factors, such as your views of educational philosophy, psychology, and child development. For example, when determining your approach to control, you will likely take into account your beliefs about what is the dominant influence on a child's development—inner forces, outer forces, or a combination of the two. You may want to review Table 2.1 on the characteristics of the discipline models and Table 2.2 on the proponents of various discipline models.

Your Management Plan

Your analysis of the philosophical views of classroom management and discipline will probably reveal whether you are inclined to use low-, medium-, or high-control approaches, each representing a different philosophical perspective. After determining your relative placement on the teacher control continuum, decide whether you want to use a particular discipline model shown in Table 2.2, synthesize two or more models, or create your own approach. Even if you choose one model, you may find that the context of the classroom and the actual events cause you to shift from that model and use elements of other approaches. You don't have to accept the entire set of actions proposed by a certain model. When determining the relative merits of the different discipline models, it may be useful to establish criteria to compare the relative characteristics, strengths, and weaknesses of each model.

There is more to developing your management plan than selecting a particular discipline model. To enact your philosophical view of classroom management and discipline, you will need to make decisions about the seven domains of responsibility in classroom management and

■ TABLE 2.3   **Clarifying Your Classroom Management Plan**

The following categories provide a framework for you to clarify and write your classroom management plan.

Philosophy on classroom management and discipline
➤ First provide background information about your personality, teaching style, and philosophy of education to reveal the origins and foundation of your classroom management philosophy.
➤ Next, describe your philosophy on classroom management and discipline for your own classroom. What are your purposes for an effective classroom management plan? To what degree do you plan to control the decision-making and actions in the classroom? To what degree will you involve students?

The classroom arrangement
➤ How will you arrange student seating, the teacher's desk, furniture arrangement, bulletin boards, technology placement, storage of materials, and the use of wall space? This could include a diagram to show the placement of these features.

Rules
➤ What behavior will you expect of your students?
➤ What rules will you display and use in your classroom?
➤ Describe how you determined the rules. Would you involve students in identifying the rules? If so, to what degree? How will you communicate the rules to the students, parents, and administrators?

Responses to misbehavior
➤ What will you do when a student misbehaves and breaks a rule? Will you have a hierarchy of consequences to deal with mild, moderate, and severe misbehavior? Specifically, what is your plan?

Procedures
➤ What procedures will you use in your classroom (e.g., distributing materials, collecting homework, transitions in and out of the room, and providing students assistance)? How will you teach the procedures to the students?

Creating a respectful, supportive learning environment
➤ What type of classroom atmosphere would you like to create? What specifically will you do to create that atmosphere? How can you maintain and reinforce appropriate student behavior? How can you promote cooperation?

Managing and facilitating instruction
➤ How will your lessons be structured? How will you begin and end your lessons? How will you group your students for instruction? How will you manage lesson delivery? How will you make modifications for diverse learners? How will you integrate technology in instruction?

Motivating students to learn
➤ How will you include motivational strategies in your instruction, evaluation, and feedback? How will you incorporate these motivational issues into all levels of your instructional planning?

Promoting safety and wellness
➤ How will you provide a physically and emotionally safe environment for students in your classroom? How will you respond to disruptive or violent behavior in the classroom? How might you prevent it?

Interacting with parents, colleagues, and others
➤ What are the reasons for communicating and interacting with parents, colleagues, and others? How will you communicate with them? How frequently?

discipline outlined in Chapter 1. Those domains can serve as organizers for your decision making to create an effective learning community.

To facilitate your thinking and decisions concerning the seven domains, Table 2.3 lists categories that could be included in your classroom management plan. Each category is discussed in this book, with some categories being addressed in an entire chapter.

MAJOR CONCEPTS

1. A continuum showing a range of low to high teacher control can be used to illustrate the various educational views expressed by educators about classroom management and discipline.

2. Low-control approaches are based on the philosophical belief that students have primary responsibility for controlling their

own behavior and that they have the capability to make these decisions.

3. Educators representative of the low-control approach are Haim Ginott, Thomas Gordon, Jim Fay, David Funk, Barbara Coloroso, and Alfie Kohn.

4. Medium-control approaches are based on the philosophical belief that students develop from a combination of natural forces within the child and outer forces of the child's environment. Thus, the control of student behavior is a joint responsibility of the student and the teacher.

5. Educators representative of the medium-control approach are Rudolf Dreikurs, Linda Albert, Jane Nelsen, William Glasser, Richard Curwin, Allen Mendler, and Spencer Kagan.

6. High-control approaches are based on the philosophical belief that students' growth and development are the result of external

conditions. Children are seen as molded and shaped by influences from the environment where they live.

7. Educators representative of the high-control approach are B. F. Skinner, Lee Canter, Fredric Jones, and Marvin Marshall.

8. When deciding on your approach to control, you will likely consider your views of educational philosophy, psychology, and child development. It may also be useful to identify whether you are inclined to use low-, medium-, or high-control approaches on the teacher behavior continuum.

DISCUSSION/REFLECTIVE QUESTIONS

1. Recall a favorite teacher you had. What level of control did that teacher use? What are the indicators of that level of control?

2. What are the merits and problems that might be associated with each of the three levels of teacher control?

3. Think of a couple examples of logical consequences that might be delivered after a student misbehaves. What are the merits for using logical consequences after a student misbehaves (as endorsed by some of the medium-control educators)?

4. How would you approach the selection of classroom rules if you were in the intervening model (high teacher control)? If you were in the interacting model (medium teacher control)? If you were in the guiding model (low teacher control)?

5. Why is the behavior modification model endorsed by B. F. Skinner included in the high-control category?

SUGGESTED ACTIVITIES

1. Think about your schooling experiences and identify teachers you had who fell in the low-, medium-, and high-control approaches. How positive were your experiences in those classes?

2. Talk with several teachers to learn about the degree of control they use when selecting rules and dealing with misbehavior. Identify which discipline model each teacher seems to reflect.

3. Select one of the discipline models outlined in Tables 2.1 and 2.2 that you believe aligns with your perspectives. Prepare a report that describes how your perspectives would be applied in a real classroom. Part of your report might be organized around the categories in Table 2.3 concerning clarifying your classroom management plan.

FURTHER READING

Charles, C. M., & Cole, K. M. (2019). *Building classroom discipline: Methods and models* (12th ed.). Boston, MA: Pearson.
In separate chapters, the book provides an overview of the discipline models of several educators. Also includes chapters examining the nature of misbehavior, working effectively with all students, and formalizing your personal system of discipline.

Hardin, C. J. (2012). *Effective classroom management: Models and strategies for today's classrooms* (3rd ed.). Boston, MA: Pearson.
In separate chapters, the book provides descriptions of many models of discipline ranging from low to high teacher control. Also includes a chapter on creating your own system.

Manning, M. L., & Bucher, K. T. (2013). *Classroom management: Models, applications, and cases* (3rd ed.). Boston, MA: Pearson.
In separate chapters, the book provides descriptions of the classroom management and discipline plans of several leading educators. Also includes chapters on understanding the need for classroom management and on building your own management plan.

© Michelle D. Bridwell/PhotoEdit

Preparing for the School Year

CHAPTER OUTLINE

Making Management and Instructional Preparations

Management Preparations

Instructional Preparations

Managing Assessment, Record Keeping, and Reporting

Establishing a Plan to Deal with Misbehavior

Preparing for the First Day

Planning for the First Day

Conducting the First Day

Organizing Your Classroom and Materials

Floor Space

Storage Space

Bulletin Boards and Wall Space

CHAPTER OBJECTIVES

This chapter provides information that will help you:

• Make instructional and management decisions and preparations before school starts.

• Determine your processes for assessment, record keeping, and recording.

- Establish a plan to deal with misbehavior.
- Plan how to conduct the first days of the school year.
- Determine how to organize your classroom and materials.

Imagine that you are going to take a two-week vacation to see the numerous state and national parks in southern Utah and northern Arizona. You gather information about the parks and attractions from a variety of sources, and then you start to plan your itinerary. Next, you make motel reservations and list all of the things you need to take with you, such as hiking shoes, water bottles, sunscreen, sunglasses, camera, and clothing. Soon before you leave on the trip, you stop mail delivery, make sure you don't have any online orders coming, and make arrangements for your pets for the days you are gone. All of these arrangements, and probably more, are needed to have a fun, trouble-free vacation.

Starting the school year also requires this type of planning. Even before school starts, you can make a number of decisions about management and instructional preparations, plans to promote a positive learning climate, arrangements for assessments and record keeping, plans for the first day of school, and arrangements for floor space, storage, and other aspects of classroom space. Early planning and decision making on these issues will help ensure a positive start to the school year. These classroom management issues are explored in this chapter.

Making Management and Instructional Preparations

If you surveyed experienced teachers about the role of management at the beginning of the school year, you would undoubtedly hear comments about management and instructional preparations before school starts and about ways to plan for the first days of the school year. Studies on classroom management have verified that the first few days of the school year set the tone for the entire year (Emmer & Evertson, 2017; Evertson & Emmer, 2017; Marzano, Marzano, & Pickering, 2003; Marzano, Gaddy, Foseid, Foseid, & Marzano, 2009).

To begin, you can make management preparations, make instructional preparations, plan to manage assessments and record keeping, and establish a plan for misbehavior. A number of these issues are addressed in this section.

There are a number of useful resources providing more details than can be discussed in this chapter. Resources are available for the *elementary* grades (Bosch & Bosch, 2015; Denton & Kriete, 2015; Jonson, 2010; Kelly, 2010; Moran, Stobbe, Baron, Miller, & Moir, 2009), *middle and secondary* grades (Bongolan, Moir, & Baron, 2010; Responsive Classroom, 2018a; Sprick, 2013; Thompson, 2011), and grades *K–12* (Bluestein, 2010; Guillaume, 2016; Kronowitz, 2012; Marzano et al., 2009; Thompson, 2018; Wong & Wong, 2018a, 2018b).

Management Preparations

It is important to carefully consider management issues such as your school environment, room and seating arrangements, materials, rules and procedures, and communication with parents.

Based on a study of experienced teachers (Schell & Burden, 2006), you could direct your attention to the following classroom management issues:

1. **The school environment.** The first step is to become thoroughly familiar with the total environment before school starts: the room, school, facilities, personnel, services, resources, policies and procedures, other teachers, children, and the community. You will then have more information on which to base decisions, will probably feel more confident about your job, and will not need to devote time in the first few weeks to gather this information.

2. **Support materials.** After examining the curriculum guide and the textbooks, you might have ideas about activities for a certain unit or lesson. Supplementary materials may be needed when the time comes to teach that lesson. This is the time to gather any additional support materials such as games and devices, pictures, DVDs, ideas for activities, charts, maps, and graphs. The school may have discretionary funds for the purchase of these types of resources. They may be obtained from school supply catalogs, a local teacher store, or even at garage sales.

3. **Filing system.** It is useful to set up a filing system for storing district and school communications and other important documents. Papers that should be kept in a filing cabinet include the district's policy handbook; correspondence from the principal, superintendent, or other supervisors; correspondence from professional organizations; lesson plans; and items on curricular content. Some teachers use file folders. A separate file folder may be created for each course unit to hold pertinent notes and resource materials. Similarly, digital files of important material should be stored in an orderly manner on your computer.

4. **Classroom procedures.** You can follow various procedures to accomplish specific tasks. Procedures may be identified regarding handing in completed work, sharpening a pencil, using the restroom, or putting away supplies. Before school starts, identify actions or activities requiring procedures that will contribute to a smoothly running classroom, and then decide what those procedures should be.

5. **Classroom helpers.** Teachers call on students at all grade levels as helpers to perform various classroom tasks. Make a list of tasks that need to be done and then decide which ones the students can perform. Give attention to how task assignment will be rotated to give every student an opportunity to help. Roles are often held for one or two weeks before being reassigned. Depending on the grade level and circumstances, some tasks may include students as line leader, light switcher, pencil sharpener, paper collector, plant waterer, whiteboard eraser, window and blind opener, and supply manager.

6. **Class lists and rosters.** It is useful to plan a means to record whether students have returned their book orders, picture money, field trip permission forms, and so on. You can prepare a generic class roster listing the students' names in alphabetical order in the left column, with blank columns on the right to check off the action. It is helpful to create the list on a computer so that an updated sheet can be easily generated when the roster changes.

7. **School/home communication.** Open communication with families is vital. Before school starts, many teachers prepare an introductory letter to families to welcome them and to inform them about the teacher, the curriculum, grading practices and standards, the homework policy, rules and procedures, and so on (discussed more fully in Chapter 11). This letter can be sent home with the students on the first day of school. Teachers can also make plans for other types of communication with families such as emails, phone calls, progress reports, or a back-to-school night.

8. **Birthdays and other celebrations.** Depending on your grade level, you may want to recognize student birthdays. Most schools have very specific policies for celebrating major holidays, such as Halloween, Christmas, Hanukkah, Martin Luther King Day, and Easter. Inquire about these policies so you will understand what is expected.

VOICES FROM THE CLASSROOM   Using a Class List for Various Purposes

Marge McClintock, fifth-grade science and social studies teacher, New Providence, New Jersey

As soon as I am given my class list of students for the year, I assign the students numbers in alphabetical order for each class. The students are told their numbers and are required to put their numbers on all of their work. This has several benefits. When homework or seatwork is handed in, I ask a student to put the papers in numerical order for me. I can see in an instant which numbers are missing and then take whatever action is needed.

Another benefit is managing the students on class trips. Although I always carry a class list with me on the trips, it is much faster to have the students call out their numbers in order when they're back on the bus or whenever roll needs to be taken.

A third benefit is in dividing the class into groups. It can be as easy as evens and odds. Or I can require the students to use higher-order math skills by saying, "All the students whose number can be factored by 3, please come to the front of the class. All students whose number can be factored by 2 and who aren't in the '3' group, please go to the back of the room. All the rest, stay where you are."

9. **Distributing textbooks.** Sometime in the first few days of school, you will need to distribute textbooks. You need to obtain the textbooks and prepare an inventory form on which to record each book number, with a space in which to write the student's name. Think about when and how the textbooks will be distributed. You might want to wait until the second or third day before distributing textbooks or distribute them just before they are needed for the first time. Attention might be given to the specific means of distribution. One way is to have students line up one row at a time and go to the table where the books are stacked. When giving the book to the student, you can record the student's name on the inventory form.

10. **Room identification.** On the first day of school, students need to locate your classroom. Especially for students new to the building, it is important to have the room clearly labeled. A poster on the outside doorway should include the room number, the teacher's name, and the grade level and/or subject (e.g., Room 211, Mr. Wagner, and World History). Some type of welcoming statement should also be placed on the whiteboard, such as "Welcome, I'm glad you're here."

11. **Room arrangement.** Room arrangement is an issue that can be decided before school starts. Take into account the fixed features in the room, instructional materials and supplies, traffic areas, work areas, boundaries for activity areas, visibility to see all students, and the purposes of various seating arrangements. Determine the arrangement in the classroom for your desk, the students' desks, tables, bookshelves, filing cabinets, and other furniture. The room arrangement you select should be consistent with your instructional goals and activities. Teacher-led instructional approaches such as presentations and demonstrations will require one type of room arrangement, whereas small-group work would require a different type of arrangement.

12. **Seat selections and arrangements.** One teacher may prefer to assign each student's seat, while another may let the students select their seats. This decision should be made before school starts. In either case, be sure that there are enough seats for the number of students you expect. You might take the age level and maturity of the students into account as you select the manner of assigning seats. You might change the seating arrangements during the school year to accommodate work groups, to move students who need close supervision to more accessible seats, or simply to provide a change.

13. **Room decoration.** It is important to make your classroom an attractive, comfortable place. Consider having some plants in the classroom, or even an aquarium. Displays of pictures, posters, charts, and maps also help cover the walls with informative and appealing materials. Attractive bulletin boards add color. You might prepare one bulletin board listing classroom information and use another one to display seasonal items. After school starts, you can have students prepare bulletin boards.

Instructional Preparations

Prior to the start of the school year, carefully consider a variety of instructional issues such as long-range plans, supplementary materials, student assessment, a folder for substitute teachers, a syllabus, and so on. Based on a study of experienced teachers (Schell & Burden, 2006), you could direct your attention to the following instructional issues:

1. **Long-range plans.** It is helpful to examine the curriculum guides and other related materials so you can recognize what should be covered by the end of the school year. Some tentative decisions need to be made on the amount of time to spend on each particular unit. Some curriculum guides include recommendations for the number of weeks to spend on each unit. Be careful not to overschedule yourself. Leave some time for review near the end of each unit or chapter, for reteaching as the situation warrants, and for unexpected occurrences such as school closings due to inclement weather. See Figure 3.1 for an illustration of plans of different durations.

2. **Supplementary materials.** For each major curricular topic in your rough long-range plans, start an ongoing list of related supplementary materials or activities. It may include field trip locations, resource people, media, games, assignments, bulletin boards, and additional books. Inquire about library or media center resources, such as audio discs or DVDs, and order and reserve them. Determine what online resources you might use and make sure you have the appropriate passwords. You might prepare other supplementary materials to use during the first few weeks of school.

3. **Skeleton plans.** A *skeleton plan* is a brief overview of intended accomplishments. It often includes a weekly list of expected accomplishments. Skeleton plans include more details than the long-range yearly plans but not the detail needed for daily lesson plans. Skeleton plans for the first three or four weeks serve as a guide for preparing the more detailed lesson plans.

4. **Weekly time schedules.** You should establish your weekly schedule before school starts and include a copy in a handy place such as in your lesson plan book. The weekly schedule is often displayed in a chart, with the weekdays listed at the top and the hours listed on the left-hand column. The principal or others probably will determine the class schedule for middle and secondary teachers in the school building, and the schedule will show what grade level and subject are taught during each class period.

5. **Daily lesson plans.** After you have completed the skeleton plans for the first three or four weeks, it is time to prepare the daily lesson plans for the first week of school. Lesson plan formats vary; one that is often used includes boxes for the days of the week and the subjects taught. In these boxes, you might include notes about objectives, a list of topics to be covered or activities to be conducted, materials, and means of assessment. Beginning and probationary teachers are often required to show the principal or assistant principal their weekly lesson plans for the coming week.

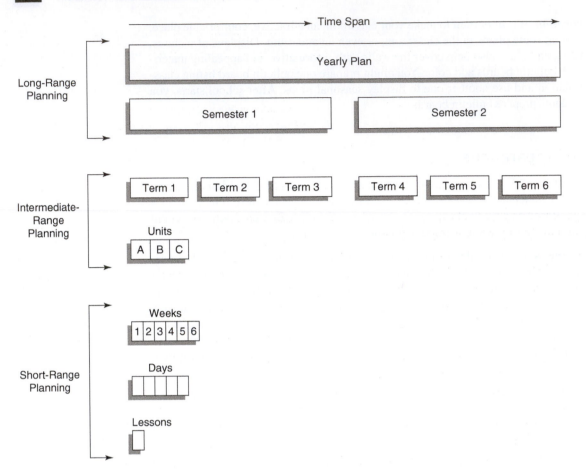

FIGURE 3.1   **Plans of different durations.**

6. **Syllabus.** You need to give students information about each course at the start of the year. You could plan and prepare this information as well as any related materials before school starts. The *course syllabus* includes the course title, the title of the textbook and any other primary resource materials, a brief course description, a list of course objectives, a content outline, course requirements (e.g., tests, homework, and projects), how grades will be calculated (e.g., the points for each requirement and the point total needed for certain grades), a description of the homework policy, the attendance and tardiness policy, and a listing of classroom rules and procedures.

7. **Policy sheets.** The syllabus might include all related classroom policies and procedures, although some teachers do not include these items. Depending on the grade level and circumstances, some teachers do not provide a course syllabus. As a result, a teacher might prepare a separate policy sheet for the students stating the classroom rules and procedures, the policy for attendance and tardiness, and the like. If a course syllabus is not used, this policy sheet might also state the grading policy.

8. **Tentative student assessment.** It is useful to make an initial assessment of the students' understanding and skills at the start of the school year so you can better recognize the abilities and differences within the class. These assessments could be conducted sometime during the first week of school, but you should think about how to plan for the assessment and

■ WHAT WOULD YOU DECIDE?   Starting with Long-Range Plans

Prior to the school year, you will need to make some long-range plans that will provide a framework for your daily and weekly plans. These general plans may be for the entire year, and then be broken down into semesters, grading periods, and units.

1. What curriculum guides and other materials will you need to gather to provide a basis for your long-range planning decisions?

2. How will you determine the amount of time to be spent on each unit for each course?

3. How will you keep a record of your long-range plans?

4. What information would you put into your plans for the first marking term? How will this help in your unit and lesson planning?

---

then make any necessary arrangements before school starts. Assessment procedures might include worksheets, oral activities, observation checklists, pretests, or review lessons. After conducting these early assessments, you should then record the results on a class roster that was drawn up earlier.

9. **Homework.** Give careful consideration to how you will evaluate students and determine report card grades. One element of student evaluation often involves homework, and preparation for developing a homework policy can be done before school starts. Prepare a homework policy in the form of a letter that is sent home to families at the start of the school year (see Chapter 11). The homework policy should explain why homework is assigned, explain the types of homework you will assign, inform parents of the amount and frequency of homework, provide guidelines for when and how students are to complete homework, let parents know you will positively reinforce students who complete homework, explain what you will do when students do not complete homework, and clarify what is expected of the parent.

10. **Backup materials.** It is useful to have some backup materials available when instruction takes less time than anticipated, when a change of plans is necessary, or when students finish their activities early. These backup materials may be related to the particular topics being covered at the time. Many teachers have a collection of puzzles, educational games, discussion questions, brainteasers, creative writing, word searches, and riddles. You can gather these materials before school starts.

11. **Opening class routine.** Students often perform better when they know that a particular routine will be regularly followed at the start of class. You can decide on the particular actions to be taken. You may need to take attendance, make announcements, and attend to other tasks at the start of the class period. The purpose of having a routine is to provide an orderly transition as students enter the room and get ready for instruction. Some teachers have students review vocabulary words or other problems related to the curriculum while other tasks are performed.

12. **Folder for substitute teachers.** A substitute teacher will take your place when you are absent. It is important to prepare materials for substitute teachers to help support what they do, maximize the learning, and minimize any off-task behavior. Many teachers keep a folder for substitute teachers that includes important information. It can be kept on your desk with the plan book.

  The type of material in a folder for substitute teachers varies, but the following information would be useful to include: a copy of the daily schedule, times of recess and lunch, a list of the classroom rules, a list of classroom procedures (e.g., morning opening, taking attendance, lunch count, lunch, dismissal, and fire drills), a list of reliable students in each class period, hall pass procedures (to go to the restroom, library, or office), information on where to find certain items (e.g., lesson plans, audiovisual equipment, and supplies), names of others to contact for information or help (e.g., a nearby teacher with room number), and a list and description of students with special needs. Much of this information can be collected before school starts, and additional information can be added as needed.

13. **Paraprofessionals.** Paraprofessionals, paraeducators, and teacher aides are among the various titles used for noncertified paid assistants in the classroom. Paraprofessionals can provide considerable assistance in the classroom under the guidance of the teacher. If you have a paraprofessional available, identify ways that you might use this person to facilitate instruction. Resources are available to give you guidance in your decisions (e.g., Ashbaker & Morgan, 2013; Doyle, 2008; Nevin, Villa, & Thousand, 2008). Guidelines are also available for paraprofessionals concerning behavioral interventions (Ashbaker & Morgan, 2015) and effective support in inclusive classrooms (Causton-Theoharis, 2009; Hammeken, 2008).

14. **Arrangements for late arrivals**. It is quite common for new students to arrive after the school year has begun. If arriving within the first week or two of the start of the school year, it may be relatively easy to get students oriented. When arriving later in the school year, orienting new students requires more effort and planning. To do so, give attention to what you would need to do to orient the new students and to prepare them academically. Research indicates that teacher support and peer acceptance have a positive impact on academic performance of students who change schools (Gruman, Harachi, Abbott, Catalano, & Fleming, 2008). Your planned actions might include reviewing the student's school records, assessing the student's current skill and knowledge levels, teaching rules and procedures, introducing the student to the class, assigning a buddy student to work with the new student during the transition, meeting with the student individually during the transition, and other facilitating actions.

Managing Assessment, Record Keeping, and Reporting

It is vital to give advance thought concerning how you will assess student achievement, record student progress and scores, and report the assessment information. Assessment always has been important in teaching. Even before the school year starts, you should decide how you will assess student learning, keep records of student performance, and report the assessment data.

Electronic gradebooks are provided in many districts, or you can purchase one you like (assuming your district does not require the same electronic gradebook for all teachers). These have a spreadsheet design in which scores for each type of assessment can be entered for each student. Electronic gradebooks facilitate record keeping and reporting of grades:

- **Assessment.** Although there are many aspects to assessment, you will need to select the means of assessment. Teacher-made tests and quizzes are common. In addition, you may choose to have students demonstrate their learning through the use of performance-based measures with (a) products (e.g., portfolios, work samples, projects, and lab reports); or (b) performances (e.g., oral presentations, presentations with media, demonstrations, debates, and athletic demonstrations). For each of these assessment approaches, you will also need to determine how you will assess the level of student proficiency. This could be done through an answer key for a test, or with the use of rubrics or other rating forms for performance-based measures.

- **Record keeping.** Once students have been assessed and you have scored their work, you must keep records in a gradebook. Gradebooks typically have a section for the daily attendance log, achievement scores, and conduct scores. All student assessment scores are placed in the gradebook, so prior thinking about your overall assessment plan will help you design the columns and labels in a useful manner. In addition to scores for performance on test

VOICES FROM THE CLASSROOM   Planning for a Substitute Teacher

Mary Pat Whiteside, middle school teacher, Palm Coast, Florida

Establishing procedures for times when you are absent helps avoid stress for you, your students, and your substitute teacher. The first step is to discuss with your students your expectations for their behavior when a substitute teacher is there. I start by having my students discuss their worst experiences with a substitute. Then I ask if they want substitutes to leave our school and go out to the community bearing tales of horror. Next, I tell students that my rule for them is to treat substitutes better than they treat me. Inappropriate behavior by them leads to punishment by me and a phone call home.

The second step is to plan for the substitute teacher. I have a folder labeled "Substitute," which includes seating charts, class attendance lists, clear plans designed for easy understanding, a folder of extra work, the location of my emergency lesson plans, and a substitute feedback sheet.

At the top of the feedback sheet, I ask that the classroom rules be enforced, and I ask for short notes from the substitute about each class's general behavior. I also ask the substitute to list any students who were uncooperative, disruptive, or tardy. I ask that the substitute not discipline my students, but instead leave me the information and I will handle any problems that arose when I return. This system works well for me, and I now look forward to returning to order instead of chaos.

items, portfolios, or other measuring techniques, some teachers have separate charts to record student proficiency for particular knowledge and skills related to the curriculum standards.

Entering the assessment scores in the gradebook is only part of your task. Then you must have a plan to translate all of the performance measures into a grade at the end of the report card period. For example, in a given subject, will you have a weight of 20% for homework, 40% for tests, 20% for a portfolio, and 20% for cooperative group projects? Furthermore, what performance level constitutes an A or a B? You need to think about your grading system before the start of the school year and establish your plan.

- **Reporting.** Your school district will likely determine a number of aspects of what will be recorded on report cards and how the information will be reported. First, the district determines what achievement and nonachievement (e.g., conduct) progress will be reported. Also, it determines what grading system will be used (e.g., letter grades, pass/fail, and checklists). There may be additional ways the district determines how grades are reported.

  In addition to report cards, you can communicate students' progress to their families in many ways, such as through parent–teacher conferences, newsletters, and open houses. During a parent–teacher conference, you may want to have a portfolio for each student ready to show representative work. For a newsletter, you may want to share information about the activities and the performance of the entire class. Give advance thought about what information you will be reporting and develop a plan for the kinds of data and materials you need to gather and report.

Establishing a Plan to Deal with Misbehavior

With an understanding of classroom management and discipline, you will need to develop a plan for dealing with misbehavior in the classroom. A seven-step plan is presented here that begins with the establishment of a system of rules and procedures. You need to provide a supportive environment during instruction and also provide situational assistance when students get off task.

If the student does not get back on task, you need to move through advancing levels of consequences. If none of these actions work, you may need to involve other personnel.

You should deal with misbehavior in a way that is effective while also avoiding unnecessary disruptions. Researchers and educators have proposed movement from low to high intervention when developing a plan to address misbehavior (e.g., Charles & Cole, 2019; Levin & Nolan, 2014; Wolfgang, 2009). Once the rules and procedures and a supportive classroom environment are in place, the teacher moves from low to high interventions, as described:

1. **Establish your system of rules and procedures.** Establish an appropriate system of rules and procedures as a foundation for dealing with discipline (discussed more fully in Chapter 4). It is vital that you select a system of rules and procedures appropriate to the situation. This system should incorporate reward or reinforcement for desirable behavior and the consequences of misbehavior. No single approach is best for all teachers and all teaching situations. For instance, rules and procedures for a tenth-grade English class would not be appropriate for a third-grade class. Furthermore, the system needs to be consistent with established school and district policies and with your own educational philosophy, personality, and preferences.

2. **Provide a supportive environment during class sessions.** Once the system of rules and procedures has been established at the start of the school year, you need to maintain a supportive environment. Actions taken in the normal course of instruction are for the purpose of guiding and reinforcing students for positive behavior (discussed more fully in Chapter 5).

   Providing a supportive environment is accomplished primarily through cueing and reinforcing appropriate behavior and getting and holding attention. Cueing and reinforcing involve stressing positive, desirable behaviors; recognizing and reinforcing desired behaviors; and praising effectively. Getting and holding attention necessitate focusing attention at the start of lessons; keeping lessons moving at a good pace; monitoring attention during lessons; stimulating attention periodically; maintaining accountability; and terminating lessons that have gone on too long. Treat students with dignity and respect and offer challenging, interesting, and exciting classes.

3. **Provide situational assistance during class sessions.** Students may get off task during a lesson. This off-task behavior may be in the form of misbehavior or may simply be a lapse in attention. Either way, you need to promptly provide situational assistance. *Situational assistance* denotes actions that you take to get the student back on task with the least amount of intervention and disruption possible. Situational assistance can be provided by removing distracting objects, reinforcing appropriate behaviors, boosting student interest, providing cues, helping students over hurdles, redirecting the behavior, altering the lesson, and other approaches (discussed more fully in Chapter 9).

4. **Use mild responses.** If a student continues to be off task after situational assistance is provided, then you need to use mild responses to correct the student's behavior. These are not intended to be punitive. Mild responses may be nonverbal or verbal (see Chapter 9). Nonverbal responses include ignoring the behavior, using signal interference, using proximity control, or using touch control. Verbal responses include reinforcing peers, calling on the student during the lesson, using humor, giving a direct appeal or command, reminding the student of the rule, and several other approaches.

5. **Use moderate responses.** If students do not respond favorably to mild responses and continue to exhibit off-task behavior, you need to deliver moderate responses (see Chapter 9). These punitive responses deal with misbehavior by removing the desired stimulus so as to minimize the inappropriate behavior. Moderate responses include the use of logical consequences and various behavior-modification techniques such as time-out and loss of privileges.

6. **Use stronger responses.** If moderate responses are insufficient, then you need to move to a more intrusive type of intervention (see Chapter 10). These stronger responses are intended to be punitive, by adding aversive stimuli such as reprimands and overcorrection. The purpose of aversive stimuli is to decrease unwanted behavior.

7. **Involve others when necessary.** If all efforts have failed to get the student to behave properly, then you need to involve other persons in the process. This occurs most commonly with chronic or severe behaviors. You may consult or involve counselors, psychologists, principals and assistant principals, teaching colleagues, college personnel, mental health centers, school social workers, school nurses, supervisors and department heads, and families (see Chapter 10). Their assistance and involvement will vary, depending on their expertise.

Preparing for the First Day

Starting the school year effectively is vitally important when implementing a system of classroom management. In addition to making management and instructional preparations before the school year starts, it is important to plan how you will conduct your first day with the students. Your planning for the first day may take into account the information you need to convey along with interactions with the students. Then you need to consider how you will conduct the first day, sort of like a lesson plan. These issues are examined in this section.

Planning for the First Day

Several principles should guide your decisions about planning the start of the school year and your actions in the first few days (Emmer & Evertson, 2017; Evertson & Emmer, 2017; Wong & Wong, 2018a, 2018b).

1. **Plan to clearly state your rules, procedures, and academic expectations.** When students arrive in your class for the first time, they may have uncertainties. They will want to know your expectations for behavior and for academic work. They will want to know what the rules are for general behavior and also the consequences for adhering to or breaking them (discussed more fully in Chapter 4). They want to know what the procedures are for going to the restroom, turning in homework, sharpening their pencils, talking during seatwork, and other specific activities. They will be interested in finding out about course requirements, grading policies, standards for work, and other aspects of the academic program.

   It is especially important to take the necessary time during the first few days of school to describe your expectations in detail about behavior and work. Emphasize and be explicit about desirable behavior. Combine learning about procedures, rules, and course requirements with your initial content activities to build a good foundation for the year.

■ **WHAT WOULD YOU DECIDE?**　Dealing with Late Students on the First Day

It's the first day of school. You've just gone over many instructional and management topics for your sixth-grade class and had some introductory, get-acquainted activities. Then two students arrive an hour late. They've missed all of that information and the introductory activities. You don't want to disadvantage the two students, but you also think you should move ahead with the rest of the class.

1. What would you do at that moment? How do you move the rest of the class ahead while still making provision for the two late students to obtain the needed introductory information and also to get to know the other students?

2. What other problems might you anticipate on the first day? How might you address those problems?

2. **Plan uncomplicated lessons to help students be successful.** Content activities and assignments during the first week should be designed to ensure maximum student success. Select relatively uncomplicated lessons at the start of the school year so that few students will likely need individual help. This allows you to focus on monitoring behavior and to respond to students in ways that shape and reinforce appropriate behavior. It provides you with opportunities to reinforce students for their academic work and to begin to develop positive relationships with students.

3. **Keep a whole-class focus.** Plan activities for the first week that have a whole-class focus, rather than small-group activities. Whole-class activities make it easier to monitor student behavior and performance. In this way, you can focus on reinforcing appropriate behavior and preventing inappropriate behavior.

4. **Be available, visible, and in charge.** You must be in charge of students at all times. Move around and be physically near the students and maintain a good field of vision to see all students wherever you stand. Move around during seatwork to check on student progress.

5. **Plan strategies to deal with potential problems.** Unexpected events can develop when you meet your students for the first time. These might include interruptions by parents, office staff, custodians, or others; late arrivals on the first day; one or more students being assigned to your class after the first day; and an insufficient number of textbooks or necessary materials. You can give advance thought to how you would deal with common, unplanned events should they occur. Treat each unexpected situation in a calm, professional manner. This will serve as a good model for your students when they confront unexpected or challenging events. Treat students respectfully and deal with some of the needed details later. For example, you can ask a late enrolling student to take a seat and begin work, and then you could handle the particular enrollment procedures later.

6. **Closely monitor student compliance with rules and procedures.** By closely monitoring students, you can provide cues and reinforcement for appropriate behavior. Better classroom managers monitor their students' compliance with rules consistently, intervene to correct inappropriate behavior whenever necessary, and mention rules or describe desirable behavior when giving feedback. Effective managers stress specific corrective feedback rather than criticism or threat of punishment when students fail to comply with rules and procedures.

7. **Stop inappropriate behavior quickly.** Inappropriate or disruptive behavior should be handled quickly and consistently. Minor misbehavior that is not corrected often increases in intensity or is taken up by other students. Quickly respond to inappropriate behavior to maximize on-task behavior. Act in a professional manner to settle the difficulty and preserve the student's dignity in front of the other students.

8. **Organize instruction on the basis of ability levels.** The cumulative record folders will indicate students' prior academic performance in reading, math, and other subjects. Select instructional content and activities to meet the ability levels of your students.

9. **Hold students academically accountable.** Develop procedures that keep students accountable for their academic work. This may include papers to be turned in at the end of class, homework, in-class activities, or other means. Return the completed papers promptly and with feedback. Some teachers give a weekly assignment sheet to each student. This sheet is completed by the student, checked by the parent, and returned to the teacher daily.

10. **Be clear when communicating information.** Effective teachers clearly and explicitly present information, give directions, and state objectives. When discussing complex tasks, break them down into step-by-step procedures.

11. **Maintain students' attention.** Arrange seating so all students can easily face the area where their main attention needs to be held. Get everyone's focused attention before

starting a lesson. Monitor students for signs of confusion or inattention and be sensitive to student concerns.

12. **Organize the flow of lesson activities.** Effective classroom managers waste little time getting the students organized for the lesson. They maximize student attention and task engagement during activities by maintaining momentum and providing signals and cues. They successfully deal with more than one thing at a time (e.g., talking with one student but also keeping an eye on the rest of the class).

Conducting the First Day

The first day of school is often a time of nervousness for teachers and students. Fortunately, you can do a number of things on the first day to address student concerns:

1. **Greet the students.** Stand by the classroom door before class begins. When students are about to enter your classroom, greet them with a smile and a handshake. As you do this, tell them your name, your room number, the subject or period, if needed; the grade level and anything else appropriate, such as the student's seating assignment. Your name, room number, section or period, and grade level or subject should be posted outside your door and on the chalkboard.

2. **Tell students about their seat assignment.** There are various ways to handle seat assignments for students. Some teachers prefer to let students select their seats, while other teachers prefer to assign seats. Either way, students should be told what to do as they enter the classroom for the first time. If you determine the seating assignment, there are several possible ways to inform students of their seat assignment as they enter the room. You might have the seating arrangement displayed on a projection screen for each class when they enter the room. Also have a copy of the seating chart in hand as the students are greeted at the door. Cover what is expected of them concerning grading. Take time to discuss the course content and some of the activities planned for the year. If you have prepared a syllabus, hand it out. Discuss the grading requirements concerning tests, homework, projects, and the like, and indicate what levels are needed for the various letter grades.

■ **CLASSROOM CASE STUDY**   A Poor Start on the Opening Day

Cheryl Templeton wanted to have an interesting opening day for her middle school language arts students. In the first class session with her fourth-period class, she briefly introduced herself, described the rules, and provided an overview of the content they would cover in the course. She then split the class of 28 students into five groups and asked each group to go to a designated area of the room where they could cluster their desks for their small-group work.

She gave directions for the groups to address some new course content and then told them to proceed with their group work. While the groups were discussing the material, Ms. Templeton was at her desk assembling some materials for her fifth-period class. Soon, it became apparent that all was not going well. The students weren't exactly sure what they were supposed to do since the directions were so long and complicated.

Since it was the first day and they didn't know each other, some group members felt uncomfortable interacting with the other students and did not participate. The content they were asked to address also seemed to be too advanced for many of the students. As a result, an increasing number of students got off task and some started to misbehave. For those actually doing the work, they weren't sure if the group was to have a single report or if each student was to turn in his/her report. They also didn't know where to turn in the report at the end of the activity.

Ms. Templeton noticed some of these actions, yet she stayed at her desk and had little interaction with the students during this activity. At the end of the class, students felt frustrated and apprehensive about what type of year they would have in this class.

Focus Questions

1. What were the errors that Ms. Templeton made in planning and conducting this class session?

2. What could she have done to avoid the problems and to have a successful class session?

3. Concerning only one dimension, what could she have done to help the students get to know each other?

3. **Correct improper room entry.** Observe students as they enter the room and take their seats. Some students may not go directly to their seats or may behave inappropriately. It is important to ask a student who enters the room inappropriately to return to the door and enter properly. Be calm, but firm; tell the students why this is being done, give specific directions, check for understanding, and acknowledge the understanding (Wong & Wong, 2018a). The communication might be something like this:

Todd, please come back to the door.
I am sorry, but that is not the way you enter our classroom every day. You were noisy, you did not go to your seat, and you pushed Ann.
When you enter this classroom, you walk in quietly, go directly to your seat, and get to work immediately on the assignment that is posted.
Are there any questions?
Thank you, Todd. Now show me that you can go to your seat properly.

During the interaction, be sure to use the student's name and be polite with a "please" and "thank you."

4. **Handle administrative tasks.** Taking attendance is one of the first administrative tasks to be done at the start of the class period. One approach is to have the students raise their hands when called to indicate that they are present and to give you an opportunity to see the face that goes with the name. As you call each name, ask the student whether you pronounced it correctly. After the first day of school, some teachers prefer not to take attendance at the start of class. Instead, they give an assignment that the students are to begin as soon as they enter the classroom. After the students are under way, the teacher can take attendance by visually scanning the room; the names do not need to be called. This approach, or one similar to it, takes very little time and allows students to move quickly into the academic work.

5. **Make introductions.** Students appreciate knowing something about the teacher. At the start of the class period, tell the students your name and some personal information, such as the number of years you have been teaching, professional development activities, family, personal interests and activities, hobbies, and other background information. This helps the students know you as a person and may be informative and comforting to them. This is also the time to let the students know that you are enthusiastic about working with them and that you will be reasonable and fair with them. Some teachers like to use this opening time to have the students briefly introduce themselves. Some get-acquainted activities for students could be included on the first day to help promote good feelings.

6. **Discuss classroom rules and procedures.** All classrooms need rules and procedures if they are to run smoothly and efficiently. Rules should be taught on the first day of class to establish the general code of conduct (discussed more fully in Chapter 4). Post the rules in a conspicuous place in the classroom. If a letter has been prepared for parents that describes the rules and procedures, this should be given to the students so they can take it home.

Some classroom procedures may be taught on the first day of school, but many teachers prefer to teach procedures (e.g., distributing materials, getting ready to leave the classroom, and handing in papers) over the next several school days instead. Procedures can be taught when the need for them first occurs. For example, when it is time to collect papers at the end of an activity, you could teach students the appropriate procedure.

7. **Present course requirements.** Before school started, you would have prepared the course requirements and syllabus. On the first day, students want to know what content will be covered and what is expected of them concerning grading. Take time to discuss the course content and some of the activities planned for the year. If you have prepared a syllabus, hand

■ WHAT WOULD YOU DECIDE?   Planning an Initial Activity in Your Classroom

On one of the first days of the new school year, you want to have an activity that provides some content review concerning what the students learned in the previous year. You also want to provide a preview for the content that will be addressed during the coming year in your class.

1. What are some ways this content review might be conducted in interesting ways to the students yet meaningful enough so that you get a picture of their current knowledge?

2. How might you provide a preview for the content that will be addressed this year? How might you use a graphic organizer for this purpose? How might you use other creative strategies for this purpose?

3. How might you relate the content to various cultural backgrounds of your students?

it out. Discuss the grading requirements concerning tests, homework, projects, and the like, and indicate what levels are needed for the various letter grades.

8. **Conduct an initial activity.** Depending on the amount of time available on the first day, many teachers plan an initial activity related to the curriculum. It should provide a review of some material that students had in the previous year or may be a preview of content to be covered. Either way, the activity should be designed so that the students can complete it without much assistance and with much success. This leaves you free to monitor the students during the activity, to provide assistance when necessary, and to take corrective action on off-task behavior.

9. **End the class period.** A routine to end the class period is needed, and this must be taught to students. Procedures need to be established and time saved for actions such as returning books and supplies, disposing of scrap paper and cleaning up the classroom, and putting away books and other materials in preparation for leaving the classroom.

Organizing Your Classroom and Materials

Decisions about room arrangement must be made before students arrive on the first day of school. Before arranging the classroom, consider (a) the movement patterns of students throughout the classroom; (b) the need for students to obtain a variety of materials, texts, reference books, equipment, and supplies; and (c) the need for students to see the instructional presentations and display materials.

Arrange and decorate your room in a manner that supports effective classroom management. Teachers organize their use of space by creating sets of procedures and expectations and by monitoring, directing, and responding to students and classroom. How you arrange your classroom will influence your selection of procedures, expectations, and ways of monitoring and interacting with your students. How you deal with these issues will influence the degree that students stay on task or get off task and misbehave. Thus, careful attention must be given to arranging the classroom and materials.

When designing and organizing your classroom and materials, you should take students' needs and interests into account and give special attention to design elements that take into account the diverse backgrounds of students. These issues and general guidelines are now presented:

1. **Design with students in mind.** Designing learning spaces that meet the needs of your students can be a high-leverage classroom management strategy, especially if students themselves are involved in some of the decision making. Research documents how a classroom designed with student feedback can positively impact emotions, engagement, and learning

(Gremmen, van den Berg, Segers, & Cillessen, 2016). Being more intentional about classroom design can help teachers manage behavior, build community, and improve learning by giving attention to such factors as flexible working spaces, quiet areas, grouping areas, colors and displays, and light and sound (Dillon, 2018). In *Strategic Classroom Design*, Jessica Martin (2019) provides guidance to design flexible classrooms leading to greater engagement and learning.

2. **Design for students with diverse backgrounds**. You probably will not have a homogeneous group of students in your class. It is more likely that you will have students with various levels of English proficiency, cognitive abilities, exceptionalities, and life experiences. They will likely represent various racial and ethnic groups.

   Due to these diverse backgrounds, you should design your classroom with much flexibility in anticipation of their diverse qualities and needs. For example, you may plan for some work areas in the room that will enable students to watch and listen to a recording, work at a computer, or interact with other students in a small-group setting. The seating pattern in the classroom might be arranged to easily permit students to turn to a partner, as in a think-pair-share activity. Bulletin boards could be used to post vocabulary words, student work, material related to content, pictures and drawings, or other items that will facilitate student learning. The bulletin board and other visual displays could be used to reflect and value the contributions and traditions of your students' ethnic groups as well as meet your students' needs for access. Consider including other classroom elements where students feel comfortable and at home in their new classroom while their academic needs are being met.

3. **Follow guidelines for good room arrangement.** Good room arrangement can help teachers cope with the complex demands of teaching by minimizing interruptions, delays, and dead times. Based on studies of effective classroom managers, there are five keys to good room arrangement (Emmer & Evertson, 2017; Evertson & Emmer, 2017):

   • **Use a room arrangement consistent with your instructional goals and activities.** You will need to think about the main types of instructional activities that will be used in your classes and then organize the seating, materials, and equipment compatibly. Teacher-led presentations, demonstrations, or recitations will require students to be seated so they can see the instructional area. In contrast, small-group work will require very different room arrangements.

   • **Keep high-traffic areas free of congestion.** High-traffic areas include the space around doorways, the pencil sharpener and trash can, group work areas, certain bookshelves and supply areas, the teacher's desk, and student desks. High-traffic areas should be separated from each other, have plenty of space, and be easily accessible. For example, try not to seat a student next to the pencil sharpener because of the heavy traffic and the possibility of inappropriate behavior.

   • **Be sure students can be seen easily by the teacher.** It is important that teachers easily see students to identify when a student needs assistance or to prevent task avoidance or disruption. Clear lines of sight must be maintained between student work areas and areas of the room that the teacher will frequent.

   • **Keep frequently used teaching materials and student supplies readily accessible.** By having easy access and efficient storage of these materials, activities are more likely to begin and end promptly, and time spent on getting ready and cleaning up will be minimized. Establishing regulated storage areas can help reduce the occurrence of students leaving materials in their desks or taking them out of the room.

   • **Be certain students can easily see instructional presentations and displays.** The seating arrangement should allow all students to see the chalkboard or the multimedia screen without moving their chairs, turning their desks around, or craning their necks. Place the primary instructional area in a prominent location to help students pay attention and to facilitate note taking.

VOICES FROM THE CLASSROOM   Creating a Center for Make-Up Work

Susan Lovelace, high school teacher, Sebastian, Florida

I realized that I was spending much time with students before and after class who wanted to know what they missed when they were absent. As a result, I organized an area for make-up work information in the back of the classroom. I purchased a dry-erase board and six pocket folders, each with a different color for each of the classes I teach. Above that board, I put a sign that reads, "What Did I Miss?"

At the end of the day, I write the assignment or activities that we covered in class that day on the dry-erase board. For each folder under the dry-erase board, I put any handouts, worksheets, or returned work in the labeled pocket folder for each class. For example, my first-period class knows they have the blue folder, so students know where to look.

Now my students know to go directly to the make-up work center to find out what they missed, and I am not using valuable time repeating make-up work information several times a day.

Floor Space

A classroom typically contains many items that take up floor space such as student desks, the teacher's desk, bookcases, tables, and activity centers. When determining how to arrange the classroom, you need to consider the functions of the space and the various factors mentioned earlier in an effort to facilitate learning and to minimize interruptions and delays.

A good starting point in creating the floor plan is to decide where you will conduct whole-group instruction. Examine the room and identify where you will stand or work when you address the entire class to conduct lessons or give directions. This area should have a whiteboard, projector screen, a table on which to place the projector, a small table to hold items needed during instruction, and an electrical outlet. Consider the following items:

- **Student desks.** Even if other arrangements are to be used later in the year, you might start the year with student desks in rows facing the major instructional area, since it is easier to manage students with this pattern. Be sure all students can see the major instructional area without having their backs to it and without having to get out of their seats. It is important to keep student desks away from high-traffic areas. Avoid placing their desks near the door, pencil sharpener, trash can, and supply areas. Leave ample aisles between the desks to enable easy movement of students and yourself when monitoring seatwork. Figure 3.2 shows a number of possible seating arrangements.

- **The teacher's desk.** Your desk should be situated so that you can see the students, but it is not essential that the desk be at the front of the room. Placement of your desk at the rear of the room, in fact, may help when monitoring students during independent work. Students facing away from you cannot discern when you are looking at them unless they turn around. This tends to encourage students to stay at their assigned tasks. Instead of sitting at their desk during independent work, many teachers prefer to move around the room to monitor and assist students.

- **Bookcases and filing cabinets.** Other items should be placed so students' visibility of whiteboards or relevant displays is not obstructed. These items should also not interfere with your monitoring of students. If a bookcase contains frequently used items such as resource books, dictionaries, or supplies, then it should be conveniently located and monitored. Seldom-used items should be stored in an out-of-the-way place. If there is only one bookcase, it is helpful to use it for frequently used items.

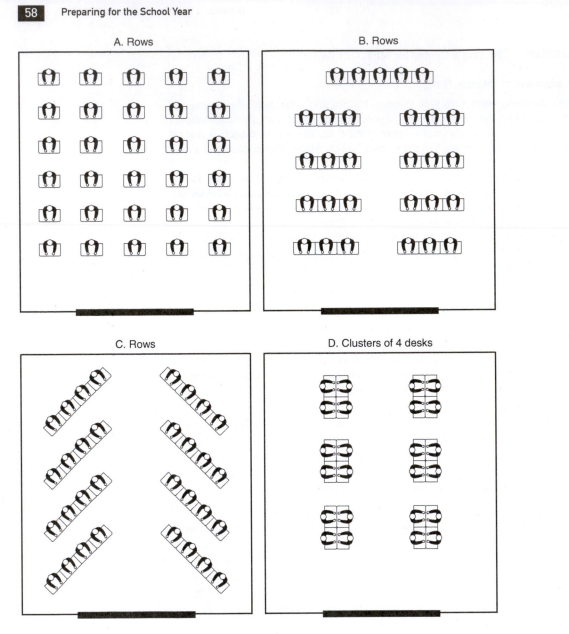

FIGURE 3.2   Possible seating arrangements.

- **Activity centers or work areas.** An *activity center* is an area where one or more students come to work on a special activity. It may be in the form of a learning center or a computer work area. One or more tables commonly serve as the work surfaces. When you select the placement of tables for this area, be sure that you can see all students in the work area, keep traffic lanes clear, and avoid congested areas. A center often will have special equipment such as a computer or other materials and supplies. Enough tables and workspace must be provided for students to work efficiently. It is useful to place the work area at the side or the back of the room and to the backs of other students.

- **Computer workstations.** Internet connections and electrical outlets will affect computer placement. Position the computers so that you can easily view them to be sure students are

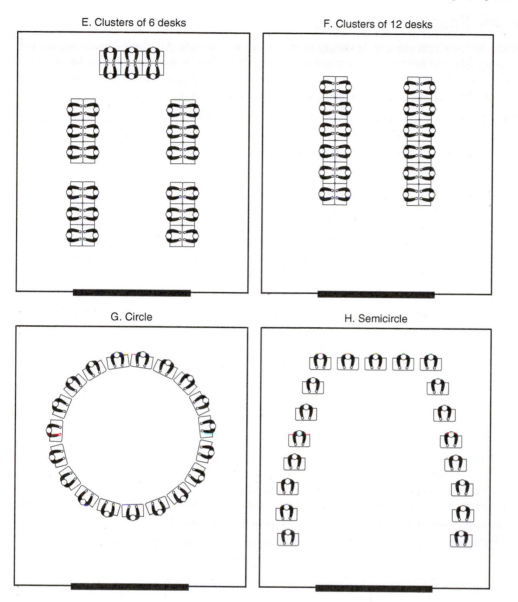

FIGURE 3.2 (continued)

on task. Some schools have computers on rolling carts to be shared among several class-rooms. In that case, you will need to select a place for the rolling cart and arrange for a clear pathway to the selected location. You also may need to arrange for space for paper, printing cartridges, and other supplies.

It might be necessary to establish special procedures for electronic devices, including computers. Some schools allow students to bring in their own devices, whether laptops, iPads, or smartphones, in which case, a strong wireless network will be important. As more computer-related technology is used in the classroom, attention needs to be given to space for student work along with guidance and support for these activities.

Storage Space

Teachers and students use a wide variety of instructional materials. All of these materials are not used every day and must be stored when not in use. Therefore, storage space must be provided for textbooks and resource books, frequently used instructional materials, teacher supplies and instructional materials, equipment, and infrequently used materials. Here are some guidelines:

1. **Textbooks and resource books.** Some textbooks are not retained by students and thus must be stored in the classroom for easy access. Resource books obtained from the school library, public library, or other sources may be available for student use. All of these books should be stored in a bookcase that enables easy access.

2. **Instructional materials.** Instructional materials that students need will vary with the subject area that you teach. These may include rulers, scissors, special paper, pencils, staplers, tape, glue, and other supplies. As with textbooks and resource books, a storage location should be selected to enable easy access to the materials. Clearly labeled containers for each of the supply items are often very helpful in maintaining an orderly supply area. These materials may be stored on shelves of a bookcase or cabinet, or on a counter.

3. **Teacher supplies.** Supplies that only you would use should be kept in your desk or in storage areas used only by you. These supplies include items such as hall passes, attendance and lunch count forms, lesson plan books, tablets, file folders, flash drives, and whiteboard markers. These items should be placed in secure places so students do not have access to them.

4. **Equipment.** The type of equipment needing to be stored will vary considerably, depending on a teacher's grade level and subject area. A physical education teacher, for example, may need to store many types of equipment and supplies when not needed for a class session. Art teachers might need to store special presses that are not used every day.

5. **Infrequently used items.** Some instructional materials are used only once a year. These include seasonal decorations (e.g., Halloween and Thanksgiving), bulletin board displays, or special project materials. Certain instructional materials may be used for only one unit, as in the case of a model of the human eye for a science class. Some teachers prefer to keep seasonal decorations or other infrequently used materials at their homes.

VOICES FROM THE CLASSROOM   Organizing Your Materials and Space

Leila Post, fourth-grade teacher, Reno, Nevada

I find that good organization makes me a better teacher. I organize my daily lessons and activities in five plastic trays lined across a counter, and they are labeled by the day of the week. On top of each tray is another tray for a second week. This allows me to plan and collect related materials for two weeks at a time. This organization also makes it easier for a substitute teacher to locate all the needed materials.

I have student supplies easily accessible on shelves, and I have labeled trays for turning in daily seatwork, homework, and center work. At each cluster of student desks, I have a plastic basket containing glue, erasers, pencils, and crayons. Each student is assigned a number at the start of the school year, and this number is used to identify all folders, mailboxes, scissors, and other items. I find classroom organization of teacher and student materials reduces wasted time, increases productivity, and teaches organizational skills to the students.

Bulletin Boards and Wall Space

Constructive use of bulletin boards and wall space can contribute to a positive classroom environment. This can be achieved by displaying relevant instructional material, assignments, rules, schedules, student work, and other items of interest. Many teachers involve students in the selection of content and the preparation of bulletin boards and the use of wall space. One approach is to select a different group of students to plan and prepare a bulletin board each month.

Some teachers prefer to dedicate each bulletin board to a certain purpose. For example, one bulletin board can be used to post classroom rules, a daily or weekly schedule, classroom helpers, lunch menus, a school map, emergency information, or any other procedural information. Another bulletin board can be used to display student work. A third type of bulletin board can be simply for decoration, with seasonal, motivational, or artistic items. Other bulletin boards can be used to post information and news articles about school or community events. In addition, bulletin boards can also be used to post content-related news articles, posters, or information.

Some of the material commonly placed on bulletin boards, such as a listing of classroom rules, can be placed on posters and displayed on the walls of the classroom if the content will not likely change during the school year. Designated areas of the chalkboard or whiteboard can also be used to display student assignments or special announcements because this information is likely to change daily.

MAJOR CONCEPTS

1. Many management and instructional preparations can be completed prior to the start of the school year.

2. Plans for dealing with misbehavior, assessment, record keeping, and reporting should be made prior to the start of the school year.

3. Early planning and decision making about classroom management and discipline issues will help ensure a positive beginning to the school year.

4. Careful attention to planning and conducting the first day of school will help provide students with a smooth beginning to

the school year and will promote their understanding of instructional and behavioral guidelines.

5. Organizing your classroom and materials includes attention to seating, floor space, storage space, bulletin boards, and wall space.

6. When designing and organizing your classroom and materials, you should take students' need and interests into account and give special attention to design elements that take into account the diverse backgrounds of students.

DISCUSSION/REFLECTIVE QUESTIONS

1. What is the reasoning for considering long-range plans (year long, semester long) before considering intermediate-term plans (terms and units) and before making more specific plans for daily lesson plans for the first couple weeks?

2. What are the benefits of planning uncomplicated lessons at the start of the school year? What might happen if the lessons are too challenging?

3. What are the merits of having a plan for systematically dealing with misbehavior?

4. What are the merits and disadvantages for placing students' seats in rows?

5. When planning to organize your classroom and materials, what are important issues that you would take into account as you make your decisions?

SUGGESTED ACTIVITIES

1. Talk with several teachers to find out how they do long-range planning for the school year. Also ask how they plan for each semester, each marking period, and each unit.

2. Think about how you will record your instructional plans (lesson plans, weekly plans, and long-range plans). Will this information be on forms or on the computer? How will you plan to store and retrieve these plans for future use?

3. Start to outline your plans for the first day of the school year. Make a list of the information you would want to convey. Make a tentative lesson plan that would include actions, content, activities, or other important elements.

4. When planning your classroom design, identify the ways your design will take into account your preferences as well as your consideration of student needs and interests. What might your classroom look like?

FURTHER READING

K–12

Guillaume, A. M. (2016). *K–12 classroom teaching: A primer for new professionals* (5th ed.). Boston, MA: Pearson.
Provides a very practical and comprehensive overview to many aspects of teaching, including issues needing attention at the start of the school year.

Kronowitz, E. L. (2012). *The teacher's guide to success* (2nd ed.). Boston, MA: Pearson.
Provides thorough descriptions of the first day, organization and management, discipline, planning, engaging learners, assessing, and professional life in balance.

Thompson, J. G. (2018). *First-year teacher's survival guide* (4th ed.). San Francisco, CA: Jossey-Bass.
Provides an excellent, thorough, yet practical guide to all aspects of starting your school year. Has a K–12 focus. Many useful charts and specific guides. Covers planning for behavior, curriculum, and instruction.

Wong, H. K., & Wong, R. T. (2018). *The first days of school: How to be an effective teacher* (5th ed.). Mountain View, CA: Harry Wong Publications.
A highly popular guide for beginning teachers. Has a K–12 focus. Loaded with very practical guidelines on positive expectations, classroom management, lesson mastery, and other vital topics.

Elementary

Jonson, K. F. (2010). *The new elementary teacher's handbook: Flourishing in your first year* (3rd ed.). Thousand Oaks, CA: Corwin Press.
Provides thorough, practical advice on topics such as organizing the classroom, managing the classroom, preparing instructional plans, dealing with discipline, assessing student work, and working with parents.

Moran, C., Stobbe, J., Baron, W., Miller, J., & Moir, E. (2009). *Keys to the elementary classroom: A new teacher's guide to the first month of school* (3rd ed.). Thousand Oaks, CA: Corwin Press.

Addresses planning, creating the environment, assessments, routines and procedures, activities in the opening days and weeks, and communication.

Responsive Classroom (2015). *First six weeks of school* (2nd ed.). Turners Falls, MA: Center for Responsive Schools.
Provides an overview of goals, responsibilities, and actions for all K–6 grades for the first six weeks. Then provides weekly guidance for each grade level. Very detailed and thorough. Useful resource.

Middle and Secondary

Bongolan, R., Moir, E., & Baron, W. (2010). *Keys to the secondary classroom: A new teacher's guide to the first months of school* (3rd ed.). Thousand Oaks, CA: Corwin Press.
Addresses the adolescent learner, starting the school year, rules and procedures, community and team building, standards-based curriculum, planning, assessment, and communicating.

Responsive Classroom (2018a). *Building an academic community: The middle school teacher's guide to the first four weeks of the school year.* Turners Falls, MA: Center for Responsive Classrooms.

Provides guidance about introducing classroom rules, fostering social-emotional and academic skills, responding to misbehavior in constructive ways, and setting a positive classroom environment.

Sprick, R. S. (2013). *Discipline in the secondary classroom: A positive approach to behavior management* (3rd ed.). San Francisco, CA: Jossey-Bass.
Addresses managing student behavior, grading and instruction, routines and procedures, classroom management plans, expectations, monitoring behavior, and consequences.

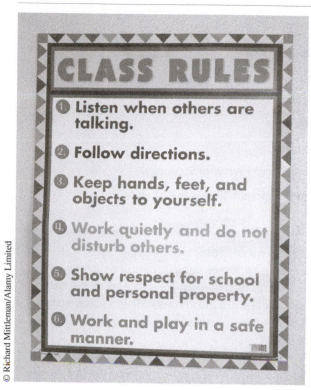

CLASS RULES

1. Listen when others are talking.
2. Follow directions.
3. Keep hands, feet, and objects to yourself.
4. Work quietly and do not disturb others.
5. Show respect for school and personal property.
6. Work and play in a safe manner.

Choosing Rules and Procedures

CHAPTER OUTLINE

CHAPTER OBJECTIVES

This chapter provides information that will help you:

- Examine the need for classroom rules.
- Use guidelines for selecting rules and procedures.
- Determine ways to teach and review the rules.
- Examine the need for classroom procedures.
- Identify guidelines for ways to select, teach, and review procedures.
- Apply strategies to help students assume responsibility for their behavior.

Think about all the traffic laws that govern the use of motor vehicles. Guidelines are set for ways to signal, turn, yield the right of way, pass other vehicles, and numerous other aspects of driving. These laws have been established in each state to ensure the safety of the driver and others. In a similar way, guidelines are also needed in the classroom to govern how the teacher and the students conduct themselves so that the learning objectives are achieved and everyone is successful.

Rules and procedures are used to guide and govern student behavior in classrooms. Even in positive learning communities where students are actively involved in arranging their learning environment, rules and procedures are necessary to guide behavior. Teachers need to consider carefully what rules and procedures are needed in order to manage the class effectively.

Your philosophical perspective on the models of discipline will greatly influence how you select rules and procedures. As discussed in Chapter 2, teachers using the intervening model (high teacher control) would likely select rules and procedures without consulting students. Teachers using the interacting model (medium teacher control) would likely have a discussion with the students and then collaboratively decide on the rules and procedures. Teachers using the guiding model (low teacher control) would likely turn the discussion over to the students and let them determine the rules and procedures.

As you consider the information on rules and procedures, reflect on your philosophical perspective concerning discipline and classroom management. One model may represent your beliefs about child development and management of student behavior. That, in turn, will give you a perspective about the degree of control you would want to take when determining rules and procedures.

Basing your classroom decisions on the principles of freedom, justice, and equality helps students look beyond their own individual cultural needs and interests and into the realm of common societal values. Your rules and procedures should respect the individual nature of each student. At the same time, all students need and deserve information about classroom expectations so that they can equally participate in protecting the common welfare needs of the group (Brady, Forton, & Porter, 2011; Moral, Wylie, & Abdus-Salaam, 2019).

Rules in the Classroom

Rules refer to general behavioral standards or expectations that are to be followed in the classroom. They are general codes of conduct that are intended to guide individual behavior in an attempt to promote positive interaction and avoid disruptive behavior. Rules guide the way students interact with each other, prepare for class, and conduct themselves during class. They are commonly stated in positive terms. In addition to general rules, teachers sometimes state rules for specific situations (e.g., cell phones must be turned off during class).

The effective use of rules involves several actions. You should examine the need for certain rules in the classroom, select appropriate rules, select the consequences, teach the rules to the students, obtain a commitment from the students about the rules, and then periodically review the rules throughout the school year. Many of the suggestions provided here are consistent with the guidance provided from the research studies on classroom management (Harlacher, 2015).

Examine the Need for Rules

Rules provide guidelines for appropriate behaviors so that teaching and learning can take place. They should be directed at organizing the learning environment to ensure the continuity and quality of teaching and learning and not simply be focused on exerting control over students.

Rules are necessary to have teaching and learning take place, and they need to be realistic, fair, and reasonable. Rules that are selected should meet the following purposes: (a) the teacher's right to teach is protected; (b) the students' rights to learning are protected; (c) the students' psychological and physical safety are protected; and (d) property is protected (Levin & Nolan, 2014).

You need to examine the way you teach and the type of classroom environment you would like to maintain when considering rules. A number of factors should be considered, including your educational philosophy, the age and maturity of the students, school rules and expectations, the type of classroom climate to be developed, and the rationale for a particular rule.

VOICES FROM THE CLASSROOM   Promoting Polite Behavior

David Young, third-grade teacher, Silverdale, Washington

During the first weeks of school, I work hard to create a positive atmosphere in my classroom and teach basic, polite behavior. As a class, we brainstorm and discuss what polite things students might do at school and in class. We then come up with a short list of things, such as saying please and thank you, waiting your turn patiently, and putting away someone else's things without even being asked.

After we have created our list, I try to catch students doing any of these polite behaviors, quickly get the class's attention, share the behavior I observed, and compliment the student. This quick celebration of polite behavior reinforces the behavior. As the year goes on, I cut back on these celebrations, but still do this occasionally. As a result, my classes have been better behaved and more polite, and I have been able to spend more time on teaching and less dealing with inappropriate behavior.

Select the Rules

After considering the need for classroom rules, you are ready to select rules that are appropriate for your classroom. Sample rules include these:

- Follow the teacher's directions.

- Obey all school rules.

- Speak politely to all people.

- Keep your hands, feet, and objects to yourself.

These rules are probably appropriate for all grade levels (K–12).

Due to differences in student maturity and developmental levels, some rules may be needed for certain grade levels. For example, students in the primary grades (K–3) often need direct guidance on many matters. Some additional rules may be appropriate for these grades: (a) follow directions the first time they are given; (b) raise your hand and wait to be called on; (c) stay in your seat unless you have permission to get up; or (d) do not leave the room without permission.

For departmentalized settings and grade levels, some rules about materials and starting class are often used. For example, rules might include bringing all needed materials to class and being in your seat and ready to work when the bell rings at the start of the period. A number of guidelines for selecting classroom rules are displayed in Table 4.1.

1. **Make classroom rules consistent with school rules.** Before you identify classroom rules, you must become familiar with school rules and recognize your responsibilities to them. For instance, school rules may identify behaviors that are specifically forbidden (e.g., student may not wear flip-flop sandals because they violate the school dress code) or specifically required (e.g., students need a hall pass when out of the classroom during class time). Some school rules, such as dress codes and cell phone use, may require a degree of interpretation when attempting to enforce the rules in the classroom. In these cases, it is useful to discuss the interpretation and enforcement of school rules with the building principal.

2. **Involve students in making the rules to the degree that you are comfortable and to the degree that the students' age level and sophistication permit.** Among other things, student involvement in selecting rules will be affected by your philosophical perspective. Many teachers do not provide for student choice in rule setting; they may clearly present the rules and discuss the rationale for them. Other teachers find that students feel greater commitment

■ TABLE 4.1   **Eight Guidelines for Selecting Classroom Rules**

1. Make classroom rules consistent with school rules.
2. Involve students in making the rules to the degree that you are comfortable and to the degree that the students' age level and sophistication permit.
3. Identify appropriate behaviors and translate them into positively stated classroom rules.
4. Focus on important behavior.
5. Keep the number of rules to a minimum (four to six).
6. Keep the wording of each rule simple and short.
7. Have rules address behaviors that can be observed.
8. Identify rewards when students follow the rules and consequences when they break them.

VOICES FROM THE CLASSROOM   Involve Students in Selecting the Rules

Laurie Robben, fourth-grade teacher, Greenwich, Connecticut

When we discuss the rules on the first day of school, I begin with a discussion of what the lunch-room would be like with no rules (no assigned tables, no order to buying lunch, no criteria for throwing away garbage). Fourth-graders are quick to surmise that lunch would be chaos. It might be fun for a while, but their lunch would soon become an unpleasant experience.

I then carry this discussion into the classroom. We brainstorm why we need rules. What problems would we face? They often say that everyone would talk at once, there would be little or no learning, and that it would be as loud as a gym. We then create a rule to avoid each possible negative outcome. We first list all possible rules and then reword the rules that are finally selected into positive statements.

Finally, I put the class into groups of four or five and have them illustrate a rule of their choice. While they perform this task, I neatly write the rules on a poster, which is displayed throughout the year.

Teresa Krell, fourth-grade teacher, Corpus Christi, Texas

On the very first day of a school year, I make sure that the students understand the guiding rule in my classroom—that no one in the class is allowed to do anything to keep them from learning. Students love the sound of this. They immediately get that they have rights in this new class. Through serious class discussions throughout the first week of school, we really nail down the implications and meanings of this rule. We talk about the hopes of their parents, grandparents, and guardians for their school year, and how none of these people would want anyone to hurt the students' feelings, hurt them physically, or keep them from learning what they need to learn on any given day of school.

After two or three days, the students write what they think the "small rules" should be for our classroom. I read these aloud, and students vote on a set of rules that will help the one big rule work. I type these up and make a poster for the room. All the students sign the poster showing that they agree, and we are off to a very problem-free year.

and are more likely to adhere to the rules if they help formulate the rules and consequences. You can be an effective manager whether or not you involve students in identifying classroom rules.

If students are involved in selecting classroom rules, you can exert different degrees of direction during the discussion of them. You may begin with a general discussion of rules used in everyday life. Rich discussions can be prompted by questions such as: What is the purpose of traffic lights? Why do people need to pass a written test about laws and a driving test to obtain a driver's license? Why were rules established for sports such as basketball and football? What would a basketball game be like without the rules?

This can be followed by a guided discussion about appropriate rules to steer students' actions in your classroom. Since students may not select all areas that you consider important, you may need to prompt the discussion at times. Teachers often guide students into selecting about five rules as a means to focus on important behavior. The degree of formality in managing the acceptance of the rules varies; you may want the class to vote on the list or you may prefer to handle approval by consensus.

3. **Identify appropriate behaviors and translate them into positively stated classroom rules.** Since rules are a general code of conduct, they should focus on the conduct desired. Students respond better when the rule is stated in a way that expresses the desired behavior.

To the extent possible, try to state rules positively. Instead of "No fighting," state the rule as "Keep your hands and feet to yourself." Instead of "No teasing, swearing, or yelling," state the rule as "Speak politely to all people."

4. **Focus on important behavior.** When identifying appropriate student behavior, you could make a list of student actions for various settings. Rules should focus on important behavior that meets one of the purposes of rules mentioned earlier. If you had a rule for every type of behavior, major and minor, you would have a very extensive list. Rules should focus only on important behavior.

5. **Keep the number of rules to a minimum (four to six).** By focusing on important behavior, the number of rules can be limited. Four to six rules is a good number for important behaviors. The rules can be written in broad enough language so they encompass related behaviors. For example, a rule about "Follow the teacher's directions" covers important behavior and is broad enough to cover a number of circumstances. By selecting rules with that degree of generality, the number can be limited to between four and six.

6. **Keep the wording of each rule simple and short.** A rule that has several conditions and qualifiers in its wording may be confusing. It is better to keep the wording simple and short so the meaning is clear and recognizable.

7. **Have rules address behaviors that can be observed.** Sometimes rules focus on an attitude, such as "Be kind to others." However, what constitutes being kind is open to many interpretations. One student might view a certain action as being unkind, whereas another student might not see it that way. To avoid problems of this nature, it is preferable that the rule address behaviors that can be observed. In this way, the behavior did or did not occur, and there is no gray area of interpretation.

8. **Identify rewards when students follow the rules and consequences when students break the rules.** Students need to know what will happen to them if they break the rules. They may then choose to follow the rule rather than incur the consequence. If the student chooses to break the rule, then that student must know that a consequence will be administered. Rewards for following the rules may include a variety of reinforcers such as social reinforcers, activities and privileges, tangible reinforcers, and token reinforcers (discussed more thoroughly in Chapter 5). Students need to be told that these reinforcers will be delivered if they follow the rules.

■ WHAT WOULD YOU DECIDE?   Selecting Your Classroom Rules

It is two weeks before school starts, and you are thinking about your classroom rules. You know some teachers select the rules themselves while other teachers involve their students in varying degrees. You think about your philosophical perspective on discipline and consider how you would like to conduct your class.

1. Do you intend to involve students in identifying rules? If so, how involved will you allow the students to be in the process?

2. How will you determine the consequences for the rules that are identified? Should students be involved in selecting consequences?

3. What type of discipline model does your approach to rule setting represent (see Table 2.1)?

Similarly, students need to be told what consequences will be delivered if they choose to break a rule. When a student gets off task, first provide situational assistance in an effort to get the student back to work. If the student stays off task, then you should deliver mild responses such as nonverbal and verbal actions. If that doesn't work, you can move on to logical consequences and other actions (discussed in Chapter 9).

Teach and Review the Rules

After the classroom rules have been identified, rules should be taught in the first class session as if they were subject matter content. This discussion should include an explanation of the rules, rehearsal, feedback, and reteaching. It is important that the students recognize the rationale for the rules and are provided with specific expectations for each rule. Specific guidelines for teaching and reviewing classroom rules are displayed in Table 4.2.

Presentation and discussion of the rules are intended to help students understand the rules, recognize their responsibilities in relation to them, and build a commitment to following them. Consider the nine guidelines in Table 4.2 when teaching and reviewing classroom rules:

1. **Discuss the rules in the first class session.** When making plans for the first day of school, include time to discuss the classroom rules in the first class session in which teachers meet the students. Students need to know the rules from the very start. You should teach the classroom rules as if they were subject matter content; this could include a handout, a projector display, discussion, practice, and even a quiz about the rules. This discussion should include an explanation of the rules, rehearsal, feedback, and repeat teaching. If different rules apply for various activities (e.g., large-group work, small-group work, labs, and independent work), these should also be clarified at this time.

2. **Discuss the reasons for the rules.** It is important that students recognize the rationale for the rules because it can build their understanding of and commitment to them. If there is a sound rationale for a rule, students are more likely to follow the rule and not challenge it. As mentioned earlier, this can start out as a general discussion about the need for rules in all aspects of life (e.g., for driving a car and for playing in a softball game). This discussion can then lead into the need for rules in the classroom to help teaching and learning.

3. **Identify specific expectations relevant to each rule. Provide examples and nonexamples. Emphasize the positive side of the rules.** Examples of specific behaviors that meet or break a rule should be identified. This will help clarify your expectations. Since the wording

■ TABLE 4.2   Nine Guidelines for Teaching and Reviewing Classroom Rules

1. Plan to discuss and teach the rules in the first class session.
2. Discuss the reasons for the rules.
3. Identify specific expectations relevant to each rule; provide examples and emphasize the positive side of the rules.
4. Inform students of the consequences when rules are followed and also when they are broken.
5. Verify students' understanding of the rules.
6. Send a copy of your discipline policy home to families and to the principal.
7. Post the rules in a prominent location.
8. Remind the class of the rules at times other than when someone has just broken a rule.
9. Review the rules regularly.

of the rules is often brief and somewhat general, this discussion allows you to clarify what will be acceptable or unacceptable behavior for each rule.

4. **Inform students of the consequences when rules are followed and also when they are broken.** Point out to the students that you are helping them make good decisions about their behavior. When the students make good decisions about their behavior, positive results will occur. When students don't make good decisions, results will be negative. Appropriate decisions are rewarded; inappropriate decisions are not. After discussing the general reasons for providing consequences, you should discuss the specific consequences that will be used.

5. **Verify students' understanding of the rules.** As in any subject matter lesson, student understanding of the rules and consequences must be verified. This may take the form of questions, a game format, or even a quiz. If there is evidence that students do not fully understand the rules and consequences, repeat teaching may be needed.

6. **Send a copy of your discipline policy home to families and to the principal.** It is helpful to send a copy of the classroom rules and consequences to the families. Include a form for the families to sign indicating that they have read the discipline policy and have reviewed it with their child. This process helps develop understanding and commitment to the policy. The form could include space for the parents to write questions or comments. This signed form should be returned to you. It is helpful to provide the principal with a copy of your policy.

7. **Post the rules in a prominent location.** The rules should then be written on a poster and displayed in a prominent place in the classroom, perhaps on a side wall where students will easily see them. This display is a constant reminder that the rules exist to guide behavior.

8. **Remind the class of the rules at times other than when someone has just broken a rule.** Rather than waiting for a rule to be broken to remind the students about a particular rule, it is better to select a time when there have been no problems to remind students about the rules. It is helpful to anticipate potential problems and remind students of the rules before the problems occur. For example, before an activity that requires students to move around the classroom, it is a good idea to remind students about the rule "Keep your hands and feet to yourselves." You alert the students about the rule and the appropriate behavior, and this presumably will minimize poking and shoving during the activity.

9. **Review the rules regularly.** At all grade levels, it is important to review the rules frequently for several weeks at the start of the school year. Daily review during the first week, three times a week during the second week, and once a month thereafter is a good approach. In the first few weeks, it may be useful for the students to evaluate their behavior and consider whether improvement is needed. Periodic review throughout the school year is then appropriate, especially right after a holiday or after the winter or spring break. Review classroom rules with each new student who might transfer into the class after the start of the school year.

Obtain Commitments

After initially teaching the rules to the students, have them express their understanding of the rules and indicate their intention to follow the rules. Although this can be done in a variety of ways, one of the most effective is to have each student sign a copy of the paper that lists the rules and includes a statement such as "I am aware of these rules and understand them." Each student thus affirms understanding of the rules. You can keep these signed sheets. An extra copy of the rules could be given to students for placement in their desk or in a notebook.

As discussed earlier, sending the discipline policy home to the families is another means of obtaining a commitment to the policy. In this way, they are informed of the policy at the start of the school year. Include your email address and school phone number on the policy so that

VOICES FROM THE CLASSROOM   Discussing and Clarifying Rules

Beatrice Gilkes, high school computer science teacher, Washington, DC

To help maintain control in the classroom, I ask my students to discuss realistic expectations for all persons in the classroom, including myself, that will help lead to the students being successful. Next, we discuss and select specific rules of behavior that affect maximum learning success in the classroom. Throughout this discussion, we emphasize three key words—love, respect, and commitment. We then commit ourselves to these rules, and their recommendations for penalties are included in the agreement. Students place this list of rules in their notebooks. This approach to getting a commitment from the students about classroom conduct has been effective for me in 40 years of teaching.

Marjorie Marks, middle school communication arts teacher, Wixom, Michigan

My rules and procedures do not vary among the three grade levels I teach, and my students are told on the first day (through verbal discussion and succinct handouts) that respect is the critical aspect of our learning environment. I emphasize that each detail of behavior, work ethic, and project outcomes are directly influenced by the level of respect we show one another and ourselves. I talk to my classes openly and warmly about this, as I do not believe that being harsh or threatening elicits a respectful, unified classroom environment.

Together, we offer examples that illustrate respectful behavior, such as being on time to class, showing kindness to your peers, sticking to a project with effort, exhibiting energy and open-mindedness, and doing what you say you're going to do. All of these represent self-respect and respect toward others. My classroom quickly becomes a Safe Zone where we do our individual best and support one another.

parents or guardians can contact you if they have any concerns or questions. If they do not, they are asked to sign and return a form that states that they are aware of the rules and understand them (similar to the form their child could sign at school).

Procedures in the Classroom

Procedures are approved ways to achieve specific tasks in the classroom. They are intended to help students accomplish a particular task, rather than prevent inappropriate behavior as in the case of rules. Procedures may be identified to direct activities such as handing in completed work, sharpening a pencil, using the restroom, or putting away supplies. The use of procedures, or routines, has several advantages: They increase the shared understanding of an activity between you and students, reduce the complexity of the classroom environment to a predictable structure, and allow for efficient use of time.

Some procedures may be sufficiently complex or critical, such as safety procedures for a laboratory or student notebook requirements, that you should provide students with printed copies of the procedures. Many procedures, however, are not written because they are very simple or their specificity and frequency of use allow students to learn them rapidly. Just as with rules, it is important to clearly state the procedures, discuss the rationale for them, and provide opportunities for practice and feedback, where appropriate (Harlacher, 2015).

Examine the Need for Procedures

As a first step, you must examine the need for procedures in your classroom. What activities or actions would benefit from having a procedure that would regularize student conduct in the performance of that action? To answer this key question, you might think about all the actions that take place in the classroom and identify those that would benefit from having an associated procedure (Smith, Fisher, & Frey, 2015).

Fortunately, you do not need to start from scratch in doing this assessment because research studies of classroom management in elementary and secondary classrooms have resulted in a framework that can be used to examine and identify typical classroom procedures. A number of the specific areas that might need classroom procedures are displayed in Table 4.3, some of which are adapted from Emmer and Evertson (2017), Evertson and Emmer (2017), Jones and Jones (2016), and Weinstein and Romano (2019).

Select the Procedures

When examining the items in Table 4.3, you need to consider the unique circumstances in your classroom. The grade level, maturity of the students, your preference for order and regularity, and other factors may be taken into account when deciding which items will need a procedure. It may turn out that you will select many items from the table because these items involve fairly standard actions in many classrooms.

After selecting the items needing a procedure, decide specifically what each procedure will be. You could draw on your own experiences when deciding on the specific procedures. You might recollect your own schooling experiences, your observations of other classrooms, your conversations with other teachers, and your own teaching experience when determining what specific procedures would be appropriate and efficient.

■ TABLE 4.3 **Areas Needing Classroom Procedures**

1. Room use procedures
   a. Teacher's desk and storage areas
   b. Student desks and storage for belongings
   c. Storage for class materials used by all students
   d. Pencil sharpener, wastebasket, sink, and drinking fountain
   e. Restroom
   f. Learning stations, computer areas, equipment areas, centers, and display areas
2. Transitions in and out of the classroom
   a. Beginning the school day
   b. Leaving the room
   c. Returning to the room
   d. Ending the school day
3. Out-of-room procedures
   a. Restroom, drinking fountain
   b. Library, resource room
   c. School office
   d. School grounds
   e. Cafeteria
   f. Lockers
   g. Fire or disaster drills

TABLE 4.3 *(continued)*

4. Procedures for whole-class activities and instruction, and seatwork
   a. Student participation
   b. Signals for student attention
   c. Talk among students
   d. Making assignments
   e. Distributing books, supplies, and materials
   f. Obtaining help
   g. Handing back assignments
   h. Tasks after work is completed
   i. Make-up work
   j. Out-of-seat procedures
5. Procedures during small-group work
   a. Getting the class ready
   b. Taking materials to groups
   c. Student movement in and out of groups
   d. Expected behavior in groups
   e. Expected behavior out of groups
6. Beginning the class period
   a. Attendance check
   b. Previously absent students
   c. Late students
   d. Expected student behavior
   e. What to bring to class
   f. Movement of student desks
7. Ending the class period
   a. Summarizing content
   b. Putting away supplies and materials
   c. Getting ready to leave
8. Other procedures
   a. Classroom helpers
   b. Behavior during delays or interruptions
   c. Split lunch periods

Teach and Review the Procedures

Students should not have to guess whether they need to raise their hands during a discussion or how to interpret subtle signals from you to determine what you want them to do. From the very first day of school, teach and review the various procedures that are needed. Effective teachers spend more time during the first four days of school on management tasks than on academic tasks. Seven steps serve as guides when teaching and reviewing classroom procedures:

1. **Explain the procedure immediately prior to the first time the activity will take place.** Rather than explain procedures for many activities and actions on the first day, plan to space out your explanation over the first several days. It is often useful to wait for a situation to arise that provides an opportunity to explain the procedure. Some procedures will likely be

taught early, such as asking to go to the restroom, while others, such as where to go during a fire drill, could be taught a few days later or just prior to the event.

2. **Demonstrate the procedure.** After the explanation, it is often useful to demonstrate what you want the students to do. For example, you could demonstrate how students are expected to use the pencil sharpener or how to get extra supplies. This will show students what actions are expected of them.

3. **Practice and check for understanding.** After your explanation and demonstration, students could then be asked to practice the procedure. They might be asked to line up in the manner explained to proceed to the next class. In this way, students actually go through the physical motions of the procedure. It is also useful to ask students about the procedures to see if they understand when and how the procedures need to be used.

VOICES FROM THE CLASSROOM   Procedures to Help Students Keep Track of Assignments

Destin Mehess, middle school science teacher, Pueblo, Colorado

I teach my students at the beginning of the school year to be responsible for their homework and assignments, and I show them the designated area where assignments are to be turned in. Each of my classes has an assignment box to place their homework and an assignment chart where the student is to check off when submitting an assignment. This chart is a visual aid that helps students keep track of what has or has not been turned in.

Students who are absent are held responsible for getting their assignments. As a result, I have an absent box that provides information about the assignments and a calendar showing the date when an assignment was given and when it is due.

The assignment box and absent box help students keep track of and be responsible for their assignments. Students do not come to class and hand me assignments or come to me after an absence asking about new assignments. They know what is expected from the first day.

■ CLASSROOM CASE STUDY   Confusion about Procedures During Seatwork

Eric Johansson was eager to start the school year with his fourth-grade class. He spent a lot of time before the school year preparing long- and short-range plans, determining the room arrangement, setting up his plan for student assessment, and addressing many other instructional considerations.

On one of the first days of school, Mr. Johansson taught a math lesson and then asked the students to work on some sample math problems individually in seatwork for the last 15 minutes of the class session. That's when the confusion began. Several students needed some help from Mr. Johansson—some of them raised their hand to have Mr. Johansson come to their desk, other students walked to his desk to see the teacher, and still others asked a nearby student for help. Three students needed to sharpen their pencils, but they didn't know if they needed to ask permission to get out of their seats or if they could go directly to the pencil sharpener.

As students completed the math problems, some of them took their completed paper to the teacher, others tried to pass it up to the front of the row, and still others walked around the room to see if there was a special basket to place completed seatwork.

At the end of the session, Mr. Johansson realized that he had not given consideration to procedures that were needed to provide clarity and guidance to the students. Then he also realized that he had not given prior thought to procedures for other classroom actions.

Focus Questions

1. For each episode of confusion in Mr. Johansson's class, what procedures would you have established if it were your classroom?

2. How might you go about teaching the seatwork procedures to your students?

3. Do you think you will have many specific procedures for the categories listed in Table 4.3 or will you have fewer, more relaxed procedures? Why? How might your students respond to your selections?

VOICES FROM THE CLASSROOM Developing Self-Regulation Strategies in Young Learners

Charity McCracken, kindergarten teacher, Nashville, Tennessee

At the beginning of kindergarten, behaviors can be severe and dangerous to students, detracting from the creation of a safe classroom environment. Many young learners have never been in a school setting and have no concept of the rules and expectations that apply. In fact, they may never have been with an adult that was not their parent. Often, our youngest learners are dealing with fears and anxieties about school and change that they cannot express. These fears can manifest themselves in behaviors such as screaming, biting, spitting, and defiance.

While it is important that students learn acceptable and unacceptable behaviors and follow the rules of kindergarten, it is equally important to begin teaching regulation strategies from the beginning. In my classroom, we start with simple ways that students can take care of themselves throughout the day. Weekly, students learn new strategies to self-regulate and deal with big emotions. We practice belly breathing, handing our heads upside down, counting backward, and a variety of yoga poses designed to relax minds and bodies.

As students build understanding of self-regulation, strategies can be suggested to them in the moment. "I can tell you are upset. Let's pick a strategy to take care of ourselves, and then we will talk about how to solve the problem." Teachers can also model these strategies in times of stress: "I am headed to the calm-down corner to breathe for a minute because I feel upset. I will talk to you when I get back." Soon, students will use strategies independently and start to deal with big emotions in healthier ways.

4. **Give feedback.** As the students are practicing the procedure, observe carefully to determine whether they do it properly. If so, provide reinforcement. If there are some problems, constructively point this out and indicate how the procedure should be done.

5. **Reteach as needed**. If a number of students have difficulty during the practice of the procedure, it may be necessary to reteach the procedure and perhaps explain it in a different way. It would then be useful to demonstrate the procedure once again and give the students another opportunity for practice.

6. **Review the procedures with the students prior to each situation for the first few weeks.** Rather than go through an activity and notice a student not following the procedure properly, it is better to remind students of the details of needed actions just before they are asked to perform them. At the end of class, for instance, you could remind students of the procedure for turning in their completed work just before you ask them to turn it in. Students appreciate the reminders instead of the criticism they might receive for not following the procedure. These reminders can be given for the first few weeks until the students have adopted the procedures.

7. **Review the procedures after long holidays.** After being away from school for many days, some students may forget some particular procedures. Therefore, reviewing the procedures after a long holiday is a useful step to reinforce them.

Helping Students Assume Responsibility for Their Behavior

Students should be given the message that they are responsible for their own behavior, and teachers should provide students with strategies and training to realize that control. Research on the impact of teaching strategies geared toward personal responsibility is strong (Schwab & Elias, 2015). Positive benefits for using self-regulatory techniques include increasing competence in specific academic areas, increasing classroom participation, and reducing behavioral problems. *Teaching Self-Discipline* (Responsive Classroom, 2018b) presents a holistic approach, focusing on rules, classroom community, support networks, and social-emotional and academic skills where students develop the intrinsic motivation to take care of themselves. Four approaches for helping students assume responsibility for their behavior are presented here:

1. **Use general classroom procedures that enhance student responsibility.** Without providing students with special training, teachers can enhance student responsibility with classroom meetings, the use of a language of responsibility, written statements of beliefs, and self-analyses.

   - **Have classroom meetings.** Classroom meetings can be used for a variety of purposes such as deciding about issues affecting the class, planning for various curricular or instructional issues, and reflecting on what has been learned. In relation to classroom management, these meetings can address causes and consequences of misbehavior and can lead to discussion, reflection, and resolution of problems. It is important to identify ground rules for the meetings to ensure that they achieve their intended purposes.
   - **Teach students the words concerning responsibility.** Certain words can be used to discuss classroom management and discipline issues, such as responsibility, rights, freedoms, and equality. To help students develop responsibility for their behavior, they need to know the vocabulary to explore and to discuss the concepts.
   - **Have students write statements of belief.** Some teachers have their students discuss and identify a classroom theme for the school year, such as "All students have a right to be treated with respect." When we take time to articulate our beliefs, we are forced to be specific about those beliefs. The class may include a narrative description in addition to the theme. Teachers also may have the class prepare a classroom constitution to outline rights and responsibilities.
   - **Use written self-analyses of behavioral incidents.** When misbehavior occurs, it is helpful to use a prescribed form to record the student's analysis of the behavioral incident. Information may include the date of the incident, location, others involved, and the nature of the incident. In addition, the form may have questions prompting the student's self-analysis and reflection of the incident with questions about how they believe they contributed to the incident, how it should be resolved, and how the student could stop this from happening again.

2. **Provide students with self-monitoring strategies.** Self-monitoring techniques are those in which students are taught to observe their own behavior, record it in some way, compare it with some predetermined criterion, and then acknowledge and reward their own successes. This is *not* a strategy to be used with an entire class. Rather, this strategy should be used with specific students for whom general management techniques are not working. This procedure involves record keeping of behavioral incidents, contingency management, monitoring, meetings, and often involvement of the parents or guardians. It follows many of the principles of behavior modification.

   Some students in your class may not regularly have behavioral difficulties, but they may benefit from your suggestions about self-control. One approach is to have students ask themselves questions when they are tempted to violate the rules or if they feel they are about to lose control. Students might ask themselves, "Is this worth the trouble it will cause me?" "Is this what I want to happen?" By pausing to question themselves, students will have an opportunity to assess the situation as well as calm down.

3. **Provide students with social skills training and problem-solving strategies.** Some students may violate classroom rules or procedures out of frustration due to poor social interactions with other students. Other students may have difficulty with challenging situations

and consequently may misbehave. The steps in social skills training and in problem-solving strategies are similar:

- When you feel like you might do something harmful or inappropriate, stop and think:
  - What are some other things you can do?
  - What will happen if you do them?
- Pick the best choice.

4. **Provide students with self-control strategies.** Teachers can teach students various self-control strategies that will help students respond to circumstances that might lead to their misbehavior. Thus, students' use of self-control strategies will help them be accountable for their behavior. Students can be taught the following strategies in an effort to calm themselves in a situation they find difficult (Curwin, Mendler, & Mendler, 2018).

   Calming techniques. Students can use these approaches to remain calm when confronted with a situation they feel is upsetting or difficult:

- **Change thoughts and images.** Teach your students that when they hear hurtful words or gestures, before they say or do anything, they should pretend the speaker said one or more ridiculous things instead. Point out that we all have the power to control our feelings by adjusting our thoughts and images.
- **Take a few deep breaths.** Teach your students to take a few deep breaths when they feel angry or scared. Have them practice counting silently to 5 or 10 with their eyes closed while inhaling and doing the same as they exhale. Suggest they breathe in calm, relaxing, fresh air, and breathe out any anger or fear they may feel.
- **Focus on positive thoughts.** What we think affects how we feel. To help students see this connection, share and explore specific positive thoughts that the students can use to remind themselves of their good qualities when somebody is trying to get them upset.
- **Think before acting to avoid and solve problems.** Some students need specific help learning how to anticipate problem situations and then practice steps to address the problem. Students can be taught to ask themselves these questions: What is my problem? What is my plan to solve the problem? Am I using the plan? How did I do?

   Anger control. Students can take the following steps to control their anger:

- Identify direct (provocations by someone) and indirect (thinking someone is being unfair) anger triggers.
- Identify physiological states related to anger (e.g., sweating, getting hot)
- Practice relaxation methods (e.g., counting backward)
- Use cognitive-behavioral methods (e.g., reminders such as "Chill out," "Take it easy," "Just stay calm," or "It's not worth the trouble").
- Conduct an evaluation, asking yourself, "How did I do?"

MAJOR CONCEPTS

1. Rules are general codes of conduct that are intended to guide individual behavior in an attempt to promote positive interaction and avoid disruptive behavior.

2. Rules that are selected should meet the following purposes: (a) the teacher's right to teach is protected; (b) the students' rights to learning are protected; (c) the students' psychological and physical safety are protected; and (d) property is protected.

3. To promote students' commitment to their learning environment, involve students in making the rules to the extent that their age level and sophistication permit.

4. Procedures are approved ways to achieve specific tasks in the classroom.

5. Teachers must first select tasks that would benefit from procedures and then determine the particular actions that students will follow.

6. A number of guidelines can be considered when selecting, teaching, and reviewing classroom rules and procedures.

7. Helping students assume responsibility for their behavior can be achieved by using selected general classroom procedures, written self-monitoring strategies, and social skills and problem-solving training.

DISCUSSION/REFLECTIVE QUESTIONS

1. What are the advantages and disadvantages of involving students in the selection of classroom rules?

2. How might your teaching style and educational philosophy influence the way that you select your classroom rules? How might you need to alter these rules if you were using cooperative learning groups?

3. How could you develop student commitment to the classroom rules and procedures as a means to promote a positive learning environment?

4. What are the benefits and potential problems of having many very specific classroom procedures?

5. How might the grade level and subject area affect your selection of rules and procedures?

SUGGESTED ACTIVITIES

1. For your grade level or subject area, select the classroom rules that you prefer to use. Next, develop a plan for teaching these rules to the students on the first day of class.

2. Prepare a letter that you might send to parents describing your classroom discipline policy.

3. Talk to two or more teachers to determine what rules and specific procedures they use. Obtain any printed guidelines that they provide students.

4. Identify tasks you would like to have performed by classroom helpers. Establish a procedure for showing the students what to do in these roles. Establish a procedure for rotating these roles to other students every week or two.

5. Identify several techniques that you can use to maintain group accountability in your class.

FURTHER READING

Brady, K., Forton, M. B., & Porter, D. (2011). *Rules in school* (2nd ed.). Turners Falls, MA: Center for Responsive Schools.
Provides guidelines for creating rules with students, practicing rules, and dealing with students who break the rules. Offers guidance for dealing with unique aspects of grades K–8.

Sprick, R. S. (2013). *Discipline in the secondary classroom: A positive approach to behavior management* (3rd ed.). San Francisco, CA: Jossey-Bass.
Addresses managing student behavior, grading and instruction, routines and procedures, classroom management plans, expectations, monitoring behavior, and consequences.

Thompson, J. G. (2011). *Discipline survival guide for the secondary teacher* (2nd ed.). San Francisco, CA: Jossey-Bass.
Provides thorough review of many aspects of discipline, such as management systems, promoting self-discipline, maintaining order, classroom climate, and preventing and responding to discipline problems.

Thompson, J. G. (2018). *First-year teacher's survival guide* (4th ed.). San Francisco, CA: Jossey-Bass.
Provides an excellent, thorough, yet practical guide to all aspects of starting your school year. Many useful charts and specific guides. Covers planning for behavior, curriculum, and instruction.

Wong, H. K., & Wong, R. T. (2018a). *The first days of school: How to be an effective teacher* (5th ed.). Mountain View, CA: Harry Wong Publications.
Is a highly popular guide for beginning teachers. Loaded with very practical guidelines on positive expectations, classroom management, lesson mastery, and other vital topics.

© Catherine Yeulet/iStockphoto

Maintaining Appropriate Student Behavior

CHAPTER OBJECTIVES

This chapter provides information that will help you:

- Build positive teacher–student relationships.
- Have a mental set for classroom management.
- Determine techniques to manage whole-group instruction.
- Apply techniques to maintain student attention throughout a lesson.
- Reinforce students effectively.

When you walk into a classroom where students are actively engaged in learning and are cooperating with the teacher and others, you can almost feel the good vibrations given off by the class. Students want to be involved and productive, and they enjoy working together. This type of classroom, however, doesn't happen by chance. Teachers take deliberate actions to establish a cooperative, responsible classroom so that students choose to cooperate and make efforts to be academically successful. Students need to feel that they are expected to be orderly, cooperative, and responsible. Developing a positive classroom climate is one of the most important ways to establish and maintain student cooperation and responsibility.

This chapter examines how you can develop a positive classroom climate and thus help maintain appropriate student behavior. Discussion in this chapter focuses on how to build positive teacher–student relationships, have a mental set for management, manage whole-group instruction, maintain student attention and involvement, and improve classroom climate with reinforcers.

Building Positive Teacher–Student Relationships

Research studies on classroom management and motivation highlight the importance of having positive teacher–student relationships in promoting appropriate student behavior and academic achievement (Bear, 2015; Davis, 2013; Schwab & Elias, 2015; Wentzel, 2016; Wubbels et al., 2015). Building caring relationships between teachers and students is necessary for several reasons. First, when students sense that a teacher cares for them, they see the teacher as more credible and as an ally rather than a foe. This increases motivation to follow directions, adhere to rules, and put effort into classroom activities and academics (Schwab & Elias, 2015).

To address the issue of teacher–student relationships, this section begins with a discussion about how to communicate caring and support in the classroom. Next, developing teacher–student relationships in urban settings is examined. Then, the issue of selecting appropriate levels of dominance and cooperation is explored when developing teacher–student relationships and maintaining appropriate student behavior.

Communicating Caring and Support

A significant body of research indicates that academic achievement and student behavior are influenced by the quality of the teacher–student relationship (Bear, 2015; Schwab & Elias, 2015;

Wubbels et al., 2015). Students prefer teachers who are warm and friendly. Students who feel liked by their teachers reportedly have higher academic achievement and more productive classroom behavior than students who feel their teachers hold them in low regard. This research suggests that you need to learn and conscientiously apply skills in relating more positively to students.

In a review of research concerning teacher–student relationships, Bear (2015) reported that positive teacher–student relationships are related to a number of social, emotional, and learning outcomes for students. Students who experience positive teacher–student relationships have greater on-task behavior, academic engagement, and academic achievement. They also are motivated to act responsibly and prosocially. They engage in less oppositional and antisocial behaviors, including bullying. The preventive value of positive teacher–student relationships is especially important for students who lack support from other sources, such as from parents, peers, and close friends.

Studies repeatedly attest to the importance that students place on teachers' willingness to "be there" for them, to listen, and to show concern for students' personal and academic lives—in short, to *care* for them. Developing a supportive community in the classroom helps to impart a sense of each student's belonging, to alleviate students' social anxieties and frustrations, and to motive students to comply with teachers' requests and act appropriately with peers (Schwab & Elias, 2015). Because of this, building caring relationships is the first step in the promotion of responsible behavior and prevention of misbehavior.

Openness, acceptance, and trust are three pillars of solid relationships with students (Scott, 2017). Openness is the ability to welcome people into your presence so that they feel safe and secure. Acceptance means being able to continue holding your students in high regard even though you see their shortcomings. Trust is mutual confidence; it is what allows people to believe that they are acting in one another's best interest.

The guidelines listed below will help you build positive relationships and communicate your caring and support to students (Cassetta & Sawyer, 2015; Charles & Cole, 2019; Marlowe & Hayden, 2013; Weinstein & Novodvorsky, 2015).

1. **Learn about your students' lives.** Teachers can promote an invitational, caring classroom by understanding students and the social factors that influence their lives. This can be done through various means, such as questionnaires at the beginning of the school year and informal interactions.

2. **Use positive human relations skills.** When learning to manage the classroom climate, appropriate human relations skills are needed. Four general human relations skills apply to almost everyone in all situations: friendliness, positive attitude, the ability to listen, and the ability to compliment genuinely (Charles & Cole, 2019). When working with students, also give regular attention, use reinforcement, show continual willingness to help, and model courtesy and good manners.

3. **Enable success.** Students need to experience success. Successful experiences are instrumental in developing feelings of self-worth and confidence toward new activities, and this in turn positively affects the teacher–student relationship. Students need to be provided with opportunities to achieve true accomplishments and to realize significant improvements. Student learning is increased when they experience high rates of success in completing tasks. Students tend to raise their expectations and set higher goals. Failure, however, is met with lowered aspirations.

4. **Communicate basic attitudes and expectations to students and model them in your behavior.** Students tend to conform not so much to what teachers say as to what they actually expect. You must think through what you really expect from your students and then see

VOICES FROM THE CLASSROOM   Relationships Are Everything

Mary Ann Settlemyre, sixth-grade teacher, Centreville, Virginia

I am an educator of 29 years teaching grades 4–6 as a classroom teacher and as a STEAM/ Outdoor Education Specialist. One thing has remained true throughout those years—*the relationship between a teacher and a student is everything!* When you walk into a classroom where there is a strong relationship between students and the classroom teacher, you can tell immediately. Students are working on their own and with the teacher, trying to figure things out, speaking kindly to other students, and more.

Each day before students even walk into my classroom, I work on student–teacher relationships. Sometimes it takes place as they come into school as I help in the car drop-off line, saying good morning, asking how they are, noticing a new haircut, and helping when they look upset. When they come to my classroom, each student greets me one-on-one. I have some standard handshakes, but students make up their own as well. Some students try to teach me words from their second language, others just want a hug.

It is simply being interested in their lives and sharing, appropriately, from your own. The difference this makes is insurmountable, and everyone feels more successful in school. All of these actions help students and staff feel more included in the learning and create a positive atmosphere for all.

that your own behavior is consistent with those expectations. If you expect students to be polite to each other, for example, you should treat your students in the same manner.

5. **Communicate high expectations.** Teacher behaviors that create positive expectations almost always enhance the teacher–student relationship, and behaviors that create negative expectations result in poor relationships and poor student self-concepts, and thus reduce learning. For example, students often put forth a solid effort when you say that work may be hard but also express confidence that they will be able to do it.

6. **Give specific, descriptive feedback**. To be supportive of students' efforts, giving specific and descriptive feedback will help students take responsibility for their successes. They will link their effort to their successes.

7. **Maintain a high ratio of positive to negative statements.** Students are sensitive to praise and criticism. Too many negative statements will cast a cloud over the student's view of the classroom. Sprick (2013) recommends three positive, reinforcing statements to a student for every negative or corrective statement given. This will help teachers to be intentionally inviting (Purkey & Novak, 1996; Purkey, Novak, & Schoenlein, 2016).

8. **Be fair and consistent.** Students want to be treated fairly, not preferentially. Your credibility is established largely by making sure that your words and actions coincide and by pointing this out to the class when necessary. If students can depend on what you say, they will be less likely to test you constantly.

9. **Show your respect and caring to students.** You must like your students and respect them as individuals. Your enjoyment of students and concern for their welfare will come through in tone of voice, facial expressions, and other routine behaviors. Middle and secondary teachers should make efforts to get to know students personally. Students who like and respect their teachers will want to please them and will be more likely to imitate their behavior and attitudes. Resources about developing caring relationships include Kaufman and Schipper (2018) and Lundy and Swartz (2011).

10. **Listen to students.** Effective use of listening skills will help students express their real concerns, needs, and wants. Teachers can help students clarify their feelings and resolve their own conflicts.

11. **Be sensitive to cultural and ethnic differences.** The student population is diverse, and students may respond to teachers' words or actions in various ways due to their background. It is important to learn about your students and take that into account in your interactions. Useful resources are available, such as *How to Teach Students Who Don't Look Like You* (Davis, 2012).

12. **Create opportunities for personal discussions and interactions.** Beyond day-to-day activities, teachers often find it helpful to set time aside to get to know their students. Some possible approaches include the following: (a) talk with students before and after class; (b) demonstrate your interest in students' activities; (c) arrange for interviews with students; (d) send letters and notes to students; (e) use a suggestion box; and (f) join in school and community events.

Relationships in Urban Settings

In a review of research on classroom management in urban settings, Milner (2015) discussed the importance of teacher–student relationships. The core of these relationships related to trust and respect, caring and committed teachers (and other adults), students' feeling connected to others in the various contexts, and students' feeling choices and perspectives in managing their own learning. Compared to suburban settings, urban schools are more likely to have students from neighborhoods with higher poverty levels, unemployment, single-parent households, immigrant populations, and crime rates (Clewell, Campbell, & Perlman, 2007). While all urban settings are not the same, teachers need to be mindful of the relationships they create.

Urban teachers need to give more attention to establishing trust, learning about their students' backgrounds and communities, and practicing good communication skills such as empathy, assertiveness, and problem solving when dealing with classroom problems. Urban students benefit from a well-managed classroom in which expectations for behavior are clear and enforced fairly and consistently. Students should believe that their teachers care for them and support their efforts. Within a safe and supportive classroom, students need opportunities to participate in decision making and to do meaningful work. Good teacher–student relationships can flourish in such classrooms.

Research on teaching in urban settings provides guidance for what teachers can do to develop and maintain good teacher student relationships (Higgs, 2014; Milner, 2015; Stairs, Donnell, & Dunn, 2012). Along with guidelines already discussed to develop good teacher–student relationships, here are some additional considerations when developing good relationships in urban settings:

- Learn about the students' community to help understand their lives and experiences. This information will inform decisions about curriculum, activities and assignments, and other aspects of classroom management.

- Share some information about yourself with the students. Some openness is desirable about your activities, interests, and values. Students are more likely to trust teachers whom they know and whom they believe are committed to their learning.

- Show students you care about them individually. Provide personalized interaction, encouragement, and support.

- Be respectful of students' cultures and provide opportunities for students to participate in the decision-making process.

Terri Jenkins, eighth-grade middle school language-arts teacher, Hephzibah, Georgia

Four years ago, I was teaching in an inner-city school with 99% minority enrollment. From the beginning, I was convinced that all of these children could learn. My goal each day was to provide material and present it in such a way that ensured every student would experience some degree of success. I will never forget one particular series of lessons.

We began reading "The Graduation" by Maya Angelou, which recounts her own graduation and valedictory address. We then learned the Negro spiritual "We Shall Overcome." The story and song were inspirational, but they weren't enough. I wanted to make the entire experience personal. I told the class that one day someone sitting in that very classroom would be responsible for giving a valedictory address at his or her own graduation, and that their next assignment was to prepare a speech and present it in class. The speeches were wonderful as I introduced each and every one of them as the valedictorian of that year. As they spoke, I could hear a new determination in their voices; I could see a new pride in their posture.

Three weeks ago, there was a soft tap on my classroom door and a welcomed face appeared. Immediately I recognized Carol, one of those students who had given her valedictory address in my eighth-grade classroom almost five years ago. After a big smile and a warm hug, she quietly spoke. "I just had to come by and personally invite you to my graduation on June 5. I'll be giving the valedictory address, and I want you to be there." With that, an irrepressible smile burst across her face. After much-earned congratulations, she looked at the tears in my eyes and said, "I did it just for you." Carol had become a believer in her dreams, a believer in herself.

Self-esteem and belief in oneself are essential. I firmly believe that self-esteem must be built through real achievement. I still strive to provide lessons designed to maximize student success and ensure achievement, and I continually verbalize my own convictions that they all can be winners. I make every effort to personalize success in the classroom. I realize that I cannot ensure success for every student in my classroom, but I now know that I truly can make a difference.

Level of Dominance

Effective classroom managers use specific techniques to establish an appropriate level of dominance in the classroom. High dominance is characterized by clarity of purpose and strong guidance in both academic and behavioral aspects of the classroom (MacKenzie & Stanzione, 2010). Thus, the teacher provides guidance about the content to be addressed and the behavior to be expected in the class. A moderate to high level of dominance and a moderate to high level of cooperation (addressed later) provide the optimal teacher–student relationship for learning (Marzano, Gaddy, Foseid, Foseid, & Marzano, 2009). The proper level of dominance will help maintain appropriate student behavior and will not interfere with developing positive teacher–student relationships. You can express dominance in the following ways:

1. **Establish rules and procedures.** The rules and procedures that you determine will help establish your dominance in the classroom (discussed in Chapter 4).

2. **Use disciplinary interventions.** When misbehavior occurs, follow it with interventions to stop the inappropriate behavior. Your use of interventions is another expression of your dominance in the classroom (discussed in Chapter 9).

3. **Exhibit assertive behavior.** One of the best ways to communicate a proper level of dominance is to exhibit assertive behavior. *Assertive behavior* involves standing up for one's

legitimate rights in ways that make it less likely that others will ignore or circumvent them. There are three primary ways that you can exert constructive, assertive behavior:

- **Use assertive body language.** This includes making and keeping eye contact, maintaining an erect posture, facing the student but not too close, and having your facial expression match the content of your message.
- **Speak in an appropriate tone of voice.** This includes speaking clearly and deliberately, using a pitch slightly elevated from normal classroom use, and avoiding emotion in the voice.
- **Persist until the appropriate behavior is displayed.** This includes not ignoring an inappropriate behavior; not being diverted by a student denying, arguing, or blaming; and listening to legitimate explanations.

4. **Establish clear learning goals.** Another way to express a proper level of dominance is to be very clear about the learning goals to be addressed in a unit, a quarter, or semester. Clear learning goals can be communicated when you: (a) establish learning goals at the beginning of a unit of instruction; (b) provide feedback on those goals; (c) continuously and systematically revisit the goals; and (d) provide summative feedback regarding the goals.

Level of Cooperation

Effective classroom managers use specific behaviors that communicate an appropriate level of cooperation. High cooperation is characterized by a concern for the needs and opinions of others and a desire to function as a member of a team as opposed to an individual. A moderate to high level of dominance and a moderate to high level of cooperation provide the optimal teacher–student relationship for learning (Marzano et al., 2009). The proper level of cooperation will help maintain appropriate student behavior and will not interfere with developing positive teacher–student relationships. You can promote cooperation in the following ways:

1. **Provide flexible learning goals.** Although you will determine the learning goals for each lesson and unit, you may provide some flexibility by allowing students to set some of their own learning goals at the beginning of a unit or by asking students what they would like to learn. This conveys a sense of cooperation.

2. **Take a personal interest in students.** All students appreciate the personal attention of the teacher, and anything that you do to show interest in students as individuals has an impact on their learning. Here are some behaviors that communicate personal interest (Marzano, Marzano, & Pickering, 2003):

- Talk informally with students before, during, and after class about their interests.
- Single out a few students each day in the lunchroom and talk with them.
- Comment on important events in their lives, such as participation in sports, drama, or other activities.
- Meet students at the door as they come into class and say hello to each student.

3. **Use equitable and positive classroom behaviors.** Teachers should ensure that their behaviors are equal and equitable for all students, thus creating an atmosphere in which all students feel accepted. These behaviors also foster positive teacher–student relationships. This can be done in many ways, such as the following:

- Make eye contact with each student in the room; freely move about all sections of the room.
- Over the course of a class period, deliberately move toward and be close to each student.

- Allow and encourage all students to be part of class discussions and interactions.
- Provide appropriate "wait time" for all students.

4. **Respond appropriately to students' incorrect responses.** When students respond incorrectly or make no response at all to a question you have posed, they are particularly vulnerable. Your appropriate actions at these critical points go a long way toward establishing a positive teacher–student relationship. Useful behaviors in these situations include the following (Marzano et al., 2009):

- **Emphasize what was right.** Give credit to aspects of the incorrect response that are correct.
- **Encourage collaboration.** Allow students time to seek help from peers.
- **Restate the question.** Ask the question a second time in a different way and allow time for the student to think before expecting a response.
- **Give hints or cues.** Provide enough guidance so that students gradually come up with the answer.

Having a Mental Set for Management

A review of research studies on classroom management has verified the importance and effectiveness of having a mental set about managing student behavior (Marzano et al., 2009). In relation to classroom management, a *mental set* is a teacher's heightened awareness of his or her surroundings and involves a conscious effort to control one's thoughts and behaviors in that setting. Using withitness and emotional objectivity will help you maintain appropriate behavior in your classroom.

Withitness

Use specific techniques to be aware of the actions of students in your classroom (withitness). Jacob Kounin (1970) is considered the first researcher to systematically study the characteristics of effective classroom managers. He coined the term *withitness* to describe a teacher's disposition (or mental set) to look at all parts of the classroom at all times to be aware of what is happening and then to demonstrate this withitness to students by quickly and accurately intervening when there is inappropriate behavior. Reflecting on the old adage, teachers who are "with-it" seem to have "eyes in the back of their heads." Such teachers do these things:

1. **Monitor regularly and react immediately.** To exhibit withitness, you should periodically and systematically scan your classroom, note the behaviors of individual students or groups

---

■ WHAT WOULD YOU DECIDE?   Deciding How Much Personal Information to Share

You've started the school year, and you want to be friendly yet professional with your students. You want to tell the students a little about yourself, your background, your experiences, and your current activities. But you are concerned about telling too much and having students think more of you as a friend than as a teacher.

1. In your everyday interactions with your students, how personal will you be with your students, and what factors will you take into account when deciding on this?

2. To what extent will you relate personal experiences to the curriculum?

3. How might the grade level and ethnic diversity of your students affect your decisions?

■ **CLASSROOM CASE STUDY**   Poor Monitoring, Unfortunate Results

Abby Leibowitz's middle-level social studies class was completing a unit on the branches of the government and the role of political parties. Since an election for the state's governor was coming up, they had examined the candidates as a way to see the distinction between the parties. To summarize that information, Ms. Leibowitz split the class into four groups and asked each group to display the parties' similarities and differences on big Post-it sheets with the use of a graphic organizer, such as a compare/contrast chart or a Venn diagram. After giving directions and forming the groups, Ms. Leibowitz was at her desk jotting some notes about a discipline incident from her last class period.

   Some students were into the task; others were not. Some groups didn't know what a Venn diagram is or had disagreements about which graphic organizer to use. Some students started to doodle with the magic markers that were to be used

on the poster paper. The students who wanted to get the poster prepared complained to the others who were off task. After a while, the noise increased, and most groups were not making much progress. Ms. Leibowitz had barely looked up during this time.

Focus Questions

1. How might Ms. Leibowitz improve her monitoring of the students' behavior and progress when they are in the groups? How could she show her withitness to the students during group work?

2. What problems might Ms. Leibowitz have foreseen with her plan? What adjustments might she have made before the lesson to have it work out better? (Foreseeing problems is part of withitness.)

---

of students, and respond quickly to inappropriate actions. When engaged in whole-group instruction, here are some specific techniques you can use to monitor students in the classroom (Marzano et al., 2003):

- Walk around the room, making sure you spend some time in each quadrant.
- Periodically scan the faces of the students in the class, making eye contact with each student if possible.
- As you scan the classroom, pay particular attention to incidents or behaviors that look like they could turn into problems.
- Make eye contact with those students involved in the incident or who are exhibiting the behavior.

2. **Foresee problems.** Another aspect of withitness is the ability to foresee potential problems and make needed adjustments to minimize behavior problems. You should mentally review what might go wrong with specific students in specific classes and consider how you might address these potential problems.

   When planning certain classroom activities, for example, you might recognize possible confusion or disruption when supplies are being distributed. With this advance thought, you could either modify the way you distribute the materials or take certain precautions when the materials are passed out. Also, you might know that specific students act in certain ways under particular conditions, such as a hyperactive student having difficulty focusing on tasks immediately after lunch. In these cases, you can give advance thought to ways to head off the potential problem behavior.

Emotional Objectivity

Use specific techniques to be emotionally objective with your students. When students misbehave, you may get upset and emotional to some degree. It is important that your disciplinary actions are not seen as an attack on the students involved, and you should try to be as objective as possible. *Emotional objectivity* is the ability to interact with students in a businesslike, matter-of-fact

VOICES FROM THE CLASSROOM   A Rubric for Participation to Guide Behavior

Lind Williams, high school English teacher, Provo, Utah

At the start of each year, I teach my students about appropriate classroom behavior. To do this, I created a rubric that displays a scale between mature and immature behaviors—I call this my Participation Grade Rubric. The rubric helps clarify what I view as active, on-task, appropriate behavior for students in class, and the rubric helps students understand what appropriate and inappropriate behavior looks like. For each behavioral indicator on the rubric, a description is included to show a high range, a mid-range, and a low range of the behavior.

Students invariably chuckle at the descriptors in the low range of the rubric because the inappropriateness of the behavior is pretty obvious. I give examples or model some of the behaviors, such as laying heads on desks, putting unfinished work away when there is still class time, making comments that ruin or derail class discussions, and breaching conversational etiquette.

I present these behavioral expectations at the start of the school year, but it takes time for students to be fully independent and self-managed in their conduct. The rubric provides some guidance about appropriate behaviors and helps the students grow in that direction.

Students are assessed with this rubric throughout the school year. When I conference with a student with problem behaviors, we can read the descriptions to see where his or her behavior lies on the rubric.

manner even though you might be experiencing strong emotions. This is particularly important when you are carrying out negative consequences for inappropriate behavior.

Your feelings of anger and frustration are only natural when dealing with misbehavior, but it is not useful to display these emotions when delivering consequences. Here are some techniques that you can use to help maintain a sense of emotional objectivity with students.

1. **Look for reasons for the misbehavior.** Maintaining emotional objectivity is much easier if you don't personalize student misbehavior. Simply trying to understand the reasons for the misbehavior can help you maintain your businesslike manner.

2. **Monitor your own thoughts.** Take time to monitor your attitudes about specific students. When your attitude about specific students is positive, it is fairly easy to interact with them. However, you might not be aware of the extent that negative attitudes about some students may get in the way of interacting with them. To help avoid any negative bias, before class each day you could: (a) mentally review your students, noting those who you anticipate having problems; (b) try to imagine these problem students succeeding or engaging in positive classroom behavior; and (c) when you interact with these students, try to keep in mind your positive expectations.

Managing Whole-Group Instruction

In many classrooms, whole-group instruction takes place quite often. Special attention needs to be given to specific skills used in whole-class instruction that help maintain appropriate student behavior. In his widely respected book *Discipline and Group Management in Classrooms* (1970), Jacob Kounin reported how instructional techniques contribute to classroom management. The implications from his research can be organized into three areas: preventing misbehavior, managing movement through the lesson, and maintaining group focus.

Preventing Misbehavior

When approaching whole-group instruction, teachers can take a number of actions to prevent misbehavior based on Kounin's work:

1. **Exhibit withitness.** As discussed earlier in this chapter, a teacher who has withitness knows what is going on in the classroom at all times, notices who is misbehaving, and responds to the misbehavior in an appropriate and prompt manner. Systematic and periodic monitoring of each student in the class is a key part of withitness because it will help prevent misbehavior from occurring.

2. **Use overlapping.** Overlapping refers to teachers supervising or handling more than one group or activity at a time. For example, a teacher working with one group of students can notice and simultaneously address a behavior incident in another part of the classroom. Teachers who are skilled at overlapping are more aware of what is going on. Thus, they have good withitness as well. As a result, teachers who overlap can effectively monitor classroom behavior and intervene when needed to keep students on task. When students know their teacher has withitness and is able to overlap, they are less inclined to get off task.

3. **Use desists.** Desists are statements by teachers to stop an inappropriate action or a misbehavior by asking or telling a student what to do. To be effective, desist statements should be specific and spoken clearly. A desist might be in the form of an appeal, such as "Shanae, please put away the comb and continue with the class assignment." Or it could be in the form of a command, such as "Wayne, stop talking with your friends and continue with your calculations in the lab activity." Effective use of desists helps keep students on task and minimizes disorder and misbehavior.

4. **Avoid satiation.** Satiation occurs when the teacher asks the students to stay on a learning task too long, and then the students begin to lose interest and enthusiasm, make more mistakes, and misbehave. This can also occur if a certain type of activity or instructional approach is used over and over again. Teachers can prevent misbehavior by avoiding satiation and thus maintaining student interest and engagement. Satiation can be minimized by (a) highlighting progress and providing feedback; (b) providing variety in the content, group structure, level of difficulty, and instructional materials and activities; and (c) offering a challenging activity to promote a greater sense of purpose and accomplishment.

Managing Movement Through the Lesson

To minimize misbehavior and to promote learning, teachers need to have the lesson proceed at a reasonable pace and avoid having the lesson go astray with abrupt changes or shifts. Kounin (1970) described the movement of the lesson in terms of momentum and smoothness, as described next. Some problems with maintaining movement through a lesson are outlined in Table 5.1.

1. **Momentum.** Momentum refers to teachers starting lessons with dispatch, keeping lessons moving ahead, making transitions among activities efficiently, and bringing lessons to a satisfactory close. Momentum deals primarily with the pacing of the lesson, and the teacher needs to avoid slowdowns in the progression through the lesson. For example, one problem in momentum is jerkiness, where the teacher fails to develop a consistent flow of instruction, going too fast sometimes and too slow at other times.

■ TABLE 5.1   Problems in Maintaining Movement Through a Lesson

These are terms that Kounin (1970) used to describe problems in momentum and smoothness when progressing through a lesson.
Dangle: Occurs when a teacher leaves a topic or activity "dangling" before completion to do something else or to insert some new material. Later, the teacher may resume the first activity (also see truncation).
Flip-flop: The teacher is engaged in one activity and then returns to a previous activity that the students thought they had finished.
Jerkiness: The teacher fails to develop a consistent flow of instruction, thus causing students to feel jerks in the lesson momentum, from slow to fast (also see thrust).
Slowdown: When teaching, the teacher moves too slowly or stops instruction too often. Thus, students lose interest or learning momentum. Fragmentation and overdwelling are two types of slowdowns.
a. *Fragmentation:* This is a type of slowdown where the teacher breaks down an activity into subparts that could be taught as a single concept; all the subdivisions are unnecessary and slow down instruction.
b. *Overdwelling:* This is a type of slowdown where the teacher dwells on an issue and engages in a stream of talk that clearly lasts longer than the time needed for students' understanding.
Stimulus bound: The teacher is distracted by some outside stimulus and draws the students' attention to it and away from the lesson.
Thrust: The teacher inserts some new information at a point where students are involved in another activity, and the new material seems irrelevant to them.
Truncation: The teacher engages in a dangle yet fails to resume the original activity (also see dangle).

2. **Smoothness.** Smoothness refers to staying on task in the lesson without abrupt changes, digressions, or divergences. Kounin described several problems when trying to maintain a smooth, continuous flow of activities throughout a lesson. Some of these problems include shifting from one topic to another, shifting back to earlier activities or content, or injecting unrelated information into a lesson.

Maintaining a Group Focus

Group focus occurs when a teacher makes a conscious effort to keep the attention of all students at all times. When this occurs, the teacher maintains efficient classroom control and reduces student misbehavior (Kounin, 1970). Group focus includes group alerting, group accountability, and high-participation formats:

1. **Use group alerting.** Group alerting refers to taking actions to engage the attention of the whole class when only individuals are responding. This includes a teacher's attempts to involve all students in learning tasks, maintain their attention, and keep them "on their toes." With group alerting, teachers create suspense before calling on a student to answer a question, keep students in suspense regarding who will be called on next, call on different students to answer questions, and alert nonperformers that they might be called on next.

2. **Maintain group accountability.** Group accountability takes place when the teacher lets the students know that their performance in class will be observed and evaluated in some manner. This assessment does not necessarily mean a grade will be recorded, only that the students' performance will be gauged. For example, the teacher might use record-keeping devices such as checklists and task cards. Other strategies include asking students to raise their hands in response to certain questions, asking students to take notes and then checking them, or asking students to write answers and then using various techniques to check them

■ WHAT WOULD YOU DECIDE?   **Holding Your Students Accountable**

After teaching students about some strategies to solve math problems, you write five brief math problems on the whiteboard at the front of the room and ask five students to go to those problems and solve them while you and the rest of the class observe. You intend to provide commentary about how the students go through the mental process of solving the problems.

1. For those who are still in their seats, how might you hold them academically accountable for the material?

2. How could you provide feedback to the students at the board as well as to those still in their seats?

3. How might the lack of a procedure for academic accountability in this setting contribute to a loss of order in the classroom?

during the class session. Student misbehavior decreases when students know they are held accountable for their learning and behavior and that the teacher knows each student's progress.

3. **Use high-participation formats.** High-participation formats are lessons that have all students performing in some way even though they may not be involved in answering a teacher's question. High-participation formats occur when each student is expected to manipulate materials, solve problems, read along, write answers, or perform a concurrent task. In this way, students do not simply sit when others are answering questions; they are actively engaged as well.

Maintaining Student Attention and Involvement

To manage a group of students effectively, you need to capture and hold student attention and encourage ongoing involvement. *Attention* means focusing on certain stimuli while screening out others. General guidelines and specific techniques for maintaining student attention and involvement are offered below.

Securing and maintaining attention is an important responsibility. If students are not engaged in the learning process, it is unlikely that they will learn the material and it is possible that they will get off task and disrupt order. Preventive steps therefore need to be taken. In addition to techniques that promote student attention to class activities, you may consider motivational strategies (discussed in Chapter 8).

Consider the following 14 guidelines to maintain student attention and involvement during your lessons:

1. **Use attention-getting strategies.** You can use certain strategies to capture students' attention at the start of a lesson. These attention-getting strategies can be used throughout the lesson to maintain student interest, and they fall into four categories: physical, provocative, emotional, and emphatic. Overuse of any one approach, however, reduces its ability to arouse and maintain attention.

   - **Physical.** Attention getters deal with any stimulus that attracts one or more of the senses (sight, sound, touch, and taste). Pictures, maps, the whiteboard, music, and manipulative objects are examples. Even your movement and vocal expression can be considered to be physical stimuli.

   - **Provocative.** Attention getters involve the use of unique or discrepant events. To create them, you could introduce contrasting information, play the devil's advocate, and be unpredictable to the degree that the students enjoy the spontaneity.

- **Emotional.** Attention getters are approaches aimed at involving students emotionally. This may be something as simple as calling the students by name.
- **Emphatic.** Attention getters place emphasis on a particular issue or event. For example, you might cue students to an issue by saying, "Pay careful attention now. The next two items are very important."

2. **Arrange the classroom so that students do not have their backs to the speaker.** When presenting material during a lesson, students should be seated so that everyone is facing the presenter (who may be you, a student, or a guest). This may seem like a simple task, but too often classrooms are arranged so that students do not have a complete view of the presenter and the instructional medium. Not only is the presenter unable to see all of the students but also the students are not able to observe all of the presenter's nonverbal behaviors.

   You may prefer to have all the student seats facing the area where you spend most of your time in direct instruction, such as by the whiteboard or by the projector. Or you may prefer to have them work in cooperative groups much of the time and thus arrange the desks in clusters. In that case, students can be asked to turn or move their chairs when you want their undivided attention.

3. **Select a seating arrangement that does not discriminate against some students.** Some teachers may spend as much as 70% of their time in front of the classroom. As a result, students at the back of the classroom contribute less to class discussions and are less attentive and less on task than those near the front. Involvement is more evenly distributed when high- and low-achieving students are interspersed throughout the room. You can enhance on-task behavior by carefully arranging the seating and moving around the room. You should experiment with seating arrangements to promote student attention and involvement.

4. **Monitor attention during lessons and provide situational assistance as necessary.** Students are much more likely to pay attention if they know you regularly watch them, both to see if they are paying attention and to note signs of confusion or difficulty. Regularly scan the class or group throughout the lesson.

VOICES FROM THE CLASSROOM   Taking Turns in Whole Group Instruction

Kathleen Trace, high school English teacher, Virginia Beach, Virginia

I use a very simple analogy to help my students stay focused while I am giving whole-group instruction. During a class period, I might introduce a topic or idea to the whole group and then give students time to work independently or in small groups, regroup as a whole group to discuss findings/ideas, go back to small groups to dig deeper, and so on.

The transition between being able to talk freely and having to be quiet and attentive is challenging for some of my students, even though they are high school seniors. Therefore, at the beginning of the school year I introduce this simple analogy: *taking turns*. I ask my students when they learned how to take turns. The answer is always in elementary school or younger. Then I tell them we'll be taking turns in this class and, since they are already experts on the skill, it should be no problem. When I am giving whole class instruction, it is "my turn" and when they are working independently or in small groups it is "their turn."

I will literally say, "My turn now," when it is time for them to stop their small group discussions and focus back with the whole group. "My turn" doesn't mean I won't be asking questions or inviting them to share ideas, but it means it is "my turn" to lead the conversation. It works, and they get it.

When students show signs of losing interest or getting frustrated, you should provide *situational assistance*—teacher actions designed to help students cope with the instructional situation and to keep students on task, or to get them back on task before problems become more serious. Situational assistance may include actions such as removing distracting objects, providing support with routines, boosting student interest, helping students over hurdles, altering the lesson, or even modifying the classroom environment.

5. **Keep lessons moving at a good pace.** Delays in a lesson may be caused by actions such as spending too much time on minor points, causing everyone to wait while students respond individually, passing out equipment individually, and so forth. Attention will wander while students are waiting or when something they clearly understand is being discussed needlessly (as in lengthy review lessons). You need to recognize what causes delays and minimize them in an effort to keep the lesson moving at a good pace.

6. **Vary instructional media and methods.** Monotony breeds inattentiveness, and the repeated and perhaps exclusive use of one approach to instruction will soon result in a classroom of bored students. Moreover, student achievement is increased when a variety of instructional materials and techniques are used. Varying media by using a projector, whiteboards, web-based virtual field trips, and online resources provides a more interesting approach to teaching any lesson.

   You should use a variety of teaching methods to solicit students' attention through the use of demonstrations, small and large groups, lectures, discussions, field trips, and the like. Using a variety of instructional techniques helps.

7. **Stimulate attention periodically.** Student attention wanders when instruction becomes predictable and repetitive. You can promote continual attention as a lesson or an activity progresses. You can stimulate attention by cueing students through transitional signals that a new section of the lesson is coming up. For example, you might say, "We have just spent the last 15 minutes considering what running water erosion is. Now let's look at the ways that farmers and other people try to stop this erosion." Or you can use challenging statements such as, "Now, here's a really difficult (or tricky or interesting) question—let's see if you can figure it out."

8. **Show enthusiasm.** Your own enthusiasm is another factor in maintaining student attention. Enthusiasm can be expressed through vocal delivery, eyes, gestures, body movement, facial expressions, word selection, and acceptance of ideas and feelings. Teacher enthusiasm has been related to higher student achievement (Good & Brophy, 2008). Students often learn more from lessons that are presented with enthusiasm and expressiveness than from dry lectures.

   You do not need to express a high degree of enthusiasm all of the time. Depending on the circumstances of the lesson, you may vary the degree of enthusiasm being expressed. For example, there may be times during a lesson when you might be very animated and vocally expressive. Other times, you may choose to be very mild mannered.

9. **Use humor.** Students appreciate a certain amount of humor in the classroom, and it can help maintain student attention. You may enjoy making silly statements or sharing funny experiences with your students. Be cautious that jokes are not used to tease or demean any student, even if expressed in a funny way, because the student may interpret these statements as being serious.

10. **Use questions effectively to maintain attention.** You can use questions to achieve various academic objectives. To maintain attention and encourage ongoing involvement, consider the guidelines in Table 5.2.

■ TABLE 5.2   **Questioning Tips to Maintain Attention and Promote Learning**

1. Prepare key questions for each lesson to provide structure and direction.
2. Phrase questions clearly and specifically.
3. Ask questions logically and sequentially.
4. Use questions that encourage wide student participation.
5. Ask questions that relate to students' own lives.
6. Vary the type of questions being asked.
7. Use variety and unpredictability in asking questions.
8. Ask the question before calling on a student.
9. Wait at least five seconds after asking the question before calling on a student.
10. Use random selection when calling on students.
11. Have students respond to classmates' answers.
12. Do not consistently repeat questions.
13. Prompt students to elaborate on their answers through the use of follow-up questions and comments.
14. When students fail to provide a complete and correct answer to your question, use cues, clues, and prompts to assist them in making connections that will lead to an answer.

11. **Maintain individual accountability.** Students should be accountable for being involved in lessons and learning all of the material. It is helpful to ask a question or require the student periodically to make some kind of response. An unpredictable pattern in the way you handle questions or responses helps maintain individual accountability and causes students to be mentally engaged in the lesson and to be more attentive.

12. **Pay close attention when students talk and answer questions.** Use active listening skills. This often entails using nonverbal skills that indicate that you are interested in what students are saying. If you do not give attention and show interest when students answer questions, you communicate to them that what they have to say is not very important, which, in turn, will discourage involvement. Nonverbal expressions of your interest might include nodding, moving toward the student, leaning forward, maintaining eye contact with the student, and showing interest in your facial expression. Verbal expressions of interest may include statements such as "Uh huh," "I see," "That's a thoughtful answer," or "I appreciate your thorough, insightful answer."

■ WHAT WOULD YOU DECIDE?   **Planning to Vary Your Methods and Media**

You recognize that varying your instructional methods and media will help maintain student attention and involvement. You are now beginning to plan an eight-day unit, and you want to deliberately plan for much variety in methods and media. Even in each class session, you want to plan for variety. (Select a unit topic in your field for this exercise as you consider the following questions.)

1. Identify five instructional strategies that you would use at some point in the unit.

2. Identify several types of media that you and your students would use. Identify how you would use each type of media to teach the content.

3. How might you design your lesson plan template to prompt your attention to include variety in your instructional methods and media?

VOICES FROM THE CLASSROOM   Curiosity, Excitement, Anticipation

Suzanne Buhner, fourth-grade teacher, Virginia Beach, Virginia

Based on my years of teaching, I have found that with student input comes curiosity, excitement, and anticipation—this is the perfect formula for increasing student engagement. When I see students at their highest level of engagement, it is when they have driven the instruction.

I can illustrate capturing student engagement with a recent example that occurred in my fourth-grade classroom. During our study of ecosystems, I introduced animal and plant adaptations with an article about invasive species. Due to one plant's harmful effects on nesting sea turtles, my students became intensely interested in eradication of this plant in our area. One student suggested that we create a *Shark Tank* experience whereby students would prepare information to be used by the general public to either learn about the negative effects of the plant or to eradicate the plant altogether.

I agreed to this experience, and students continued to research the plant by polling local residents, speaking with local garden associations, writing to journalists for assistance in spreading the word about the plant, and asking parents to take them on expeditions to places along the coast to look for the plant. Throughout the unit, I provided information and activities designed to help students meet curriculum learning objectives and pass mandatory assessments. I rearranged language arts and writing lessons to accommodate their needs, rather than strictly following given pacing guides. In the end, student scores on benchmark assessments for both writing and science were above average.

Due to this positive *Shark Tank* experience, I now plan all units of study to include some type of inquiry—inquiry the students and I plan together. Some units start with an issue to solve, others begin with a traditional introduction and then we add inquiry throughout via journal articles, artifacts, and guest speakers. What lies at the heart of student engagement? Simply ask the students to get involved!

13. **Reinforce students' efforts and maintain a high ratio of positive to negative verbal statements.** Students attend more fully if a positive learning environment has been created. One of the best means for accomplishing this is to respond positively to their efforts. On the one hand, positive and encouraging statements are very important for all students, and they can be motivated by positive reinforcement. On the other hand, a teacher who consistently belittles students' efforts will create a negative learning environment that will likely lead to inattention and off-task behavior. Make many more positive and encouraging statements than negative statements. Think about it from the students' point of view—would you like to be in a classroom where you hear mostly negative statements or positive statements?

14. **Terminate lessons that have gone on too long.** When the group is having difficulty maintaining attention, it is better to end the lesson than to struggle through it. This is especially important for younger students, whose attention spans are limited. Nevertheless, some teachers continue lessons in order to maintain a certain schedule. This can be counterproductive since students may not learn under certain conditions and in any case will have to be taught again. It is always helpful to give advance thought to a backup activity for each lesson. For example, you may select a different instructional technique for covering the same lesson objectives.

Improving Classroom Climate with Reinforcers

A *reinforcer* is an event or consequence that increases the strength or future probability of the behavior it follows. Reinforcement is used to strengthen behaviors that are valued and to motivate students to do things that will benefit them. It is important to recognize the general principle of reinforcement: *Behaviors that are reinforced will be retained; behaviors that are not reinforced will be extinguished.* You need to carefully consider whom to reinforce, under what conditions, and with what kinds of reinforcement (Reeve, 2015).

The awarding of reinforcers must be contingent on the student's behavior. If a student does what is expected, then an appropriate reinforcer can be awarded. Students are thus reinforced for their appropriate actions, and that behavior is strengthened. In the absence of the needed behavior, students do not receive reinforcers.

Types of Reinforcers

Several techniques of reinforcement are available, including recognition, activities and privileges, tangible reinforcers, and token reinforcers. Many of these reinforcers can be used with both individual students and the entire class.

Recognition

Recognition is a social reinforcer serving as a positive consequence to appropriate behavior. Social reinforcers may be expressed by verbal or written expressions, nonverbal facial or bodily expressions, nonverbal proximity, and nonverbal physical contact. Social reinforcers are especially valued by students when given by people important to them. Social forms of approval are especially useful when reinforcing student behavior if you and the students have a good relationship. *Praise* is an expression of approval by the teacher after the student has attained something, and social reinforcers are often used to express this praise.

Most recognition should be done privately with the student, but some may be done publicly. You need to consider carefully student characteristics when deciding how to deliver praise. A seventh grader, for example, might be somewhat embarrassed by being praised in front of the class. Recognition should always be contingent on performance of appropriate behavior. You should be specific about the behavior that resulted in the praise and the reasons for giving it.

Activities and Privileges

Activity reinforcers include privileges and preferred activities. After students complete desired activities or behave in appropriate ways, you can then reinforce them with various activities and privileges. Some of these reinforcers could be various jobs as a classroom helper. Activity reinforcers are often very effective for reinforcing the entire class. A list of sample activities and privileges that can be used as reinforcers is provided in Table 5.3.

It is important to verify that certain behaviors are desirable. When you and the student are on good terms, just performing certain tasks such as straightening the room or washing the whiteboards with you can be rewarding. Many other activities and privileges have an intrinsic value that doesn't depend on the student's relationship to you. Running errands, studying with a friend, going to the library, being first in line, or choosing an activity are each likely to be a positive incentive that produces satisfaction in its own right. You may have students fill out a sheet at the beginning of the school year to identify activities and reinforcers that they would appreciate.

Tangible Reinforcers

Tangible or material reinforcers are objects that are valued in and of themselves: certificates, awards, stars, buttons, bookmarks, book covers, posters, ribbons, plaques, and report cards. Food also may serve as a tangible reinforcer: cookies, sugarless gum, popcorn, jellybeans, candy, or raisins. If you are interested in using food (M&Ms, cookies, etc.), recognize some

■ TABLE 5.3   Examples of Activity and Privilege Reinforcers

Privileges
Playing a game
Helping the teacher
Going to the library
Decorating a bulletin board
Working or studying with a friend
Reading for pleasure
Exploring approved websites on the computer
Writing on the whiteboard
Earning extra recess time

Classroom jobs
Distributing or collecting papers and materials
Taking attendance
Adjusting the window shades
Taking a note to the office
Watering the plants
Stapling papers together
Erasing the whiteboard
Operating the projector
Controlling the mouse for the SMART Board
Shutting down the computers

cautions. Some parents may object to certain foods (such as those high in sugar), and there may be cultural differences related to food. Students may be allergic to certain foods such as nuts, wheat, soy, or dairy, and there may be health and state regulations governing dispensing food in schools.

Since tangible reinforcers serve as external or extrinsic reinforcement, their use should be limited. Other types of reinforcers are generally more available and more reinforcing in natural settings than tangible reinforcers. When you give awards, it is a good idea to distribute them so as to include a good number of the students. Don't give awards only for outstanding achievement; award for improvement, excellent effort, good conduct, creativity, and so on.

VOICES FROM THE CLASSROOM   Using Incentives to Foster Positive Behavior

Yvonne Smit, second-grade teacher, Centreville, Virginia

Each Monday as part of our morning meeting, we set a class focus for the week. To give the class ownership, the students come up with the focus; however, it is definitely guided by me. I might say, "What do you think of our hallway behavior?" and inevitably someone will comment that it's very loud and walking silently should be our focus. Our focus is posted on the board. I will remind students of it several times during the day and also share it with parents in our daily news. To incentivize this, I tie in the focus to our schoolwide behavior system in which classes are recognized for positive behavior.

When we have been recognized in our schoolwide behavior system a predetermined number of times, we have a celebration. In our class, the celebration is not determined until we have reached our target number, in efforts to keep the focus on positive behavior and not a reward. Sometimes the celebration is extra recess, sometimes it is a cookie, but again, that is decided by our class. It's a fun way to encourage positive behavior.

Token Reinforcers

A *token reinforcer* is a tangible item that can be exchanged for a desired object, activity, or social reinforcer at a later time. Tokens may be chips, points, stars, tickets, buttons, play money, metal washers, happy faces, or stickers. The backup reinforcer is the reward for which tokens can be exchanged. Token reinforcement is useful when praise and attention have not worked. Tokens are accumulated and cashed in for the reinforcer.

Using Reinforcers Effectively

It is important to recognize the general principle of reinforcement: behaviors that are reinforced will be retained; behaviors that are not reinforced will be extinguished. You need to consider carefully whom to reinforce, under what conditions, and with what kinds of reinforcement. Reinforcement is likely to be effective only to the extent that (a) the consequences used for reinforcers are experienced as reinforcers by the student; (b) they are contingent on the student achieving specific performance objectives; and (c) they are awarded in a way that complements rather than undermines the development of intrinsic motivation and other natural outcomes of behavior.

MAJOR CONCEPTS

1. Positive teacher–student relationships can be developed by communicating caring and support, adjusting to your students, and taking actions to create an appropriate level of dominance and cooperation.

2. To develop good teacher–student relationships in urban settings, teachers should focus on trust and respect, caring, helping students feeling connected to others in the various contexts, and providing students choices in managing their own learning.

3. An optimal teacher–student relationship consists of equal parts of dominance and cooperation.

4. Effective classroom managers have a mental set for management in which they consciously have high awareness of the actions in the classroom and respond quickly when misbehavior occurs.

5. Successful management of whole-group instruction can be achieved by deliberate actions to prevent misbehavior, manage movement through the lesson, and maintain a group focus.

6. A variety of approaches can be used that cause students to pay attention to the class activities at all times.

7. A reinforcer is an event or consequence that increases the strength or future probability of the behavior it follows. Reinforcement is used to strengthen behaviors that are valued and to motivate students to do things that will benefit them.

8. Recognition, activities and privileges, tangible reinforcers, and token reinforcers can be used to reinforce desired student behavior.

DISCUSSION/REFLECTIVE QUESTIONS

1. From your experiences and observations, what are the characteristics of good teacher–student relationships?

2. When considering the teacher–student relationship, give some examples of high and low dominance by a teacher. Also give some examples for high and low cooperation.

3. Give some examples where a teacher demonstrates "withitness" in a lesson. Give some examples where a teacher did not demonstrate withitness. What happened then?

4. When considering whole-group instruction, describe some examples where a teacher does not have good momentum and smoothness when proceeding through a lesson.

5. From your experiences in K–12 classrooms, describe ways your teachers maintained attention and involvement in lessons.

6. Why would attention-getting strategies promote student involvement? What precautions could you identify for their use?

7. How might your selection and use of reinforcers be affected by grade level or subject area?

SUGGESTED ACTIVITIES

1. Talk with several teachers and ask them to describe how they develop positive relationships with their students.

2. Ask several teachers how they maintain control of the class without being too dominant or negative.

3. Reflect on your schooling experiences and identify some strategies that your teachers used to capture and maintain students' attention, interest, and involvement.

4. Talk with several teachers to see how they reinforce students (e.g., recognition, activities and privileges, tangible reinforcers, or token reinforcers).

FURTHER READING

Anderson, M. (2016). *Learning to choose, choosing to learn: The key to student motivation and achievement*. Alexandria, VA: Association for Supervision and Curriculum Development.
Focuses on ways to offer students choices about their learning, which helps boost student learning, motivation, and achievement. Provides a step-by-step process to help you plan and incorporate choice in your classroom. Is a good resource.

Curwin, R. L., Mendler, A. N., & Mendler, B. D. (2018). *Discipline with dignity* (4th ed.). Alexandria, VA: Association for Supervision and Curriculum Development.
Provides many ways to build responsibility, relationships, and respect in your classroom. Focuses mainly on discipline but with student involvement and choice in mind. Is a thorough resource.

Lopez, I. (2017). *Keeping it real and relevant: Building authentic relationships in your diverse classroom*. Alexandria, VA: Association for Supervision and Curriculum Development.
Provides ways to design and leverage an effective learning environment. Considers relationships, interventions, work ethic, and reflective practices for teachers to improve.

Middleton, M., & Perks, K. (2014). *Motivation to learn: Transforming classroom culture to support student achievement*. Thousand Oaks, CA: Corwin Press.
Provides ways to create and sustain a classroom community that is highly engaged. Focuses on positive relationships, choices for students, meaningful tasks, challenge and support for students, and classroom practices and strategies. Many good ideas.

© Susie Fitzhugh/The Image Works

Communication Skills for Teaching

CHAPTER OBJECTIVES

This chapter provides information that will help you:

- Use language effectively to promote student learning and appropriate conduct.

- Apply the guidelines for effective use of teacher language in the classroom.

- Communicate firm limits for student behavior.

- Use supportive language in the classroom.

- Apply listening skills to enhance learning and address behavior.

- Exhibit appropriate nonverbal communication in the classroom.

Teachers talk all day long. Everything they say communicates information and is designed to achieve certain purposes. Teacher talk can positively or negatively affect just about everything in the classroom—the classroom climate, student motivation, behavior, student performance, and other factors. With their language, teachers can either support student decision making, responsibility, teamwork, and initiative or encourage students to be passive in the classroom to do only what they are told to do.

This chapter focuses on communication skills for teachers in relation to classroom management. The power of teacher language and the purposes of teacher communication in the classroom are first identified. Then there are separate sections concerning guidelines for teacher language, communicating firm limits for behavior, characteristics of verbal communication, using supportive language, listening, and nonverbal communication.

The Power of Language

In recent years, there has been considerable interest in how teachers use their language to promote learning and to guide student behavior. Entire books have been written on this topic, as illustrated by the following examples:

- *What We Say and How We Say It Matter* (Anderson, 2019)

- *The Power of Our Words: Teacher Language that Helps Children Learn* (Denton, 2014)

- *Use Your Words: How Teacher Talk Helps Children Learn* (Mooney, 2005)

- *What Do You Say When . . .? Best Practice Language for Improving Student Behavior* (Holloman & Yates, 2010)

- *Inviting Students to Learn: 100 Tips for Talking Effectively with Your Students* (Edwards, 2010)

- *Talking, Listening, and Teaching: A Guide to Classroom Communication* (Farrell, 2009)

The language that teachers use and the manner in which they express that language can profoundly affect students in the classroom. The term *teacher language* refers to the professional use of words, phrases, tone, and pace to enable students to engage in active, interested learning and develop positive behaviors (Denton, 2014, p. 3).

What teachers want to achieve in the classroom will influence their communication and their use of language. The overall role of the teacher is to guide and support student learning, which can be broken down into many smaller elements. In relation to classroom management, teachers try to achieve three important purposes in the classroom: (a) to create a positive learning community; (b) to provide instruction and support student engagement; and (c) to guide and correct student behavior.

Teachers can achieve these purposes through the intentional use of language—this is the power of language. Learning to use teacher language to its full positive potential means becoming aware of your habitual ways of speaking and the positive and negative messages that these may be sending to students (Denton, 2014). It means stepping back to hear ourselves and to reflect, "What did I say? What message did I convey? What tone did I use?" Teachers then can try and practice new words, phrases, tones, and pacings to replace any ineffective language patterns.

Research on teacher communication provides guidance for effective practice. In a review of research on teacher communication, Raczynski and Horne (2015) report on communication in three areas: listening, speaking, and helping to solve problems. In another review of research, Wubbels et al. (2015) report that specific behaviors associated with teacher warmth and closeness, such as eye contact, open body position, and teacher self-talk, have been found to be associated with positive student behaviors such as on-task student behavior.

General Guidelines for Teacher Language

Students need to know that teacher words have meaning when providing instruction or addressing a misbehaving student. Students also need to know that words correspond with actions. Here are some general guidelines for using language to affirm meaning and action, to address various aspects of instruction and behavior management, and to engage in guidance and conversation with students. These guidelines underpin the additional, more specific strategies offered later in this chapter and represent a synthesis of those offered by Charney (2002, pp. 235–245), Denton (2014, pp. 12–31), and Mooney (2005, pp. 18–20):

1. **Keep it simple and brief.** When giving directions, long explanations are often counterproductive since students may not identify or remember all of the parts, and students may not

even follow along during the entire explanation. Short, simple directions and explanations are essential if we expect specific actions.

When giving directions, do not give warnings about consequences if students don't heed the reminders and directions. Warnings tell students that we think it is unlikely they will behave well. Such warnings are generally not effective and too often come across as threats.

2. **Use direct language—say what you mean.** Teachers sometimes use indirect language as a means to get students' compliance, such as praising some students' behavior in the hopes of getting the other students to comply. A more effective strategy is to *give directions clearly and directly, telling students what you want them to do*. Instead of an indirect statement such as "I like the way that Ethan and Joline are ready for our activity," say, "I would like everyone's attention before we start our activity." A warm, matter-of-fact tone conveys authenticity, respect, and directness.

Another common pattern is to phrase directions as a question, perhaps as a means to soften our commands to students, such as "Could you all go back to your seats now?" By contrast, "Everyone go back to your seats now" tells students what you want. If students do not comply, they know they are defying you and that they will receive consequences. Therefore, *use statements rather than questions when giving directions*.

3. **Follow through on your words—mean what you say.** When students know that teachers will follow through on their words, students are likely to take the words seriously. There should be consequences for not following directions, and consequences are more effective if they are made clear ahead of time and are anticipated. At the start of the school year, you can discuss potential consequences if students do not follow the rules and procedures. Taking action at the early signs of off-task or disruptive behavior is best, and students get the message that you mean what you say. Your words carry the most weight when the students see that you back them up with action.

4. **Focus on observable words and actions.** Rather than using abstract terms, focus on concrete concepts and behaviors. Instead of saying, "Be responsible," you could tell the students specifically what is expected. If expectations include abstract concepts such as being responsible or treating each other with respect, you can have a discussion to clarify what those expectations look like in real words or actions. This helps communicate expectations more clearly.

5. **Use words that invite cooperation and convey faith in students' abilities and intentions.** Because language is such a powerful shaper of identity and perceptions, it is important that you carefully use language to open, rather than close, the doors of possibility for students. Our language conveys our assumptions and expectations, which then influence students. "Show me how you will follow the rules in the hall," conveys an expectation that students know how to follow the rules they practiced and will do so. Also, take time to notice the positives that students exhibit and comment on them. This is reinforcing.

6. **Know when to be silent.** The skillful use of silence can be just as powerful as the skillful use of language. Silence allows for students' voices. It allows for thinking, interacting, and decision making. There are four aspects of the skillful use of silence in the classroom (Denton, 2014).

- **When asking questions,** *provide wait time* **(i.e., teacher silence) for several seconds.** This will enable students to think about the question and their possible response. Also, pause for a while before responding to students. In addition, speaking more slowly allows for thought processes.
- **Listen to what students have to say.** Listening to what students have to say models respectful interaction in a community of learners, and it helps students learn when they need to formulate and express their ideas. Skillful listening means letting students complete their statements rather than interrupting them. It means maintaining eye contact and pausing before our reply.

- **Refrain from repeating directions.** Teachers can give directions once, check to see if there are any questions, and stop. Then during an activity, instead of repeating the directions, teachers can provide help with prompts or questions. Students can be given a chance to remember and figure things out themselves.
- **Resist the temptation to use voice-overs.** A voice-over is a repeating of a student's response right after it has been uttered. By not repeating, you allow the student's voice to stand on its own, indicating to the class the importance of listening to each other. That is the power of silence.

7. **Be aware of the signals your body language, tone and volume of voice, and facial expression send.** Your body language, gestures, tone of voice, and other nonverbal expressions should be consistent with your spoken words (nonverbal communication is discussed later in this chapter). If students see a mismatch between a teacher's words and body language, they may lose trust in the teacher or simply get confused. Generally, the nonverbal signal is believed whenever there is a mismatch. Therefore, teachers need to be aware of the signals they are sending through their body and match their nonverbal signals to the verbal messages they are expressing.

8. **Make sure you have student attention before you proceed.** Whether talking with one student or the entire class, it is important to capture the students' attention before you proceed with what you plan to say. In a whole-class setting, teachers may use some type of signal, sound, movement, or statement to capture students' attention that the class is about to begin. When speaking to a single student, face-to-face communication works best, along with eye contact.

VOICES FROM THE CLASSROOM   Three Tips for Teacher Talk

Cristina Fontana, first-grade teacher, Guilford, Connecticut

Using effective language in the classroom and when conversing with students is crucial. Below are some guidelines that I keep in mind when I converse with students.

Less is more. I have found that the less I address the whole class, the more students listen when I do address them. Less teacher talk allows for conversations to be more student directed. Student-led conversations foster agency and encourage sharing of ideas.

I have found that proper planning prior to a lesson is what has helped me to talk less. Before a lesson, I plan out the intended learning as well as possible prompting questions to allow students to get to the end goal.

Wait time. It is important to allow adequate wait time after posing a question or asking for student input. Extending my wait time has increased student participation. When we do not allow for proper wait time, the students who take longer to process or compose ideas may get discouraged. Students may also start to think, "I don't need to think of the answer, Johnny will answer for me." Wait time slows down the conversation and allows students to process the ideas that are being shared.

Depending on the lesson, I may wait for every student to have an answer to share with the group. Asking students to put their thumbs up on their knees when they have an answer and waiting for each student to do so gives every student the amount of processing time he/she needs to arrive at an answer. This fosters student agency and teaches students that all of their ideas are important and valued.

Ask open-ended questions. When asking closed questions (i.e., yes or no responses) the conversation has nowhere to go. To help me realize when I was using closed questioning, I started audio recording my lessons. I then listened to the questions I asked and thought about how I could change the questions to be more open-ended. For example, rather than asking, "Did the character change?" I would ask, "How did the character change?" That small change can take the answer from a simple yes or no to a discussion or debate.

You have two computer centers in your classroom, each with four computers. Since this is the first time students will be using the centers this year, you describe the guidelines for their use and your expectations about conduct before having the first group of students at the center. Then, you notice that two students at the computers are not following the behavioral guidelines you stated.

1. Identify specifically how you would apply the guidelines for effective teacher language when presenting the guidelines and behavioral expectations to the students.

2. Similarly, identify how you would apply the guidelines for effective teacher language when you noticed two students misbehaving at the computers.

Communicating Firm Limits for Behavior

Teachers identify rules for the classroom and then enforce the rules when necessary. When a student exhibits a behavior that violates a rule, teachers typically interact with the student verbally before delivering a consequence. However, many teachers hold up the wrong signals to stop misbehavior. They don't realize that their stop signs don't really require stopping or that their attempts to say "no" actually sound like "yes," "sometimes," or "maybe" to their students. In these cases, the teacher's limits are soft, not firm, and the students know it. *Setting Limits in the Classroom* (MacKenzie & Stanzione, 2010) provides the basis for much of this information, and it is a useful guide.

Soft Limits

Soft limits are rules in theory but not in practice. Soft limits can be ineffective verbal messages or ineffective action messages; sometimes they are both at the same time. The verbal message seems to say stop, but the action message says stopping is neither expected nor required. All soft limits are mixed messages that invite testing and power struggles.

Soft limits don't stop behavior, don't encourage acceptable behavior, and don't promote positive learning about the rules or authority. Firm limits are more effective.

Examples of Soft Limits

Soft limits come in a variety of forms as verbal messages or action messages. Either way, students are not compelled to adhere to the rule in question and feel free to continue with their behavior. Soft limits are ineffective. Here are some examples:

Soft Limits—Verbal Messages

- "Would you cooperate just once in a while?"

- "You'd better shape up."

- "Would you do me a favor and pay attention?"

- "Come on, get your act together."

Soft Limits—Action Messages

- Allowing students to walk away from a mess.

- Cleaning up students' messes for them.

- Overlooking a misbehavior when you are in a good mood.

- Giving in to persistent nagging.

Types of Soft Limits

Here are some typical types of soft limits (MacKenzie & Stanzione, 2010). Realize that you should *avoid the following soft limit behaviors and use firm limits instead*. In most cases, the firm limits are simply the opposite of the soft limit behaviors that are noted.

1. **Wishes, hopes, and shoulds.** "I really wish you would put away your supplies before the end of class." Wishes, hopes, and shoulds are another way of saying, "Stopping is nice, but you really don't have to until you are ready." Compliance is optional, not required.

2. **Repeating and reminding.** Teachers who repeat and remind are teaching students to ignore and tune out. For example, a teacher might ask a student to put away a personal booklet and then remind the student again when it is not done. When students wonder how far they can go, they simply do not comply until they realize they must do so.

3. **Speeches, lectures, and sermons.** If a student comes in from recess late, for example, the teacher might go on about how disruptive this is since the class has already begun and directions need to be restated for her. The student learns that showing up late is okay if she can tolerate the teacher's lectures about the event.

4. **Warnings and second chances.** Teachers sometimes give a student a warning before delivering a consequence. But if teachers give several warnings without a consequence, then students learn that they will be given additional chances and they can keep doing the behavior. Students will likely continue to test until the consequence is delivered.

5. **Cooperate, okay?** "Amber, you're supposed to put away your materials before starting the next activity. Okay?" Okay to whom—the student or the teacher? Does that mean cooperation is optional? When teachers add "Okay" to the end of requests, the clarity of the message is obscured.

6. **Statements of fact.** Students at the beginning of class are talking with some not even in their seats. The teacher says, "I'm ready to start. It's too noisy. I can't get started until it's quiet." This soft message was intended to tell the students to stop talking and get in their seats, but many students continue to test the message. A clearer signal is needed. Statements of fact do not convey the intended message.

7. **Ignoring the behavior.** If a student is clowning around, for example, a teacher may ignore it with the hope that it will go away. Especially if the behavior shows up repeatedly, ignoring the behavior just gives a green light to the student. Instead, a teacher should tell the student to stop and should deliver appropriate consequences if the behavior continues.

8. **Unclear directions.** Sometimes teachers make statements that are open to interpretation. "Don't take too long on this task in your small groups." What does "too long" mean? Five minutes? Ten minutes? Unclear or open-ended directions invite testing and set up conflicts. It is better to be specific when stating expectations.

■ WHAT WOULD YOU DECIDE?   **Poor Guidance with Soft Limits**

Near the end of some seatwork, you give directions to the students to soon be ready for their next large group activity. After a couple of minutes, you see an idle student and you say, "Austin, you are supposed to be getting ready for the next activity. Okay?" Even after you leave Austin's area, you then notice that he is not moving. But you decide not to go back to him because he might complain about you nagging him.

1. What specific problems with soft limits are illustrated in this example?

2. If you were the teacher, how specifically might you have used firm limits to better address the situation?

Firm Limits

In contrast to soft limits, firm limits are clear signals that students understand and that teachers enforce. The key to giving a clear message with your words is to say only what needs to be said in a clear, firm, and respectful manner. Using firm limits will reduce testing. Using firm limits does not mean that a teacher is harsh or nasty with students. Here are four useful guidelines for providing clear, firm signals:

1. **Keep the focus of your words on behavior.** Keep the focus of your message on what you want the student to do or stop doing, not on attitude or feelings or the value of the student. The goal is to reject the unacceptable behavior, not the student performing the behavior. A clear, focused behavioral message is less likely to be perceived by the student as a personal attack.

2. **Be direct and specific.** A clear message should inform students, directly and specifically, about what you want them to do or not to do. If necessary, be prepared to tell them how and when you want them to do it. The fewer the words, the better.

3. **Use your normal voice.** The tone of your voice is important. Your normal tone expresses control, but a raised voice indicates loss of control. Your tone should convey that you are firm, in control, and resolute in your expectation that the students will do what you have asked. Firm limits are not stated harshly.

4. **Use nonthreatening body language.** Our body language conveys a message about our comfort level, feelings, and expectations in discipline situations. When our body language is congruent with a neutral or positive message, students are more likely to receive the message in a supportive and instructive manner. Threatening body language, on the other hand, increases the likelihood of defensive responses from students.

5. **Specify the logical consequence for noncompliance.** Some students will test your rules and authority in an effort to see how far they can go. Teachers can prevent a lot of testing and power struggles by simply providing students with information about consequences that will be delivered if they continue being noncompliant. For example, "Lydia, put away the comb. If you have it out during class again, I will keep it at my desk until the end of the day." In this way, you are providing the student with information she needs to make an acceptable choice to cooperate.

Examples of Firm Limits

Firm limits also come in a variety of forms as verbal messages or action messages. They send a message that compliance is expected and required. They send messages in clear, direct, concrete behavior terms. Here are some examples:

Firm Limits—Verbal Messages

- "I expect you to be back in five minutes."
- "If you shove, you will go to the back of the line."
- "You won't be ready to leave until your desk is clean."
- "You can finish your assignment during class time or during recess."

Firm Limits—Action Messages

- Removing an object from a student who does not put it away when asked.
- Separating a student from others for misbehaving in a small-group activity.
- Temporarily removing a privilege for abusing that privilege.
- Holding students accountable for cleaning up their messes.

Using Statements or Directives

When talking to students about their behavior, teachers may state their opinions, ask questions, or give directives. Giving statements or directives is more clear and straightforward. The use of opinions and questions are indirect ways of guiding and correcting student behavior and generally are less effective.

If a student is making a tapping noise during a test, for example, the teacher may express an opinion ("I am concerned that this noise will distract other students"), ask a question ("Will you stop tapping?"), or give a directive ("Stop tapping now"). Using indirect language, such as with opinions and questions, may be a less harsh and sometimes easy way to gain compliance. However, soft commands such as those don't always lead to compliance. It is often better to be more clear and direct by stating a directive in a nonthreatening, matter-of-fact tone.

Think about these statements from the students' perspective at the end of small-group work: "I think it's time to get back to your regular seats" (opinion). "Will you get back to your regular seats?" (question). "Please go back to your regular seats now." (directive). There is less ambiguity and more clarity for the students when using a directive statement.

Characteristics of Verbal Communication

Verbal communication takes into account the use of words and the effect that your words have on your students. We give special attention to three characteristics of verbal communication for teachers: the clarity of their words, the appropriateness of their word choice, and the way teachers deliver their words (Simonds & Cooper, 2011).

Clarity

Clarity refers to the precision of your communication to your students regarding the desired behavior. Clarity in teaching helps students understand better, work more accurately, and be more successful. Effective teachers exhibit a high degree of clarity by providing very clear and explicit directions, instructions, questions, and expectations. If you are constantly asked to repeat questions, directions, and explanations or if your students do not understand your expectations, you are not exhibiting clarity in your instructional behavior.

Clear directions, instructions, and expectations ensure that students know what is expected of them and can act accordingly as they work on classroom activities, assignments, and other tasks. If you are not very clear when giving directions, for example, students may not complete the assignment in the way you intended, may become confused, and may need additional time and attention to later complete the assignment in the manner intended. In a review of the research on teacher clarity, Simonds and Cooper (2011) reported that teacher clarity has been linked to student achievement, satisfaction, and student's perception of teacher caring.

To be clear in the classroom, (a) inform the learners of the objective; (b) provide learners with advance organizers; (c) check for task-relevant prior learning and reteach, if necessary; (d) give directions slowly and distinctly; (e) know the ability levels of students and teach to those levels; (f) use examples, illustrations, and demonstrations to explain and clarify; and (g) provide a review or summary at the end of each lesson.

Appropriateness

Teachers should be sure that the language used in the classroom is appropriate to the topic and the students. Vocabulary and word choice used in presenting academic content should be at the level students will understand, with content and terms not too shallow or not too deep. Rather than talking to students in a way that is below their developmental level, it is better to communicate in the same voice as we would with other adults; this avoids students feeling like they are being talked to as if they were younger children.

Teachers should select words and use language that is positive and that expresses faith in students' abilities and intentions. Words should convey a belief that students want to cooperate, listen, and learn. Negative expressions, such as the use of sarcasm, would not be appropriate or in line with these purposes.

Teachers should strive to use language that is inclusive. Inclusive language considers and respects all types of people regardless of gender, race, sexual orientation, and other factors. Inclusive language respects students and avoids making assumptions about what people can or cannot do. For example, teachers may want to avoid using gender terms to describe what people do or which gender should be in certain jobs or social roles.

Verbal Delivery

Effective teachers do not speak in a monotone all day long. They vary the volume of their voice, the speed in which they speak, and the way they express ideas. Verbal delivery involves the following factors (Simonds & Cooper, 2011).

- *Articulation* is the clear formation of words. This involves how completely and accurately the letters and syllables are expressed when a person speaks.

- *Pronunciation* is how a word is said and stressed. This involves knowing which syllable is the strongest and which vowel sound is used. Is it a long *a* or a short *a*? For effective verbal communication, teachers should be certain to pronounce words correctly.

- *Volume* is how loud or soft words are expressed. Teachers may vary the volume of their voice to add some dramatic effect, perhaps speaking louder when they want to stress a point. The volume of your voice should be appropriate to the size of the room and your audience. You will want to project your voice so students at the farthest point in the room can hear you without appearing to be shouting.

- *Rate* is the speed that you talk. You will want to vary the speed of your talk, speaking faster or slower at various times. Pay attention to your students to see if your speed of talking is suitable. Talking too fast on a regular basis, for example, may make it difficult for some students to keep up with you. Talking too slow may bore students.

- *Pauses* are moments of brief silence during a verbal presentation. Pauses can be used to emphasize a point, collect your thoughts, or transition to a new point.

- *Pitch* is the highness or lowness in the quality of sound of your voice. When you vary your pitch, you are using inflection to help communicate your ideas. Without this variation, you will have a monotone voice, which can become irritating to students.

- *Vocal variety* involves the way you use volume, rate, pauses, and pitch in your verbal communications. Vocal variety allows you to become more conversational and expressive. Think about ways you can vary your voice so your students become interested in what you have to say.

The tone of your voice is important when managing student behavior. *Tone* is the mood, atmosphere, or feeling you create through the use of your verbal communication. Your normal voice tone expresses control, whereas your raised voice sends the opposite message—loss of control. Your tone should convey that you are firm, in control, and resolute in your expectations

VOICES FROM THE CLASSROOM   The Meaning of Our Words

Suzanne Buhner, fourth-grade teacher, Virginia Beach, Virginia

I recently asked my students to research and name a favorite idiom. Two of my fourth graders engaged in deep discussion about the idiom "talk is cheap." What I heard surprised me as they were discussing how teachers sometimes tell students to do their best and be brave enough to make mistakes "because that is how you learn." But when mistakes are made or a poor grade achieved, teachers then dole out consequences such as lecturing about the actions, phone calls home, and extra work. Both students agreed, "talk is cheap" means that you say one thing but do another, much like when teachers tell students mistakes are OK but then give out consequences when mistakes happen.

We opened dialogue with the entire class about this and created a list of phrases teachers commonly use to encourage positive behavior and academic success. As a class, we then defined words like *good, better, best*. Now we record wording examples that match our definitions of those three words, and we also created a look-for list of mistakes for each of the three words. Based on our chart of good and bad examples for the use of those three words, we have created interesting data charts and analyses of our mistakes, and this has led to building critical thinking and metacognition skills. I see students thinking more about their actions.

The greatest change has perhaps occurred in my practice. I no longer jump to conclusions when student behaviors (aka mistakes) occur. My new "talk" goes something like this, "My interpretation of _____ leads me to think _____. Am I on the right track?" I now am more cognizant of my teacher talk and its consequences.

that the students will do what you have asked (MacKenzie & Stanzione, 2010). Diffily and Sassman (2006) describe this as "developing your teacher voice." The best way to communicate this expectation is simply to state your message matter-of-factly in your normal voice, but with a noticeable degree of firmness.

Using Supportive Language

Teachers can use supportive language to guide and support effective instruction, classroom management, and discipline. Language that expresses guidance, caring, and support can positively affect teacher–student relationships and the climate in the learning community. Although there are many dimensions of language for these purposes, the following sections offer suggestions for supportive language in relation to classroom management and discipline.

Being Intentionally Inviting

Establishing a positive classroom community is an important goal for all teachers, and many deliberate actions need to be taken to create this positive environment. To do so, teachers need to be intentionally inviting and supportive of students. In *Inviting School Success*, Purkey and Novak (1996) describe four types of teacher behaviors toward students: intentionally disinviting, unintentionally disinviting, unintentionally inviting, and intentionally inviting.

Inviting messages are intended to inform people that they are able, valuable, and responsible; that they have the opportunity to participate in their own development; and that they are cordially summoned to take advantage of these opportunities. Conversely, a disinviting message informs recipients that they are irresponsible, incapable, and worthless and cannot participate in activities of any significance. To create a positive, caring learning community, teachers need to use inviting messages and be intentionally inviting by giving deliberate attention to how they state and deliver their words. Teachers should strive to use inviting messages that express to students that they are able, valuable, and responsible. There are five elements of invitational education giving teaching purpose and direction: intentionality, care, optimism, respect, and trust (Purkey, Novak, & Schoenlein, 2016)

1. **Intentionality.** By focusing on being intentionally inviting and supportive of their students, teachers become more accurate and dependable in their decision making and behaviors, leading to more clear purpose and direction. Education is never neutral; everything adds to the educative process.

2. **Care.** Warmth, empathy, and positive regard are important aspects of caring. With invitational education, teachers have the ability and desire to care about students, their growth, and their accomplishments.

3. **Optimism.** Teachers should take the optimistic view that students want to learn and will learn in a cooperative and supportive environment. They believe that students have untapped potential and that they are only beginning to use their knowledge and skills.

4. **Respect.** Students are to be seen as able, valuable, and responsible and should be treated accordingly. Teachers believe that students have inherent worth, self-directing power, and personal and social accountability.

5. **Trust.** Teachers establish trust through a pattern of inviting actions, rather than by a single inviting act. It takes time, effort, and collaboration to establish trustworthy interactions. In doing so, teachers need to be reliable, genuine, truthful, intentional, and competent.

Reinforcing Language

Reinforcing language involves statements that identify and affirm students' specific positive work and behavior. We want to build on students' strengths, and reinforcing language helps achieve that purpose. Teachers can use reinforcing language in various situations such as: (a) to coach students on key behaviors when they practice social and academic skills ("That is the correct way to create a Venn diagram"); (b) to help a group move past a stuck point (by noticing and commenting on correct behavior); (c) to point out an individual student's "leading edge" behaviors (by noticing and commenting on a student's important improvement in behavior or academic work); and (d) to make students aware of their growth by describing their learning histories (by drawing attention to how the student has changed from a previous time) (Denton, 2014).

Reinforcing language can be used to highlight many important student strengths. Here are some guidelines when using reinforcing language (Denton, 2014):

- **Name concrete, specific behaviors.** This goes beyond simply telling students they did a good job. Reinforcing statements should be concrete and specific, communicating exactly what aspects of students' behavior, products, or processes are working well. Be specific and mention only what the student did. For example, "I noticed you speaking up more in the group discussions. That helps us know your ideas."

- **Use a warm and professional voice.** Speak to students in adult language without being overly sentimental. Use words in a warm and professional tone that will assure students they are being recognized as intelligent, capable people. Avoid language that may appear that you are talking down to students.

- **Emphasize description of the action over your own personal approval.** When we make statements that focus on our feelings, we send implicit messages to students that the purpose of the good behavior is to please us. Instead, focus your words on the student's actions. For example, a teacher might observe, "You took your time to proofread your material today before turning it in" instead of "I loved how you proofread your material today before you turned it in."

- **Consider adding a question to extend student thinking.** To extend students' thinking, teachers can follow their statements about their positive behaviors with open-ended questions. The goal is to help students become more aware of the behaviors named, to deepen their understanding of how the behavior is useful, or to help them see what they can do to improve further. For example, a teacher might ask, "You have been working on improving your writing skills. What has helped you the most in that process?"

- **Find positives to name in all students.** Reinforcing language should be used with all students, not just the best performers. Even when a student's work is not where we want it to be, we can comment on positive aspects or growth. However, teachers should be selective in their statements by describing only those behaviors that are truly important and relevant. For example, "I noticed that you sharpened your pencil first today to be prepared for class."

- **Avoid naming individuals as examples for others.** "See how well Tiffany is cleaning up her lab table." The teacher may make this statement with the intention of encouraging other students to also clean their area effectively. But such statements can be damaging because they elevate some students at the expense of others. All who are not lauded have been, by implication, devalued or criticized. Instead, focus your statements on what has been done well without mentioning individual students.

Reminding Language

Reminders help us stay organized and on track with our activities. In everyday life, when we give reminders, we tell our listeners what it is they should remember. Reminders in classrooms, however, should prompt the students to do the remembering themselves ("What are some things we should remember about safety before we begin this lab activity?" "Jason, what are you supposed to be doing right now?").

Used in this way, reminding language helps students develop the feelings of autonomy and competence that lead to self-control and intrinsic motivation. These guidelines can make classroom reminders more effective (Denton, 2014):

- **Start by establishing expectations clearly.** When discussing a behavioral expectation, be sure students understand the specific behavior. Illustrate the behavior with examples. Next, teachers can model the expected behavior to ensure understanding. This interactive modeling can have the following steps: say what you will model and why, model the behavior, ask students what they noticed, invite one or more students to model, again ask students what they noticed, have all students practice, and provide feedback.

- **Phrase a reminder as a question or a statement.** A reminder may be in the form of a question, such as "What are you supposed to be doing right now?" In doing so, teachers should use a neutral vocal tone, rather than an angry or exasperated tone. Reminders also can be in the form of a statement that communicates the belief that students know what is expected, such as "Cleanup time," or "I'll begin when everyone is ready."

- **Use a direct tone and neutral body language.** When we use a direct vocal tone and keep our body language neutral, we communicate calmness and faith that students have the desire and ability to do well and be responsible. Students are more likely to take these reminders as honest, helpful prompts.

- **Use reminders proactively or reactively.** When thinking about an upcoming activity and the challenges or difficulties students might experience, proactive reminders can be given to students before the activity begins to highlight any guidelines or expectations. Reactive reminders can be given during the activity when students are starting to get off track but before the inappropriate behavior is well established.

- **Use reminders when the student and you are both calm.** Reminders are most effective when both the teacher and student are feeling calm. The teacher needs to give the reminder in a neutral but direct tone. The student needs to be calm to think what the appropriate behavior is and act accordingly.

- **Keep reminders brief.** Stating reminders in one or two short sentences usually is sufficient. Generally, the fewer words we use, the better.

- **Watch for follow-through.** After giving a reminder, teachers need to watch to make sure students act as desired. If students follow through correctly after a reminder, teachers can acknowledge it with a nonverbal expression such as a smile, nod, or wink. No words are necessary. If students do not follow through on the reminder, more direct language is needed.

■ CLASSROOM CASE STUDY   Poor Use of Limit Setting and Supportive Language

Terrell Green planned some small-group activities for his tenth-grade geometry class. Instruction had been completed on a new topic, and Mr. Green wanted the students to work in small groups to work out some sample problems together. He provided each group with paper, rulers, compasses, and protractors to work out the problems.

After a while, some students in the groups were using the rulers to swat other students. Most students were on task, but one or two in each group were hitting with the rulers. Several times, Mr. Green said, "Rulers are not for hitting," but he didn't follow up with any other statements or actions. Later, he said to two students, "Will you stop hitting with the ruler?" but he had no follow-through. After about 10 minutes, he realized that he had not stated any guidelines or cautions with the use of the supplies at the start of the activity.

This activity disturbed Mr. Green, and he seemed to be at a loss for what to do. He didn't interact with the students who were on task, and he simply walked around to be physically close to those who were hitting. After the lesson, he reflected about what happened and what he might have done differently to get a better outcome.

Focus Questions

1. How did Mr. Green use statements and questions? What was the problem with his use of those statements and questions?

2. How might Mr. Green have used *reminding* language to guide and correct those misbehaviors?

3. How might he have used *redirecting* language in this situation?

Redirecting Language

Reinforcing positive behaviors and reminding students about how to behave can be very helpful in classroom management and discipline. However, there are times when teachers simply need to give students clear, nonnegotiable commands about what to do.

Redirecting statements should guide students to act differently while preserving their dignity and sense of belonging in the classroom. Here are some points to remember when using redirecting language (Denton, 2014):

- **Be direct and specific.** Call the student by name and state exactly what you want the student to do. By including the student's name, you get his or her attention. By stating exactly what you want the student to do, you avoid any misinterpretation as compared to general statements. The redirection needs to be given in a calm, even tone without sounding upset or angry.

- **Name the desired behavior.** Instead of, "Many of you are wasting time," state, "We will begin when you are all seated with your materials ready."

- **Keep it brief.** Get the students' attention first in a few direct words, such as "Pencils down, I want your attention now." After you have their attention, then you can give them directions for the next actions.

- **Phrase redirections as a statement, not a question.** Instead of, "Can you put your backpacks away?" say, "Put all backpacks on the hooks now." Statements provide directives and firm limits, rather than questions that give the illusion of choice when, in fact, the teacher wants a particular response. Questions also give students an opportunity to say "No" and engage in a power struggle.

- **Follow through after giving a redirection.** After giving redirecting language, observe the students and step in with clearer directions or consequences if students don't follow the redirection. This tells students we mean what we say.

Listening

Effective communication is essential in the classroom for instruction and behavior management. Listening is a vital part of effective communication, and it is a key element in developing positive teacher–student relationships, addressing classroom problems, and enhancing instruction and supporting student learning.

What Is Listening?

Listening is more than passively receiving a student's words. It involves searching for the student's intended meaning, which means paying attention to what's being said beneath the works and using responding strategies to explore the words and the meaning. Listening and responding is actually a three-step process (Denton, 2014): (a) take in the words; (b) figure out the true meaning of the words by looking at tone, context, and other signals for clues; and (c) think about how to respond.

Listening involves more than hearing what the other person is saying. It is more than taking turns speaking, with responses sometimes unrelated to what the other person just said. The meaning of the words must be explored. There are four tools to develop the art of listening (Larrivee, 2009):

1. **Control the impulse to talk and just remain silent.** Avoid the tendency to jump in with your own ideas or solutions before hearing from the student.

2. **Demonstrate acceptance.** Provide verbal and nonverbal support for what the student is saying.

3. **Provide an invitation to talk.** This often involves open-ended, nonevaluative questions that invite the student to talk more.

4. **Use active listening skills.** Use listening strategies (discussed later) such as paraphrasing and clarifying to seek the real meaning of the messages.

Why Listen?

Teachers need to listen in order to communicate effectively when dealing with instruction and behavior management. Effective listening serves many purposes. In *The Power of Our Words*, Denton (2014) gives six reasons why we need to listen in the classroom:

1. **Listening lets us know the child.** Listening helps teachers understand their students, and this helps teachers make better decisions about curriculum, classroom management, and discipline. Students, then, are more likely to feel that they belong and are important in the classroom community.

2. **When we listen, children learn about themselves.** By listening to students and reflecting back to them what we heard, teachers can help students become more conscious of their own interests, talents, worries, and questions. This self-awareness is important if students are to learn at their best.

3. **Listening builds a sense of community.** When teachers listen and reflect back to students what they said, other students hear this interaction and thus understand each other better. Also, when teachers listen to all students, this sets a standard and a tone for respect and empathy that are fundamental to a strong learning community.

4. **Listening makes our questioning more effective.** When asking questions, it is important that teachers listen to the students' answers and follow up as needed to identify and explore the meaning of their responses. If teachers do not show they listened and understood student replies, students will likely be less engaged in these interactions in the future.

5. **When we listen, students take their learning more seriously.** When teachers follow up student statements with questions seeking meaning, students begin to take their ideas and words more seriously. They see that the teacher cares and is interested in them and their ideas.

6. **Our listening helps students become better communicators.** By listening and reflecting back what we understood, teachers can help students improve their communication skills. In this way, teachers model for students how to be good listeners themselves—how to take in a speaker's words, how to search for the intended meaning, and how to respond.

■ **WHAT WOULD YOU DECIDE?**   Knowing Each Other Through Listening

You know that there is a fairly high enrollment change each year in your school, so you realize that it is helpful at the start of the school year to help students in your class to get to know each other. Three important purposes of listening are to help the teacher to know the student, help students learn about each other, and help build a sense of community.

1. What might you do to listen and get to know individual students?

2. What might you do to help the students get to know each other?

3. How might this information help you when you plan for instruction and interact with the students?

Listening Strategies

Several listening strategies can be used to achieve the purposes just described. Within the four levels of listening, there are nine listening strategies (Larrivee, 2009):

Level 1: Passive listening. The teacher just listens without any interaction with the student.

- **Silence.** Remaining a silent listener allows the student to express ideas and feelings. This is passive listening.

Level 2: Acknowledgment. These responses indicate that the teacher is really listening.

- **Nonverbal support.** Nonverbal messages help communicate that you are really paying attention. These include nodding, smiling, or leaning forward. This is an acknowledgment of what the person is saying.

- **Encouragers.** Minimal verbal expressions also can offer acknowledgment of what is being stated and serve as an encouragement to continue. Expressions by the teacher such as "Oh," "I see," and "Uh-huh" let the student know to continue.

Level 3: Invitation to talk further. This is a deliberate statement encouraging the student to speak.

- **Opening.** The teacher may provide a more deliberative invitation to talk by asking open-ended, nonevaluative questions to encourage students to talk more. Some examples are, "Would you like to tell me what happened?" "That's interesting. Want to tell me more?"

Level 4: Active listening. This involves teacher responses that include additional interaction to more fully explore the meaning of the ideas being expressed. It provides feedback to the student that the teacher understands.

- **Reflecting.** Reflecting and the next four strategies are those used in active listening. These strategies involve interaction with the student and provide feedback to the student that the teacher understands. With reflecting, teachers verbalize the feelings and attitudes that they perceive lie behind the message ("You seem disappointed with your assignment." "Paige really irritates you when she acts like that."). This interaction often leads to a discussion about the origin of a problem and can lead to a solution.

- **Exploring.** This strategy calls for questioning in an open-ended way to extend a student's thinking and to expand a student's range of options. For example, "Can you tell me more about. . .?" "What's causing you the most trouble?"

- **Paraphrasing.** Paraphrasing calls for translating or feeding back to the student the essence of the message the teacher just heard, but in a simpler, more concise and precise way. In paraphrasing, you make sure that you are clear about what the student said. It demonstrates understanding of what was said and communicates that you care enough about what the student said to get it right.

- **Perception checking.** The purpose of perception checking is to make sure you are interpreting what the student said in the way it was intended. To do so, you pose a question and ask for feedback. After a student describes an incident, for example, the teacher might say, "I'm not sure I understand. Was it Tyler's statement that made you mad?"

- **Clarifying.** Sometimes there is a need to sort out something that is confusing. Clarifying involves restating what the student has said to clear up any confusion. Often, it involves stating your own confusion and asking for help to clarify your understanding. For example, "Can we stop here? I really don't understand what you mean. Can you tell me more?" "Earlier you said. . .Now you seem to be saying. . .I'm confused."

Using Nonverbal Communication

How teachers deliver their messages can be as significant as what information is being communicated. It is important to be aware of the types of nonverbal communication and the ways that you can use it in instruction and in addressing issues concerning classroom management and discipline.

Nonverbal communication does not occur in a vacuum, but instead occurs alongside verbal communication. We want our nonverbal and verbal communications to be congruent. In other words, if we are expressing positive ideas with our words, then our physical, nonverbal expressions should also send a positive message. When the messages are not congruent, the nonverbal signal is often the message that is recognized as the real message. Thus, it is important for teachers to examine and reflect on their use of words, but also to identify and reflect on their expression of nonverbal communication to effectively manage a classroom.

People from different cultures and ethnic groups may interpret nonverbal communication in a different way than the teacher. Gestures and the use of personal space, for example, may be interpreted quite differently by various cultures. Thus, it is important that teachers be familiar with the ways that culture influences communication in the classroom (Powell & Powell, 2015).

Nonverbal communication can have a positive effect on student behavior. In a review of literature, Wubbels et al. (2015) reported that specific behaviors associated with teacher warmth and closeness, such as eye contact, open body positioning, and teacher self-talk, have been found to be associated with positive student behaviors such as on-task student behavior.

As a mild response to student misbehavior, nonverbal responses are discussed more fully in Chapter 9, including actions such the use of nonverbal signals, standing near the student, and other measures.

Types of Nonverbal Communication

There are many aspects of nonverbal communication, commonly organized into two categories—proxemics and kinesics (Knapp, Hall, & Horgan, 2014).

Proxemics deals with how people use space, including seating arrangements, the general physical environment, and personal space. Communication is affected by the type of seating arrangements in a classroom, such as the various ways rows of seats or clusters of desks can be arranged, as illustrated in Chapter 3. Other parts of the classroom environment include the teacher's desk, filing cabinets, tables, activity centers or work areas, computer workstations, storage units, and other features that also affect traffic flow and communication in the classroom. Personal space also influences communication and behavior. As a general rule, personal space is 1.5–3 feet in length. Invasion or encroachment of personal space tends to increase a person's anxiety and leads to uncomfortable feelings. Teachers should respect the student's personal space.

Kinesics deals with the communication aspects of the body, such as facial expression, eye behavior, vocal intonation, touching, body movement and gestures, and dress and personal appearance (Leathers & Eaves, 2008). Teachers' nonverbal behaviors through these features influence instruction and behavior. Kinesic behavior can communicate that you like or dislike your students or the subject you are teaching.

The following sections on nonverbal communication focus on kinesics in which teachers communicate nonverbally to their students concerning classroom management issues.

Teachers' Use of Nonverbal Communication

As previously noted, we will concentrate on kinesics in this section—the ways that teachers communicate nonverbally through their facial expressions, eye behavior, vocal intonation, body movements and gestures, and other ways. Useful resources for teachers on nonverbal communication are available, including *Body Language: An Illustrated Introduction for Teachers* (Miller, 2005) and *Nonverbal Behavior in Interpersonal Relations* (Richmond, McCroskey, & Hickson, 2012).

Eye Contact

Eye contact signals that you want to communicate with another person. Eye contact, for example, can be a way to encourage further involvement in a conversation. Students indicate they are more comfortable with a teacher who, when speaking, listening, or sharing mutual silence, looks at them 50% of the time than a teacher who looks at them 100% of the time (Simonds & Cooper, 2011). Thus, teachers who stare at students at length may create anxiety.

Direct eye contact usually communicates interest and attention, whereas lack of direct eye contact communicates disinterest and inattention. Teachers who use moderate eye contact can monitor and regulate their classrooms more easily. Generally, when students feel teachers looking at them, they stop their disruptive behavior.

Facial Expressions

Facial expressions may include raising eyebrows, smiles, frowns, winks, and other movements that can express a variety of meanings and emotions. A teacher can use facial expressions to manage interactions, regulate communication, signal approval or disapproval, and reinforce or not reinforce. Sometimes, teachers may not want to communicate what they are thinking or feeling.

A teacher who smiles and has positive facial expressions will be perceived as approachable. A teacher's dull expression may be perceived by students as indicating disinterest in them or the subject matter. Teachers need to consider what messages they are sending with their faces.

Touch

Touch involves making physical contact with a student. Touch can communicate many things such as caring, emotional support, approval, or encouragement. Touch also can be used to quiet or calm a student or to take some action to suppress inappropriate behavior.

The amount of touching between teachers and students typically declines steadily from kindergarten to sixth grade. Less touching occurs in middle school and high school. However, a pat on the back may be appropriate at times and very appreciated by a student. A touch on the back, hand, arm, or shoulder is acceptable to many students. A brief touch is considered acceptable; the longer the touch is, the more it becomes unacceptable. Talk to your principal to be certain you understand the guidelines and legal considerations of appropriate touching.

Physical Stance and Movement

Our body language is often expressed by our physical stance and movements that we make. Our body language conveys a message about our comfort level, feelings, and expectations in guidance and discipline situations. When our body language is congruent with a neutral or positive message, we increase the likelihood that the message will be received in a supportive manner.

Threatening body language, however, increases the likelihood of a defensive response by students. Glaring or staring at students, standing too close, standing rigidly with arms crossed, or looking down on students are examples of intimidating body language that raises the threat level and increases the likelihood of a defensive response from students (MacKenzie & Stanzione, 2010).

Signals

Gestures and various types of signals can guide and direct students without any spoken word. Signals can be used to direct students to perform certain actions, but the signal and the action must be taught to students if they are expected to successfully follow them.

Teachers can identify situations that would benefit from a signal, select an appropriate signal, and then teach the students about the signal. There may be visual, auditory, or musical signals:

- **Visual.** Nonintrusive visual signals can be used to give directions without speaking or interrupting what is already happening in the classroom. The simplest signals are those that just come naturally such as holding up your hand, palm facing out as a sign for stop, placing your index finger across your lips for quiet, or using a crooked index finger gesturing to come (Diffily & Sassman, 2006). Teachers may create unique visual signals to convey certain directions, often with the use of fingers and hands or arm motions.

- **Auditory.** Teachers sometimes use sound to signal to the students that it is time for class to start or for some other activity or event. Sound is intended to get the attention of all students to alert them to the next event. This may be done with a bell, chimes, or some type of noise-maker. Some teachers prefer to clap their hands or count down with numbers as a signal. Students must be informed of the signal and their expected behavior once the signal has been sounded.

- **Musical.** A song or some type of musical sounds may be used as a signal to students that some event will immediately follow and that their cooperation and preparation is required. The use of musical sounds as a signal is more common in the elementary grades but may be used in the upper grades. This may involve the use of recorded sounds or songs.

VOICES FROM THE CLASSROOM   Using Body Language and "The Teacher Look"

Lynne Hagar, high school history and English teacher, Mesquite, Texas

I am a small woman, but I can effectively control 30 senior students just by using my voice and my body language. When I want a certain behavior to stop, the first thing I do is to look at the student. Even if that student is not looking at me, he or she eventually becomes aware that I am staring. Then I point at the student and nonverbally indicate that the behavior is to stop. A finger placed on my lips indicates that talking needs to stop.

Often, a questioning or disapproving look or gesture can stop undesirable behaviors right there. I may have to move into a student's personal space or comfort zone to stop a behavior, but a combination of a look and physical proximity is effective about 90% of the time. I might even casually rest my hand on the student's desk, never stopping teaching, and stay put for a minute or so until I'm sure the student is back on task.

My advice is to practice "the look" in the mirror until you get it right. It shouldn't be a friendly look, but it doesn't have to be angry, either. Learn to say in your manner, "I am in charge here." Also, move around the classroom. Getting close to your students is essential, not only when you are correcting them but also when you want to reassure them or reinforce their positive feelings about you and your classroom. A friendly touch on the shoulder as you are helping a student with a problem or a hug when a student has a big success can go miles toward cementing your positive relationship with that student.

Nonverbal Teacher Behaviors

Teachers use nonverbal communication in the classroom to achieve various purposes. In a comprehensive study involving the observation of elementary and secondary teachers, Love and Roderick (1971) identified the following means by which teachers can use nonverbal communication to achieve selected purposes:

- **Accept student behavior.** Smiles, affirmatively shaking your head, pats on the back, winks, and hands placed on shoulder or neck all indicate acceptance.

- **Praise student behavior.** Clap, raise your eyebrows and smile, or nod affirmatively while smiling.

- **Display student ideas.** Writing comments on board, putting students' work on bulletin board, and holding up student papers.

- **Show interest in student behavior.** Establish and maintain eye contact.

- **Move to facilitate student–student interaction.** Physically move away from the student group to not interfere with student–student interaction.

- **Give directions to students.** Point with the hand, look at specified area, employ predetermined signal (such as raising hand for students to stand up), reinforce numerical aspects by showing that number of fingers, extend arms forward and beckon with the hands, point to student for answers.

- **Show authority toward students.** Frowns, stares, raised eyebrows, foot tapping, negatively shaking your head, walking or looking away from the deviant, or snapping fingers all display authority.

- **Focus students' attention on important points.** Use a pointer, walk toward the person or object, tap on something, thrust your head forward, or thrust your arm forward to emphasize verbal statements.

- **Demonstrate or illustrate.** Perform a physical skill, manipulate materials and media, or illustrate a verbal statement with a nonverbal action.

- **Ignore student behavior.** Students are sometimes brought to attention with this nonverbal response when they might ordinarily expect a response.

Teachers might consider the following nonverbal behaviors when trying to restore classroom control (Farrell, 2009): (a) use extended eye contact; (b) shake their head to indicate no; (c) use facial expressions of disapproval; (d) use gestures to put off the behavior; (e) move closer to the site of the disruption; and (f) make use of approval facial expression when order is restored.

MAJOR CONCEPTS

1. The term *teacher language* refers to the professional use of words, phrases, tone, and pace to enable students to engage in active, interested learning and develop positive behaviors.

2. Teachers can follow general guidelines for using language to affirm meaning and action, to address various aspects of instruction and behavior management, and to engage in guidance and conversation with students.

3. Three important dimensions of verbal communication are clarity, appropriateness, and vocal delivery.

4. Soft limits are rules in theory but not in practice. Firm limits are clear signals that students understand and that teachers enforce.

5. The use of opinions and questions are indirect ways of guiding and correcting student behavior. Giving directives is more clear, straightforward, and effective.

6. Teachers can use supportive language to guide and support effective instruction, classroom management, and discipline. Supportive language includes being intentionally inviting and using reinforcing, reminding, and redirecting language.

7. Listening is a vital part of effective communication, and it is a key element in developing positive teacher–student relationships, addressing classroom problems, and enhancing instruction and supporting student learning.

8. Teachers communicate nonverbally through their facial expressions, eye behavior, vocal intonation, body movements and gestures, and other ways. We want our nonverbal and verbal communications to be congruent.

DISCUSSION/REFLECTIVE QUESTIONS

1. Select one of the items listed in the section on General Guidelines for Teacher Language. Why is that item important to promote student learning and positive student behavior? Give some examples for how that item would be demonstrated in a classroom.

2. Identify an example of a behavior problem in the classroom. For that behavior, list several examples of soft limits and firm limits a teacher might use in response. Why are the firm limits better?

3. Select two guidelines listed in the section on Reinforcing Language. Why are those items particularly useful? What might be the effect on a classroom if a teacher did not use reinforcing language?

4. When considering Redirecting Language, what would happen if a teacher was not direct and specific, did not name the desired behavior, or follow through after giving a redirection?

5. In the section "Why Listen?" six reasons are given. From your perspective, what are the three most important reasons? Why?

6. During a classroom discussion, how might a teacher's use of active listening strategies promote more discussion and enhance the depth of the discussions?

7. From your K–12 schooling experience, what are some ways your teachers expressed nonverbal communication? What messages were they communicating in your examples? How did the nonverbal communication influence students in the classroom?

SUGGESTED ACTIVITIES

1. Make a list of six examples of classroom misbehaviors or situations where students need guidance. For each example, write a firm verbal message or a firm action message that you might use in response to the behavior.

2. View a video of a teaching episode or observe an actual classroom. Pay attention to three aspects of verbal communication by the teacher: clarity, appropriateness, and vocal delivery. What did you notice in the teacher's communication for each of those aspects?

3. Identify two examples of positive student work and two examples of positive student behavior. For each, indicate how you could use reinforcing language for these behaviors.

4. Talk with several teachers about how they use nonverbal communication in their teaching. Ask about facial expressions, eye behavior, vocal intonation, body movements, signals, gestures, and other ways. Ask how they use this communication in instruction and behavior management.

FURTHER READING

Charney, R. S. (2002). *Teaching children to care: Classroom management for ethical and academic growth, K–8* (Rev. ed.). Turners Falls, MA: Center for Responsive Schools.
Three chapters address dimensions of teacher language in classroom management and instruction. Other chapters examine building and supporting classroom communities.

Denton, P. (2014). *The power of our words: Teacher language that helps children learn* (2nd ed.). Turners Falls, MA: Northeast Foundation for Children.
Provides guidelines for teacher language. Discusses several specific areas: envisioning, open-ended questions, listening, reinforcing language, reminding language, and redirecting language. Very useful resource.

Diffily, D., & Sassman, C. (2006). *Positive teacher talk for better classroom management*. New York: Scholastic.
Discusses the characteristics and importance of teacher language. Then provides guidance for language when welcoming students, setting the tone for the year, helping students manage their behavior, supporting learning, and using signals.

Edwards, J. (2010). *Inviting students to learn: 100 tips for talking effectively with your students*. Alexandria, VA: Association for Supervision and Curriculum Development.
Discusses reasons for communicating invitationally with students, along with strategies and purposes. Then describes 100 specific tips to apply these strategies.

© KidStock/BlendImages/Getty Images, Inc.

Knowing and Connecting with Your Students

Creating an Inclusive Classroom
    Teaching Students Who Are Different from You
    Creating a Supportive, Caring Environment
    Varying Your Instruction
    Providing Assistance with the Response to Intervention

CHAPTER OBJECTIVES

This chapter provides information that will help you:

- Select ways to know and connect with your students.

- Describe ways in which diversity is exhibited in students.

- Recognize ways that students are challenged, thus affecting their achievement.

- Identify how some students are challenged with adverse conditions.

- Create a supportive, inclusive, and caring classroom.

- Vary your instruction with student characteristics in mind.

- Provide assistance when needed by applying the Response to Intervention.

Just think about the diversity apparent in a typical classroom. There may be a wide range of student cognitive and physical abilities. Students may have different degrees of English proficiency, and some may have a disabling condition such as a hearing disorder. A wide range of ethnic characteristics may be evident, and various socioeconomic levels are likely to be represented. You may have some struggling or disengaged learners in your classroom, and some students may be considered to be at risk due to challenging circumstances in their lives. These examples are just a few of the human and environmental variables that create a wide range of individual differences and needs in classrooms. Individual differences need to be taken when making decisions regarding instruction, classroom management, and discipline.

How can you get to know and connect with your students? What are the sources of student diversity? How can your understanding of adverse student conditions help guide your decisions to provide opportunities for all students to learn? How can you create an inclusive and caring classroom? These issues are explored in this chapter.

Implications for Diverse Classrooms

Students who are in the classroom affect classroom management and instruction. Schools in the United States are very diverse and have students from different economic, cultural, ethnic, and linguistic backgrounds. In addition, you may find that your classroom has students with a range of ability levels or achievement, groups of students with skills below grade level, and students with special needs. All of these factors contribute to the diversity in your classroom.

For you and your students to be successful, you may need to make adjustments in instructional and management practices to meet the needs of different groups in your class. For example, you may find a wide variety of academic ability in your classroom and consequently need to vary your curriculum, instruction, and assessments. You also may have several students whose primary language is not English, and similar adjustments may need to be enacted. Your job is to enhance student learning, and adjustments based on student characteristics will be necessary.

As discussed in Chapter 1, there are several domains of responsibility for classroom management. Understanding of your students will likely influence your decisions about ways that you will organize the physical environment, manage student behavior, create a supportive learning environment, facilitate instruction, and promote safety and wellness. To be an effective classroom manager in a diverse classroom, you should make a commitment to do these things:

- Get to know all of your students.

- Create an inclusive classroom by making instructional and management modifications based on an understanding of your students.

- Create a classroom environment that promotes positive behavior and enhances student learning.

Getting to Know Your Students

The more information teachers have about their students, the better able they are to meet students' needs and support student learning. With a better understanding of their students, teachers can be more effective in their selection of instructional strategies, their adjustments for individual differences, and their interactions with the students and their families.

When starting the school year, many educators maintain that the foundation for a successful, caring learning environment must be built. This can be done by establishing an environment where students feel safe and valued (Wormeli, 2016). Don't waste the first week; establish relationships, not just routines (Tucker, 2016). Getting information and establishing relationships with your students in the opening days of school are vital.

Types of Information

Several types of information would be useful for teachers to achieve these purposes. Teachers would benefit from information about each student concerning these areas:

1. **Academic abilities, needs, and interests.** Is the student a gifted or a struggling learner? What is the student's reading level? What is the student's performance on achievement tests? What are the student's strengths and weaknesses in relation to the academic work? What are the student's academic interests?

2. **Special needs, learning problems, or disabilities.** Are there any emotional or physical disabilities? Does the student have a learning disability of any kind? What accommodations or modifications are needed? Are there any health problems?

3. **Personal qualities related to diversity.** What is the student's preferred learning style? Is the student a second language learner? How does the student's culture or socioeconomic status

(**SES**) influence behavior or learning? Are there any gender or sexuality issues that might influence the student? Is the student considered at risk for any reason?

4. **The student's life and interests.** What are the student's interests? How do the family and community influence the student? What does the student like to do in spare time? What are the student's ambitions?

5. **Problematic or atypical parent custodial arrangements.** Many family arrangements and conditions exist, and it is useful for teachers to know which family member to contact, along with any other special considerations. One parent may have custody of a child with conditions to limit contact with the other parent. The student may be living with grandparents or other relatives. The student may have a parent away from the home, due to military obligations, prison, or other reasons. The student may have gay or lesbian parents.

Cumulatively, information about students, their families, and their living environment provide "funds of knowledge" about the students' abilities, interests, and life experiences. In *Funds of Knowledge*, Gonzalez, Moll, and Amanti (2005) maintain that people are competent and have knowledge, and their life experiences have given them that knowledge. Thus, first-hand research experiences with families allow teachers to document student competence and knowledge. This information can provide teachers with insights into students' capabilities and experiences and can aid in decisions to connect with students and meet their instructional needs. This information also can help teachers make connections with families and help make instruction more meaningful for students.

Choosing to see your students' patterns of thinking, feeling, and behaving can also help bridge cultural differences. For this purpose, Scott (2017) recommends that teachers study their students: (a) the social structures that shape students' lives, (b) their day-to-day interactions, (c) their language/dialect, (d) their cognitive processes, (e) their motivational influences, (f) their goals, and (g) their media influences.

VOICES FROM THE CLASSROOM   Learning the History of Your Students

Darrian Bruce, high school history teacher, Knoxville, Tennessee

I work in a very diverse school that has a high number of students in poverty. Many of our students have frequent absences and experience significant distractions outside of school. Having a relationship with students is crucial to getting them to perform in the classroom. If students feel like their teachers' care, they are more likely to come to school and actively engage in class.

Every year, I have my students write a personal history on the first day. I tell them that they can share whatever they like in their personal history. Some students tell me really deep personal information while others stick to more surface-level stories and facts. I then take the time to write letters back to each one of my students. I make connections between their life and hobbies and mine. If we have similar interests, I point that out to them. Sometimes I make movie, music, or book suggestions based on what they mentioned.

I try to empathize with difficult life experiences that they share. They are always surprised to get a letter back from me. I get lots of smiles when they read what I have written. Many students keep their letters in the front of their binders for the rest of the year. It takes a lot of time to write to every student, but the benefit is well worth it. It shows my students that I care about them, and it helps them to see that I am a human, too. In that small act of writing a letter, the beginning of a positive relationship is formed.

Sources of Information

Some information about your students can be obtained from existing records, such as the student's cumulative record. Much information can be obtained directly from the students and their families. While there are many ways you can obtain information about the students in your class, here are some commonly used sources:

- **Viewing cumulative records.** The school office will have a cumulative record folder for each student. That folder includes personal information, home and family data, school attendance records, scores on standardized achievement tests, year-end grades for all previous years of schooling, and other teachers' anecdotal comments. Other types of additional information may be included, such as which family member to contact (or not to contact). Collectively, the cumulative record provides considerable information. Recognize, however, that material in the cumulative records does not provide a full picture of the student.

- **Using student questionnaires.** Asking students simple, get-to-know-you questions on the first day can provide much information. Open-ended questions such as these can provide much insight into your students (Hayward, 2016): What are your academic strengths and weaknesses? What do you want me to know about you? What activities are you involved in out of school? What don't you want me to do? What is one goal you'd like to set right now?

  Asking students to fill out a questionnaire can provide much insight into their actions, interests, and skills. Include questions that provide helpful information as you (a) select curricular content, instructional activities, and strategies; (b) determine your way of interacting with the students in the class; (c) identify how to address the diversity of learners in the class; (d) address any challenges, problems, or disabilities the students may have; and (e) try to get to know all your students to enable their successful learning. Some open-ended questions can yield useful information (e.g., It helps me learn when . . . , or, What I appreciate about my family is . . .).

- **Using family questionnaires and contacts.** Information from families about their own children also can provide great insight into the qualities and needs of the students in your class. A brief questionnaire may be prepared for parents at the start of the school year. Items may include asking how parents describe their children, what makes their children special, what their children do at home, their children's strengths and weaknesses, and parents' hopes for their children during the school year. In addition, teachers may see some parents at back-to-school night or at parent–teacher conferences.

- **Observing and interacting with students.** Arrange for icebreaker activities for students to get to know each other at the start of the school year. Much information about each student can be learned simply by watching students interact during these icebreakers. Informal observation and interaction with students also provide opportunities to learn more about each student.

Using the Information

To know how to use the information you gather, think about the reasons you wanted that information in the first place—to be more effective in your selection of instructional strategies, adjustments for individual differences, and interactions with the students and their families. Gathering information is not sufficient. You must read, review, and mentally process the information to guide the decisions you will make in the classroom.

It may be useful to first summarize the information you have on each student, and perhaps on the class as a whole. Whether you have a class of 22 fifth-grade students or 143 high school students in several classes makes a big difference in how you might summarize the information. Some teachers may read through the information about each student from the various sources reviewed earlier and then simply make mental notations. Other teachers may want to summarize results of each question on a student questionnaire, for example, to get a picture of the entire class. Still other teachers may have a card for each student, with key information listed on the card. For certain types of information (e.g., the preferred type of learning approaches), it may be helpful to make a list of students so that you pay proper attention to the students on that issue.

    The main thing is to get to know your students and show that you care for them. They need to know that you will do your best and will not give up on them when challenges occur. As described by Powell (2010), you can intentionally take actions each day to relate to your students and to create a culture of belonging and safety that strengthens the students' self-concept, confidence, resiliency, and cognitive processes.

Student Diversity

Individual differences abound, and adapting instruction to student differences is one of the most challenging aspects of teaching. The first step in planning to address the diversity of students is to recognize those differences. While there are many sources of student diversity, this section explores four significant sources: cultural diversity, language, gender, and exceptionalities.

Cultural Diversity

The racial/ethnic enrollment of students enrolled in public elementary and secondary schools in fall 2015 was 49% Caucasian, 26% Latino, 15% African American, 5% Asian/Pacific Islander, and 3% two or more races (National Center for Education Statistics [NCES], 2019a). This represents a wide range of races, cultures, and countries of origin. By fall 2027, the percentage of

■ WHAT WOULD YOU DECIDE?   Your Culture Is Different

Many classrooms have students from a variety of ethnic and cultural backgrounds. It is possible that you will feel disconnected from your students because you have a different ethnicity or different cultural background from your students.

1. What can you do so that you and your students feel comfortable with one another?

2. What can you do so that the different backgrounds do not contribute to misunderstandings and off-task behavior?

Caucasian students is projected to drop to 45%, Latino enrollment to increase to 29%, and African American enrollment to be at about 15%.

Cultural diversity is reflected in the wide variety of values, beliefs, attitudes, and rules that define regional, ethnic, religious, or other cultures. Minority populations wish their cultures to be recognized as unique and preserved for their children. The message from all cultural groups to schools is clear—make sure that each student from every cultural group succeeds in school.

Culturally responsive teaching is instruction that acknowledges cultural diversity (Gay, 2005, 2018). It attempts to accomplish this goal in three ways: (a) accepting and valuing cultural differences; (b) accommodating different cultural interaction patterns; and (c) building on students' cultural backgrounds. Culturally responsive teachers use the best of what is known about good teaching, including strategies such as these (Cole, 2008; Gallavan, 2011a, 2011b; Rothstein-Fisch & Trumbull, 2008):

- Connecting students' prior knowledge and cultural experiences with new concepts by constructing and designing relevant cultural metaphors and images.

- Understanding students' cultural knowledge and experiences and selecting appropriate instructional materials.

- Helping students to find meaning and purpose in what is to be learned.

- Using interactive teaching strategies.

- Helping learners construct meaning by organizing, elaborating, and representing knowledge in their own way.

In a culturally relevant classroom, the student's culture is seen as a source of strength on which to rely, not a problem to be overcome or as something to be overlooked (Ladson-Billings, 2009). Teachers can weave a range of cultural perspectives throughout the curriculum to make education more relevant for students who see their cultures recognized. In doing so, teachers need to be aware of a variety of cultural experiences to understand how different students may learn best. Learning about the various cultures is important. Resources such as *Through Ebony Eyes* (Thompson, 2007a) and *Up Where We Belong* (Thompson, 2007b) provide information about helping African American and Latino students in school.

Each cultural group teaches its members certain lessons about living. Differences exist among cultures in the way members conduct interpersonal relationships, use time, use body language, cooperate with group members, and accept directions from authority figures. You need to treat each student as an individual first because that student is the product of many influences.

Caring is considered to be critical to culturally responsive management where teachers display concern for the students' overall development through developing good positive relationships while setting and maintaining high academic and behavioral standards (Cartledge, Lo, Vincent, & Robinson-Ervin, 2015). Many resources are available concerning cultural diversity (e.g., Banks, 2016; Gollnick & Chinn, 2017) and the instructional implications (Mazur & Doran, 2010; Thompson & Thompson, 2014).

As you consider individual differences due to cultural diversity, you should do the following:

1. Examine your own values and beliefs for evidence of bias and stereotyping.

2. Regard students as individuals first, with membership in a cultural group as only one factor in understanding that individual.

3. Learn something about students' family and community relationships.

4. Consider nonstandard English and native languages as basic languages for students of culturally diverse populations, to support gradual but necessary instruction in the majority language.

5. Allow students to work in cross-cultural teams and facilitate cooperation while noting qualities and talents that emerge.

6. Infuse the curriculum with regular emphasis on other cultures, rather than provide just one unit a year or a few isolated and stereotyped activities.

Language

There is tremendous language diversity in the United States, and it is not uncommon for a school district to have students representing numerous languages. Students who are *English language learners* (ELLs) participate in language assistance programs that help ensure that they attain English proficiency and meet the same academic content and achievement standards that all students are expected to meet. In 2015–2016, there were 4.85 million ELLs in the United States, comprising 10% of all students in grades K through 12 (Office of English Language Acquisition [OELA], 2018b). In 2015–2016, the most common languages included Spanish (80%), followed in descending order by Arabic, Chinese, Vietnamese, Somoli, and Haitian/Haitian Creole (OELA, 2018a). ELLs in US public schools are reported as speaking over 400 different languages and dialects. The great majority of these students spend most or part of their time in English-only classrooms (Nieto & Bode, 2018).

Some students whose first language is not English may have acquired sufficient English language skills to perform in English-only classes. Others have not acquired sufficient skill in speaking, reading, or writing English, and they need additional assistance. Schools have various types of programs to deliver assistance.

ELLs benefit from (a) clear goals and objectives, (b) well-designed instructional routines, (c) active engagement and participation, (d) informative feedback, (e) opportunities to practice and apply new learning and transfer it to new situations, (f) periodic review and practice, (g) opportunities to interact with other students, and (h) frequent assessments, with reteaching as needed (Marzano, 2017).

If you have some students in your classroom who speak limited or no English, here are some strategies to use in communicating and teaching (Kottler & Kottler, 2007; Kottler, Kottler, & Street, 2008):

- Provide predictable, clear, and consistent instructions, expectations, and routines.

- Identify and clarify difficult words and passages.

- Provide extra practice in reading words, sentences, and stories.

- Increase time and opportunities for meaningful talk.

- Encourage English speaking while honoring students' first language and culture.

- Use a variety of *reading* supports such as text tours to preview the reading material, graphic organizers (story maps, character analyses), and text signposts (chapter headings, bold print).

- Use a variety of *writing* supports, such as group composing, graphic organizers, and drawing-based texts.

Gender

There are obvious differences between males and females, and some of those differences influence their performance at school. Researchers have found females generally are more extroverted, anxious, and trusting; are less assertive; and have slightly lower self-esteem than males of the same age and background. Females' verbal and motor skills also tend to develop faster than those of males (Berk, 2018; Berk & Meyers, 2016; Sadker & Silber, 2007).

These gender differences are caused by a combination of genetics and environment. These differences are examined in *Boys and Girls Learn Differently* (Gurian & Henley, 2010), which includes discussions concerning elementary, middle, and high school classrooms. Concerns about the performance by boys in schools are examined in sources such as *The Minds of Boys*

■ WHAT WOULD YOU DECIDE?   Students with Limited English Proficiency

You've accepted a teaching position in a school district with much student diversity. At the start of the school year, you realize that several of your students have limited English proficiency and two students barely speak English at all. Besides English, there are four languages represented.

1. Where would you get resources for teaching students with limited English proficiency?

2. How might you use paraprofessionals, parent volunteers, and even the other students as assistants in your instruction of students with limited English proficiency?

■ CLASSROOM CASE STUDY   Adjustments for English Language Learners

Jason Kulpinski teaches high school history in an urban school in which 42% of the students are Hispanic and many are English language learners. To introduce his classes to some of the major events and themes of US history, Mr. Kulpinski uses short texts, which are texts that can be read in one sitting and that combine both words and pictures to tell a story. He has found that all the students in his classes have benefited from reading the short texts. The short texts provide ELLs with background knowledge on the content they will learn in the course. Without this background, many students would have no prior knowledge as a reference point for learning new content in the unit. With a design that incorporates both words and pictures providing context clues, the short texts help struggling readers and English language learners to negotiate meaning from the material.

Mr. Kulpinski has seen many of his hesitant readers grow in confidence after they have read several short texts and have been able to comprehend the content. Class discussions also have been enhanced by the use of short texts.

Focus Questions

1. How does Mr. Kulpinski's strategy of using short texts help him teach diverse learners?

2. How do all learners in the classroom benefit from this strategy?

3. If you had Mr. Kulpinski's class, what other strategies might you use to teach the content while reaching the English language learners?

(Gurian & Stevens, 2007), *Teaching the Male Brain* (James, 2015), and *Teaching the Female Brain* (James, 2009).

There are also gender differences in career preparation and career choice. Teachers should keep both boys and girls academically motivated, especially in science, technology, engineering, and math areas, where gender-based differences in career choices still exist. To address this, you take the following actions (Gurian & Stevens, 2010; Gurian, Stevens, & King, 2008):

- Provide students with a mix of successful male and female role models.

- Make sure that girls take an active part in math and science classes, especially given boys' tendency to be more assertive in such settings.

- Use more hands-on experiments and group activities and less teaching by telling and lecturing.

- Allow students to investigate real-world problems, both large and small.

- Encourage students to see that academic achievement is more a product of effort than of natural ability.

You can make your classroom more gender friendly for all students by following these guidelines: incorporate movement in instruction, make learning visual, give students choice and control, provide opportunities for social interaction, find ways to make learning real, blend art and music into the curriculum, connect with your students, promote character development for the benefit of the individuals and the classroom environment, and encourage equal participation (Gurian et al., 2008; James, 2015).

Exceptionalities

Exceptional students include those who need special help and resources to reach their full potential. Exceptionalities include both disabilities and giftedness (Bateman & Cline, 2016). The Individuals with Disabilities Education Act (IDEA) committed the United States to a policy of mainstreaming students who have handicapping conditions by placing them in the least restrictive environment in which they can function successfully while having their special needs met. The degree to which they are treated differently is to be minimized. The *least restrictive environment* means that students with special needs are placed in special settings only if necessary and only for as long as necessary; the regular classroom is the preferred least restrictive placement (Vaughn, Bos, & Schumm, 2018).

According to the 2017 Digest of Education Statistics (NCES, 2017a), 13.2% of children 3–21 have disabilities and are served under IDEA (this does not include gifted or talented learners). Categories for special education services include learning disabilities; speech or language impairment; intellectual disability; emotional or behavioral disabilities; other health impairments; multiple disabilities; impairments in hearing, orthopedics, or sight; deafness/blindness; traumatic brain injury; and autism spectrum disorder (Bryant, Bryant, & Smith, 2016).

Gifted or talented learners are those with above-average abilities, and they need special instructional consideration. According to the 2017 Digest of Education Statistics (NCES, 2017b), 6.4% of public school students are enrolled in gifted and talented programs. Resources about teaching gifted students are also available (e.g., Cash, 2017; Heacox & Cash, 2014; Smutny & von Fremd, 2011; Turnbull, Turnbull, Wehmeyer, & Shogren, 2020; Winebrenner & Brulles, 2014).

Teachers often make accommodations and modifications to their teaching to meet the learning needs of students with exceptionalities (Polloway, Patton, Serna, & Bailey, 2018; Salend, 2016). An *accommodation* is an adjustment in the curriculum, instruction, learning tasks, assessments, or materials to make learning more accessible to students. For example, a student might have an adapted test with fewer test items. The student may also have the same test but take it orally in a one-on-one situation with the teacher, or he or she might be given extra time to take a test. Different materials might be used to teach the same content, or additional practice or various instructional approaches may be used. In any case, accommodation is *not* a watering down or change in the content or a change in expected learner outcomes.

A *modification* is a change in the standard learning expectations so that they are realistic and individually appropriate. The curriculum or instruction is altered as needed. Modifications are used for students for whom all possible accommodations have been considered and who still need additional measures to help them progress. For example, students with skill deficits in reading or math may need modifications in assignments or the level of the content and reading materials, or they may need an alternative assignment or test.

Adverse Conditions and Student Achievement

Teachers need to get to know all of their students and take their qualities into account when making instructional decisions. Some students, however, may have experienced challenging circumstances in their lives and, as a consequence, their performance in school may be negatively affected. Due to these conditions, some students do not perform well and do not live up to their potential. There may be an achievement gap between their potential and their actual performance.

Some students may struggle because they have difficulty learning at an average rate. Due to environmental and personal influences, other students may be considered at risk of being successful in school or in their role as a member of society. Students living in poverty often are challenged, and low-income students do not perform well on the National Assessment of Education Progress (NAEP) texts given annually to samples of fourth, eighth, and twelfth graders (US Department of Education, 2015). Other students may be seriously disengaged and may have simply given up in school. Finally, some students face significant adverse conditions in their lives that influence their effort and performance in school.

Teachers need to get to know and connect with all of their students to create a successful learning environment. By understanding the unique circumstances and adverse conditions that some students face, teachers will be more able to provide appropriate strategies and learning environments to promote achievement and success for all students. These issues are explored in the following sections.

Opportunity/Achievement Gaps

Underachieving students do not perform well academically and do not live up to their potential. An *achievement gap* is the difference in academic achievement, especially measured by standardized tests, among groups of students based on their race, ethnicity, SES, native languages, sex, and exceptionalities. Students in lower socioeconomic groups and those living in poverty factor into this achievement gap (Johnson, Musial, Hall, & Gollnick, 2018).

Holding low expectations of students contributes to gaps in learning and achievement primarily through the types of learning opportunities teachers provide students (Weinstein, 2002). Budge and Parrett (2018) recommend several strategies for holding high expectations: (a) build on relationships to make learning relevant; (b) provide for rigor and risk taking; (c) be a "warm demander" by being insistent and supportive; (d) act from an empathic perspective; (e) hold a growth mindset and encourage the same in students; (f) interrogate your mental map; and (g) employ caring, clear, and consistent communication of expectations. These strategies will provide opportunities for learning and will help reduce the achievement gap.

In *Minding the Achievement Gap One Classroom at a Time*, Pollock, Ford, and Black (2012) maintain that student engagement and achievement can be increased through intentional teaching with the following structure in each lesson:

- *Goal*: Set and present a learning goal in a manner that students can understand.

- *Access*: Conduct an activity to help students access their prior knowledge.

- *New information*: Present and help students acquire the new information related to the lesson goal.

- *Apply*: Give students the opportunity to apply a thinking skill or practice their new knowledge in a new situation.

- *Goal review*: Conclude the lesson by prompting students to engage in goal review, generalizing their understandings and reviewing their progress toward the goal.

Drawing on evidence from successful schools, Boykin and Noguera (2011) offer strategies for increasing minority student engagement and boosting their levels of achievement. Increasing student engagement is the first success factor they identified, which happens on three levels: behavioral engagement, cognitive engagement, and affective engagement. The second success factor is strengthening student self-efficacy ("I can do this task"), goal setting, and a belief that working hard at an intellectual task will lead to mastery. The third success factor is to build positive classroom dynamics between teachers and students to develop a culture of learning in which students see themselves as having a significant role to play.

When trying to close the achievement gap and create success for urban students, Rajagopal (2011) identified many strategies to engage learners and promote success, as illustrated by the following examples:

- Incorporate culture, background, prior knowledge, vocabulary, music, and sports into the curriculum.

- Make success personal and visible by using individualized student contracts and rewards that enforce high expectations.

- Scaffold content to individual student's abilities, and make sure each student "gets it" before moving on.

- Use cooperative learning and one-on-one tutoring for students who have the most difficulty completing the in-class assignments.

Additional resources are available to address the achievement gap in urban schools and with high-poverty schools (e.g., Barr & Parrett, 2007; Curwin, 2010; Howard, 2020; Muhammad, 2015; Parrett & Budge, 2012).

VOICES FROM THE CLASSROOM   Student-Generated Goals

Kathleen Trace, high school English teacher, Virginia Beach, Virginia

I teach a writing-based class to high school seniors. At the beginning of the year, students take a pretest that is not graded but is scored with a rubric on various elements of the writing craft. This is their first point of reference for what their strengths and weaknesses are as a writer.

A few years ago, I found that having a whole class focus on a specific goal for a writing assignment failed to challenge all students, so I began to integrate student-generated goals into our writing routine. Before each writing assignment, students set a specific goal for themselves for that particular piece of writing. They also list at least two strategies they can use to achieve that goal.

After they go through the writing process for that piece of writing and get feedback from peers and from me, they return to their goal sheet and make notes on their progress, citing specific evidence of where in their writing they did or did not achieve their goals. From there, as we move to the next piece of writing, they may revise their goal or generate a new one and the process continues. This works great for writing, but I can also see it used for various other types of skills.

Struggling Learners

A student who is considered a *struggling learner* cannot learn at an average rate from the instructional resources, texts, workbooks, and materials that are designated for the majority of students in the classroom. This student often has a limited attention span and deficiencies in basic skills such as reading, writing, and mathematics. He or she needs frequent feedback, corrective instruction, special instructional pacing, instructional variety, and perhaps modified materials (Protheroe, Shellard, & Turner, 2004). In *Helping Struggling Learners Succeed in School*, Harriet Porton (2013) takes a comprehensive approach by considering planning, grouping, management, instructional strategies, and assessment

In *How to Support Struggling Students,* Jackson and Lambert (2010) state that effective support is ongoing, proactive, targeted, accelerative (rather than remedial), learning focused, and managed by the teacher as an advocate. They suggest strategies before, during, and after instruction to support struggling students. Marlowe and Hayden (2013) maintain that the best way to teach children who are hard to reach is to have a relationship-driven classroom. Positive teacher–student and student–student relationships influence discipline, classroom dynamics, and student engagement in learning.

In *Teaching Boys Who Struggle in School,* Kathleen Cleveland (2011) examines what causes boys to struggle in school and offers recommendations. She suggests (a) replacing an underachieving boy's negative attitudes about learning; (b) reconnecting each boy with school, with learning, and with a belief in himself as a competent learner; (c) rebuilding learning skills that lead to success in school and life; and (d) reducing the need for unproductive and distracting behaviors as a means of self-protection.

For the struggling learners in your class, you should (a) frequently vary your instructional technique; (b) develop lessons around students' interests, needs, and experiences; (c) provide for an encouraging, supportive environment; (d) use cooperative learning and peer tutors for students who need remediation; (e) provide study aids; (f) teach content in small sequential steps with frequent checks for comprehension; (g) use individualized materials and

■ WHAT WOULD YOU DECIDE?   Struggling Learners in Your Classroom

In your first year of teaching, you have six students in your classroom who are struggling with the academic work. They appear to be willing to do the work but have difficulty with the reading, complicated directions, and assignments with several parts and steps. Each student also needs continual guidance and reinforcement. You would like to make a plan to help them, but you are not certain how to go about this.

1. First, have you ever been a struggling learner in your K–12 schooling or witnessed a student who was? What did the teacher do to help? What else might have been done?

2. In this example in your first year of teaching, what other educators might you turn to for information, ideas, and support?

3. What are some ways that you might make the assignment directions less complicated and easier to understand? How might you set up a procedure for more frequent feedback to the students?

---

individualized instruction whenever possible; (h) use audio and visual materials for instruction; and (i) take steps to develop each student's self-concept (e.g., assign a task where the student can showcase a particular skill).

Students at Risk

Other environmental and personal influences may converge to place a student at risk. *Students at risk* are children and adolescents who are not able to acquire and/or use the skills necessary to develop their potential and become productive members of society. Conditions at home, support from the community, and personal and cultural background all affect student attitudes, behaviors, and propensity to profit from school experiences.

Students potentially at risk include children who face adverse conditions beyond their control, those who do not speak English as a first language, talented but unchallenged students, those with special problems, and many others. At-risk students often have academic difficulties and thus may be low achievers.

Students at risk, especially those who eventually drop out, typically have some or all of the following characteristics (Ormrod et al., 2020): a history of academic failure, older age in comparison with classmates, emotional and behavioral problems, frequent interaction with low-achieving peers, lack of psychological attachment to school, and increasing disinvolvement with school.

Effective use of classroom instructional strategies can help reach at-risk students (Snow, 2005). These strategies include whole-class instruction, cognitively oriented instruction, small groups, tutoring, peer tutoring, and computer-assisted instruction. Here are some general strategies to support students at risk:

- Identify students at risk as early as possible.

- Create a warm, supportive school, and classroom atmosphere.

- Communicate high expectations for academic success.

- Provide extra academic support.

- Show students that they are the ones who have made success possible.

- Encourage and facilitate identification with school.

VOICES FROM THE CLASSROOM   Empowering Students Through Goal Setting

Cristina Fontana, first-grade teacher, Guilford, Connecticut

Having high expectations for all students is essential to student success. I found the act of goal setting to be a powerful way to set specific expectations for all students. During reading instruction in my first-grade classroom, I start the goal-setting process by having an exploratory reading conference with each student. I ask him/her various questions about reading engagement, characters, plot, and setting. Additionally, I listen to the student orally read in order to determine his/her ability to work with print. I then use this information to decide on the next step for the student as a reader. For example, during an exploratory conference, a student may make frequent errors while reading aloud. This tells me this student's area of focus needs to be decoding.

After the exploratory conference, I then have a goal-setting conference with the student. During this conference, I give the student a self-assessment rubric focused on his/her potential areas of need. The student then assesses him/herself to see which skills he/she is able to do consistently, is able to do sometimes, or is not able to do yet. For example, the student who needs to focus on print work will use a rubric focused on print work and ask him/herself, "Do I catch myself when I make mistakes? Do I know strategies to fix my mistakes? Can I use those strategies to figure out hard words?"

The student and I then use the answers from the self-assessment rubric to create a reading goal. For example, if the student responds, "No, I do not catch my mistakes," we can then use this to create a goal that says, "I will catch my mistakes in my reading." The goal-setting process allows each student to set high expectations and have input on his/her own learning trajectory.

Involving students in the creation of goals is important, as it gives students ownership and agency over their learning and empowers them to meet their goals. Goal setting allows for all students to be working at their own pace on the skills they need to become better readers.

Students in Poverty

Socioeconomic status is a measure of a family's relative position in a community, determined by a combination of parents' income, occupation, and level of education. There are many relationships between SES and school performance. SES is linked to intelligence, achievement test scores, grades, truancy, and dropout and suspension rates (Brown, Geor, & Lazaridis, 2014).

Students' school performance is correlated with their SES: higher-SES students tend to have high academic achievement, and lower-SES students tend to be at greater risk for dropping out of school (Books, 2004; Lee & Bowen, 2006). As students from lower-SES families move through the grade levels, they fall further and further behind their higher-SES peers. Students from higher-SES families, however, may face pressure from their parents to achieve at a high level, which can lead to anxiety and depression.

To better address the learning needs of students living in poverty, some educators seek to understand the characteristics of the students and their culture and then make appropriate decisions about curriculum and instruction. In *A Framework for Understanding Poverty,* Ruby Payne (2005, 2008) strongly advocates seeking this understanding. However, others have been critical of this approach as stereotyping students living in poverty (e.g., Bomer, Dworin, May, & Semingson, 2008; Gorski, 2008).

Taking these factors into account, you should (a) capitalize on students' interests; (b) make course content meaningful to the students and discuss the practical value of the material; (c) make directions clear and specific; (d) arrange to have each student experience some success; (e) be sure that expectations for work are realistic; and (f) include a variety of instructional approaches, such as provisions for movement and group work. Additional useful resources include *Teaching with Poverty in Mind* (Jensen, 2009), *Engaging Students with Poverty in Mind* (Jensen, 2013), *Why Culture Counts: Teaching Children of Poverty* (Tileston & Darling, 2008), and *Reaching and Teaching Students in Poverty* (Gorski, 2018).

In *Disrupting Poverty: Five Powerful Classroom Practices*, Budge and Parrett (2018) report that school and classroom cultures in high-poverty, high-performing schools are based on five values: caring relationships, high expectations and support, commitment to equity, professional accountability for learning, and courage and will to take action. When bringing these values to life in a classroom, teachers disrupt the negative effects of poverty on learning and instead provide opportunities to learn and achieve.

Often, children in low-income families, especially children of poverty, lag behind their more affluent peers in academic, physical, emotional, and social development. They may not have the going-to-school skills that many students have, and they will benefit from specific strategies and support from the teachers. Here are some suggestions (Hargis, 2006):

- **Provide free learning materials.** Seek out free resources or donations for extra instructional materials or special field trips or activities. Have extra supplies available in case some of your students don't have them.

- **Facilitate after-school programs.** Schools may be the only safe place in the neighborhood, and many students may not want to leave at the end of the school day. Provide opportunities for activities or study after school.

- **Subsidize school expenses.** Dances, sports, or other events can be expensive. Work with others in your school to find ways to keep costs low or to provide donations.

- **Treat students with respect.** Ensure that your classroom is emotionally and physically safe. Interact with your students in a respectful manner.

- **Teach procedures in a step-by-step manner to clarify expectations.** Point out expectations, describe why the procedure exists, and show how to complete the strategy.

- **Permit students to work together.** This enables students to discuss problems and solutions together, and also allows students to help another student with something they do well.

Seriously Disengaged Students

Students who are seriously disengaged are not simply underachievers; they've given up. Student disengagement can take many forms, including lack of effort and participation, acting out and disrupting class, disaffection and withdrawal, and failure to become involved in classroom learning activities and responsibilities (Fredricks, 2014). Disengaged students are in all types of school districts, but the rate may be higher in urban districts due to the higher levels of poverty and other factors. Nationwide, rates of disengagement are higher among males, youths from an ethnic group other than white or Asian, youths from lower SES households, and youths in special education (Yazzie-Mintz, 2007).

Disengagement leads to the gradual process by which students begin to withdraw from school. Cumulative negative schooling experiences contribute to students dropping out of school. Dropout rates vary dramatically by racial/ethnic group, SES, and school location. Hispanic and African American students are significantly less likely to complete high school than are their white and Asian counterparts (Rumberger, 2011). Youths who do not complete high school are more likely to experience unemployment, underemployment, and incarceration. Failure to graduate from high school also results in lower earnings, poorer health, greater reliance on public assistance, and increases in crime (Rumberger, 2011).

Increasing engagement is seen as the key to addressing problems of low achievement, higher levels of student boredom and alienation, and high dropout rates. *Student engagement* refers to the "degree of attention, curiosity, interest, optimism, and passion that students show when they are learning or being taught, which extends to the level of motivation they have to learn and progress in their education" (Glossary of Education Reform, 2016).

There are various causes of disengagement, including outside school factors and curricular factors (Fredricks, 2014). As the teacher in one classroom, you can give attention to what you can control in your own classroom. You can promote student engagement through effective planning after considering your students' interests, the pacing of the lesson, and the learning process. Some key elements to consider when planning for enhanced student engagement include activities and assignments, grouping of students, instructional materials and resources, structure and pacing, creating a positive classroom community, establishing classroom norms and expectations, procedures and routines, and physical space (Wray, 2017).

In *Engaging Students with Poverty in Mind*, Eric Jensen (2013) described five core rules for engagement that will help build a foundation for student success:

1. **Upgrade your attitude.** Students keenly sense teachers' attitudes toward them, so a positive, optimistic attitude is crucial.

2. **Build relationships and respect.** Show you care by sharing a bit of yourself every day, respecting your students, and using interactive language.

3. **Get student buy-in.** Create hooks that pull students into the content and activities.

4. **Embrace clarity.** Use precise and brief words and have well-defined actions.

5. **Show your passion.** Show your interest in the content and your teaching through verbal and nonverbal communication.

When trying to reach the hard to teach, Echevarria, Frey, and Fisher (2016) maintain that the way forward is to apply five essential practices of excellent instruction: (a) provide access to the core curriculum; (b) establish a climate that supports students as individuals and learners; (c) set high expectations for success; (d) provide language instruction; and (f) provide assessment-informed instruction.

Students Challenged with Other Adverse Conditions

You may have students who have difficulty with their academic work and their behavior due to exceptionally challenging circumstances in their lives. Some students may have been the victims of circumstances beyond their control, such as having been abused or neglected, living in extreme poverty, or having parents who are abusing alcohol or drugs. Other students may do things that place themselves at risk, such as being prone to violence, abusing alcohol or drugs, having eating disorders, or being depressed.

These are not your usual students, and the origins of their academic or behavioral problems initially may not be apparent. Significant deviations in a student's behavior may signal the presence of a problem. Some students exhibit those deviations from the first day they walk into your classroom.

When you notice atypical behavior, it is helpful to ask yourself a few questions to clarify the situation (Kottler & Kottler, 2007): What is unusual about this student's behavior? Is there a pattern to what I have observed? What additional information do I need to make an informed judgment? Whom might I contact to collect this background information? What are the risks of waiting longer to figure out what is going on? Does this student seem to be in any imminent danger? Whom can I consult about this case? These questions can provide guidance for analyzing the situation and deciding on a course of action.

Students may have to deal with adverse conditions such as:

1. **Substance abuse.** Substance abuse can profoundly affect the behavior of individuals. Students may be affected in two ways—they may be the children of substance-abusing parents or the students themselves may be abusing drugs and alcohol.

2. **Students who have been abused or neglected.** Many children suffer from physical, emotional, or sexual abuse, and many more may be the victims of neglect by their parents or guardian.

3. **Students prone to violence, vandalism, and bullying.** Violence and crime occur in communities, and that often shows up in schools to some degree. Some students seem prone to violent behavior, and they can cause considerable disturbance in schools. Some of these disruptive behaviors in schools are disturbing but not serious.

4. **Students living in poverty.** Many aspects of student behavior and performance may be influenced by conditions of poverty.

5. **Students facing serious challenges.** Some students face serious and exceptionally challenging situations in their lives that greatly influence their attendance and performance in school. Some of these serious challenges are homelessness, eating disorders, depression, suicide, and natural disasters.

A number of resources are available, providing teachers with ways to support students living with trauma, violence, chronic stress, or other adverse conditions (Fisher, Frey, & Savitz, 2020; Jennings, 2018; Souers, 2019; Zacarian, Alvarez-Ortiz, & Haynes, 2017). Teachers can work to meet the students' academic needs while also using strategies to foster resilient learners and to provide hope in addressing the students' challenging circumstances.

Creating an Inclusive Classroom

Understanding the sources of student diversity is not enough. You must use that information as the basis of many classroom decisions when creating a positive learning environment, selecting a responsive curriculum, determining instructional strategies, and providing assistance. A number of useful resources offer guidance about these issues, including *Culturally Proficient Instruction* (Nuri-Robins, Lindsey, Lindsey, & Terrell, 2011), *Building Culturally Responsive Classrooms* (Gaitan, 2006), *How to Teach Students Who Don't Look Like You* (Davis, 2012), and *Finding Joy in Teaching Students of Diverse Backgrounds* (Nieto, 2013).

Teaching Students Who Are Different from You

One of the challenges many teachers face is connecting with students of diverse backgrounds. The reality is that the background of many teachers does not reflect the demographic reality of their students. Many teachers are white, while there is an increasing number of African American, Hispanic, Asian students, and children who live in low-income families. White teachers often do not know or understand the lives and culture of their students (Howard, 2016).

There is evidence of a mismatch between ethnically diverse students and white teachers' communication styles and interactions, which can often result in higher conflict in the classroom (Delpit, 1995). This misalignment helps explain the finding that African America youth, particularly boys, are disciplined more frequently and harshly than students in other racial or ethnic groups (Cartledge et al., 2015; Skiba & Rausch, 2015).

One reason for the higher level of conflict in diverse classroom is that many teachers hold lower expectations for their African American, Hispanic, and low-income students. Most teachers are often unaware that they hold these differential expectations and are treating groups differently. When teaching students who are different from you and avoiding differential expectations, teacher can focus on the following three approaches.

Culturally Responsive Teaching

Culturally responsive teaching involves purposely responding to the needs of culturally, ethnically, and linguistically diverse students in the classroom through instructional processes and culturally relevant curriculum. Rather than viewing students from a deficit perspective, teachers should view ethnically and culturally diverse students' experiences as valuable assets that can be incorporated in the classroom.

The instructional approaches for culturally responsive teaching reviewed earlier in this chapter will help teachers focus on the students and overcome any division between the teacher's and students' cultures. A first step is to be mindful of one's own perceptions and prejudices of students. Next, teachers can seek out information to understand the cultural characteristics and contributions of different ethnic groups. Finally, teachers need to understand ethnic groups' cultural values, traditions, and communications. Then, decisions about curriculum and instruction can be made to demonstrate culturally responsive teaching.

Teacher–Student Relationships

Positive teacher–student relations are associated with positive behavior and achievement gains. Having close and caring relationships with teachers has been found to be especially important to engagement of low income and African American and Hispanic youths (Garcia-Reid, Reid, & Peterson, 2005).

Especially when teaching students who are different from you, McKinley (2010) suggests that teachers do the following when establishing teacher–student interactions, with a high focus on how you interact and treat students:

- **Demonstrate caring.** This involves actions such as encouraging a sense of family and community, listening to and encouraging mutual sharing of personal experiences related to the curriculum, and creating an inviting environment that reflects personal caring.

- **Exhibit fairness and respect.** This involves actions such as creating situations for all students to succeed, respecting every person, and promoting student interactions based on principles of democracy, equity, and justice.

- **Show low favoritism.** This involves actions such as treating all students equally well and providing each student with equitable access to learning resources and opportunities to learn.

- **Show low friction.** This involves actions such as ensuring that students and teachers treat each other with civility, gentleness, and support and handling disagreements with discussion and respect for alternative positions.

Exhibiting Caring

Exhibiting caring is part of establishing positive teacher–student relationships, but there is more. Students need to know how much you care for them. Students who have positive relationships with their teachers experience less stress, behave more appropriately, and feel more excited about their learning. Students almost always work harder for teachers they like (Cornelius-White & Harbaugh, 2010).

Caring can be exhibited in various ways. When exhibiting caring, Jensen (2013) suggests that teachers share a bit of themselves every day with their students, such as a story about everyday life they are experiencing. Teachers also should find out about their students every day. Try to engage every student, every day. Students need to know that you are on their side, not an adversary. Jensen also suggests using positive language when interacting with students, with respectful words and phrases.

■ WHAT WOULD YOU DECIDE?   You Are Different from Your Students

You accepted a teaching position in a different town from where you grew up. As you start the school year, you realize that you have students from several ethnic groups, three languages, various religions, and even several types of family arrangements. You are different from your students—they don't look like you, talk like you, or think like you. You feel the need to take steps to get to know your students to better meet their needs:

1. What can you do so that you and your students get to know each other and feel comfortable with one another?

2. What can you do so that the different backgrounds do not contribute to misunderstandings and off-task behavior?

Creating a Supportive, Caring Environment

How students feel about the classroom can make a big difference in the way they participate in the classroom. Your attitude toward the students and the curriculum can influence these student feelings. To create a supportive, caring environment, you should translate your attitude into the following actions:

1. **Celebrate diversity.** Student diversity exists in many ways, as reviewed earlier in this chapter. Students don't want to be criticized because they have some characteristic that is different from others. Through your actions, recognize that each student contributes to the rich variety of ideas and actions in the classroom. Show that you appreciate and value the diversity that is reflected in the students in the classroom. In turn, students will feel appreciated rather than feeling different, and this will make them feel more comfortable in the classroom.

2. **Have high expectations for students and believe all students can succeed.** Teachers may sometimes consider certain sources of student diversity—cognitive ability, language, disabilities, SES, for example—as having a negative effect on student performance. Thus, teachers may lower expectations and adjust the content and activities accordingly. However, this is a disservice to the students when they are not given the opportunity to address meaningful and challenging content and to develop their knowledge and skills. It is important to hold high expectations for all students and to believe all students can succeed. Students appreciate the challenge and will find the classroom more stimulating and worthwhile than a classroom with lowered expectations.

3. **Give encouragement to all students.** Students who perform well academically often receive words of praise, reinforcement, and encouragement from teachers. There may be many students in a classroom who do not perform at the highest academic levels, but they would appreciate hearing encouraging statements as well. Encouraging words and guiding suggestions will help all students feel that they are being supported in their efforts.

4. **Respond to all students enthusiastically.** When students see their teacher is welcoming and enthusiastic about each student, they feel more comfortable in the classroom and are more willing to participate fully. Warm greetings when students enter the classroom, conversations with individual students, and positive reactions when students contribute to classroom discussion are just a few ways that enthusiasm might be expressed. The main thing is that each student needs to feel valued, and they see this through enthusiastic teacher responses.

5. **Show students that you care about them.** When students know that you care for them and that you are looking out for them, it makes all the difference in the world. Students then feel valued, regardless of their characteristics, and are more likely to participate actively in the classroom. Even when the teacher needs to deal with a student concerning a problem, the student recognizes that the teacher's actions are well intended.

6. **Create an antibias educational environment.** Sometimes when students interact with others who are different from them, they may talk or act in ways that express disapproval.

VOICES FROM THE CLASSROOM   Treat Students with Kindness

Sandra Allen-Kearney, fifth-grade teacher, Fort Pierce, Florida

At the beginning of every year, I give all students a fresh slate when they enter my classroom, regardless of their past experiences. I treat all children with kindness, fairness, and consistency. I work very hard to help my at-risk, behaviorally challenged students feel loved and cared for, while setting the limits they desperately seek.

This philosophy has taken time and patience to nurture, but the rewards are tremendous. One day, I went to pick up my students from physical education, and I saw one of my most challenging students wearing his jacket backward. I calmly asked him to put it on correctly, and he quickly complied.

At this, the physical education teacher's mouth dropped. She confronted the student in an angry voice, "I told you to put on your jacket properly in class several times, and you refused. I even put you in time-out for refusing to obey me, and you still wouldn't do it. Why did you put your jacket on the right way when Mrs. Kearney asked you to, when you wouldn't do it for me?"

His simple reply was, "Because she's nice to me." I will never forget that moment, or that young man, when all of my hard work paid off in that one sentence. As we walked back to class, I had to turn away and wipe my eyes when he wasn't looking.

Teachers need to take steps to overcome this bias. In an antibias classroom, teachers intervene with immediate actions and follow-up activities to counter the cumulative, hurtful effects of these messages. In an antibias classroom, children learn to be proud of themselves and of their families, to respect human differences, to recognize bias, and to speak up for what is right (Derman-Sparks & Edwards, 2010). Antibias resources are available, such as from Teaching Tolerance (http://tolerance.org), which provides numerous classroom resources and publications on discipline, civil rights, race, inclusion, and related antibias topics.

Varying Your Instruction

To meet the needs of the diverse students, instruction cannot be one-dimensional. A variety of instructional approaches is needed to challenge all students and to meet their instructional needs. Useful resources include *The Differentiated Classroom* (Tomlinson, 2016), *The Inclusive Classroom: Strategies for Effective Differentiated Instruction* (Mastropieri & Scruggs, 2018), and *Planning and Organizing Standards-Based Differentiated Instruction* (Chapman & King, 2014). Several ways to vary your instruction are highlighted here:

1. **Differentiate with the universal design for learning.** Teachers at any grade level can use the *universal design for learning (UDL)* to meet the needs of all students by adapting the curriculum and delivery of instruction. UDL is an instructional approach that helps meet the challenge of diversity by suggesting flexible instructional materials, techniques, and strategies that empower educators to meet students' varied needs (National Center on Universal Design for Learning, 2011; Hall, Meyer, & Rose, 2012). Version 2.0 of the UDL Guidelines was released in 2011. To create the flexible design and delivery of instruction in UDL, teachers must provide multiple means for learners to (a) acquire information; (b) demonstrate what they know; and (c) engage in learning by tapping on their interests, providing appropriate challenges, and motivating students to learn (Salend & Whittaker, 2017).

2. **Challenge students' thinking and abilities.** You should (a) start where the learner is (i.e., in concert with the pupil's level of development); (b) then begin to mismatch (i.e., use a different approach from what the student prefers) by shifting to a slightly more complex level

of teaching to help the student develop in many areas; and (c) have faith that students have an intrinsic drive to learn. These practices complement the recommendations of Lev Vygotsky, Lawrence Kohlberg, and others to nudge students beyond comfort zones of learning into just enough cognitive dissonance to facilitate growth.

3. **Group students for instruction.** Grouping makes differentiation of instruction more efficient and practical. When each group is challenged and stimulated appropriately, students are motivated to work harder. Differentiated materials can be used more easily. On the other hand, labeling can be stigmatizing if grouping is based on variables such as ability or achievement. Grouping too much and changing groups too infrequently can obstruct student integration and cooperation.

    With the proper planning, structure, and supervision, grouping is a useful way to provide for individual differences. When using grouping arrangements, you should follow these guidelines:

    - Include activities that mix group members frequently.
    - Adjust the pace and level of work for each group to maximize achievement. Avoid having expectations that are too low for low groups. Students tend to live up or down to teachers' expectations.
    - Form groups with care, giving attention to culture and gender.
    - Structure the experience and supervise the students' actions.
    - Prepare students with necessary skills for being effective group members, such as listening, helping, cooperating, and seeking assistance.

4. **Consider differentiated assignments.** *Alternative or differentiated assignments* can be provided by altering the length, difficulty, or time span of the assignment. Alternative assignments generally require alternative evaluation procedures. Enrichment activities qualify as alternative assignments when directed toward the individual student's needs. Resources are available concerning ways to vary assessments, such as in *Differentiated Assessment Strategies* (Chapman & King, 2012).

5. **Have students participate in all class activities.** Regardless of the source of their diversity, all students like to participate in class activities such as discussions, projects, group activities, or computer-based activities. They enjoy the opportunity for involvement and interaction, and they seek the challenge. These activities also provide an opportunity for individual expression and serve as a vehicle for recognition and appreciation.

6. **Provide opportunities for students to try different types of activities.** Although certain class activities and instructional strategies may seem well suited for a particular student, it is important to involve the student in many different types of activities to challenge the student and the student's thinking and understanding. Project-based learning, for example, provides opportunities to differentiate instruction with a variety of activities and roles (Bender, 2012; Boss & Larmer, 2018).

7. **Use authentic and culturally relevant pedagogies.** Each instructional strategy has particular strengths, and some of the strengths may match up well with students with particular needs (Murawski & Spencer, 2011). Direct instruction, for example, has been used effectively in teaching basic skills to students with special needs. Cooperative learning has been shown to be effective in urban classrooms with diverse student populations and in positively changing the attitudes of nondisabled students toward their peers who have disabilities.

    Instructional approaches should be selected that develop classrooms that are multicultural and inclusive. Techniques can be used to anchor instruction in students' prior knowledge and help them learn the new content. Instructional approaches can be selected that are seen by the student as realistic and culturally relevant (Tomlinson, 2017).

8. **Use authentic and fair assessment strategies.** Some students demonstrate their learning better through certain types of assessment. Since there are many types of students in classrooms, a variety of methods for evaluating student learning should be used. Using a variety of approaches, such as written or oral tests, reports or projects, interviews, portfolios, writing samples, and observations, will circumvent bias. In addition, evaluation of student learning should be at several levels—recall, comprehension, application, analysis, synthesis, and evaluation.

Providing Assistance with the Response to Intervention

Many classrooms include students who can benefit from special assistance in their learning. When creating an inclusive, multicultural classroom, these students cannot be overlooked because they may not advance in their learning without such assistance.

1. **Provide special individualized assistance to all students.** Teachers often provide individualized assistance to students who have difficulty learning. This assistance can make a big difference in helping the student overcome hurdles and can lead to better understanding. However, other students can benefit from this type of assistance as well. By providing assistance to all types of diverse learners, teachers express their interest in the student, provide support for student learning, and have the opportunity to challenge the students in new ways.

2. **Work with students with special needs.** As a first step, teachers need to know district policies concerning students with special needs and know what their responsibilities are for referrals, screening, and the preparation of individualized educational plans (IEPs). Learning materials and activities can be prepared commensurate with the abilities of students with special needs. Positive expectations for student performance are a means to promote student learning.

3. **Provide assistance through the Response to Intervention.** *Response to Intervention* (RTI), as referenced in the Individuals with Disabilities Improvement Act of 2004, was conceived as a method to ensure that students receive early intervention and assistance before falling too far behind their peers. RTI requires that these students receive supplementary support, guided by regularly gathered assessment data, referred to as progress monitoring. When planning for instruction, teachers need to take into account the needs of all their students, and struggling students require extra attention and assistance. Thus, all levels of planning need to take these students into account as RTI is applied.

■ WHAT WOULD YOU DECIDE?   Vary Your Instruction to Meet Needs

Let's say you are planning to teach a lesson on soil erosion (or another topic that you think the students might not be too excited about). Yet you recognize that varying your instruction will help meet the learners' needs and may motivate them to be actively engaged.

1. What type of activities might you select to challenge students' thinking?

2. How might you use differentiated assignments and provide students with opportunities to try different types of activities?

3. How might you vary your assessment strategies?

4. How might you need to make adjustments for English language learners?

VOICES FROM THE CLASSROOM   Using the Response to Intervention (RTI)

Margaret Price, first-grade teacher, West Bloomfield, Michigan

After administering district assessments, the data are analyzed and used to plan and implement interventions for those children who are not meeting the district standards. Based on the data, two children from my first-grade classroom were significantly below our district standard in reading.

With our RTI arrangements, Tier 1 intervention consisted of having these students meet with me five days a week for an individual 10-minute guided reading lesson. I would also individually conference with them either in reading or writing at least three days a week. In addition, they would have the lesson repeated another two times a week with one of our bilingual paraeducators.

Although the student needs were different, the lesson format is similar for each child. The lessons consist of reading or guided writing, working with the alphabetic principle (word study), and learning concepts about print. At the end of a six-week period, the students are assessed again to determine how much growth they have made. A determination is then made to continue the intervention or to alter it for more acceleration.

RTI requires that all teachers at all levels (K–12) assess students systematically and provide levels of support for students who need assistance (Allington, 2009; Howard, 2009). Most RTI models include three levels, or tiers (Fisher & Frey, 2010); see Figure 7.1. In *RTI Success*, Whitten, Esteves, and Woodrow (2019) provide guidance for strategies to establish, maintain, and evaluate the use of RTI in the classroom.

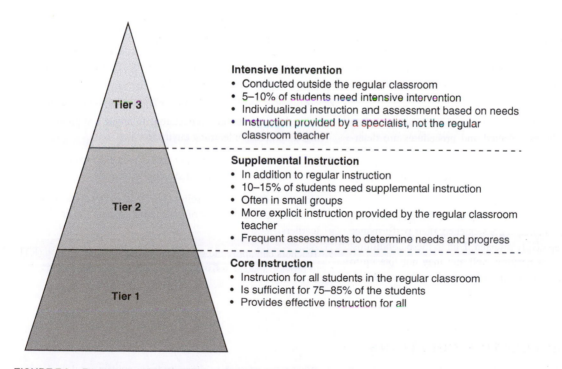

Intensive Intervention
- Conducted outside the regular classroom
- 5–10% of students need intensive intervention
- Individualized instruction and assessment based on needs
- Instruction provided by a specialist, not the regular classroom teacher

Supplemental Instruction
- In addition to regular instruction
- 10–15% of students need supplemental instruction
- Often in small groups
- More explicit instruction provided by the regular classroom teacher
- Frequent assessments to determine needs and progress

Core Instruction
- Instruction for all students in the regular classroom
- Is sufficient for 75–85% of the students
- Provides effective instruction for all

Tier 3
Tier 2
Tier 1

FIGURE 7.1   **Response to intervention: a three-tiered model.**

- **Tier 1: Core instruction.** This is regular classroom instruction, and it involves assessing, instructing, and diagnosing learning difficulties. The focus is on quality teaching and implementing systems to determine which students respond to this instruction and which students do not. Approximately 75–85% of students should make sufficient progress through core instruction alone.

- **Tier 2: Supplemental phase.** This phase can occur either in the regular classroom or as an adjunct to the classroom. In this phase, teachers begin to monitor how students respond to various interventions that are put in place to provide them with assistance. In Tier 2, students receive instruction in addition to that received in Tier 1, and assessment occurs more frequently in order to determine responsiveness and to plan subsequent interventions. This intervention often takes the form of additional small-group instruction, which complements the core instruction. About 10–15% of students at one time or another need supplemental interventions. These interventions may last up to 20 weeks, and more frequent assessments take place during this time. The regular classroom teacher typically provides this intervention, sometimes with guidance and support from other educators in the building.

- **Tier 3: Intensive intervention.** Some students do not benefit from the supplemental interventions in Tier 2 and will benefit from even more intensive interventions; 5–10% of students will require this level of intensive intervention. Students in Tier 3 often receive instruction on a one-to-one basis from a curriculum specialist, learning coach, speech-language pathologist, or related intervention specialists. The regular classroom teacher typically does not provide this intervention.

MAJOR CONCEPTS

1. In an effort to get to know students, teachers can select the types of information they need, identify the sources for that information, and then use that information to be more effective in their selection of instructional strategies, their adjustments for individual differences, and their interactions with the students and their families.

2. Individual differences need to be taken into account when instructional methods are selected and procedures are determined for classroom management.

3. Important sources of student diversity are cultural diversity, language, gender, and exceptionalities.

4. Some students may have experienced challenging circumstances in their lives and, as a consequence, their performance in school may be negatively affected. Due to these conditions, some students may not perform well and may not live up to their potential. There may be an achievement gap between their potential and their actual performance.

5. Teachers may need to address students who have to deal with challenging circumstances in their lives. These may include struggling learners, students at risk, students in poverty, seriously disengaged students, and students challenged with other adverse and often serious conditions.

6. Information about the sources of student diversity can be used as the basis of classroom decisions to create a supportive, caring, and inclusive learning environment.

7. A variety of instructional approaches is needed to challenge all students and to meet their instructional needs.

8. Universal design for learning (UDL) is a way to adapt a curriculum and the delivery of instruction to meet the needs of all learners.

9. Teachers can apply the steps in Response to Intervention (RTI) to provide special assistance to students in their learning.

DISCUSSION/REFLECTIVE QUESTIONS

1. What is the value of obtaining information about your students? How might you use that information to improve instruction and management in your classroom?

2. What types of student diversity were evident in classrooms in your own K–12 schooling experience? In what ways did your teachers seem to take those student characteristics into account in

the selection of content, the use of instructional approaches, and the use of classroom management and discipline procedures?

3. What are some challenges you might experience in dealing with students with limited English proficiency? What could you do to overcome those challenges to promote student learning?

4. If you had some seriously disengaged students in your class in your first year, what would you do to try to reach them? Are there other educators in the school you could turn to for ideas and help?

5. What are some ways that you might create a supportive, caring, and inclusive classroom?

6. How might you vary your instruction through the use of instructional methods, materials, activities, and assessments?

SUGGESTED ACTIVITIES

1. Identify several ways that you will gather information about your students at the start of a new school year. Start to outline and prepare any materials or processes you would need for this task.

2. Using the categories of differences addressed in this chapter as a guide, ask several teachers to describe individual differences they notice in their students. How do the teachers take these differences into account in their instruction and classroom management procedures? What difficulties have they experienced?

3. In anticipation of needing to address disengaged students, start reading and investigating characteristics of seriously disengaged students, and identify and list actions that you could take in your classroom to address their needs.

4. Select a unit that you might teach and identify specific ways that you could vary your instruction over a two-week unit when taking student diversity into account.

FURTHER READING

Davis, B. M. (2012). *How to teach students who don't look like you: Culturally relevant teaching strategies* (2nd ed.). Thousand Oaks, CA: Corwin Press.
Provides background knowledge about diverse learners and understanding our own perspectives about diversity. Provides guidance for creating a supportive learning community and for selecting instructional strategies for diverse learners.

Gollnick, D. M., & Chinn, P. C. (2017). *Multicultural education in a pluralistic society* (10th ed.). Boston, MA: Pearson.
Provides descriptions of human differences due to class, ethnicity and race, gender, exceptionality, religion, language, and age. Discusses education that is multicultural.

Tomlinson, C. A. (2016). *The differentiated classroom: Responding to the needs of all learners* (2nd ed.). Boston, MA: Pearson.
Describes ways that teachers can differentiate content, process, and product according to a student's readiness, interests, and learning profile.

Vaughn, S. R., Bos, C. S., & Schumm, J. S. (2018). *Teaching students who are exceptional, diverse, and at-risk in the general education classroom* (7th ed.). Boston, MA: Pearson.
Provides a comprehensive discussion about diverse student characteristics and thoroughly describes instructional modifications that are suitable. Also examines inclusive instructional approaches for the subject areas and for reading.

Whitten, E., Esteves, K. J., & Woodrow, A. (2019). *RTI success: Proven tools and strategies for schools and classrooms* (revised and expanded ed.). Minneapolis, MN: Free Spirit Publishing.
Is a comprehensive resource that describes RTI, setting up support teams, creating and sustaining learning environments, conducting assessments, and grouping students.

© Diane Collins and Jordan Hollender/Digital Vision/Getty Images, Inc

Planning and Conducting Instruction

CHAPTER OBJECTIVES

This chapter provides information that will help you:

- Select ways to structure lessons and group students.

- Identify ways to hold students academically accountable.

- Determine ways to motivate your students.

- Address administrative actions that are commonly taken at the start of a lesson.

- Take actions that can be used at the start of a lesson to capture student interest and focus attention on the learning objectives.

- Take actions that contribute to effective group management during the middle part of a lesson.

- Conduct actions at the end of a lesson to provide for lesson summary and enable students to prepare to leave.

- Manage seatwork, assignments, records, and paperwork.

When planning for a vacation trip, you often need to plan ahead. Do you want to stay in one place and relax, or do you want to visit a number of areas? Would you like to schedule several events for each day, or would you like to leave the daily schedule open? What types of accommodations would you like? To ensure an enjoyable vacation, you need to give these questions attention.

Similarly, you need to give advance thought to the type of classroom you would like to have. How structured do you want your classroom and lessons? How do you want to group your students for instruction? How will you hold the students academically accountable? How can you motivate your students to learn? How will you handle various aspects of lesson delivery? How will you manage student work? These issues will be explored in this chapter. How you attend to these issues will make a difference in managing instruction and student behavior.

Planning Decisions Affect Behavior Management

Preparing daily lesson plans is a vital task for effective classroom management and discipline because effective, engaging lessons can keep students on task and can minimize misbehavior. You need to consider the degree of structure that will occur in each lesson. The grouping planned for the instructional activities will also affect student interaction. Furthermore, students are more likely to stay on task and be engaged in instruction when they know that they will be held academically accountable. Also, decisions need to be made about motivating students to learn.

The Degree of Structure in Lessons

Many instructional strategies can be used, ranging from teacher-centered, explicit approaches to the presentation of content to student-centered, less-explicit approaches. *Teacher-centered approaches* include lectures, demonstrations, questions, recitations, practice and drills, and reviews. *Student-centered approaches* include inquiry approaches, discovery learning and problem solving, role-playing and simulation, gaming, laboratory activities, computer-assisted instruction, and learning or activity centers. Various types of grouping and discussion methods may be student or teacher directed, depending on how they are used. Teacher-centered approaches are often more structured than student-centered approaches. As a result, the management issues will vary depending on the approach used.

When deciding on your instructional strategy, you need to weigh the advantages and disadvantages of the various strategies along with the lesson objectives. Effective teachers use several strategies, ranging from teacher directed to student directed. The lesson objectives may determine what type of approach is most appropriate. Some content may lend itself to inquiry and discovery techniques, whereas other content may be better handled with direct instruction. Over time, students should be given the opportunity to learn through a variety of instructional strategies.

Grouping Students for Instruction

Group students in the way most appropriate for the instructional strategies and objectives. Focus on a group as a collection of individuals who learn. Within groups, each individual student observes, listens, responds, takes turns, and so on. Groups can be large or small. Whole-group, small-group, and independent work are options to consider; each affects student conduct and order.

Whole-Group Instruction

In *whole-group instruction*, the entire class is taught as a group. It allows you to (a) lecture, demonstrate, and explain a topic; (b) ask and answer a question in front of the entire class; (c) provide the same recitation, practice, and drill exercises; (d) work on the same problems; and (e) use the same materials. Although instruction is directed to the whole group, you can still ask individual students to answer questions, monitor students as they work on assigned activities, and work with individual students. Even with whole-group instruction, however, you need to consider individual student differences.

Small-Group Instruction

There are times when the objectives can be better met with small groups called *small-group instruction*. In small-group instruction, students tend to be more actively engaged, and teachers can better monitor student progress. Groups of four students often work well. If there are more than six in a group, generally, not everyone will actively participate.

Since group work helps develop relationships, it is useful to vary the membership of the groups based on gender and ethnicity. Students with disabilities can be placed in groups with nondisabled students to integrate them into the mainstream classroom. Although there may be good reasons for planning a homogeneous group for certain activities, educators in general recommend the use of heterogeneous groups (Johnson & Johnson, 2017).

There are various ways to establish fixed or flexible groups, such as fixed groups, ability groups, cluster grouping, within-class groups, cooperative learning groups, cross-grade groups, and others (Brulles & Brown, 2018). Useful guides are available when planning to use grouping, such as *Designing Groupwork* (Cohen & Lotan, 2014). Three types of groupings are discussed here: ability grouping, cooperative learning, and peer tutoring.

1. **Ability grouping.** *Ability grouping* involves the clustering of students who are judged to be similar in their academic ability into classes for instruction. There are two common types of ability grouping: between-class grouping and within-class grouping:

   - *Between-class grouping* involves having separate classes for students of different abilities. When reporting research on between-class ability grouping, Slavin (2018) noted that grouping arrangements made on the basis of standardized test scores are not effective in reducing the range of differences that affect the specific class. In addition, the quality of

VOICES FROM THE CLASSROOM   Grouping Students for Instruction

Saralee Wittmer, second-grade teacher, Amarillo, Texas

Students in my room are arranged in small groups of four students according to ability. I shuffle the mix every four to six weeks. Students get the chance to work with all other students and can sit close to the teacher, at the back of the room, close to the door, and up by the chalkboards.

Students are encouraged to discuss lessons with each other within their groups. It's amazing how much they learn from each other if we will only give them the opportunities. I can tell what the class might not have gotten from my lesson presentations by listening carefully to them when they are in their groups.

Gladis Diaz, fifth-grade teacher, Reno, Nevada

When preparing to group my students, I have them complete some cooperative activities so that I can see their skills and personalities. This helps me place them in homogeneous groups and establish the roles for each person in a group. Each group has a leader, a recorder, a go-getter, a speller, and an organizer. I choose the leader who remains in that role throughout the school year. The roles of the others rotate four times during the school year. I meet with the group leaders at least twice a week to discuss their role for the week and to be sure everything is running smoothly.

instruction often is lower in lower-track classes, and students feel stigmatized by their assignments to low tracks. The disadvantages of between-class ability grouping suggest that it should be avoided when possible (Oakes, 2005).

- *Within-class grouping* involves creating subgroups within a class, with each subgroup being fairly homogeneous in terms of ability. A small number is better than a large number of groups. In this way, group assignments can be flexible, role models for low achievers are available, teacher morale is higher, and the stigmatizing effect is minimized. Within one classroom, you may group students for various activities or subjects. For example, middle school and secondary teachers may use ability groups for only part of a class period and whole-group activities or other approaches for the rest of the class time. You may group students to work on selected projects or activities.

2. **Cooperative learning.** *Cooperative learning* is a grouping in which students work in small, mixed-ability learning teams to help one another learn academic content. Such groups can be formed at various grade levels and in different subject areas. Through cooperative learning, students understand that they are responsible not only for their own learning but also for the learning of their team members. Cooperative learning approaches are often used to supplement other instructional practices.

    Cooperative learning occurs in three different ways: (a) assignment of individual students to specific responsibilities within a larger group task or project; (b) assignment of students to a shared project or task; or (c) assignment to groups to study and be responsible for group members' learning. There are several common types of cooperative learning techniques. Additional resources on cooperative learning include Gillies (2007, 2015), Jacobs, Power, and Inn (2003), Johnson, Johnson, and Holubec (2007, 2009), Jolliffe (2007), and Udvari-Solner and Kluth (2018).

3. **Peer tutoring.** *Peer tutoring* involves students teaching students. The two types of peer tutoring are cross-age tutoring, in which older students work with younger ones, and peer tutoring, in which students within the same class work together. There are several advantages of peer tutoring (Johnson & Johnson, 2017): (a) peer tutors are often effective

in teaching students who do not respond well to adults; (b) peer tutoring can develop a bond of friendship between the tutor and tutored, which is important for integrating slow learners into the group; (c) peer tutoring allows the teacher to teach a large group of students while giving slow learners the individual attention they need; and (d) tutors benefit by learning to teach.

Peer tutoring can be used at all grade levels. Before having students work in pairs, you will need to clarify the purposes of the tutoring, obtain the necessary materials, and provide an appropriate work area where the students can work without disturbing other students. You might offer some guidance about working and studying together.

Independent Work

You might give students opportunities to work on tasks of their own choosing, or you may assign activities that enable students to work alone. This is *independent work*. Good and Brophy (2008) found that one-third of elementary teachers attempt to individualize instruction and that one-fifth of secondary teachers attempt to do so.

When assigning independent work, you may involve students in any of a number of instructional strategies. In inquiry and discovery instructional approaches, students learn about the process of discovery by collecting data and testing hypotheses. Teachers guide students as they discover new meanings, practice the skills, and undergo the experiences that will shape their learning. These approaches include computer-assisted instruction, learning centers, learning stations, laboratories, discovery techniques, and others.

Holding Students Academically Accountable

Procedures to help manage student work must be selected. *Academic accountability* means that the students must complete certain activities related to the instructional objectives. Teacher responsibilities for holding students academically accountable are displayed in Table 8.1, some of which are adapted from Emmer and Evertson (2017), Evertson and Emmer (2017), and Jones and Jones (2016).

■ TABLE 8.1   Holding Students Academically Accountable

Take into account the grade level and subject area when decisions are made on the following issues in an effort to hold students academically accountable.

1. The Grading System
   a. Select a grading system.
   b. Select types of evaluation measures.
   c. Determine how grades will be assigned.
   d. Address nonachievement outcomes.
   e. Communicate the grading system to students.
   f. Design a gradebook.
   g. Report grades and communicate to parents.
2. Assignments
   a. Post assignments.
   b. State requirements and grading criteria for assignments.
   c. Make long-term assignments.

■ TABLE 8.1   *(continued)*

3. Work and Completion Requirements

    a. Identify work requirements.

        (1) Use of pencil or pen

        (2) Headings on papers

        (3) Writing on the back of the paper

        (4) Neatness and legibility guidelines

    b. Identify completion requirements.

        (1) Due dates

        (2) Late work

        (3) Incomplete work

        (4) Missed work

    c. Make provisions for absent students and make-up work.

        (1) Assignment lists or folders

        (2) Due dates

        (3) Places to pick up and drop off absent assignments

        (4) Regular times to assist students with make-up work

4. Monitoring Progress and Completion of Assignments

    a. Determine when and how to monitor in-class assignments.

    b. Determine when and how to monitor longer assignments, projects, or works in progress.

    c. Determine when and how to monitor in-class oral participation or performance.

    d. Determine which activities will receive a grade and which will be used only for formative feedback for the student.

    e. Select checking procedures that will be used in class.

        (1) Students exchanging papers

        (2) Marking and grading papers

        (3) Turning in papers

5. Providing Feedback

    a. Decide what kind of feedback will be provided to students, and when it will be provided.

    b. Determine what records students will keep concerning their progress.

    c. Select incentives and rewards.

    d. Record scores in the gradebook.

    e. Post selected student work.

Consider these five guidelines when holding students academically accountable:

1. **Determine a system of grading (e.g., letter grades or numerical grades and measures for nonachievement outcomes).** This decision may have been made for you by the school district as reflected in the report card format. Use a variety of evaluation measures (e.g., tests, written or oral reports, homework, ratings, and projects) throughout the marking period and describe the grading system to the students.

2. **Make decisions about assignments.** Decide on where and how you will post assignments, as well as the requirements and criteria for grading. Students should understand that completed assignments are part of the grading system.

3. **Decide on work and completion requirements.** Students need to have guidelines or work requirements for the various assignments. Details about due dates, late work, and missed assignments due to absence should be explained. The relevant procedures will help students understand expectations held of them and should minimize questions on a case-by-case basis.

4. **Monitor student progress and completion of the assignments.** You may want to use some in-class activities as formative exercises for students but not count performance on these in your grading. The activities may be written, oral, or performance demonstrations. Student progress should be monitored. In many cases, the entire class is at work on the designated activity; this enables you to walk around and observe each student carefully to see how the student is progressing.

5. **Provide students with feedback about their progress.** Feedback on in-class activities may take the form of statements to the individuals or to the class. Students may exchange papers to evaluate progress on formative exercises. Papers or projects that are to be part of the report card grade should be collected, graded, and returned promptly. In this way, students receive regular feedback about their progress throughout the marking period. Computer programs available for maintaining a gradebook can easily generate progress reports for both students and teacher.

Planning for Motivation

Many educators use the word *motivation* to describe those processes that can arouse and initiate student behavior, give direction and purpose to behavior, help behavior to persist, and help the student choose a particular behavior. Of course, teachers are interested in a particular kind of motivation in their students—the motivation to learn (Anderman & Anderman, 2014; Gregory & Kaufeldt, 2015; Middleton & Perks, 2014; Wentzel & Brophy, 2014; Wentzel & Miele, 2016).

Before examining specific motivational strategies, it is important to consider three aspects of planning for motivation:

1. **Develop a comprehensive approach to motivation.** The message about motivation from research and best practice is clear—develop a comprehensive approach to motivate students to learn instead of looking at one or two classroom variables in isolation. Much of the information about motivation addresses important topics such as needs, satisfactions, authority, and recognition. These issues should not be considered in isolation, and the ways teachers address these issues show up in their decisions about instructional tasks, evaluation, recognition, and other areas.

2. **Adjust motivational strategies to your instructional situation.** Motivational strategies discussed in this chapter come from research and best practice, and thus they provide a framework for classroom decisions. It is likely, however, that you will need to evaluate your own situation—grade level, subject area, student characteristics—to determine which strategies are most appropriate in your context. Some strategies might need to be modified to work successfully in your classroom. Some strategies might be used a great deal while others might not be used at all. Your professional assessment of your situation will guide the selection and use of the motivational strategies.

3. **Build motivational issues into all levels of your instructional planning.** Your instructional planning actually includes many time frames: the course, the semester, the marking period, each unit, each week, and each lesson.

You need to think globally to help students see the big picture as well as the importance of each smaller piece of content. Your long-range planning should take the topic of relevance into account, and the relevance should be apparent in each unit and lesson. Therefore, your planning for motivation needs to be conducted for all levels of planning.

As you consider how to incorporate the motivation concept of relevance, for example, into your instruction, you would think about ways to apply that concept in each time frame listed here. How might you help students see the relevance of the entire course, and how might that be reflected in your course syllabus and introduction to the course? How might you highlight the relevance of the content during each marking period and each unit? Similarly, students would appreciate seeing the relevance of the content that is covered in each week and in each lesson. Select assignments that connect to students' lives since students are more likely to be motivated to complete these assignments with a higher degree of excellence (Dabrowski & Marshall, 2018).

There are various ways to organize the way you incorporate motivational aspects into your instruction. Based on the research on motivation, Wentzel and Brophy (2014) organized strategies in two categories: strategies for increasing expectations for success and strategies for increasing perceived value. Quate and McDermott (2009) suggest the six Cs for creating a context that motivates students and nurtures engagement: (a) caring classroom community; (b) checking in and checking out (i.e., assessment); (c) choice; (d) collaboration; (e) challenge; and (f) celebration. Sullo (2009) offers suggestions centering on relationships, rules and procedures, rewards, enthusiasm, expectations, and student characteristics and needs. The *Handbook of Motivation in Schools* (Wentzel & Miele, 2016) provides much background and suggestions for practice.

The instructional strategies that you use, the tasks that you ask the students to complete, and the way that you interact with students during instruction all influence students' motivation to learn (Kaplan & Patrick, 2016; Reeve, 2015; Schunk, Meece, & Pintrich, 2014). As you prepare your plans, try to incorporate the 12 motivational strategies displayed in Table 8.2 into your instruction.

■ TABLE 8.2   Motivational Strategies for Instruction

1. Capture Student Interest in the Subject Matter
   a. Take time to understand what students perceive as important and interesting.
   b. Select topics and tasks that interest students.
   c. Set the stage at the start of the lesson.
   d. State learning objectives and expectations at the start of the lesson.
   e. Use questions and activities to capture student interest in the subject matter.
   f. Introduce the course and each topic in an interesting, informative, and challenging way.

2. Highlight the Relevance of the Subject Matter
   a. Select meaningful learning objectives and activities.
   b. Directly address the importance of each new topic examined.
   c. Adapt instruction to students' knowledge, understanding, and personal experience.
   d. Have students use what they previously learned.
   e. Illustrate the subject matter with anecdotes and concrete examples to show relevance.

3. Vary Your Instructional Strategies to Maintain Interest
   a. Use several instructional approaches throughout the lesson.
   b. Use games, simulations, or other fun features.
   c. Occasionally do the unexpected.

4. Plan for Active Student Involvement
   a. Try to make a study of the subject matter as active, investigative, adventurous, and social as possible.
   b. Vary the type of involvement when considering the students' learning and cognitive styles.

5. Select Strategies That Capture Students' Curiosity
   a. Capitalize on the arousal value of suspense, discovery, curiosity, exploration, and fantasy.
   b. Use anecdotes or other devices to include a personal, emotional element in the content.

6. Select Strategies with an Appropriate Degree of Difficulty
   a. Assign moderately difficult tasks that can be completed with reasonable effort.
   b. Divide difficult tasks into smaller parts that are achievable without requiring excessive effort.
   c. Focus on higher-order learning outcomes.
   d. Monitor the level of difficulty of assignments and tests.

7. Group Students for Tasks
   a. Plan to use a variety of individual, cooperative, and competitive activities.
   b. Promote cooperation and teamwork.

8. Design the Lesson to Promote Student Success
   a. Design activities that lead to student success.
   b. Adapt the tasks to match the motivational needs of the students.
   c. Communicate desirable expectations and attributes.
   d. Establish a supportive environment.
   e. Use familiar material for initial examples, but provide unique and unexpected contexts when applying concepts and principles.
   f. Minimize performance anxiety.

9. Allow Students Some Control over the Lessons
   a. Promote feelings of control by allowing students a voice in decision-making.
   b. Monitor the difficulty of the goals and tasks that students choose for themselves.

■ TABLE 8.2   *(continued)*

10. Express Interest in the Content and Project Enthusiasm

   a. Model interest and enthusiasm in the topic and in learning.

   b. Project enthusiasm.

   c. Introduce tasks in a positive, enthusiastic manner.

   d. Expect interest, not boredom, from the students.

11. Provide Opportunities to Learn

   a. Focus lessons around mid-level concepts that are substantive but not overwhelming to students.

   b. Make the main ideas evident in presentations, demonstrations, discussions, and assignments.

   c. Present concrete illustrations of the content and relate unfamiliar information to your students' personal knowledge.

   d. Make explicit connections between new information and content that students had learned previously, and point out relationships among new ideas by stressing similarities and differences.

   e. Elaborate extensively on textbook readings rather than allowing the book to carry the lesson.

   f. Guide students' thinking when posing high-level questions.

   g. Ask students to summarize, make comparisons between related concepts, and apply the information they are learning.

12. Support Students' Attempts to Understand

   a. Model thinking and problem solving, and work with students to solve problems when the students have difficulty.

   b. Keep the procedures in instructional tasks simple.

   c. Encourage collaborative efforts by requiring all students to make contributions to the group.

VOICES FROM THE CLASSROOM   Planning for Motivation and Opportunities to Learn

Janet Roesner, elementary teacher, Baltimore, Maryland

It is important to identify the learning goals and the indicators of learning for each unit—this provides a clear focus when planning the unit. Next, a teacher needs to determine the skills and type of thinking the students will need in order to be successful in the lesson. These acquired skills then become strategies for success and can be applied to all areas of learning.

One important question to ask when planning a unit is, "How will this learning be meaningful?" Making meaningful connections to the students' background knowledge, experiences, and interests is key to motivating the learners. Giving students opportunities to decide on real-life assessments that are clearly related to the learning goals is very motivating. In this way, interest peaks, application of knowledge soars, and students succeed.

Each lesson in a unit must make meaningful connections to the learning goal. In this way, students begin to learn for understanding rather than for just completing the work.

Managing Lesson Delivery

You've finished your planning. You've selected the instructional strategies. You've prepared and gathered the instructional materials. Now it is the day of your lesson. You're all ready to begin, but wait. You also must recognize that you can take certain actions during your instruction that will help students stay on task and achieve the lesson objectives.

You can use a number of strategies at certain points in a lesson to manage the group effectively, maintain order and control, and fulfill various administrative and academic objectives. If these actions are not handled appropriately, it is likely that students will be more inclined to be off task and possibly misbehave. As a result, it is important to examine these lesson delivery tasks from the perspective of management and order in the classroom.

The Beginning of a Lesson

A successful lesson beginning can greatly contribute to a meaningful learning experience for students. The beginning of a lesson should be designed to handle various administrative tasks, capture the students' interest, and focus their attention on the learning objectives to be addressed during the lesson. An effective beginning can increase students' ability to focus on the objectives.

Actions you take at the start of a lesson help establish an atmosphere in which students have the "motivation to learn" (Wentzel & Brophy, 2014). *Motivation to learn* draws on the meaningfulness, value, and benefits of the academic task to the learner. For example, math problems may be developed relating to student interests, such as selling products for a youth-group fundraiser. Thus, the focus is on learning rather than on merely performing. Often, students can be motivated at the beginning of a lesson by emphasizing the purpose of the task or the fact that students will be interested in the task.

Prior to beginning the substance of a lesson, take attendance and solicit student attention. At the beginning of the lesson, your actions include providing daily review, providing a set induction, introducing lesson objectives, distributing and collecting materials, and giving clear, focused directions.

Taking Attendance

Elementary teachers in self-contained classrooms commonly take attendance first thing in the morning, whereas middle school and high school teachers take attendance at the start of each class. Tardiness also must be noted, and teachers need to follow school policies when recording and responding to tardy students. It is helpful not to hold up the beginning of class to take attendance. You should plan an opening activity for students to do while you take attendance. Some teachers have the first activity posted on the board for the students to do while attendance is taken. It is important to have a seating chart for each class; a substitute teacher will find this to be especially useful.

Getting Attention

Students should understand that they are expected to give full attention to lessons at all times. A lesson should not begin until you gain their full attention. There should be a predictable, standard signal that tells the class, "We are now ready to begin the lesson." The type of signal will vary with teacher preferences. For example, you can raise your hand, ring chimes or a bell, stand in a certain location, or make a statement. After giving the signal, pause briefly to allow it to take effect. Then when you have attention, move quickly into the lesson.

There are at least three ways to solicit attention at the beginning of a lesson. These approaches are designed to secure the students' attention and reduce distractions that might occur at the beginning of a lesson (Jones & Jones, 2016):

1. **Select a cue for getting students' attention.** Students often need a consistent cue to focus their attention. These cues may include a special phrase that the class has chosen to indicate that you want immediate attention, or it may be a nonverbal cue such as closing the door at the beginning of class.

2. **Do not begin until all students are paying attention.** It is important not to begin a lesson until all students are paying attention to the teacher. Teachers who begin lessons without the attention of all their students spend much more time repeating directions. Also, a teacher who begins a lesson in such a fashion is a poor role model since this indicates that it is all

right to talk while others are talking. Teachers sometimes just stand silent, waiting—students soon get the message.

3. **Remove distractions.** Some students cannot screen out distracting stimuli. You can help remove distractions by closing the door, having the students remove unnecessary materials from the tops of their desks, adjusting the blinds, or taking other appropriate actions.

Providing Daily Review

A lesson can start with a brief review of previously covered material, correction of homework, and review of prior knowledge that is relevant to the day's lesson. The purpose of daily review is to determine if the students have obtained the necessary prerequisite knowledge or skills for the lesson. This review may last from three to eight minutes, and the length will vary according to the attention span of the learners and the nature of the content. Daily review is especially useful for teaching material that will be used in subsequent learning. Examples include math facts, math computation and factoring, grammar, chemical equations, and reading sight words.

You can conduct daily review at the beginning of a lesson to provide additional practice and overlearning for previously learned material and to allow the teacher to provide corrections and reteaching in areas where students are having difficulty. Vary the methods for reviewing material.

Checking homework at the start of class is one form of review. Game formats, such as a trivia game, can be used as a means for review. You can conduct review through discussion, demonstration, questioning, written summaries, short quizzes, individualized approaches, and other methods of instruction. During reviews, students might answer questions at the chalkboard, in small groups, or as a whole class. Some additional techniques include asking questions about concepts or skills taught in the previous lesson, having students meet in small groups of two to four to review homework, and having students prepare questions about previous lessons or homework and ask them to one another or the teacher can ask them to the class.

In addition to daily review, the learning of new material is also enhanced by weekly and monthly reviews. Weekly reviews may occur each Monday, and monthly reviews every fourth Monday. These reviews provide additional opportunities for you to check for student understanding, ensure that the necessary prior skills are adequately learned, and also check on your pace of instruction.

VOICES FROM THE CLASSROOM   Using Clickers for Daily Review

Cindy Burkes, third-grade teacher, Las Vegas, Nevada

We use a classroom performance system (CPS) for a variety of purposes, including daily review. This system enables me to enter a series of questions into a PowerPoint presentation, and it includes a handheld "clicker" (like a remote control) for students to record their answers to these questions. On my computer screen, I can immediately see the results for each question and each student.

I begin each day with "The Daily Four," which are two review questions and two preview questions that students answer using their clickers. The instant feedback on student performance provided by the clickers helps me determine if remediation is needed or if future lessons can be pared down, thereby eliminating the need for in-depth lessons when a quick overview will be sufficient.

Establishing Set

Set induction is the activity at the beginning of the lesson that is used to induce students to a state of wanting to learn. This activity helps establish the context for the learning that is to follow and helps students engage in the learning. Typically, the set is brief, lasting only long enough to develop student readiness to accomplish the lesson's objective. Set induction helps students see what the topic of the lesson is in a way that is related to their own interests and their own lives. Madeline Hunter (1994) used the term *anticipatory set* to describe this concept, pointing out that the activity is intended to develop a mental readiness (or "set") for the lesson.

For example, a health lesson on the topic of first aid might begin with the reading of a newspaper report about a recent fire or accident. After reading the article, you could ask the students what they would do if they were the first ones to arrive after the accident. A number of ideas are likely to be generated in this discussion. Then you could bring that opening discussion to a close by saying that today's lesson will be about that exact topic—what type of first aid to administer for various conditions. Then you would move into the first part of the lesson. This set induction activity helps create interest in the lesson in a way that students can relate to their own lives.

Effective set induction activities should meet four criteria:

1. **Get the students interested in what is to be taught during the lesson.** This is referred to as an initiating activity. For example, you might begin a lesson on creative writing by turning off the lights in the room and explaining to the students that you will take them on an adventure to a distant planet. As the room remains dark, they are to imagine their trip into outer space.

2. **The set induction activity must be connected to the lesson.** An activity that is designed to get the students' attention but is not connected to the lesson does not meet this criterion.

3. **Students must understand the material and/or activity.** The information contained in the initiating activity must be stated in a clear manner so students will not only understand the activity but also know how it is connected to later content. Later, the set induction activity can be referred to while teaching the lesson.

4. **The set induction and the content of the lesson should be related to the students' lives or to a previous lesson.** Students will be more interested in a lesson if they can relate the material to their own lives. For example, a lesson concerning measurement might include measuring ingredients to bake a cake or some other practical application. Also, you can reduce anxiety by relating the lesson to material already learned by the students.

■ WHAT WOULD YOU DECIDE?   Holding Students Accountable

Let's assume that you are teaching a math lesson and that you are having five students complete sample problems at the whiteboard while the rest of the students remain in their seats, watching the five students at the board. You are watching the students at the board work on the problems and are offering comments and suggestions to them as they are taking steps to solve their problems.

1. For students still in their seats, how might you hold them academically accountable for the material?

2. How could you provide feedback to the students at the board as well as to those still in their seats?

3. How might the lack of a procedure for academic accountability in this setting contribute to a loss of order in the classroom?

Introducing Lesson Objectives

At the start of a lesson, you should clearly describe its purpose. In addition, it is helpful to discuss the activities and evaluation process, since these procedures help reduce student anxiety about the lesson. At the beginning, some teachers will clearly explain the objectives, the activities, and evaluation procedures to be used; others will write these elements on the board for the students, or they will wait for an appropriate point in the lesson, such as after the set induction.

By using set induction activities and introducing lesson objectives, a teacher gives students an *advance organizer* that provides a framework for the new content and helps the students relate it to content they already know. Advance organizers help students by focusing their attention on the subject being considered, informing them where the lesson is going, relating new material to content already understood, and providing structure for the subsequent lesson. Students learn more, in less time, when they are informed of the lesson objectives. Furthermore, students are more likely to become involved and derive more satisfaction and enjoyment from an activity that has a definite aim.

Consider the alternative if you do *not* clearly communicate the learning goals to enable the students to understand the goals. Students may go through the motions of an activity without understanding its purpose or its relationship to other content. Students may be concerned only with completing the assignment, rather than attempting to understand the purposes and objectives behind the assignment. Some students, in fact, may become passive when they see no academic purpose and consider assignments to be busywork with no specific learning objective.

Distributing and Collecting Materials

Teachers often need to distribute materials to students. Students' maturity should be considered when determining the most appropriate time and way to do so. Handouts, maps, and student guides can be distributed at the beginning of class to focus student attention on important material and to avoid disruptions during the lesson. Materials can be handed to students as they enter the room to save time during the lesson. You may prefer to distribute materials at the point in the lesson when they are actually needed.

Materials should be strategically located in the classroom to provide easy distribution and to minimize disruptions. For example, frequently used resource books should be located where there is sufficient room when the books are needed. Procedures should be established for their distribution. You may have one row of students at a time get the resource books, have one student in each row get enough copies for that row, have students pick up a copy as soon as they enter the room, or give each student a copy as soon as they enter the room.

Some materials that are distributed need to be collected later in the lesson, and appropriate ways to collect these materials should be selected. The manner of collecting the materials may be the same as or different from the way they were distributed.

Giving Clear, Focused Directions

To give clear and focused directions, you first must carefully plan them. Directions are often given at the beginning of a lesson; of course, directions might also be given for activities throughout a lesson.

When *planning for directions*, you should (a) have no more than three student actions that are required for the activity to be described; (b) describe the directions in the order that students will be required to complete the tasks; (c) clarify what type and quality of product is expected; (d) make the description of each step specific and fairly brief; (e) provide written (on the chalkboard, a transparency, or a handout) and oral directions; (f) give the directions just before the activity; and (g) make provisions for assisting students who have difficulty.

VOICES FROM THE CLASSROOM   Giving Directions

Ron Butler, high school social studies teacher, Gillette, Wyoming

There are several parts of giving directions for class activities. First, I give detailed, step-by-step descriptions for what I want the students to do. This may include mentioning the pages in the textbook and the specific actions that I want the students to take. Second, I seek feedback from the students to see if they understand the directions. Especially when there are several steps in the directions, I ask a randomly selected student to repeat the directions to ensure that the students hear them again. At any time, I can correct any misunderstandings they have. Third, I screen the steps on the overhead projector so the students can refer to them as they move along.

When actually *giving directions*, you need to (a) get student attention; (b) present the directions; (c) check to see if students understand the directions ("Do you have any questions about what you need to do?"); (d) have the students begin the tasks; and (e) remediate if necessary if one or more students are not following directions. Clearly state what books and materials are needed.

It is often helpful to demonstrate the actions expected of the students by doing one problem or activity together. Students then see what is expected of them before they begin to work independently. Once students begin work, you should walk around to see if they are following the directions and to be available to answer student questions. If many questions arise, it may be useful to gain everyone's attention for further explanation.

The Middle of the Lesson

A number of teacher behaviors during lesson delivery contribute to effective group management. These include pacing the lesson, providing smooth transitions, avoiding satiation, having a task orientation, ensuring academic learning time, being clear, and exhibiting enthusiasm.

Pacing the Lesson

Pacing is the speed at which the lesson proceeds. It is the rhythm, the ebb and flow, of a lesson. Effective pacing is neither too slow nor too fast. Adjustments in the pace of the lesson are made as the need warrants. To pace a lesson effectively, you should not dwell too long on directions, should distribute papers in a timely and efficient manner, and should move from one activity to another smoothly and without interruption. Classrooms that lack effective pacing will drag at times or will move along at a pace where the students are unable to grasp the material. You should, however, recognize that it takes more time for students to mentally and physically transition from one activity to another than it does the teacher.

Use the following guidelines to pace a lesson effectively (Good & Brophy, 2008; Jones & Jones, 2016):

1. **Develop awareness of your own teaching tempo.** As you gain more experience in the classroom, you will be more aware of your own personal pace in the classroom. A good means of determining your pace is to audio- or videotape your performance. In this way, you will be able to determine how fast you talk, how you move around the classroom, and how much wait time you provide your students.

2. **Watch for nonverbal cues indicating that students are becoming puzzled or bored.** Monitor student attentiveness and then modify the pacing of the lesson as needed.

If high-achieving students are looking puzzled, they and perhaps most of the class may be lost. The content may be too complex or it is being covered too quickly. A good indication that your pacing is too slow is if students are becoming restless and inattentive—looking out the window or fiddling with materials on their desks. You might select several students to notice on a regular basis throughout the lesson as indicators of your pacing.

3. **Break activities up into short segments.** Many teachers go through an entire activity before beginning discussion or review. However, it is more effective to break the activities up into shorter segments and to ask questions or review these shorter segments rather than the entire activity.

4. **Provide short breaks for lessons that last longer than 30 minutes.** Long lessons can cause inattentiveness and disruptive behavior. A three- to five-minute break can allow the students to return fresh to the activity. These breaks can be short games related to the activity or a stand-up-and-stretch interlude. A brief activity where students can get up to mingle or just stand up and stretch can also provide enough of a break.

5. **Vary the instructional approach as well as the content of the instruction.** Students often become restless with only a single instructional approach. A lesson plan that incorporates several instructional strategies will result in better attentiveness.

6. **Avoid interrupting the flow of the lesson with numerous stops and starts.** *Jerkiness* is a term that refers to behaviors that interfere with the smooth flow of the lesson. This occurs when the teacher (a) interrupts an ongoing activity without warning and gives directions to begin another activity; (b) leaves one activity dangling in midair, begins another, only to return to the first; or (c) leaves one activity for another and never returns to the first activity. In such instances, students never experience closure to the activities they were engaged in prior to the switch. Sudden reversals of activities tend to leave students flustered over not completing the previous activity and unprepared to begin the new activity.

7. **Avoid slowdowns that interfere with the pace of the lesson.** *Slowdowns*, or delays in the momentum or pace of a class, can occur due to overdwelling or fragmentation. *Overdwelling* occurs when too much time is spent on directions or explanations. Overdwelling also occurs when the teacher becomes so enthralled with the details of the lesson or a prop being used for a demonstration that students lose sight of the main idea. For example, an English teacher may get so carried away describing the details of an author's life that the students barely have time to read the author's works. Another example is a science teacher who gets carried away describing the laboratory equipment so that the students have little time to conduct any experiments.

   Fragmentation is another form of slowdown in which the lesson is divided into such minute fragments that some of the students are left waiting and become bored. For example, the directions for an experiment may be broken down into such minute, simple parts that the students feel belittled, or an activity may be done by one row of students at a time, leaving the rest waiting.

8. **Provide a summary at the end of a lesson segment.** Rather than plan for a single summary at the end of a lesson, it might help the pacing of the lesson to provide a summary after each main point or activity. For example, students might be asked to write a one-sentence summary of each scene as the class reads a play orally.

Providing Smooth Transitions

Transitions are movements from one activity to another. A smooth transition allows one activity to flow into another without any breaks in the delivery of the lesson. Transitions that are not smooth create gaps in delivery.

Transition time can occur when (a) students remain at their seats and change from one subject to another; (b) they move from their seats to an activity in another part of the classroom; (c) they move from somewhere else in the classroom back to their seats; (d) they leave the classroom to go outside or to another part of the school building; or (e) they come back into the classroom from outside or another part of the building.

Disorder and misbehavior can arise during transition times. More disruptions occur during transitions (including hitting, yelling, and other inappropriate actions) than during non-transition time. There are several reasons why transitions can be problematic. First, you may have difficulty getting the students to finish an activity, especially if they are deeply engaged in it. Second, transitions are more loosely structured than instructional activities, and there typically is more freedom to socialize and move around the room. Third, students may "save up" problems or tensions and deal with them during the transition time. For example, a student may ask to use the restroom, complain to you about another student, or ask permission to get something from a locker. Finally, there may be delays in getting students started in the new activity.

To reduce the potential for disorder during transitions, you should prepare students for upcoming transitions, establish efficient transition routines, and clearly define the boundaries of lessons. V. F. Jones and Jones (2016) offer several suggestions for effective transitions:

1. **Arrange the classroom for efficient movement.** Arrange the classroom so you and the students can move freely without disturbing those who are working.

2. **Create and post a daily schedule and discuss any changes each morning.** Posting a daily schedule will aid in the elimination of confusion in the students.

3. **Have material ready for the next lesson.** Prepare and gather materials for the next lesson to ensure that class time is not taken and that activities flow smoothly.

4. **Do not relinquish students' attention until you have given clear instructions for the following activity.** All too often, teachers allow the class to become disruptive while they pause between activities or lessons to prepare for the next lesson. It requires considerable time and energy to regain students' attention.

5. **Do not do tasks that can be done by students.** Have students take responsibility for their own preparations for the next class session. This will enable you to monitor student actions.

6. **Move around the room and attend to individual needs.** By moving around the room, you will be able to notice any minor disturbances that might expand into major problems.

7. **Provide students with simple, step-by-step directions.** Clearly state exactly what you want your students to do during the time given for the transition.

8. **Remind students of key procedures associated with the upcoming lesson.** Reviewing standard procedures and discussing unique procedures for an upcoming activity help promote smooth transitions because students know what is expected of them.

9. **Develop transition activities.** After lunch or physical education, for example, students are excited and may not be ready for quieter work. Given this, you could choose structured transition activities to prepare the students for the next class session. These might include reading to students, discussing the daily schedule, having students write in a journal, or doing some type of activity that may not necessarily deal with the content of the next class session. After this transition time, they will likely be more ready to begin the next class session.

> **VOICES FROM THE CLASSROOM   Transitions Between Activities**
>
> **Carla Roman, kindergarten teacher (National Board Certified Teacher), Miami, Florida**
>
> After providing whole-class instruction, I often ask students to work in small groups. I have found it is useful to provide a break from their small-group work when they are getting tired or having trouble staying focused on what they are doing.
>
> Providing a break as a transition to another activity can take many forms. Sometimes, it may be just some time to rest. Other times, it may involve singing and asking the students to do certain actions. In this way, they are provided a "break" from what they are currently doing, and to them it seems like a game. Actually, it provides an opportunity to listen and to follow directions, and students are more ready to get back on task for the next activity.

Avoiding Satiation

Satiation means that students have had enough of something, and this may lead to boredom, restlessness, and off-task behavior. For example, students may enjoy seeing a video, writing a creative story, or working in pairs on a project. When those activities are used too often or for too much time, however, students will start to lose interest, become bored, and likely get off task. You need to guard against planning activities that will lead to satiation.

As Kounin (1970) reported in his classic research, there are three ways to avoid satiation. First, have students experience progress, which is the feeling they get when steadily moving toward some significant objective. Pacing and group focus help achieve this sense. To promote feelings of progress, you need to avoid dwelling on one topic too long. Second, provide variety as an effective way to avoid satiation. At the same time, classroom routines are necessary to preserve order and organization. You need to sense when enough is enough. Instructional variety helps invite inquisitiveness, excitement, and interest.

Third, select an appropriate degree of challenge in the students' academic work. Students do not tire of success if the success is a genuine test of their abilities and culminates in personally relevant accomplishments. When the challenge is sufficient to court and fortify the best efforts of students, satiation is seldom a problem.

Being Task Oriented

Task orientation has to do with your concern that all relevant material be covered and learned, as opposed to being mired in procedural matters or extraneous material. The more time dedicated to the task of teaching a specific topic, the greater the opportunity students have to learn. Task-oriented teachers provide an appropriate amount of time lecturing, asking questions, and engaging students in activities directly related to the material that is to be learned. Students have higher rates of achievement in classrooms of task-oriented teachers.

Task-oriented teachers are goal oriented, and they plan instructional strategies and activities that support these goals. In addition, task-oriented teachers have a high, but realistic, set of expectations for their students. To be task oriented in the classroom, you should (a) develop unit and lesson plans that reflect the curriculum; (b) handle administrative and clerical interruptions efficiently; (c) stop or prevent misbehavior with a minimum of class disruption; (d) select the most appropriate instructional model for objectives being taught; and (e) establish cycles of review, feedback, and testing.

Ensuring Academic Learning Time

Academic learning time is the amount of time students are successfully engaged in learning activities. However, the amount of time that students are actively engaged, or on task, can vary

■ **WHAT WOULD YOU DECIDE?**   Having Smooth Transitions

Assume that you have planned a lesson in which your students view a video as a whole class, then have small-group discussions about the video, and finally individually outline some content and answer some questions from the textbook. Thus, there are several transitions in which students shift to a different type of activity.

1. What information and directions might you provide at the start to promote smooth transitions between the lesson segments?

2. What might you do during the lesson to guide students to the next lesson segment with a smooth transition?

greatly across and within classrooms. On the one hand, low-achieving students often go off task due to frustrations about not understanding class material. High-achieving students, on the other hand, tend to go off task after they have completed their assigned work. Therefore, you should ensure that all students can be successfully engaged in classroom tasks while also ensuring that high-achieving students are engaged throughout the lesson. Provide feedback and correctives to students who need assistance, and at the same time, monitor the rate of student progress through the lesson.

For new material that students have not yet mastered, expect a lower success rate initially but set a goal of higher success rates as students receive feedback on their performance and gain confidence. As a general rule, students should have a success rate of approximately 80% on most initial tasks. The rate of success should be somewhat higher when students are engaged in independent work, such as homework or independent seatwork. The goal is to ensure that students are given meaningful tasks to complete, are given feedback and correctives when needed, and are ultimately able successfully to complete all assigned tasks.

Being Clear

Clarity refers to the precision of your communication to your students regarding the desired behavior. Clarity in teaching helps students understand better, work more accurately, and be more successful. Effective teachers exhibit a high degree of clarity by providing very clear and explicit directions, instructions, questions, and expectations. If you are constantly asked to repeat questions, directions, and explanations, or if your students do not understand your expectations, you are not exhibiting clarity in your instructional behavior.

Clear directions, instructions, and expectations need to be given. Students then know what is expected of them and can act accordingly as they work on classroom activities, assignments, and other tasks. If you are not very clear when giving directions, for example, the student may not complete the assignment in the way you intended, may become confused, and may need additional time and attention later to complete the assignment in the manner intended.

To be clear in the classroom, (a) inform the learners of the objective; (b) provide learners with advance organizers; (c) check for task-relevant prior learning at the beginning of the lesson; (d) give directions slowly and distinctly; (e) know the ability levels of students and teach to those levels; (f) use examples, illustrations, and demonstrations to explain and clarify; and (g) provide a review or summary at the end of each lesson.

Exhibiting Enthusiasm

Enthusiasm is an expression of excitement and intensity. It is quite obvious that a teacher who is enthusiastic and vibrant is more entertaining to observe than an unenthusiastic teacher. However, teacher enthusiasm has also been related to higher student achievement (Good & Brophy, 2008). Enthusiasm has two important dimensions: (a) interest and involvement with the subject matter; and (b) vigor and physical dynamism. Enthusiastic teachers are often described as stimulating, dynamic, expressive, and energetic. Their behavior suggests that they are committed to the students and to the subject matter. While teachers often expect students to be interested in *what* they say, students more often react to *how* enthusiastically it is said.

Enthusiasm can be conveyed in a variety of ways. These include the use of animated gestures, eye contact, voice inflection, and movement around the room. A teacher who is enthusiastic in the classroom often manages to develop enthusiastic students. Constant, highly enthusiastic actions are not necessary and, in fact, may be counterproductive. Instead, a variety of enthusiastic actions, ranging from low to high degrees of enthusiasm, would be appropriate.

The Ending of a Lesson

As stated earlier, an effective lesson has three important sections: a beginning, a middle, and an end. All three sections must be planned and implemented effectively if a lesson is to be successful. Simply ending a lesson when the bell rings or when you have covered the planned material is not appropriate. In such cases, students are not given the opportunity to place the lesson in a context with other related lessons or are not permitted to ask questions that might clarify a misunderstood point from the lesson. Providing a summary is imperative for a successful lesson. Furthermore, students need time at the end of the lesson to get ready to leave the classroom.

Providing Closure to Part of a Lesson

Closure refers to actions or statements that are designed to bring a lesson presentation to an appropriate conclusion. Closure has three purposes (Shostak, 2014):

1. **Draw attention to the end of a lesson segment or the lesson itself.** Often students need to be cued that they have arrived at an important segment of the lesson or that it is time to wrap things up. They might be cued with a statement that it is time to summarize key concepts.

2. **Help organize student learning.** It is the teacher's responsibility to relate the many pieces of the lesson to the whole. Some students are able to see this by themselves while others need assistance. To accomplish this purpose, you might provide a diagram, illustration, outline, or other type of summary indicating how all the content of the lesson is related.

3. **Reinforce the major points to be learned.** You might emphasize or highlight certain concepts at this point. The major objective is to help the student retain the information presented in the lesson for future use.

   Closure is important because students instinctively structure information into patterns that make sense to them. If a learning experience is left with some uncertainties, students may draw inaccurate conclusions as they create their own patterns of understanding from the material, thus detracting from future learning.

■ WHAT WOULD YOU DECIDE?   Providing Closure

Let's assume that you are teaching a history lesson in which a series of significant dates have been identified and related events have been discussed. You have planned for three to four minutes for closure at the end of the lesson to help students organize their learning and to reinforce the major points in the lesson.

1. How might you bring closure by helping students organize their learning and see how all the dates and events are related?

2. How might you involve students in this closure?

The second and third purposes involve summarizing, which is addressed later. The time at the end of a lesson segment or the lesson itself can be used to make homework assignments. Between lesson segments, students may be given 5–10 minutes to start the homework assignment while you move around the room to answer questions that might arise.

Summarizing the Lesson

Providing a *summary* of the main points of a lesson can help students gain a better idea of the content and clarify any misunderstandings. You should plan to stop the lesson several minutes before the bell rings to begin the summation. Make sure that you have the attention of all students before the summary begins. You should avoid merely reiterating the content covered during the lesson. Ask several questions that encourage the students to relate key aspects of the lesson or to evaluate key points. Also ask their opinions about what they believe are the key points.

To add interest and variety, vary the way that the lesson summary is conducted. Some days may involve simply a series of questions for students. On other days, you may ask several students to go to the chalkboard to solve a problem and discuss the thought process involved. A game format could be used as a means of summary, such as questions out of a hat or a "Trivial Pursuit" type of approach. Several creative approaches could offer the desired variety of lesson summaries.

The summary should be used to determine if the students have grasped the main ideas of the lesson. For example, your summary might reveal that several students do not understand the key concepts of a math lesson. It would be foolish to teach the next math lesson as though all students understand the concept. Therefore, you can use the information gathered during the summary to adjust the next day's lesson plan.

Getting Ready to Leave

At the end of the lesson, middle, junior high, or senior high school students usually need to leave the classroom and go to their next class. The bell will ring at the end of the class period and students will have just a few minutes to get to their next class in another room in the building.

You should plan to complete all instruction and lesson summary by the end of the class period so students are not delayed in moving to the next class. You should not teach right up to the bell because time needs to be allowed for several other events.

First, you must allow time for students to return any books, supplies, or materials to the appropriate locations. Also, students need time to throw away any scrap paper and to straighten up the classroom. They need time to put away their own books, papers, pencils, or other materials before leaving. You may plan to reserve one to four minutes at the end of a lesson to allow sufficient time for these final actions to be completed before the bell rings. Students then should be dismissed on time. You need to schedule this time when planning lessons.

Managing Student Work

Students prepare homework and seatwork as a regular part of their instruction. To effectively manage this student work, guidelines are offered here for managing seatwork effectively, collecting assignments and monitoring their completion, maintaining records of student work, managing the paperwork, and giving students feedback. It is helpful to develop a plan to organize your instructional records, grading and assessment records, classroom management records, parental contact records, and special needs and accommodation records.

Managing Seatwork Effectively

Seatwork involves students working on assignments during class that provide practice or review of previously presented material. Students spend hundreds of hours during a school year doing seatwork privately at their desks. It is imperative that you structure seatwork so that it is done effectively while enabling students to experience a high rate of success.

Guidelines for successfully implementing seatwork in the classroom come from a variety of sources (Jones & Jones, 2016; Weinstein & Novodvorsky, 2015; Weinstein & Romano, 2019). The following 12 recommendations represent a synthesis from these sources:

1. Recognize that seatwork is intended to practice or review previously presented material. It is not suited for students to learn new material.

2. Devote no more time to seatwork than is allocated to content development activities.

3. Give clear instruction—explanations, questions, and feedback—and sufficient practice before the students begin their seatwork. Having to provide lengthy explanations during seatwork is troublesome for both you and the student. In addition to procedural directions, explain why the activities are being done and how to do the seatwork.

4. Work through the first few problems of the seatwork together with the students before having them continue independently. This provides a model for completing the work and provides an opportunity for the students to ask questions for clarification about the content or procedures.

5. Decide if you will allow talking during seatwork. It is often desirable to start out with no talking during seatwork to have students work alone. After a month or two, teachers sometimes allow students to talk quietly with others to seek or provide help. Clarify when quiet talking is allowed.

6. Circulate from student to student during seatwork, actively explaining, observing, asking questions, and giving feedback. Monitoring students to provide this positive and corrective feedback is very important.

7. Determine how students will seek your help. When students are working at their seats and need help, ask them to raise their hands. You can then go to them or signal them to come to you at an appropriate time.

8. Determine when students can get out of their seats. To eliminate unnecessary wandering around the room during seatwork, decide when and for what purpose students can get out of their seats. For example, students may get supplies, sharpen pencils, or turn in papers only when necessary.

9. Have short contacts with individual students (i.e., 30 seconds or less).

10. Break seatwork into short segments rather than one long time slot. Rather than having one lengthy presentation of content followed by an extended period of seatwork, break up instruction into a number of segments, followed by brief seatwork after each segment.

11. Arrange seats to facilitate monitoring the students (e.g., face both small groups and independently working students).

12. Establish a routine to use during seatwork activity that prescribes what students will do when they have completed the exercises. Students may complete an additional enrichment assignment for extra credit, or they may use the time for free reading or to work on assignments from other classes.

■ CLASSROOM CASE STUDY Managing Lesson Delivery

Logan Reynolds's twelfth-grade English class just finished reading George Orwell's *1984*, one of his favorite books to teach. The students participated in panel discussions and debates, and the desks were arranged in a circle to promote discussion. Mr. Reynolds encouraged lively conversations by asking probing questions and engaged his students in role-playing and simulation activities. His animated nature during class discussions motivated the students to become actively involved. Students also responded to a number of journal prompts at the beginning of each class session just prior to discussion. These prompts required students to reflect on the underlying ideas presented in their readings and to make connections to present-day concerns.

The class next moved to a unit on Shakespeare. Although Mr. Reynolds was not particularly interested in the works of Shakespeare, he understood the importance of introducing his class to classics such as *Macbeth*. Since Mr. Reynolds was concerned about the complexity of Shakespeare's works, he decided that lecturing about the material was the best way to promote student learning, and the desks were put into rows for this approach. As a result, student interactions were minimal, with no room for debate, role-playing, and simulation games. Mr. Reynolds felt those activities would only complicate study of an already obscure literary subject. Mr. Reynolds conducted all of his class meetings in a similar fashion, asking students to read a certain number of pages for homework and be prepared for the lectures, with only brief opportunities for discussion. Mr. Reynolds became concerned when his students were not very engaged in the brief class discussions and seemed to lose focus and interest.

Focus Questions

1. What factors contributed to the high level of student involvement in the unit on *1984*? To the low level of student involvement in the unit on Shakespeare?

2. Based on what you know about managing lesson delivery and other instructional factors, what suggestions do you have for Mr. Reynolds when teaching the unit on Shakespeare?

Collecting Assignments and Monitoring Their Completion

Whether it is homework or seatwork, you need to establish a process for collecting assignments and monitoring their completion.

- **Institute a regular procedure for collecting assignments.** Papers can be collected during class by asking students to pass them in a given direction until you have all papers in your hands. As an alternative, students may be asked to place their completed assignments in a certain basket, tray, or drop box at a designated time during class. Once students know this collection procedure, assignments can be gathered quickly and efficiently.

- **Have a procedure for grouping papers by subject or class session.** In an elementary classroom, assignments on a variety of subjects may be submitted during the day. It is useful to have a separate drop box for each subject. In this way, only papers of a certain subject are in a drop box, and you don't need to spend time sorting through all the papers to pick out just the math papers or just the social studies papers. Similarly, middle and secondary classrooms should have a different drop box for each class period. Thus, students in the fourth hour would place their assignments in the box for their class period.

- **Keep a record of whose papers have been turned in.** If you evaluate the papers quickly, you will know who has or who has not submitted the assignments when you record the grades in your gradebook. If there is a delay in grading, you may have a checklist to record who has submitted the assignments. In this way, you can follow up with students who did not submit the materials. Some teachers also have students keep an assignment notebook for homework and seatwork to record the items that were due and what was turned in.

Maintaining Records of Student Work

Records of student progress and completion are entered in your gradebook. For elementary classes, you may organize your gradebook by having a separate section for each subject area. The date and description of the assignment can be entered at the top as a subject heading, and each students' scores can be placed in the appropriate column on the line for his or her name. Similarly, middle level and secondary teachers can have separate sections of the gradebook for each of their class sections. It is useful to establish a coding system to indicate a student absence or other information related to the assignment.

Gradebook software can be used to record the submission of assignments and the scores that students received. Progress reports for individual students can be easily prepared, and these are useful to show the students and parents.

Managing the Paperwork

Homework and seatwork involve a lot of paperwork, and it is easy to become overwhelmed by the volume of papers you deal with on a regular basis. Here are five guidelines to effectively manage your handling of the papers:

1. **Assess, record, and return assignments quickly.** Make a commitment to assess and return all assignments in a day or two. Delays in your return of assignments often lead to a backlog of assignments to be graded. That situation puts a lot of pressure on you, and it is not fair to the students because they need to receive feedback as quickly as possible.

2. **Be realistic about your grading capabilities.** Plan sufficient time in your schedule to assess and record the assignments. If you are making frequent assignments and getting behind in the grading, it is time to reassess your use of assignments. Strategically, space out the assignments that are to be graded. Long assignments take time to assess. Instead, short and specific assignments may be effective in monitoring student learning, and they take less time to assess.

3. **Recognize that every seatwork assignment does not need to have a grade.** Every subject or every class period does not need an assignment that must be graded by you every day. Therefore, you do not need to receive papers each day. Students can be assessed in class and given feedback in various ways without asking them to submit the paperwork to you to be assessed. For example, you can assign seatwork and then check each student's work and give feedback during class.

4. **Institute a system for coding the papers for each subject or class section.** As mentioned previously, have a system for collecting assignments from your students. Using color-coded folders for each subject or each class period can be a helpful technique for organizing the paperwork.

5. **Have a predetermined way to return papers to the students.** When returning papers to students, keep them in labeled folders by the subject or class period. You could organize the papers by rows or groups to facilitate the return. Plan a certain way to return the papers each time. You may choose to use student helpers in returning the papers.

■ WHAT WOULD YOU DECIDE?   **Giving Students Feedback**

You regularly use seatwork in your classroom, and you provide prompt feedback. However, several students often have difficulty with the seatwork, often do not perform well, and need more feedback and guidance. There seems to be a divide in the class—those who get it and those who do not.

1. If you shifted to providing more feedback during class while the students are working on the assignments, what

are some ways you might provide feedback with that new approach?

2. How might you provide students with more immediate feedback rather than having them wait to receive the graded assignment back from you the next day?

3. How might you use other students in the class to provide this needed guidance and feedback?

Giving Students Feedback

You will assign seatwork and homework to help students learn, and it is important that students receive feedback about this work. Follow these guidelines for giving students feedback:

- **Provide frequent and regular feedback.** Students need fairly immediate feedback about their performance so they have an opportunity to correct any errors in their knowledge or skills before moving ahead to new material. Thus, plan for ways for students to demonstrate their learning and for ways that you can provide frequent and regular feedback about their learning.

- **Develop ways to provide feedback to students in class.** To provide prompt feedback and to avoid assigning homework every day, develop ways to provide feedback to students after instruction and practice have taken place in class. For example, you could have students work on problems at the board and give feedback, show answers on an overhead screen, or have students help review one another's work.

- **Take corrective actions promptly with students who do not perform well.** Don't wait until several poor assignments have been turned in or until it is time to submit the report card grade before meeting with a student who is not performing well. Some students may need more assistance to learn the content, and this feedback and assistance should come early without delay.

MAJOR CONCEPTS

1. The degree of structure in a lesson and the manner in which students are grouped for instruction need to be taken into account when managing instruction and promoting appropriate behavior.

2. Students are more likely to stay on task when they are held academically accountable for their work.

3. Plan for motivating students to learn by developing a comprehensive approach to motivation, adjusting motivational strategies to your instructional situation, and building motivational issues into all levels of your instructional planning.

4. When beginning a lesson, teachers need to take attendance, solicit attention, provide daily review, provide a set induction, introduce lesson objectives, distribute materials, and give clear, focused directions.

5. When conducting a lesson, effective teachers pace the lesson appropriately, provide smooth transitions, avoid satiation, have a task orientation, ensure academic learning time, and exhibit clarity and enthusiasm.

6. An effective teacher ends a lesson with a summary of important concepts and allows students time to get ready to leave the room after the lesson.

7. Managing student work involves managing seatwork effectively, collecting assignments and monitoring their completion, maintaining records of student work, managing the paperwork, and giving students feedback.

DISCUSSION/REFLECTIVE QUESTIONS

1. Why would a teacher decide to use a variety of whole-group, small-group, and independent work for instruction? Which type of instructional approach did you prefer as a learner?

2. How might the selection of accountability procedures be affected by differences in grade level and subject areas?

3. How do students benefit when a teacher begins a lesson by clearly introducing the lesson objectives? How are students affected if a teacher does not introduce the lesson objectives?

4. Recall several examples when your teachers were not clear in providing directions, instructions, or expectations. What effect did this lack of clarity have on you as a student?

5. From your own school experiences, what approaches to review did you find the most useful? What are the merits of using different approaches for review?

6. How did your K–12 teachers collect assignments done in class? Turned in as homework? Which approaches were most efficient and effective?

SUGGESTED ACTIVITIES

1. Look at Table 8.2 concerning motivational strategies for instruction, and then select a lesson topic you likely will teach. Describe how you will apply at least five items in that table to motivate your students during the lesson.

2. Ask several teachers to describe the various ways that they begin lessons and end lessons. Do they have standard procedures for the beginning and ending of lessons that they find effective?

3. List a number of approaches that you could use to summarize a lesson. Include some strategies where you would direct the review, as well as some approaches where students might take the lead in their review.

4. Talk with several teachers about the procedures they use to manage seatwork, collect and monitor assignments, maintain records, and manage paperwork. Then outline the ways that you will handle these responsibilities in your own classroom.

FURTHER READING

Burden, P. R., & Byrd, D. M. (2019). *Methods for effective teaching* (8th ed.). Boston, MA: Pearson.
Provides an overview of all aspects of teaching methods, including topics such as planning, classroom management, instructional strategies, and assessment. Includes content on lesson delivery.

Dean, C. B., Hubbell, E. R., Pitler, H., & Stone, B. (2012). *Classroom instruction that works: Research-based strategies for increasing student achievement* (2nd ed.). Alexandria, VA: Association for Supervision and Curriculum Development.
Provides a thorough yet concise review of proven instructional strategies to promote student learning. Examines homework and practice, cooperative learning, cues, questions, advance organizers, summarizing, and other strategies.

Marzano, R. J. (2017). *The new art and science of teaching*. Alexandria, VA: Association for Supervision and Curriculum Development.
Provides research-based guidelines for many aspects of lesson delivery, planning, management, student involvement, and assessment.

Thompson, J. G. (2018). *The first-year teacher's survival guide* (4th ed.). San Francisco, CA: Jossey-Bass.
Offers recommendations about many aspects of lesson delivery and related issues such as planning, instruction, classroom climate, management, and behavior.

© Lisa F. Young/iStockphoto

Responding to Inappropriate Behavior

CHAPTER OUTLINE

CHAPTER OBJECTIVES

This chapter provides information that will help you:

- Describe the principle of least intervention.

- Identify ways that situational assistance can be provided.

- Apply mild and moderate responses to misbehavior.

- Avoid certain disciplinary practices.

- Recognize the limitations of punishment and guidelines for its effective use.

- Identify ways to address chronic misbehaviors.

- Confront bullying.

Even with an effective management system in place, students may lose interest in a lesson and get off task. You must be prepared to respond with appropriate strategies to restore order. How should you respond to students who are simply off task? What options do you have when a student misbehaves? What are some practices to avoid? What are some guidelines in the use of punishment? How can chronic misbehavior be addressed? How can bullying be confronted? These issues are addressed in this chapter.

A Three-Step Response Plan

The teacher must decide when and how to intervene when students are off task or are misbehaving. An *intervention* is an action taken by the teacher that is intended to stop the disruptive actions and return the student to the academic activities.

Intervention decisions are typically based on the teacher's knowledge of who is misbehaving, what the misbehavior is, and when it occurs. Decisions about the type of intervention may depend on the student's history of inappropriate behavior. However, you should not automatically jump to conclusions if an incident involves a student with a history of behavior problems. It is helpful to discuss the problem with the student to clarify the problem from both your perspective and the student's before considering possible interventions.

The *principle of least intervention* states that when dealing with routine classroom behavior, misbehaviors should be corrected with the simplest, least intrusive intervention that will work (Slavin, 2018). If the least intrusive intervention does not work, then you move up to a more intrusive approach. The main goal is to handle the misbehavior in an effective manner that avoids unnecessarily disrupting the lesson. To the extent possible, the lesson should continue while the misbehavior is handled.

How do you apply this principle of least intervention? When you notice students starting to lose interest in the lesson or beginning to get off task, you can provide situational assistance—these are actions to help the student cope with the situation and keep the student on task. Then if the student is still off task, you can select mild responses to get the student back on task. If mild responses are not effective, next you can use moderate responses. Based on the principle of least intervention, this three-step response plan is displayed in Table 9.1.

■ TABLE 9.1   A Three-Step Response Plan to Misbehavior Using the Principle of Least Intervention

Teacher response	Step 1: Provide situational assistance	Step 2: Use mild responses	Step 3: Use moderate responses
Purpose	To help the student cope with the instructional situation and keep the student on task	To take nonpunitive actions to get the student back on task	To remove desired stimuli to decrease unwanted behavior
Sample actions	• Remove distracting objects. • Provide support with routines. • Reinforce appropriate behaviors. • Boost student interest. • Provide cues. • Help students over hurdles. • Redirect the behavior. • Alter the lesson. • Provide nonpunitive time-out. • Modify the classroom environment.	**Nonverbal responses** • Ignore the behavior. • Use nonverbal signals. • Stand near the student. • Touch the student. **Verbal responses** • Call on the student during the lesson. • Use humor. • Send an I-message. • Use positive phrasing. • Remind students of the rules. • Give students choices. • Ask, "What should you be doing?" • Give a verbal reprimand.	**Logical consequences** • Withdraw privileges. • Change the seat assignment. • Have the student write reflections on the problem. • Place student in a time-out. • Hold student for detention. • Contact the family. • Have the student visit the principal.

Situational Assistance

Students sometimes pause from the instructional task to look out the window, daydream, fiddle with a comb or other object, or simply take a brief mental break from the work. In these examples, students are not misbehaving—they are simply off task for a short time. You should take steps to draw students back into the lesson and to keep students on task.

Some inappropriate behaviors are of such short duration and are so insignificant that they can be safely ignored. Your use of situational assistance might be considered a "forgiveness step" for the student by recognizing that the off-task behavior is minor or fleeting and by allowing the student to get back on task without penalty.

To communicate to the student that you have noticed off-task behavior, you should first provide *situational assistance*—these are actions designed to help the students cope with the instructional situation and to keep them on task or to get them back on task before problems worsen. Problem behaviors thus can be stopped early before they escalate or involve other students.

If students remain off task after situational assistance has been provided, move on to *mild responses*. These nonverbal and verbal nonpunitive responses are designed to get the student back on task. The continuum of responses to misbehavior (see Table 9.1) illustrates that situational assistance is the starting point when dealing with off-task behavior. The following techniques can be used to provide situational assistance to help get students back on task.

1. **Remove distracting objects.** Students sometimes bring objects to school that may be distracting, such as combs, key, or magazines. Suggestions regarding cell phones are found in "Dealing with Chronic Misbehaviors." When you see that such an object is keeping the students from the assigned tasks, simply walk over to the student and collect the object. The student should be quietly informed that the object can be picked up after class. Be kind and firm; no discussion is necessary. Inform students that they should store such objects in an appropriate place before school.

2. **Provide support with routines.** Students appreciate and often find comfort in knowing what is going to happen during the class period or during the day. It is helpful to announce and post

the daily schedule. Even for a single lesson, students often appreciate knowing at the start what activities are planned for the lesson. Knowing the schedule provides students with a sense of security and direction. Routines for entering and leaving the classroom, distributing classroom papers and materials, and participating in group work contribute to this sense of security.

3. **Reinforce appropriate behaviors.** Students who have followed the directions can be praised. This communicates to the student who is off task what is expected. A statement such as, "I'm pleased to see that Juan has his notebook ready for today's lesson," communicates to others what is expected. Appropriate behavior is reinforced while giving a signal to students who are off task. While commonly used in elementary classrooms, this approach may be considered a little juvenile by middle and secondary students.

4. **Boost student interest.** Student interest may wane in time as the lesson proceeds. You should express interest in the student's work when he or she shows signs of losing interest or being bored. Offer to help, noting how much work has been completed, noting how well done the completed part of the task is, or discussing the task. These actions can help bring the student back on task. Interest boosting is often needed when students do individual or small-group class work.

5. **Provide cues.** Sometimes, all the students are asked to do one thing, such as to prepare their materials or to clean up at the end of class, and cues can be given in these cases. *Cues* are signals that it is time for a selected behavior. For example, you may close the door at the start of class as a cue that instruction is about to begin and that everyone is expected to have all materials ready. The lights could be flipped or a bell sounded to signal time to begin cleanup or to finish small-group work. You can select an appropriate cue and explain its use to the students. This conveys behavioral expectations and encourages constructive on-task behavior.

6. **Help students over hurdles.** Students who are experiencing difficulty with a specific task need help in overcoming that problem—help over a hurdle—to keep them on task. Hurdle helping may consist of encouraging words from you, offering to assist with a specific task, or making available additional materials or equipment. In this way, you help before the student gives up on the assignment or becomes disruptive.

7. **Redirect the behavior.** When students show signs of losing interest, you can ask them to answer a question, do a problem, or read as a means of drawing them back into the lesson. Students should be treated as if they were paying attention and should be reinforced if they respond appropriately. It is important not to embarrass or ridicule students by saying that they would have been able to answer the question if they had been paying attention. Simply by asking a content-related question, you will show students that you are trying to draw them back into the lesson. Redirecting student behavior back into the lesson discourages off-task behavior.

■ WHAT WOULD YOU DECIDE? Using Cues or Signals

Imagine that your students are working in cooperative learning groups on a four-day project. When they come into the room, they immediately go to their groups and start work. On some days and during some of the class sessions, you need to get the attention of all students so that you can give some additional information.

1. How can you use a cue to indicate to students that you want them to stop their work momentarily and to give you their attention at that time?

2. Identify some ways to give a cue to the students indicating that it is time to finish their work and to prepare to leave the class.

8. **Alter the lesson.** Lessons sometimes do not go as well as you would like, and students may lose interest in the lesson for a variety of reasons. The lesson needs to be altered in some way when students are seen daydreaming, writing notes to friends, yawning, stretching, or moving around in their seats. When altering the lesson, select a different type of activity from the one that has proven unsuccessful. For example, if a whole-class discussion proves unsuccessful, you might have students work in pairs on a related issue that still deals with the lesson's objectives. In your initial planning, take student interests and abilities into account and provide a variety of activities in each lesson.

9. **Provide nonpunitive time-out.** Students who become frustrated, agitated, or fatigued may get off task and become disruptive. When you notice this happening, provide a nonpunitive time-out. A *time-out* is a period of time that the student is away from the instructional situation to calm down and reorganize his or her thoughts. The student then returns to the task with a fresh perspective. When a time-out is needed, you can ask the student to run an errand, help you with something, go get a drink, or do some other task not related to the instructional activity.

10. **Modify the classroom environment.** The classroom environment itself may contribute to off-task behavior. The arrangement of desks, tables, instructional materials, and other items in the classroom may give rise to inefficient traffic patterns or limited views of the instructional areas. Other factors include the boundaries between areas for quiet student and group projects and access to supplies. Once misbehavior develops, you may need to separate the students or change the setting in some way. Examine the disturbance and identify the element that contributes to it.

Mild Responses

Students may misbehave even after you have developed a system of rules and procedures, provided a supportive instructional environment, and given situational assistance to get misbehaving students back on task. Minor infractions of rules may be considered behavioral interruptions, including actions such as talking when another student is talking, not sitting when asked, throwing harmless objects, using an unauthorized electronic device, or disrupting a lesson in some manner. In these cases, mild responses should be used to correct the student's behavior.

VOICES FROM THE CLASSROOM   Start with Small Steps

Cindy Zepeda, high school English/language arts teacher, Fort Worth, Texas

Whenever students are off task or misbehaving, I prefer a subtle approach to correcting behavior whenever possible. Standing near a student will sometimes take care of a problem, or gently tapping on their desk as I walk by. If that doesn't work, I'll give a verbal cue. From there, I escalate to warnings about actions that might be taken such as changing seats, making a phone call to their home, or emailing their coach.

At that stage, I usually have a hallway conference with the student. I always start these with, "What's going on?" in an effort to find out factors that might be contributing to the student's behavior. Sometimes the students don't know why they're acting out, or they know but don't trust me enough to say, and I respect that. Sometimes the cause is easy to fix with a snack or a sympathetic ear. Sometimes I'm very direct about what they need to do. But the bottom line is always that the work gets done.

My students and I start each day fresh. We learn from yesterday's mistakes, but we don't hold on to them. No matter how much a student misbehaved yesterday, today he can be a superstar.

Mild responses are nonpunitive ways to deal with misbehavior while providing guidance for appropriate behavior. Nonverbal and verbal mild responses are meant to stop the off-task behavior and to restore order. The three-step response plan shown in Table 9.1 illustrates the movement to more directive responses if situational assistance is not successful.

Nonverbal Responses

Even with situational assistance, students may get off task. Nonverbal responses are taken as a nonpunitive means to get the student back on task. *Nonverbal responses* may include ignoring the behavior, nonverbal signals, standing near the student, and touching the student. These approaches are taken in increasing order of teacher involvement and control.

1. **Ignore the behavior.** Intentionally ignoring minor misbehavior is sometimes the best course of action as a means to weaken the behavior. This is based on the reinforcement principle called *extinction*; that is, if you ignore a behavior and withhold reinforcement, the behavior will lessen and ultimately disappear. Minor misbehaviors that might be ignored are pencil tapping, body movements, hand waving, book dropping, calling out an answer instead of raising a hand, interrupting the teacher, whispering, and so on. Behaviors designed to get your attention or that of classmates are likely candidates for extinction or ignoring the behavior.

   There are limitations to ignoring the behavior. One risk is that students may conclude that you are not aware of what is happening, and they may continue the behavior. Hostile or aggressive behaviors may be too dangerous to ignore.

2. **Use nonverbal signals.** A nonverbal signal can be used to communicate to the disrupting student that the behavior is not appropriate. Signals must be directed at the student. They let the student know that the behavior is inappropriate and that it is time to get back to work. Nonverbal signals may include making eye contact with the student who is writing a note, shaking a hand or finger to indicate not to do some inappropriate action, holding a hand up to stop a student's calling out, or giving "the teacher look." These actions should be done in a businesslike manner. You need to move to the next level of intervention if these disruptive behaviors persist.

3. **Stand near the student.** Using your physical presence near the disruptive student to help him or her get back on task is *proximity control*. This is warranted at times when you can't get the student's attention to send a signal because he or she is so engrossed in an inappropriate action. For example, a student may be reading something other than class-related material or may be writing a note. While doing this, the student may not even look up at you. As a result, signals will not work. While conducting the lesson, walk around the room and approach the student's desk. The student will then likely notice your presence and put the material away without a word being spoken.

■ WHAT WOULD YOU DECIDE?   Using Nonverbal Responses

Students are working in small groups on an activity, and you notice a group in which two students are off task. They are not misbehaving or causing disruption; they just are not working on the activity.

1. How can you respond nonverbally to get these two students back on task? What factors might affect your decision on the particular method?

2. At a later time, you are making a presentation to the whole class when you notice two other students off task. What nonverbal responses might you make in that situation?

Some proximity control techniques are somewhat subtle, such as walking toward the student, while other approaches such as standing near the student's desk are more direct. If students do not respond to proximity control, you need to move to a more directive level of intervention.

4. **Touch the student.** Without any verbal exchange, you may place a hand on the student's shoulder in an effort to achieve calm, or take the student's hand and escort the student back to his or her seat. *Touch control* involves mild, nonaggressive physical contact that is used to get the student on task. It communicates that you disapprove of the action. Talk to your principal to be certain you understand the guidelines and legal considerations of appropriate touching.

When deciding whether and how to use touch control, you may take into account the circumstances of the behavior and the characteristics of students. Students who are angry or visibly upset sometimes do not want to be touched, and some do not want to be touched at any time. How well touch will be received depends on where it occurs and how long it lasts. A touch on the back, hand, arm, or shoulder is acceptable to many students, whereas touch to the face, neck, leg, chest, or other more personal area is often unacceptable. Brief touch is considered acceptable; the longer the touch is, the more it becomes unacceptable.

Verbal Responses

Although nonverbal mild responses may be effective, verbal responses can be used as nonpunitive, mild responses to misbehavior. Their purpose is to get the student back on task with limited disruption and intervention. Various verbal responses are described as follows.

1. **Call on the student during the lesson.** You can recapture a misbehaving student's attention by using his or her name in the lesson, such as, "Now, in this next example, suppose that Kimberly had three polygons that she. . . ." You can then ask a question of the student to recapture his or her attention. Calling on the student in these ways allows you to communicate that you know what is going on and to capture his or her attention without citing the misbehavior. If you call on students in these ways only when they misbehave, they will sense that you are just waiting to catch them misbehaving, and this strategy will backfire by creating resentment.

2. **Use humor.** Humor can be used as a gentle reminder to students to correct their behavior. Humor directed at the situation or even at yourself can defuse tension that might be created due to the misbehavior. It can depersonalize the situation and thus help resolve the problem. You must be careful that the humor is not sarcastic. *Sarcasm* includes statements that are directed at correcting or making fun of the student; these statements are intended to criticize or embarrass the student. Instead, humor is directed at or makes fun of the situation or the teacher. The student may then reconsider his or her actions and then get back on task.

3. **Send an I-message.** An *I-message* is a statement you make to a misbehaving student that prompts appropriate behavior without giving a direct command (Gordon, 2003). An I-message has three parts: (a) a brief description of the misbehavior; (b) a description of its effects on you or other students; and (c) a description of your feelings about the effects. For example, you might say, "When you tap your pen on the desk during the test, it makes a lot of noise and I am concerned that it might distract other students." I-messages are intended to help students recognize that their behavior has consequences for other students and that you have genuine feelings about the actions. Since I-messages leave the decision about changing the behavior up to the student, they are likely to promote a sense of responsibility.

4. **Use positive phrasing.** *Positive phrasing* is used when inappropriate off-task behavior allows you to highlight positive outcomes for appropriate behavior. This usually takes the form, "When you do X (behave in a particular appropriate way), then you can do Y (a positive outcome)." For example, when a student is out of her seat, you might say, "Renee, when you return to your seat, then it will be your turn to participate in the activity." Through the use of positive phrasing, you redirect students from disruptive to appropriate behavior by simply stating the positive outcomes.

5. **Remind students of the rules.** Each classroom needs to have a set of rules that govern student behaviors, along with a set of consequences for breaking them. When students see that consequences of misbehavior are in fact delivered, reminders of the rules can help them get back on task because they want to avoid the consequences. When one student is poking another student, for example, you might say, "Delores, the classroom rules state that students must keep their hands and feet to themselves." This reminder often ends the misbehavior because the student does not want the consequence. If the inappropriate behavior continues, you must deliver the consequence; otherwise, the reminder will be of little value because students will recognize that there is no follow-through.

6. **Give students choices.** Some students feel defensive when confronted about their misbehavior. As a result, you can give them choices about resolving the problem. This allows the student to feel that he or she settled the problem without appearing to back down. All of the choices that you give to the student should lead to resolution of the problem. If a student is talking to another nearby student, you might say, "Harvey, you can turn back in your seat and get back to your project, or you can take the empty seat at the end of the row." In this way, Harvey has a choice, but the result is that he gets back to work in his seat or in the seat at the end of the row.

7. **Ask, "What should you be doing?"** Glasser (1998a) proposes that teachers ask disruptive students questions in an effort to direct them back to appropriate behavior. When a student is disruptive, you might ask "What should you be doing?" This question can have a positive effect because it helps redirect the student to appropriate behavior. Of course, some students may not answer this question honestly or may refuse to reply at all. In that case, you should make statements related to the question, for example, "Keith, you were swearing and name-calling. That is against our classroom rules. You should not swear or call others names." If the student continues to break the rule, then appropriate consequences should be delivered.

8. **Give a verbal reprimand.** A straightforward way to have students stop misbehaving is to simply ask or direct them to do so. This is sometimes called a *desist order* or a *reprimand*, and it is given to decrease unwanted behavior. Verbal reprimands are effective with many mild and moderate behavior problems, but by themselves are less successful with severe behavior disorders (Kerr & Nelson, 2010).

    A *direct appeal* involves a courteous request for the student to stop the misbehavior and to get back on task. You might say "Martina, please put away the comb and continue with the class assignment." A direct appeal often gives the student a sense of ownership for deciding to get back on task and to do as you requested. The student feels a sense of responsibility.

    As an alternative, you could use a *direct command* in which you take the responsibility and give a direction in a straightforward manner, such as "Wayne, stop talking with your friends and get to work on the lab activity." With the direct appeal and the direct command, the student is expected to comply with your directions. If the student defies your request or command, you must be prepared to deliver an appropriate consequence.

VOICES FROM THE CLASSROOM   Giving Students Choices

Terri Jenkins, middle school English teacher, Hephzibah, Georgia

Avoiding conflict is important for classroom survival. This is especially true if the student is trying to seek power or attention. By giving the student a choice in resolving a problem, you defuse the situation and avoid a conflict.

For example, a student may be talking with a neighbor while you are giving instructions. You might say, "Brian, I really need quiet while I am giving directions so that everyone can hear. You have a choice: (a) you may remain where you are and stop talking to Mary or (b) you may reseat yourself somewhere else in the classroom. Thanks." Then you should walk away.

In this way, students have the power to make a choice. They do not feel challenged and usually respond appropriately. The behavior stops, and little instructional time is lost. Choices should not be punitive or rewarding; they should be designed to stop the misbehavior.

When giving choices, you should be polite and courteous, being careful that the tone of your voice is emotionless. After stating the choices, you should say thank you and then walk away from the student. In this way, it becomes obvious that you expect the student to comply.

Moderate Responses

Following situational assistance and mild nonverbal and verbal responses, students might continue to misbehave. In that case, moderate responses should be used to correct the problem. The three-step response plan shown in Table 9.1 illustrates the movement to more directive responses if mild responses are not successful.

Moderate responses are intended to be punitive ways to deal with misbehavior by removing desired stimuli to decrease the occurrence of the inappropriate behavior. Moderate responses include logical consequences and behavior modification techniques. Because student behaviors that warrant moderate responses are more problematic than mild misbehaviors, it is often useful to discuss specific problems with the principal, other teachers, or the school counselor. The family can be contacted at any point to inform them of their child's actions and to solicit their help.

A *logical consequence* is an event that is arranged by the teacher that is directly and logically related to the misbehavior (Dreikurs, Grunwald, & Pepper, 1998). The consequence should be reasonable, respectful, and related to the student action. For instance, if a student leaves paper on the classroom floor, then he or she must pick the paper off the floor. If a student breaks the rule of speaking out without raising his or her hand, you will ignore the response and call on a student whose hand is up. If a student marks on the desk, then he or she will be required to clean the marks off. Students are more likely to respond favorably to logical consequences because they do not consider the consequences mean or unfair. Logical consequences should be related to the student's action and be reasonable and respectful (Schwab & Elias, 2015).

At the start of the school year, you should think of two or three logical consequences for each of the classroom rules and inform students of them. When logical, reasonable consequences are preplanned, you are not under the pressure of thinking up something appropriate at the time the misbehavior occurs.

Some consequences might be designed to restore property or a condition that was damaged by the student. This practice is considered *restorative justice* in which the student takes steps to remedy the problem he or she created (Brown, 2018; Holtham, 2009; Meyer & Evans, 2012). For property damage, the student helps clean, repair, or pay for damages. The consequences are focused on teaching improved behavior to prevent a recurrence of the problem, and to the degree possible, to repair whatever physical or emotional damage was done (Smith, Fisher, & Frey, 2015).

Some examples of logical consequences include the following:

- **Withdraw privileges.** As a regular part of the classroom activities, you may provide your students with a number of special privileges such as a trip to the library, use of a computer, use of special equipment or a game, service as a classroom helper, or other valued privilege. If the misbehavior relates to the type of privilege offered, a logical consequence would be to withdraw the privilege. For example, if a student mishandles some special equipment, then the student would lose the privilege of using the equipment.

- **Change the seat assignment.** Students may talk, poke, or interact with other students in nearby seats. Sometimes, a problem occurs because certain students are seated near each other. Other times, just the placement of seats enables easy interaction. If inappropriate interaction occurs, a logical consequence would be to relocate the student's seat.

- **Have the student write reflections on the problem.** It is often useful to ask the student to reflect on the situation to help him or her recognize the logical connection between the behavior and the consequences. You may ask the student to provide written responses to certain questions; this might be done during a time-out.

  These questions may include the following: What is the problem? What did I do to create the problem? What should happen to me? What should I do next time to avoid a problem? Written responses to these or similar questions help students see their behavior more objectively and promote more self-control. You may choose to have the student sign and date the written responses for future reference. The written responses can be useful if family members need to be contacted at a later time.

- **Place the student in a time-out.** Sometimes, a student is talking or disrupting the class in such a way that interferes with the progress of the lesson. In such a case, the student can be excluded from the group; this is called a *time-out*. Removing the student from the group is a logical consequence of interfering with the group. An area of the room should be established as the time-out area, such as a desk in a corner or partly behind a filing cabinet. As a general rule, a time-out should last no longer than 10 minutes.

VOICES FROM THE CLASSROOM   Using an OOPS Sheet for Reflections

Lisa Bietau, fourth-grade teacher, Manhattan, Kansas

When my students misbehave, I sometimes ask them to fill out an OOPS sheet to have them reflect on their behavior. OOPS stands for "Outstanding Opportunity for a Personal Stretch." The sheet has a place for their name and date at the top. Then there are several other areas that the student needs to fill in: (a) Describe the problem. (b) What other choices did you have to settle the situation without difficulty? (c) How might you handle this differently if it happens again?

After the student fills out the OOPS sheet, I meet with the student privately to discuss the situation briefly and to review the options and solutions that the student wrote. This reflection and discussion with me helps the students understand my expectations and recognize that they have a responsibility to consider reasonable options when they meet a challenging situation.

I sign the OOPS sheet and make a copy for my files. The original is then sent home with the student to obtain the parent's signature. All of the student's privileges are suspended until the signed sheet is returned. If the sheet is not returned the next day, I call the parents and another copy is sent home if necessary. I have found that students show more self-control after completing the OOPS sheet.

- **Hold the student for detention.** *Detention* means detaining or holding back a student when he or she normally would be free to go and do other things. The student is deprived of free time and perhaps the opportunity to socialize with other students. Detention may include remaining after class or staying after school. During detention, the student could be asked to complete the assignment that was not completed during class time. Students will soon see the logic that time wasted in class will have to be made up later, on their own time in detention. Make sure your use of detention is consistent with school guidelines.

- **Contact the family.** If a student shows a pattern of repeated misbehavior, then you may need to contact the family. The logic here is that if all earlier attempts to extinguish the misbehavior do not work, it is appropriate to go to a higher authority. Parents, guardians, or other family members may be notified by a note or a letter to inform them of the problem and to solicit their involvement or support. You may choose to call them instead. If the situation is fairly serious, a conference with the parents may be warranted.

- **Have the student visit the principal.** In cases of repeated misbehavior or serious misbehavior, such as fighting, students may be sent to the school office to see the principal. The principal may talk with the student in an effort to use his or her legitimate authority to influence the student to behave properly. Some schools have specific procedures to be followed when students are sent to the principal. When the behavior problems reach this point, additional personnel, including the school counselor or psychologist and the family, need to be consulted to help the student.

Cautions and Guidelines

Before school starts, it is best to have a plan to address off-task behavior and misbehavior when it occurs. However, teachers may make decisions in the heat of the moment when responding to misbehavior, and these responses may not be appropriate. You should be aware of some disciplinary practices to avoid and some guidelines for using punishment.

Some Practices to Avoid

Research and practice suggest that some interventions are inappropriate or unsuccessful when trying to restore control. Disadvantages outweigh advantages in the use of harsh reprimands, threats, and physical punishment. Furthermore, practitioners have identified additional approaches that have questionable effectiveness. The message is clear—teachers should avoid the following practices.

1. **Harsh and humiliating reprimands.** A harsh reprimand is very negative verbal feedback. Teachers may be carried away with this verbal thrashing and humiliate the student. Research reports suggest that the use of harsh reprimands is a very ineffective, inefficient, and costly strategy. Harsh reprimands include speaking to the student in an exceptionally stern manner, yelling, and screaming. All of this may progress to the point where the student is humiliated.

2. **Threats.** A threat is a statement that expresses the intent to punish the student if he or she does not comply with the teacher's wishes. Most practitioners and researchers believe the disadvantages of using threats outweigh any possible benefits. Teachers may warn students to alert them to potential consequences, but a threat often expresses more severe consequences than would normally be expected and may be stated when the teacher has lost emotional control.

3. **Nagging.** Continual or unnecessary scolding only upsets the student and arouses the resentment of other students. The teacher may consider these scoldings as mini-lectures, but they are seen as nagging from the students' point of view.

4. **Forced apologies.** Forcing a student to express an apology that is not felt is a way of forcing him or her to lie. This approach solves nothing.

5. **Sarcastic remarks.** Sarcastic remarks are statements that the teacher uses to deride, taunt, or ridicule the student. While the teacher may consider these statements as a means of punishment, they create resentment; they may lower the student's self-esteem and may lower the esteem of the teacher in the eyes of students.

6. **Group punishment.** Group punishment occurs when the entire class or group is punished because of the misbehavior of an individual. The intent is for peer pressure to help modify the individual's behavior. However, the undesirable side effects of group punishment are likely to outweigh the advantages. It forces students to choose between the teacher and a classmate. Even if they go along with the teacher, the punishment engenders unhealthy attitudes.

7. **Assigning extra academic work.** When assigning extra academic work as a punishment, the teacher implies that the work is unpleasant. It is often in the form of homework that is not normally required. The student then associates schoolwork with punishment. This is not a message that teachers should convey.

8. **Reducing grades.** Penalizing a student academically for misbehavior again creates an undesirable association. Students who are penalized for misbehaving may develop an attitude of "What's the use?" toward academic work. Furthermore, reducing grades for misbehavior confounds the grade, which is intended to report only the student's academic progress.

9. **Writing as punishment.** After students misbehave, teachers may have them copy pages out of a dictionary, encyclopedia, or other book, or have them write a certain statement ("I will not do such and such again.") a number of times. Unfortunately, this approach leads to hostility from students, gives the impression that writing is a bad thing (English teachers will get upset about the message being conveyed here), and is not logically linked to what students may have done.

10. **Physical labor or exercise.** A teacher may use push-ups or some other physical action as punishment. However, the teacher may not be familiar with the student's physical abilities, and the student could get hurt. In addition to concerns about the student's safety, having students do extra exercises in physical education in response to misbehavior may cause the student to lose interest in the physical activities when the teacher assigns them as punishment.

11. **Corporal punishment.** Corporal punishment is a strategy in which the teacher inflicts physical pain on the student to punish him or her for misbehaving. Paddling, spanking, slapping, and pinching are examples. There are many disadvantages to using physical consequences (Hyman, 1997). Other negative behaviors often emerge, such as escape (running away from the punisher), avoidance (lying, stealing, cheating), anxiety, fear, tension, stress, withdrawal, poor self-concept, resistance, and counter-aggression. Many districts have a policy either prohibiting the use of corporal punishment or establishing specific guidelines for its limited use.

VOICES FROM THE CLASSROOM   Discouraging Disruptions

Yvonne Smit, second-grade teacher, Centreville, Virginia

I send my second-grade students to a break area just outside of our classroom for some physical activity to help them release their energy and regain a calm mind and calm body. When I see excessive wiggling or whispering and students are not responding to cues to stop that behavior, I will say, "Hey, Justin, run out and do 100 jumping jacks, real quick." I have a designated area for this, right outside our classroom in the hallway, where I can still keep eyes on them.

For students who are slow at decision making, I state the type and amount of physical activity I want them to do. Other students can make their own choices, "Hannah, go out and do some jumps or sit-ups, and I'll see you back in two minutes." It is important to present this with a neutral tone of voice and not as a punishment, but rather as a strategy to help regain focus.

Guidelines for Punishment

The later steps of the principle of least intervention may involve punishment. *Punishment* is an act of imposing a penalty with the intention of suppressing undesirable behavior. There are two procedures for achieving this purpose: (a) withholding positive reinforcers or desirable stimuli through techniques such as logical consequences and behavior modification approaches such as time-out and loss of privileges; and (b) adding aversive stimuli through actions where students receive a penalty for their misbehavior. Withholding positive reinforcers is considered to be less harmful than adding aversive stimuli.

Especially for beginning teachers, dealing with misbehavior that requires moderate or severe responses can be very troubling. It is often helpful to talk with the principal, other teachers, or school counselors to obtain ideas and advice for dealing with students who exhibit more serious misbehavior. In addition, it is often useful to contact the student's parents at any point to inform them of any concerns you might have and to solicit their help in working with the student.

You should express confidence in students' ability to improve and punish only as a last resort when students repeatedly fail to respond to more positive treatment. Apply punishment as part of a planned response, not as a means to release your anger or frustration.

The following factors are important to consider when effectively using punishment:

1. **Discuss and reward acceptable behaviors.** Acceptable behaviors should be emphasized when classroom rules are first discussed. Make it clear to students why the rules exist. Discuss the reasons for not engaging in the behavior considered to be inappropriate. Most students will behave appropriately if they know what is expected.

2. **Clearly specify the behaviors that will lead to punishment.** Clarifying acceptable behaviors for the students may not be enough. To help the students understand, identify and discuss examples of behaviors that break the rules and lead to punishment.

3. **Use punishment only when rewards or nonpunitive interventions have not worked, or if the behavior must be decreased quickly because it is dangerous.** Punishment should be used as a last resort when other techniques have failed.

4. **Administer punishment in a calm, unemotional manner.** If you deliver punishment while still emotionally upset, you may select an overly harsh punishment and may also provoke the student into further inappropriate reactions. Punishment should not be an

◼ CLASSROOM CASE STUDY   Responding to a Classroom Incident

Marilyn Schmidt is a middle school social studies teacher who just started her second year of teaching. On one of the opening days, she was presenting some new material to the entire class when she noticed three students talking near the back of the classroom, and one of them was also sending a text message.

Ms. Schmidt decided not to wait for anything more to happen before acting since she wanted to show that she was in control. She already was somewhat upset from her previous class period when the students were unruly, so she wanted to send a strong message that nonacademic talking would not be tolerated in this class. She told the three students that they would need to come after school for a half hour of detention. The three students protested this decision and began to argue with Ms. Schmidt. She told them if they did not agree to come in for detention, then the whole class would have an additional project to complete.

After one of the three students said a few more words in protest, Ms. Schmidt demanded that the student apologize for those statements. If the student did apologize, Ms. Schmidt said that she would remove the whole-class punishment. The student ended up apologizing but didn't really mean it. There seemed to be a lot of tension for the rest of the class period. Ms. Schmidt got the three students to stop talking, but at what price?

Focus Questions

1. In what ways did Ms. Schmidt *not* follow the sequential steps in the three-step response plan when addressing misbehavior?

2. Identify the disciplinary practices that she used but should have avoided.

3. Identify the ways she did not follow the guidelines for the use of punishment.

4. How might Ms. Schmidt have addressed the situation more appropriately and successfully?

---

involuntary emotional response, a way to get revenge, or a spontaneous response to provocation.

5. **Deliver a warning before punishment is applied to any behavior.** The warning itself could reduce the need for punishment. If the student does not correct the behavior after the warning, punishment should be delivered at the next occurrence.

6. **Apply punishment fairly to everyone who exhibits the targeted behaviors.** You should treat both genders the same way, and low-achieving and high-achieving students the same way.

7. **Apply punishment consistently after every occurrence of the targeted misbehavior.** Behaviors that reliably receive punishment are less likely to be tried by students than behaviors that occasionally go uncorrected.

8. **Use punishment of sufficient intensity to suppress the unwanted behaviors.** Generally speaking, the greater the intensity, the longer lasting the effect. But this does not mean that you need to resort to extreme measures. For example, the loss of positive reinforcement because of inappropriate behavior is better than shouting, "Don't do that!" with increasing intensity.

9. **Select a punishment that is effective, that is not associated with a positive or rewarding experience, and that fits the situation.** Not all aversive consequences that you select may be seen as punishment. Some students, for instance, might think that it is a reward to be placed in a time-out area in the classroom. In that case, a different consequence should be used that is not seen by the student as being positive or rewarding.

10. **Avoid extended periods of punishment.** Lengthy, mild punishment such as missing open study time for a week may have a boomerang effect. Punishment with a short duration is more effective.

Dealing with Chronic Misbehaviors

Chronic misbehaviors are troublesome behaviors that students repeatedly or compulsively perform. They include tattling, clowning, cheating, lying, stealing, profanity, rudeness toward the teacher, defiance or hostility, and failure to do schoolwork. This behavior is recurring and inappropriate, and teachers can take actions to minimize their presence in the classroom (Crowe, 2009; Foley, 2012; Gootman, 2008; Kapalka, 2009; Khalsa, 2007b; Wilson, 2013). Strategies to address some common chronic misbehaviors are presented here:

1. **Tattling.** Tattling occurs when students report minor infractions or perceived injustices to the teacher. Tattling is not disruptive, but it can become a problem when students commonly report minor, petty complaints. To prevent tattling from occurring in the first place, let students know what kinds of information they should and should not report to you. You need to know about an incident where a student got hurt, for example, but not when some other student is not doing the schoolwork.

   Many teachers, especially in the primary grades, have an explicit lesson about tattling. They describe the difference between reporting important information to the teacher and reports that are tattling about minor infractions.

2. **Clowning.** Students who clown behave in silly or funny ways or may play practical jokes. This clowning is disruptive to the class. Figuring out the source of the student's clowning can help determine what to do about it (Gootman, 2008). Some students may use clowning to cover up a deficiency; they may clown during a math lesson because they are weak in math. Clowning may also be a vehicle for a student to achieve success—to gain some recognition, fame, and popularity among other students. Still, clowning may be a way of venting frustrations and pressures that students may experience from school, home, or other factors.

   Keeping a record of who, what, when, where, and how for clowning incidents can help pinpoint the source. Then you can meet privately with the student to discuss the pattern of the clowning behavior and why it is disruptive. Help the student figure out ways to meet his or her needs without being disruptive.

3. **Cheating.** Cheating involves students getting answers or projects from someone else and turning them in as their own. Students may cheat for several reasons. They may cheat if teachers' expectations are too high and they may not be capable of mastering the material. Students then may see cheating as a way out. Other students may simply not be prepared or they may have test anxiety.

   It is best to minimize the temptation to cheat by determining the difference between helping and cheating, demonstrating expected behaviors for various activities, and having students identify appropriate and inappropriate actions. In addition, it is important to minimize the opportunity to cheat by determining desk placement during tests and by giving attention to policies, procedures, and submission guidelines for other types of student products.

4. **Lying.** Lying involves saying something that is not true in a conscious effort to deceive somebody. Students may have many reasons for lying, such as trying to protect their self-image, to mask their vulnerable points, or to inflate their image in front of others. They may feel afraid, feel insecure, or fear rejection. Students may lie to protect themselves from punishment or if we are too strict with them.

   The best response is to express concern about the student's need to lie by saying, "I wonder why you couldn't tell me what really happened." This approach makes it easier for the student to talk about the reason he or she felt compelled to lie. Stay calm and encourage them to discuss why they felt they needed to tell a lie. In doing so, try not to overreact or get angry with the student. Focus on the student's reasons and feelings that led to the lie. Encourage

■ **WHAT WOULD YOU DECIDE?**   **Addressing Cheating in Your Classroom**

On three successive quizzes in your class, you notice that four students have always received the same score. You are suspicious that this is more than a coincidence.

1. Under what circumstances would you talk with these four students about their scores?

2. What could you do about the questions and the formatting of the quiz to minimize cheating?

3. What could you do about room arrangement and your monitoring of students during a quiz to minimize cheating?

students to be honest about their feelings, and use a calm problem-solving approach to help students address a problem that caused them to lie in the first place.

5. **Stealing.** Stealing involves taking something that belongs to somebody else without the owner's permission. Students in early grades may still be learning the difference between sharing and taking what doesn't belong to them. Students may impulsively steal because they want something, or they may take something from another student because they are angry with the other person.

   If an incident of stealing takes place and you know the culprit, you can have a private conversation with the student about what happened. Describe what you saw and have the student return the item, replace it, or make restitution. Help the student figure out options other than stealing. You may need to respond more forcefully, depending on the value of the property and the frequency of stealing. In such cases, you may need to contact the principal and the family. Because of legal implications, it is wise to discuss an incident with the principal before conducting a search of backpacks, lockers, or a student's clothing.

6. **Profanity.** Profanity occurs when students use abusive, vulgar, or irreverent language. Age plays a role in the use of profanity. Young children may simply be restating language they heard on television, by family, or by friends with little or no understanding of the meaning. An instructional response is appropriate here, rather than a disciplinary one (e.g., "We don't use words like that in school"). For older students, such language may have become a regular part of their vocabulary, or they may use profanity when they are angry with another person. In such cases, students need to see what is acceptable and unacceptable in school. Stress that using language to hurt others will not be permitted and that there are other acceptable ways to express anger.

7. **Rudeness toward the teacher.** Students might be rude to the teacher by using disagreeable or discourteous words or actions that are outside acceptable standards. Rudeness might be expressed in talking back, arguing, making crude remarks, or showing inappropriate gestures. It is best to avoid overreacting, arguing, or getting into a power struggle. A low-key, respectful response is more suitable. When rude behavior is first evident, you should inform the student that the behavior is inappropriate, and you might refer to a classroom rule that relates to respectful behaviors. If the actions continue, you should meet with the student privately to identify the reason for the behavior and possibly to deliver consequences. If the rude behavior continues, you may need to consult with the principal or counselors about additional responses.

8. **Defiance or hostility toward the teacher.** Defiance occurs when a student refuses to obey or conform to teacher directions. These actions may be open, bold, or even hostile, and defiance may be in the form of a confrontation with the teacher during a class session. The best way to deal with defiance is to try to defuse it by keeping it in private and handling it individually with the student. Put the student off by saying that you will discuss the situation in a few minutes when you have time. Avoid a power struggle and remain objective. Listen to the student's point of view but don't engage in an argument. State the consequence clearly and implement it.

One February, I found myself dealing with continuous disruptions and off-task behaviors in my ninth-grade English class. This became a chronic problem. Students were shouting out irrelevant comments, not finishing assignments during group work, and constantly engaging inside conversations. I kept trying to address these issues with individual students, but I was spending way too much time talking to these students in the hallway. It felt like a game of whack-a-mole.

I knew a lot of students were frustrated by the disruptive behavior of their peers, but they were not willing to "call them out" during class. So I decided to leverage those feelings in a way that would be productive and anonymous: *a whole-class restorative conversation.*

First, I gave students an anonymous survey that asked them for both their positive and negative observations of our class, as well as how those observations made them feel. I also asked them to reflect on their own behavior, how their classmates made them feel, and what they could do to improve their performance and behavior in class. I put together their responses in a two-column handout sorted by "positives" and "ways to improve." Comments ranged from "My classmates help me when I need it" to "My classmates act like little kids and can't stay quiet."

The next day, I gave the students this handout and asked them to silently read the comments and to circle three items that resonated with them. Then I had them work with a partner to share and discuss their observations. Next, they worked with their partner to identify two key positive behaviors they wanted to see more of and to write two action steps per behavior for how to achieve those outcomes. We ended this process with a whole-class discussion in which students shared their reactions and their suggestions for achieving a more positive culture.

I was pleased to find that the class took all of this very seriously, and the students who had been silent were willing to speak honestly about their frustrations. Behaviors did not improve overnight, but I did notice that more students were willing to step up and remind their classmates of our goals. We checked in about these goals every Friday for several weeks, and by the end of the school year that class was much more productive and cohesive than it had been in February.

Here are some guidelines when students become defiant. First, stay in control of yourself. Direct the rest of the class to work on something while you speak to the student in a private area away from the rest of the students. Stand a few feet away from the defiant student (i.e., don't get in his face). Acknowledge the student's feeling by saying something like, "I can see that you are really angry." Avoid a power struggle in the conversation (e.g., "I am the boss here, and I am telling you what to do"). As a means to defuse the situation, offer the student a choice of actions for what the student needs to do next (Weinstein & Romano, 2019).

9. **Failure to do work in class or homework.** You should first examine how you hold students academically accountable in your class (see Chapter 8) and make any needed adjustments to ensure accountability. Next, you should plan to maintain accurate records of the schoolwork and respond early when you recognize students who are regularly not completing their class work.

You also should examine the nature of assignments and homework. Is the material too difficult to be completed independently? Is it too boring? Is it too long? Could the material be mastered with a shorter assignment? Was there sufficient preparation in class before students were to do the seatwork or homework? Are there other ways to provide practice and to assess student progress without having seatwork and homework every day? Your reflection on these questions may lead to your adjustment of the assignments and expectations.

When selecting seatwork and homework, it is often helpful to break it up into parts whenever possible. Work on the first few questions in class as a group before asking students to complete the rest on their own. Monitor students closely to see that they are able to handle the work independently. Be sure to review, collect, and grade all assignments.

10. **Inappropriate use of electronic devices.** Millions of students of all ages carry their cell phones and other electronic devices to school each day. Student use of these devices during school hours has the potential for creating problems, so many schools have adopted schoolwide policies for their use. Students may misuse their phones by texting, bullying other students (i.e., cyberbullying), or taking unflattering photographs or recordings of teachers. They may be used to cheat on tests or assignments, and they may be stolen.

Teachers should take a common-sense approach when dealing with these electronic devices. First, follow the guidelines in your schoolwide policy for these devices. Second, make sure all students are aware of the policy, understand when they can and cannot use these devices, and are aware of the consequences for not following the school policy. Third, be consistent in your enforcement, and students should be self-disciplined about the use of these devices.

If there is no school policy, it is useful to establish a policy for your classroom. For example, you may have a clear and consistent expectation that phones will be silenced during class and stored in a backpack, unless they are being used in classwork. To discourage cell phone use, teachers may require that backpacks be placed on the floor, and the teachers may walk around the room during class to monitor this. Moving around will also help teachers notice students using headphones for music.

Bullying

Bullying is when a person, or group of persons, uses power to harass or intimidate one or more people who have less power. Bullying takes the form of belittling weaker students, calling them names, and threatening or harassing them. For elementary students, the bully may be the student who pushes them out of the cafeteria line or bothers them on the school bus. For older students, bullying might even be in the form of harassment on social media through photographs or text messages (Espelage, 2015). The *Handbook of Bullying in Schools* (Jimerson, Swearer, & Espelage, 2009) provides a thorough discussion of bullying behaviors, assessment and measurement of bullying, and research-based prevention and intervention approaches.

Characteristics of Bullying

Regardless of the type of bullying, three characteristics are apparent:

1. **Imbalance of power.** People who bully use their power to control or harm, and the people being bullied may have a hard time defending themselves.

2. **Intent to cause harm.** The person bullying has a goal to cause harm. Actions done by accident are not bullying.

3. **Repetition.** Incidents of bullying happen to the same person over and over by the same person or group.

Bullies may do many things to harass or dominate others, such as make verbal threats, boss people around, take people's money, put people down, make obscene gestures, attack people physically, intimidate people, gossip, leave people out, spread rumors, tease, hit, or hurt others in many possible ways.

Nationwide, about 20% of students report being bullied during the school year. Some of those bullying activities may take place in the classroom. You can take steps to create a positive classroom community to minimize bullying from taking place, but you also can take steps to inform students of their responsibilities.

1. How might you inform your students about bullying—its characteristics, types, and effects?

2. How might you inform your students of their responsibilities for appropriate conduct and also for reporting any bullying actions?

3. What can you do to create a positive classroom environment where bullying behavior is minimized?

There are two types of kids who are more likely to bully others. First, some are well connected to their peers, have social power, are overly concerned about their popularity, and like to dominate or be in charge of others. Second, others are more isolated from their peers and may be depressed or anxious, have low self-esteem, be less involved in school, be easily pressured by peers, or not identify with the emotions or feelings of others. Students who have any of the following factors also may be more likely to bully others: are aggressive or easily frustrated, have less parental involvement or are having issues at home, think badly of others, have difficulty following rules, view violence in a positive way, or have friends who bully others (US Department of Education, 2019).

Bullies tend to be average students academically. Bullies may have an inflated self-concept but usually have low self-esteem or feel inferior to others, which reflects a strong need to dominate with threats. Bullies lack empathy for their victims and feel justified in their actions. Reciprocal aggressive behavior by the victim usually does not stop the bully (Khalsa, 2007a).

Bullying is most commonly learned, with modeling and reinforcement by parents and peers playing major roles and influences (Roberts, 2006). Bullies tend to come from homes whose parents are authoritarian, hostile, and rejecting. Parents may have poor problem-solving skills and use fighting as a solution to conflicts; their children then imitate these behaviors. Bullies are often emotionally underdeveloped, and they are unable to understand or empathize with others' perspectives or regulate their own behavior (Berk, 2019; Berk & Meyers, 2016).

Types of Bullying

There are several types of bullying (Breakstone, Dreiblatt, & Dreiblatt, 2009; Englander, 2013; Khalsa, 2007a):

1. **Physical bullying** is action oriented. It includes hitting, shoving, kicking, pushing, spitting, and taking or damaging a person's property.

2. **Verbal bullying** involves the use of words to hurt or humiliate another person. It includes teasing, name-calling, insulting, put-downs, and making threats or rude comments.

3. **Relational bullying,** also known as social aggression, is the use of relationships to hurt others. It includes preventing people from playing with others, using the silent treatment, and spreading rumors and lies.

4. **Sexual bullying** involves hurtful teasing and comments about sexuality, sexual preference, physical development, and sexual experiences as a way to undermine an individual's self-esteem and self-confidence. Victims may even be physically threatened or injured. Some experts would not consider these actions sexual bullying; they would call them sexual harassment. Harassment of girls and young women ranges from name-calling to touching, and even rape.

5. **Cyberbullying** involves the use of technology to hurt or humiliate others. It includes using computers, phones, and the internet. The most common places where cyberbully occurs are

(a) social media such as Facebook, Instagram, Snapchat, and Twitter; (b) text messages; (c) instant message; (d) email; and (e) other means to send, post, or share negative, harmful, false, or mean content about someone else (US Department of Education, 2019). The anonymity of the internet distinguishes cyberbullying from other types of bullying. This anonymity can make bullies even more insensitive to the hurtful nature of the bullying incidents (Willard, 2006).

Reports on Bullying

The National Center for Educational Statistics regularly gathers data on educational issues. The information on bullying that follows was from the 2017 School Supplement to the National Crime Victimization Survey (National Center for Education Statistics [NCES], 2019b) concerning students ages 12–18.

- **Frequency of bullying.** About 20% of the students reported being bullied at some time during the school year. Between 2005 and 2017, the percentage of students ages 12–18 who reported being bullied at school during the school year decreased from 29% to 20%.

- **Bullying by gender.** Female students reported more bullying (23.8%) than male students (16.7%).

- **Bullying by grade level.** For grades 6–12, sixth grade had the highest percentage of students reporting being bullied (29.5%) with each later grade level having a successively lower percentage. Twelfth grade had the lowest level (12.2%).

- **Bullying by community size.** Towns and rural communities had higher levels of reported bullying than cities and suburbs. The percentages were: rural (23.8%), towns (26.9%), suburbs (18.1%), and cities (19.9%).

- **Type of bullying.** In descending order of frequency, the types of bullying were: subject of rumors (13.4%), made fun of or insulted (13.0%), pushed, shoved, tripped, or spit on (5.3%), excluded from activities on purpose (5.2%), threatened with harm (3.9%), tried to make them do things they did not want to do (1.9%), and property destroyed on purpose (1.4%).

- **Location of bullying.** In descending order of frequency, the bullying was reported in the following locations: in the hallway or stairwell (43.4%), inside the classroom (42.1%), cafeteria (26.8%), outside on school grounds (21.9%), online or by text (15.3%), on the school bus (8.0%), or somewhere else in the school building.

- **Effects of bullying.** Bullied students reported effects in the following ways: an adult was notified (46.3%), feelings about self (26.8%), schoolwork (19.4%), relationships with family and friends (18.6%), and physical health (13.7%).

- **Perceived relationship to bullying.** Bullied students reported that they perceived the bullying was related to their: appearance (29.8%), race (9.4%), disability (7.5%), ethnic origin (7.3%), gender (7.2%), religion (4.6%), or sexual orientation (3.5%).

- **Cyberbullying.** In 2017, about 15% of students in grades 9–12 reported being electronically bullied during the previous 12 months. However, females reported a higher frequency of cyberbullying (19.7%) than males (9.9%).

- **LGBTQ Youth.** Lesbian, gay, bisexual, transgender, or questioning (LGTBQ) youth and those perceived to be LGBTQ are at an increased risk of being bullied. Results from the 2017 Youth Risk Behavior Survey show that more high school students who self-identify as lesbian, gay, or bisexual report being bullied on school property (33%) and cyberbullied (27.1%) in the past year, which were higher than the levels for their heterosexual peers (17.1% and 13.3%, respectively) (US Department of Education, 2019).

Ken Jackson, high school counselor, Atlanta, Georgia

Students who are lesbian, gay, bisexual, transgender, or questioning (LGBTQ) are often the targets of bullies. Since these characteristics are not typically exhibited until adolescence, bullying of LGBTQ students occurs more often in middle school and high school.

I am a high school counselor, and I recently needed to address an incident with two students. Claudia is a self-identified lesbian, rather small in stature, and a relatively successful student taking advanced placement courses. One day, she approached me relatively timidly but very upset. She explained that she was experiencing harassment in one of her classes from a varsity football player. He was talking to her in class, telling her to have sex with him, using explicit language to describe what he wanted them to do. He spoke softly so the teacher could not hear, and he had a female varsity athlete giving him support for his taunting. After Claudia kept refusing, the other student then began making statements about her being a lesbian and continued to mess with her.

As the school counselor, I gave Claudia some options and strategies. With her permission, I met with the classroom teacher to discuss how to help Claudia without making things more difficult since the teacher had not heard any of the remarks. The teacher decided to rearrange some classroom groupings to separate the students, place Claudia closer to the teacher's desk, and make the commitment to monitor students more closely. With these adjustments, Claudia felt that she could trust the teacher and go to the teacher for support should there be a recurrence. I followed up with Claudia several times to make sure she felt supported, and the situation had significantly improved.

Effects of Bullying

Bullying has serious and long-lasting effects for both bullies and their victims. Students who are bullied have a higher risk of depression and anxiety that may persist into adulthood, including feelings of sadness and loneliness, changes in sleep and eating patterns, and loss of interest in activities. They are more likely to have health complaints, decreased academic achievement and school participation, and increased thoughts about suicide that may persist into adulthood; they are also more likely to skip or drop out of school, and to retaliate through extremely violent measures (US Department of Education, 2019).

People who bully others are more likely to get into fights, vandalize property, and drop out of school; have a higher risk of abusing alcohol and other drugs in adolescence and as adults; are more likely to engage in early sexual activity; are more likely to be abusive toward their romantic partners, spouses, or children as adults; and are more likely to have criminal convictions and traffic citations as adults (US Department of Education, 2019). Even bystanders, students who witness bullying, are more likely to have increased use of tobacco, alcohol, or other drugs; have increased mental health problems, including depression and anxiety; and miss or skip school.

Confronting Bullying

Adult intervention is one of the best defenses against bullying. Teachers need to recognize the warning signs of bullying and intervene when it happens, sending the message that bullying is not acceptable. Although there is no set formula for how teachers should respond to bullying incidents, here are some actions to consider:

- **Intervene immediately.** Separate the students involved. Do not immediately ask about or discuss the reason for the bullying.

- **Get the facts.** Speak to the students involved, both participants and observers, and ask what happened. Request more information. Get all sides of the story before taking any action.

- **Tell the students you are aware of their behavior.** Talk to the students involved separately. Make it a teachable moment. Helping the students and bystanders understand what happened and why it happened may help prevent future incidents.

- **Consider an appropriate intervention.** Base your decision on the circumstances, the severity and history of the incident, and the students involved.

- **Follow up with the students.** Follow up on the incident and monitor the students involved to ensure the bullying does not continue.

- **Report the incident to the right person.** The school may have a reporting policy about bullying incidents, and a report may need to be submitted to the school administrator, a counselor, or a member of the school safety committee. This report will help the school track the incidents and the responses. Some states have laws that require incidences to be reported.

Teachers can take steps to deal with aggression and to encourage cooperation. Teachers can present themselves as a nonaggressive model. They can ensure that their classroom has enough space and appropriate materials for all students, thus minimizing the source of some conflicts. They can make sure students do not profit from aggressive behaviors by delivering appropriate consequences. They can teach directly about positive social behaviors. Teachers can also provide opportunities for learning tolerance and cooperation. Furthermore, states and school districts are developing safe school laws and policies that promote changing the behaviors of bullies. They include procedures for reporting and investigating incidents.

A number of books are available for teachers with information along with classroom activities and discussions to address bullying. These include *How to Stop Bullying and Social Aggression* (Breakstone et al., 2009), *How to Bullyproof Your Classroom* (Crowe, 2012), and *No Kidding about Bullying* (Drew, 2017). Useful sources also include Coloroso (2017), Dillon (2012, 2015), Kaiser and Rasminsky (2017), Roberts (2016), and Swearer, Espelage, and Napolitano (2009). A web search will reveal a number of sources to address bullying.

MAJOR CONCEPTS

1. The principle of least intervention states that when dealing with routine classroom behavior, misbehavior should be corrected with the simplest, least intrusive intervention that will work. If that doesn't work, then move up to a more intrusive, directive approach.

2. Situational assistance is designed to help students cope with the instructional situation and to keep them on task.

3. Mild responses are nonpunitive ways to deal with misbehavior while providing guidance for appropriate behavior. Nonverbal and verbal approaches can be used.

4. Moderate responses deliver punishment by removing desired stimuli as a means of decreasing inappropriate behavior.

5. Research and practice suggest that some interventions are inappropriate or unsuccessful when trying to restore order, and these practices should be avoided.

6. Due to inherent problems in the use of punishment, teachers should follow certain guidelines when using punitive responses.

7. Chronic misbehaviors are troublesome behaviors that students repeatedly or compulsively perform. They include tattling, clowning, cheating, lying, stealing, profanity, rudeness toward the teacher, defiance or hostility, and failure to do schoolwork.

8. Bullying is when a person, or group of persons, uses power to harass or intimidate one or more people who have less power. Bullying may be physical, verbal, relational, sexual, or cyber.

DISCUSSION/REFLECTIVE QUESTIONS

1. What are some positive aspects of the principle of least intervention?

2. What are the benefits of providing situational assistance?

3. What student misbehaviors would you be willing to deliberately ignore for a short time? What situations would you not ignore?

4. In your K–12 schooling, what inappropriate interventions have you experienced or observed? What were the effects on the students?

5. Can chronic or challenging misbehaviors be adequately addressed in the three-step response plan shown in Table 9.1, which applies the principle of least intervention?

6. What difficulties might teachers experience when trying to identify and address problems with cyberbullying done by their students?

SUGGESTED ACTIVITIES

1. Ask several teachers to describe how they deal with misbehavior. Do they have an overall plan such as the principle of least intervention that escalates the interventions?

2. Identify examples of consequences and punishments that teachers might deliver. Determine where those actions fall in the three-step response plan and judge whether the punishments are appropriate.

3. Ask teachers what types of chronic misbehavior they encounter and discuss how they address these misbehaviors.

4. Search the topic of bullying on the internet. From many resources and the many topics, identify 10 significant guidelines that teachers might follow in addressing bullying.

FURTHER READING

Crowe, C. (2012). *How to bullyproof your classroom*. Turner Falls, MA: Northeast Foundation for Children.

Describes bullying and gateways behaviors. Has a K–5 focus. Provides ideas for preventative approaches dealing with rules, working together, students knowing each other, and approaches to teach children about bullying.

Foley, D. (2012). *Ultimate classroom management handbook* (2nd ed.). Indianapolis, IN: JIST Publishing.

Offers many practical suggestions concerning managing student behaviors, seat assignments, peer pressure, common problems, dealing with disruption, incentives, connecting with your students, preparing students for work, providing an environment for achievement, rewarding success, and managing the classroom.

Thompson, J. G. (2011). *Discipline survival guide for the secondary teacher* (2nd ed.). San Francisco, CA: Jossey-Bass.

Provides thorough coverage of many topics including developing a comprehensive plan for classroom management and discipline, developing a positive classroom environment, promoting self-discipline, maintaining order with effective instruction, and preventing and addressing misbehavior.

Wilson, M. B. (2013). *Teasing, tattling, defiance and more: Positive approaches to 10 common classroom behaviors*. Turners Falls, MA: Northeast Foundation for Children.

Provides helpful description for ways to address common or chronic misbehaviors, such as teasing, cliques, defiance, disengagement, silliness and showing off, too much physical contact, and meltdowns.

chapter

10

© Mike Abrahams/Alamy Limited

Dealing with Challenging or Violent Students

CHAPTER OUTLINE

CHAPTER OBJECTIVES

This chapter provides information that will help you:

- Identify characteristics of challenging and violent students.
- Develop a plan for working with challenging students in your classroom.

- Teach students alternatives to disruption and violence.
- Develop an action plan for responding to disruption in your classroom.
- Determine when and how to seek outside help.

It's bound to happen. You have planned an exciting lesson for your students, and two students who often cause disturbances create some problems partway through the lesson. You have to stop what you are doing to deal with these students. Since they don't respond well to some of your usual disciplinary techniques, you know that they will disturb tomorrow's class and that of the day after. Some of the students, in fact, may have a tendency to be physical and violent. What do you do with these challenging students?

The first step is to understand these challenging students—their behaviors and the influences on their behaviors. Next, you need to make a commitment and a plan to work with them. Furthermore, you can teach students alternatives to disruption and violence. Finally, you need to be ready to respond to disruptive or violent behavior if it does occur. This chapter explores these issues.

Understanding Challenging and Violent Students

Challenging students are constantly disruptive, demand attention, openly confront your authority, or do not complete any assigned work. They disrupt learning, interfere with the work of others, and may prompt other students to misbehave. Your regular classroom management system may not work with challenging students. Before considering how to deal with these students, it is helpful to identify the behaviors challenging students actually exhibit, recognize influences that may have contributed to the development of the difficult behaviors, and understand that the behaviors of challenging students may be the early signs of serious problems.

Behaviors

According to Rhode, Jenson, and Reavis (2020), about 2–5% of all students are considered being a *tough kid* who has excessive noncompliant and aggressive behavior or behavior deficits in self-management, social, and academic skills. In some school environments, percentages for difficult students may be even higher. Tough kids who persistently break rules and sometimes become involved in serious misbehavior are an ongoing challenge in the classroom.

Characteristic behaviors of challenging and violent students are outlined in Table 10.1. These include *behavior excesses* where students do too much of a behavior. This may include noncompliance and aggression. The behaviors also include *behavior deficits* where students are unable to adequately perform a behavior (e.g., self-management, social skills, and academic skills).

Schools reflect society. If there are problems in the school community, similar problems may show up in schools. Violent or challenging students may be involved with thefts, robbery, assaults, bullying, gangs, drugs, hate-related words or graffiti, fights, weapons, illegal substances, alcohol, and marijuana. However, many indicators of school crime and safety show a *decrease* in recent years in the occurrence of many indicators, as illustrated by the items listed below (National Center for Education Statistics [NCES], 2018). The most serious forms of violence (robbery, aggravated assault, homicide, rape, and sexual assault) rarely occur in schools. There are schools where violence and fear are prevalent, but these schools are the exception rather than the rule.

■ TABLE 10.1   Characteristic Behaviors of Challenging or Violent Students

1. **Behavior excesses:** Too much of a behavior
   a. Noncompliance
      (1) Does not do what is requested
      (2) Breaks rules
      (3) Argues
      (4) Makes excuses
      (5) Delays
      (6) Does the opposite of what is asked
   b. Aggression
      (1) Tantrums
      (2) Fights
      (3) Destroys property
      (4) Teases
      (5) Verbally abuses
      (6) Is cruel to others
2. **Behavior deficits:** Inability to adequately perform a behavior
   a. Self-management skills
      (1) Cannot delay rewards
      (2) Acts before thinking; impulsive
      (3) Shows little remorse or guilt
      (4) Will not follow rules
      (5) Cannot foresee consequences
   b. Social skills
      (1) Has few friends
      (2) Goes through friends fast
      (3) Noncooperative; bossy
      (4) Lacks affection
      (5) Has few problem-solving skills
      (6) Constantly seeks attention
   c. Academic skills
      (1) Generally behind in academics, particularly reading
      (2) Off task
      (3) Fails to finish work
      (4) Truant or frequently tardy
      (5) Forgets acquired information easily

Here are some crime and safety indicators for schools in the United States (NCES, 2018):

- **Victims.** In 2017, 2% of students ages 12–18 reported being victimized at school during the previous six months. One percent of students reported theft, 1% reported violent victimization, and less than 0.5% reported serious violent victimization. All of these percentages were lower than those reported in 2001. In 2015–2016, 69% of public schools recorded one or more violent incidents of crime, 15% recorded one or more serious violent incidents, and

39% recorded one or more thefts. (*Violent crimes* include violent incidents and simple assault. *Serious violent crimes* include rape, sexual assault, robbery, and aggravated assault.)

- **Fear.** Between 2001 and 2017, the percentage of students ages 12–18 who reported being afraid of attack or harm at school during the school year decreased from 6% to 4%, and the percentage who reported being afraid of attach or harm away from school during the school year decreased from 5% to 3%.

- **Bullying.** Between 2005 and 2017, the percentage of students ages 12–18 who reported being bullied at school during the school year decreased from 29% to 20%. In 2017, about 15% of students in grades 9–12 reported being electronically bullied during the previous 12 months.

- **Hate language.** In 2017, about 6% of students ages 12–18 reported being called hate-related words at school during the school year, representing a decrease from 12% in 2001. About 23% of students reported seeing hate-related graffiti at school during the school year in 2017, representing a decrease from 36% in 2001.

- **Fights.** The percentage of students in grades 9–12 who reported being in a physical fight anywhere decreased between 2001 and 2017 (from 33% to 24%), as did the percentage of students in these grades who reported having been in a physical fight on school property (from 13% to 9%).

- **Weapons.** In 2017, about 16% of students in grades 9–12 reported that they had carried a weapon anywhere at least one day during the previous 30 days and 4% reported carrying a weapon on school property at least 1 day during the previous 30 days. The percentage of students in grades 9–12 who reported carrying a weapon on school property during the previous 30 days decreased from 6% in 2001 to 4% in 2017.

- **Gangs.** Between 2001 and 2017, the percentage of students ages 12–18 who reported that there were gangs at their school during the school year decreased overall (from 20% to 9%), as well as for students from urban areas (from 29% to 11%), suburban areas (from 18% to 8%), and rural areas (from 13% to 7%).

- **Alcohol.** The percentage of students in grades 9–12 who reported using alcohol on at least 1 day during the previous 30 days decreased from 47% to 30% between 2001 and 2017.

- **Marijuana.** In 2017, about 20% of students in grades 9–12 reported using marijuana anywhere at least once in the past 30 days. Interestingly, this rate was higher for students identifying themselves as gay, lesbian, or bisexual, at about 30% of these students.

- **Illegal drug availability.** The percentage of students in grades 9–12 who reported that illegal drugs were made available to them on school property in the last 12 months decreased from 29% to 20% in 2017.

There are many useful websites providing information to help understand disruptive and violent student behavior and providing guidance about solutions. Some sites are the National School Safety Center (www.schoolsafety.us) and Stop Bullying (www.stopbullying.gov).

Influences

For many of these students, underlying influences may contribute to their persistent misbehavior. Many of these students come from homes where they have been emotionally or physically abused or neglected. Some of them may have had traumatic childhoods as a result of suffering from organic conditions, such as attention deficit-hyperactivity disorder (estimated to affect 4% of school-age children), fetal alcohol syndrome, or the effects of being born to mothers addicted to cocaine. Some of the students may live in a home environment where one or more adults are addicted to alcohol, crack, or other drugs. Many students come from home environments where parents have little influence or control over their children's behavior.

Many students who chronically misbehave come from home environments in which the parents themselves have had a negative school experience. The student then carries this distrust to school with the expectation that school will not be a positive experience. The student also may have limited trust in adults and teachers. Thus, the student enters school with negative influences and expectations. Every failure diminishes his or her self-esteem and often leads to anger and distrust. These are the difficult students, the tough kids who must be reached. Some students may have emotional and behavioral problems that contribute to their challenging actions (Cole & Shupp, 2012).

The risk of violent behavior in schools is heightened with the increased occurrence of gangs and weapons. A street gang is a group of people who form an allegiance for a common purpose and engage in violent, unlawful, and criminal activity. Many gang members are of school age, and when they come to school, confrontations often arise.

Schools have struggled over how to address the influence of gangs. Strategies fall into three categories: (a) prevention—stopping the problem before it begins by teaching children skills so they will never become violent; (b) intervention—singling out those kids who have shown violent behavior and working one on one to change their ways; and (c) suppression—keeping weapons out of schools by using police-style tactics to make schools safe. Many educators maintain that we must teach children how to avoid violence—how to keep conflicts from escalating, how to deal with anger, how to recognize dangerous situations, and how to avoid weapons. Resources are available for dealing with gangs and school violence (Jimerson, Nickerson, Mayer, & Furlong, 2012).

Early Signs of Serious Problems

Some of the behaviors exhibited by challenging students are troublesome while others are quite serious. Aggressive behaviors such as fighting, throwing tantrums, vandalizing, stealing, and exhibiting abusive behavior very seriously affect the student and the learning environment. Because of the immediacy of the events, you cannot ignore these actions. Immediate attention is needed.

Some challenging students, however, exhibit behaviors that may not demand immediate attention, yet they also may be a sign of serious problems. A student who does not comply with directions, has limited self-management skills, or has limited social or academic skills may be considered a challenging student. Whether overtly aggressive or passively noncompliant, challenging students exhibit behaviors that can disrupt their learning and that of others. Some students may show early signs of serious problems through their behavior in the following ways:

- **Changes in physical appearance.** Students may reveal underlying problems through sudden changes in their physical appearance. This may be evident in deterioration in posture, dress, and grooming habits, or in changes in weight. Bruises and cuts may be signals of abuse, neglect, or even self-mutilation.

- **Changes in activity level.** Excessive tardiness, lethargy, absenteeism, and sleepiness may result from various problems, including depression and substance abuse. Students may also deal with problems by exhibiting hyperactivity, overaggressiveness, impulsivity, or lowered frustration and tolerance levels.

- **Changes in personality.** When students experience emotional disturbances, they may express uncharacteristic personality characteristics. These may include sudden expressions of sadness, easy agitation, or anger.

- **Changes in achievement.** When students are dealing with problems, they may have a decline in their ability to focus on the school activities, to complete the activities, or to perform at their previous achievement level.

- **Changes in health or physical abilities.** Complaints about frequent headaches, stomachaches, dizziness, unhealed sores, and frequent bathroom use lead to a concern about a student's health. These changes may be an indication of other difficulties the student is experiencing.

- **Changes in socialization.** Although students who are suddenly quiet and withdrawn may not cause disruption in the classroom, this change might signal a problem in the student's life that may be later expressed in more outward and potentially disruptive behavior. Contributing factors to these changes could be very serious and beyond your influence to address or remedy. You should be prepared to contact other specialized professionals in an effort to help students who show signs of serious problems. Professionals may include counselors, psychologists, nurses, social workers, or even police officers. It is often helpful to consult with the school principal before making contacts with those outside the school.

Students who are prone to violent behaviors often exhibit a number of behaviors prior to any violent acts. The US Department of Education and the Department of Justice published a guide for schools (Dwyer & Osher, 2000) that contains a list of early warning signs that can alert teachers to a student's potential to violence, as well as signs that violence is imminent (see Table 10.2).

■ TABLE 10.2   Early and Imminent Warning Signs of Violence

Early warning signs
  Social withdrawal
  Excessive feelings of isolation and being alone
  Excessive feelings of rejection
  Being a victim of violence
  Feelings of being picked on and persecuted
  Low school interest and poor academic performance
  Expression of violence in writings and drawings
  Uncontrolled anger
  Patterns of impulsive and chronic hitting, intimidating, and bullying behaviors
  History of discipline problems
  Past history of violent and aggressive behavior
  Intolerance for differences and prejudicial attitudes
  Drug use and alcohol use
  Affiliation with gangs
  Inappropriate access to, possession of, and use of firearms
  Serious threats of violence

Imminent signs of violence
  Serious physical fighting with peers or family members
  Severe destruction of property
  Severe rage for seemingly minor reasons
  Detailed threats of lethal violence
  Possession or use of firearms and other weapons
  Other self-injurious behaviors or threats of suicide

Planning to Work with Challenging and Violent Students

Many schools have taken actions to address violent behavior with formal violence prevention programs, increased school security, zero-tolerance policies, and programs in character development, problem resolution, and anger control. To be successful with challenging and possibly violent students in your own classroom, you must assume responsibility for addressing the situation and take steps to have the student behave within acceptable limits (Applebaum, 2009; Canter & Canter, 2008; Kaiser & Rasminsky, 2017; Kapalka, 2009; Mendler & Curwin, 2007; Otten & Tuttle, 2011). Resources such as *Motivating Defiant and Disruptive Students to Learn* (Korb, 2012) link motivation with classroom management and discipline strategies. Here are six things that you could do to meet that challenge:

1. **Establish rules, procedures, consequences, and reinforcements for the classroom.** It is vital to develop a comprehensive classroom management and discipline system for all students in the classroom. This is the foundation for any additional actions that you need to take when addressing the special challenges of working with difficult students.

2. **Make a commitment to help challenging students succeed.** These students are sometimes accustomed to teachers trying to help them but then later giving up. Actually giving up on the student only reinforces and perpetuates the problem behavior; it will not go away without intervention. The inappropriate behavior will continue unless you make the commitment to help the challenging student.

   In doing so, you must clearly communicate your concern to these students. They must know that you will do everything possible to help them succeed. Since you may not be in a position to change any of the underlying contributing factors for the misbehavior, you should focus on the inappropriate classroom behaviors. This commitment is a vital step in overcoming problem behaviors.

3. **Establish a plan to deal with each challenging student.** Because there are different types of challenging students, you may need to use a different approach with each type. In addition, each student has his or her own personality, academic history, and circumstances to be considered. For these reasons, it is helpful to establish a plan to deal with the unique characteristics of each challenging student.

   Handling each incident as a separate act is not sufficient. Preplanned, sequential actions are needed to address the problem behaviors systematically. Approaches to be used in the classroom as part of this plan are addressed in the next section. Fortunately, some useful guidelines and materials are available (e.g., Colvin & Scott, 2015; Jenson, Rhode, & Reavis, 2020; Morgan, Young, West, & Smith, 2012; Rhode et al., 2020).

4. **Keep documentation and anecdotal records.** It is important to keep a written record of the incidents of misbehavior and the actions you have taken in a separate folder for each challenging student. This documentation will help you see any patterns in the behavior. If at a later point you need to consult the parents, principal, counselor, psychologist, or others about the student, this documentation will help them better understand the nature and scope of the problems. There are several types of documentation:

   - **Anecdotal record.** Keep a written *anecdotal record* to document specific events of misbehavior. An anecdote is a brief, narrative description of an incident. It should include the student's name, the date and time of the incident, the location of the incident, a brief description of the student's behavior, and a brief description of your response.

Two students in your classroom are involved in a heated argument about a lost notebook. One student has no previous problems in class, whereas the second student has had a series of difficulties getting along with others in the classroom.

1. Will you make a written anecdotal record of this incident for both students' files?

2. What factors will you take into account as you decide whether to have a written record?

3. Why is it important to have a written record of certain incidents?

- **Incident reaction sheet.** Ask the student to fill out an incident reaction sheet outlining an incident of misbehavior. Students could write this while in time-out. The incident reaction sheet provides the student with an opportunity to evaluate his or her behavioral choices while calming down. Questions may require the student to describe the rule that was broken, why the student chose to misbehave, who was bothered by the misbehavior, what more appropriate behavior could be chosen next time, and what should happen to the student next time the misbehavior occurs. This reaction sheet should be kept on file as documentation of the incident, and it may be shown to others such as the family, principal, or counselor as the need warrants.
- **One-on-one meetings.** Keep a record of any one-on-one meetings with the student as a means to document the series of interactions and decisions that were made in consultation with the student.
- **Behavioral contracts.** Keep a copy of any contracts that were developed with the student or in consultation with others.

  In addition to these four types of documentation, your folder of documentation might include notes or records of phone conversations concerning the student.

5. **Focus attention on preventing disturbing or violent behavior.** Think comprehensively about prevention strategies. These may include teaching students alternatives to disruption and violence, knowing the early warning signs for violent behavior, being attentive to student interactions, building a positive classroom community, and taking actions to de-escalate confrontational situations.

6. **Make plans for ways to respond to disruptive or violent behavior.** Decide how you will address aggressive behavior and even how you will respond to physical fights. Thinking about these issues in advance will enable you to make quick, appropriate decisions in the event of an incident.

   When addressing dangerous behavior in the classroom, a three-pronged approach can help prevent and de-escalate classroom crises (Murphy & Van Brunt, 2018):

- **Prevent disruptions.** First, prevent classroom disruptions or dangerous behaviors to the extent possible with a focus on mutual respect and clear expectations about appropriate behaviors and how frustrations should be handled.
- **Reduce the escalation.** Second, if such behaviors occur, use crisis de-escalation skills (e.g., adopt a cool and collected manner, avoid shaming or embarrassing the student, stay solution focused, and ensure that supportive resources are in place for the teacher and student alike).
- **Set up an approach to deal with future risk.** Third, institute a community-based, systemic approach to reduce future risk (e.g., interact with the school's behavioral intervention team, psychologists, and parents as needed).

VOICES FROM THE CLASSROOM   Have a Plan to Deal with Challenging Students

Celeste Hanvey, sixth-grade teacher, McKinney, Texas

When I find out a student of mine has had a history of, or has begun to exhibit, violent behavior, I make a plan. I have found that students who are disruptive and frightening often want an audience. Before the behavior begins, I work with a teacher nearby to arrange for another available classroom for students to go to in the event that I need to evacuate the other students from my classroom. My students are then taught a key word or signal that means to get up and go to that safe place as quietly and quickly as possible, thus leaving only the violent or very disruptive student in my classroom. Once the audience (the other students) has been removed, it is only then when I am able to speak with the troubled student to get to the root of the problem.

I would only need to follow these procedures for very violent or disruptive students in rare situations. This is only part of a plan to deal with challenging students. Other aspects of a plan include conferences with the student, consulting with other educators and the family, and the delivery of supports and consequences.

Teaching Students Alternatives to Disruption and Violence

When confronted with a challenging conflict, students may not have the skills to defuse a situation and thus may resort to disruption and violence as a first step. Students, however, can be taught strategies that emphasize self-control and problem solving. Students can be taught ways to deal with anger, use problem-solving strategies, and use new behavioral skills such as social skills, conflict resolution skills, and self-management skills. By using these skills, students are less likely to exhibit disruptive behaviors or become violent.

Dealing with Anger

Anger is a feeling indicating the person feels frustrated and thwarted. Everybody gets angry at some time or other, and figuring out what to do with anger is the tough part. Hidden anger often leads people to a breaking point where they explode with pent-up feelings, but letting anger get out of hand also can lead to many problems. In the classroom, help students manage anger constructively, calm their own anger, and deal with other people's anger (Curwin, Mendler, & Mendler, 2018; Gootman, 2008).

Managing Anger Constructively

People who are angry may take actions without thinking much about the situation. Here are some ways to manage anger constructively (Johnson & Johnson, 2005):

1. **Recognize and acknowledge your anger.** Anger is a natural, normal human feeling. It does not need to be feared or rejected. Repressed anger does not vanish: It may erupt suddenly in physical or verbal assaults or as overreactions to minor provocations. Recognize how you get angered and what your responses are.

2. **Decide whether to express your anger.** You might find something upsetting, but you might or might not want to express your anger. Clarify the situation to be certain someone has done something aggressive or provocative in nature. Then decide whether to express your anger directly or keep it hidden. Detach and let go if you decide not to express your anger.

3. **Express your anger directly and descriptively when it is appropriate to do so.** Express your anger to the appropriate person and make your point in descriptive, accurate, and brief terms as a means to describe your concerns and to lay the groundwork for settling the difficulty.

4. **When direct expression is not appropriate, express your anger indirectly or react in an alternative way.** When not expressing anger openly, you may still have feelings that need to be expressed. This can be done privately by some verbal or physical expression, physical exercise, psychological detachment, or relaxation.

5. **When the other person is angry, focus on the task or issue.** You can control and contain your anger and better manage the situation by staying focused on the goal to be achieved, not on what the other person is saying or doing.

6. **Analyze, understand, and reflect on your anger.** Get to know yourself so that you recognize the events and behaviors that trigger your behavior and the internal signs that signal you are becoming angry. This will help you understand your anger and stop anger before it develops.

Calming One's Own Anger

There are many easy-to-learn things that make it possible to calm yourself when you are angry (Curwin & Mendler, 1997). These include the following:

1. **Count from 1 to 10.** Plan on this counting before doing anything when you are upset. You may repeat this counting if you are still feeling angry. What did you say or do to the person who upset you? After the counting, how did your feelings change?

VOICES FROM THE CLASSROOM   Guidelines for Working with Challenging Students

Michael Abbott, teacher in an alternative high school, Livonia, Michigan

Our alternative high school has a high percentage of students who would be considered at risk and challenging to work with. There is a sign in the school that says, "Soft on people, hard on issues." Probably nothing has helped me in my relationships with my students as much as this simply stated philosophy. To me, it says a great deal about human relationships and provides the following guidance as I work with challenging students:

- Self-esteem is easily damaged.

- People respond well to gentleness.

- It is not necessary to be cruel to be effective.

- People respond well if they know the issues.

- Expectations must be clear.

- Anticipate problems (be proactive rather than reactive).

- State consequences before anything has happened.

- Be consistent.

- Follow through.

2. **Count from 10 to 1.** Counting backward from 10 to 1 works the same way as counting from 1 to 10, but just in reverse order.

3. **Count backward by 5, starting at 100.** This type of counting requires a little more thinking and thus helps calm the anger.

4. **Breathe in deeply.** Just breathe in deeply and then let the air out slowly. Repeat this several times. By focusing on your deep breathing for three to five minutes, you can calm your anger.

5. **Breathe in deeply and count together.** This approach combines deep breathing and counting. Silently say the number "one" each time you exhale. Doing this for two minutes or more can slow down and calm the anger.

6. **Count by fives and breathe.** This is similar to the exercise in which you say "one" when exhaling. In this exercise, you silently count to five while inhaling, count to five while briefly holding your breath, and count to five while exhaling.

7. **Use calming words.** Many students find that they can calm themselves down by silently saying words that make them feel better. This approach could be combined with deep breathing. For example, students might think of words such as *calm down*, *chill out*, *stay cool*, or *relax*. Students could silently say the first word (e.g., *calm*) when inhaling and the second word (e.g., *down*) when exhaling. This can be repeated several times.

Dealing with Another Person's Anger

It is important to not let other people's anger make you angry. There are many things you can do to keep calm when someone is bothering or threatening you. Here are some ways to respond to other people's anger constructively (Johnson & Johnson, 2005):

1. **Let others feel angry.** Remember that anger is a natural human feeling, and that everyone feels angry at some time. It is better for the anger to be expressed than hidden, as long as there is no violence or aggression.

2. **Don't get angry back.** When another person is angry, the first step is to control your own feelings. Losing your temper will only escalate the problem.

3. **Recognize that the use of aggression by the other person is an expression of feeling weak and helpless.** The angry person probably does not know what to do when angry and thus may be aggressive. Help the person back off, cool down, and try something else.

4. **Focus attention on the task, not on the anger.** Focus both your attention and the attention of the angry person on the task to be completed. Don't get sidetracked or baited into a quarrel when the other person is angry.

5. **Explain the situation.** Your explanation of the situation can help the angry person see the circumstances from a new perspective, understand the cause of his or her anger, and lead to calming of the anger.

Techniques for Solving Problems

In addition to dealing with anger, students need to be good at figuring out how to solve problems that they have or that others give them. When students confront a conflict, they need problem-solving strategies to help them act effectively without doing damage to themselves or others.

VOICES FROM THE CLASSROOM　　Dealing with an Angry Student

Lynne Hagar, high school history and English teacher, Mesquite, Texas

John walked into my classroom at the start of the school year ready to fight me all the way. This pugnacious redhead walked, talked, and acted tough as nails, but when I spoke to him sharply, he blushed.

How should I handle this firecracker of a student? Experience had taught me that a lot of love and consistency would solve many of his problems. I tried to react calmly to John's insulting comments, trusting that once he began to respond to my teaching, he would show more respect. When he became disruptive, I asked him privately to tell me if I had done something to offend him or to lose his respect. John was surprised that a teacher would be concerned about the reasons for his behavior and astonished that I had admitted I was capable of doing something wrong.

Once we had a basis for our relationship, I found something to say to John every day—not necessarily a compliment, just an acknowledgment that I recognized he was there. I tried my best to really listen when John talked to me, making eye contact and coming close to his desk. Sometimes I touched his arm in a friendly way when he entered the room, or I laid my hand on his shoulder as I passed his seat. I put long comments on his papers and added stickers when his work began to show improvement.

I soon realized that John attended school every day without fail; it was the best place in his life—the only place where he felt safe enough to express his feelings. I gave John opportunities to let his anger out on paper and to write about his feelings. I found out about things he was proud of and then built writing lessons around subjects such as rodeo-riding and fast cars.

There's something about struggling with a difficult student and succeeding in gaining his or her trust that gives a teacher a special warmth for that student. It's very rewarding in a unique way.

Students can use a 10-step process for dealing with problem situations before they do something hurtful to themselves or others (Curwin & Mendler, 1997).

1. **Stop and calm down.** Give yourself time to think and respond when something upsetting occurs. Pay attention to the signs that your body gives you when it feels tense. If angered, use some technique previously discussed to calm your anger.

2. **Identify what the problem is.** Clarify your concerns in specific, behavioral terms. Think about the causes of the problem, who was involved, and whether you contributed to the problem in some way. Consider whether you need to talk to others to help come up with a solution.

3. **Decide on your goal.** Determine specifically what you want to have happen.

4. **Think of as many solutions to the problem as you can.** Brainstorm about the many different actions you can choose to take to solve the problem.

5. **For each possible solution, think of all the things that might happen next.** Anticipate consequences for these possible solutions.

6. **Choose the best solution.** From your list of possible solutions, select one solution that has the most desired consequences.

7. **Choose a back-up solution in case the first one doesn't work out.** Always have a back-up plan ready. You need to have at least one more possible solution ready in case the first one doesn't work out.

8. **Plan your solution and make a final check.** Mentally rehearse when, where, and how a best solution will be implemented. Also anticipate potential obstacles and how to deal with them.

9. **Carry out your solution.** Carry out your decision and see how it works. If it does not work, then try another solution.

10. **Evaluate.** When evaluating your decision making concerning a particular problem, there are three important questions to consider: Did I reach my goal? If the same problem occurs again, what will I do? Are there any people (parents, friends, and teacher) who might help me as I figure out the best solution?

Developing New Behavioral Skills

Another way to help students seek alternatives to disruption and violence is to teach them new behavioral skills that help them effectively function in the classroom. A number of authors have developed programs in which students are taught new behavioral skills, such as social skills, conflict resolution skills, and self-management skills. Although it is beyond the scope of this book to provide a detailed description of each of these programs, a brief description is provided for a representative sample of the available programs.

- **Social skills.** Cooperative skills are those that help students get along socially. These skills include communication, cooperation, problem solving, conflict resolution, and team building (Otten & Tuttle, 2011). Burke (2008) provides comprehensive descriptions and specific activities to teach cooperative social skills to K–12 students. Her program addresses basic interactions, communication skills, team-building skills, and conflict resolution. Separate sections of Burke's book discuss students who have trouble accepting responsibility, students who need help with their interpersonal skills, students with behavior problems, and students with special needs. Activity descriptions, checklists, forms, and related transparency masters are included.

- **Conflict resolution and self-management skills.** Some programs provide a set of individual or interactive activities for students to complete to develop self-management and conflict resolution skills (e.g., Henley, 2003; Morgan et al., 2012).

  Conflict resolution programs help students develop skills to deal with conflicts they might experience in the classroom. Conflict resolution programs typically involve instruction about the steps in dealing with conflict and the related skills necessary to work through the conflicts (Winslade & Williams, 2011).

■ WHAT WOULD YOU DECIDE?   Teaching Students Conflict Resolution and Self-Management Skills

Students in your fourth-grade class seem to have disagreements all the time. Even during recess and noninstructional time, they pick at each other and say mean things. They don't seem to have the social skills and the ability to settle disagreements in a reasonable manner. You've reached the point where something must be done. You decide to find instructional materials to teach your students how to deal with conflicts themselves:

1. After selecting some ready-made instructional lessons on conflict resolution, you must take class time for this

instruction and the student interaction. How can you justify taking time away from content instruction?

2. Why don't teachers teach some of these skills even when there are no major problems?

3. What is the value of teaching conflict resolution and self-management skills?

- **Reducing school violence through conflict resolution.** In *Teaching Students to be Peacemakers* (2005), D. W. Johnson and R. T. Johnson offer specific guidance to help students deal with conflicts in a constructive manner. They examine conflicts in a comprehensive way and then provide guidance in teaching students skills in the following areas: negotiating, conflict strategies, managing anger, mediating conflicts, managing developmental conflicts, and peacemaking. Conoley and Goldstein (2004) also provide abundant guidance for school violence intervention.

Responding to Disruptive or Violent Behavior

Teachers who have a plan to respond to disruptive or violent behavior are often more successful than teachers who do not have a plan. Without a plan, teachers continually feel stressed and ill-equipped to deal with challenging students, and this may contribute to teachers leaving teaching. A number of specific approaches can be used to respond to disruptive behavior (Colvin & Scott, 2015). Outside help is available if necessary.

Approaches to Use in the Classroom

The goal is to help challenging students be successful. To achieve that goal, you need to be committed to a preplanned, sequential set of actions to have the student stop misbehaving and get back on task. A set of actions is discussed here to achieve that goal. Communication with parents is vital when dealing with difficult students. One of the following steps is to consult and inform parents, but this contact can occur at any point as the need warrants, even when you are assessing the situation.

Assess the Situation

Before taking any actions to remedy the situation, it is vital to gather information and be reflective about the student, the behaviors, the environment, and yourself.

1. **Find out about the characteristics of the challenging students and the influences in their lives.** In this way, you will have a better understanding of the students, and this information may help you decide on appropriate actions to help the student succeed. You may obtain this information by talking with the student, through a questionnaire about interests, by asking other teachers who come in contact with the student, or other means.

2. **Examine your classroom management system.** This is a necessary step to see if there are any factors in the classroom contributing to the misbehavior of challenging students. This should include a review of rules and their consequences, procedures, space usage, motivation, lesson delivery, reinforcement, and efforts to monitor students and promote cooperation.

3. **Analyze the problem behavior and your response.** It is important to identify precisely what the student is doing to create a problem. Some of the student behaviors may be similar to those listed in Table 10.1. Various checklists and observation systems are available to help record the behaviors (Rhode et al., 2020). One useful format is to list the type of student behavior and your related response.

   This step of looking at your own actions can be quite enlightening. To borrow from William Glasser (1969), ask, "What am I doing? Is it working?" If it is not working, stop doing it! When asking these questions, your attention is focused on selecting an appropriate, workable response. By looking at the student's behaviors and your related responses, you can often determine the reason for the misbehavior. You then can act in ways not to reinforce the motive behind the student's misbehavior.

Meet with the Student

Some consequences used to stop misbehavior may have only short-term effects with challenging students. These students need help in making better decisions about their behavior. Thus, a one-to-one conference with the student is needed when the behavior is chronic or serious, or if there is a sudden change in behavior. The purpose of the conference is to provide caring and guidance to the student. You should listen to the student's concerns, firmly clarify your own expectations, and then work together to arrive at a practical course of action. There are several guidelines to consider when meeting with the student (Canter & Canter, 2008):

1. **Meet with the student privately.** The conference should be confidential, and there should be no other students around to overhear or disrupt the meeting. The conference should also be brief, with a maximum of 10–15 minutes.

2. **Show empathy and concern.** The conference is intended to help the student explore alternative, more appropriate behaviors. Therefore, you should help the student gain insight into his or her present behavior and choose more responsible behavior. The student should understand that this meeting is to help him or her, rather than punish. The student should also know that you are concerned and that you care.

3. **Question the student to find out why there is a problem.** It is important to listen to the student's point of view rather than assume you know why the student is misbehaving. Question the student about what the problem may be. It might be that the work is too hard or that there is something happening at home or with other students who are contributing to the misbehavior.

    Questions should be stated in a caring, nonaccusational manner. Avoid questions such as "What is your problem?" Instead, use questions such as "Did something happen today to get you so upset?" or "Can you tell me what's causing you to be so upset?" After asking the question, listen carefully to the student and don't interrupt. Let the student talk. By doing so, you will have more information and fuller understanding of the student and the circumstances that contribute to the misbehavior.

4. **Determine what you can do to help.** Based on the answers to your earlier questions, you may discover there is a simple method to get the student back on track, such as moving his or her seat away from another student. In most cases, however, the solution is more difficult to find.

■ WHAT WOULD YOU DECIDE?   Meeting with a Disruptive Student

A student has been misbehaving in your class, primarily due to limited self-management and social skills. It has reached the point where you decide that a special, private meeting is warranted to express your concern, provide guidance, clarify your expectations, and seek a practical course of action to overcome the problems:

1. What materials might you need to gather, and how might you prepare for this meeting?

2. How might you prepare for and conduct the meeting differently if the student instead showed behavior excesses such as noncompliance and aggression?

5. **Determine how the student can improve his or her behavior.** Part of the meeting should focus on what the student can choose to do differently in the future to avoid problem behaviors. Talk about the situation and listen to the student's input.

   At this time, it may be necessary to reteach appropriate behaviors for certain classroom activities. Most students need only a single explanation of procedures for classroom activities such as independent seatwork, discussion, cooperative groups, and entering and leaving the room. Other more difficult students need to be taught how to behave and be reminded often. While you will have previously taught appropriate procedures to the entire class, this one-to-one meeting with the difficult student provides an opportunity to reteach and clarify these procedures and expectations.

6. **State your expectations about how the student is to behave.** The student must understand that you are very serious about not allowing the misbehavior to continue. While expressing a caring attitude to work with the student to solve the problem, the student must realize that predetermined consequences will be used if he or she chooses to continue to misbehave. Therefore, near the end of the meeting, you might say something like: "I'm going to work with you to solve this problem. I know that you can behave responsibly. But you must remember that fighting is not acceptable. Anytime you choose to fight, you will be choosing to go to the principal."

7. **Disarm criticism.** Some difficult students may become argumentative and critical and may actually blame you for all the problems they have in class. In that case, take steps to disarm the criticism by letting the student speak. Also, ask the student for more information concerning why he or she is upset with you. This approach can help calm the student down, and he or she will see you as being concerned. This additional information will likely help address the problem.

8. **Document the meeting.** In addition to anecdotal records you keep concerning the student's behavior in class, it is important to keep records of any one-to-one meeting you have with the student. This documentation should include the date of the meeting, a summary of the ideas generated in the meeting, and any conclusions that were drawn.

Consult and Inform Others

You may want to consult with others to get more information or advice about how to deal with the challenging student in the classroom. The principal, school counselor, psychologist, or other teachers who currently or previously came in contact with the student may be consulted for more information. They could also share their experiences in dealing with the student and perhaps offer recommendations for strategies that you could take in the classroom. The student's family members are also a source of information about the student. Consultations are intended to help you deal with the student in the classroom; no referrals for outside services are made at this point.

Rather than wait until the behavior becomes very serious, inform the principal or family members about the problems. They will then know what you are doing and may be able to support you as the situation warrants. If the problems become more serious, the principal and family will appreciate this earlier contact rather than being surprised by a crisis at a later time. At a later time, the principal and parents may be involved in actions to address the problems if they persist or become more severe.

Provide Positive Support

Students need to receive reinforcement for their appropriate behavior through social reinforcers, activities and privileges, tangible reinforcers, and token reinforcers. Reinforcement encourages the student to continue the rewarded behavior. Challenging students especially need to be reinforced for their appropriate behavior. Even though it may be easy to overlook delivering reinforcement to difficult students, they need to receive their fair share of rewards for their appropriate behavior. You may choose to make notes in your plan book as reminders to reinforce difficult students at regular intervals.

Challenging students need to receive additional positive support beyond what is given to all students in the class (Canter, 2010; Rhode et al., 2020). One way is to call the student at home before the school year begins. (You will know which students to call based on information you hear from the student's teachers from the previous year.) In this way, you can ask the student for ideas about how the school year could be successful and to express your confidence that you and the student will work together to have a good year.

You could contact the student's family to express your caring about their child, get input about the student's experiences the previous year, get input on what the child needs from you this year, emphasize that the student will be most successful if you and the family work together, and express confidence that by working together the child will have a more successful experience at school. This early contact helps build a positive relationship with the family before problems arise.

Another approach that can be used with all students but is especially useful with challenging students is to have them fill out a student interest inventory at the start of the school year. Based on the questions you ask and the responses provided, you will have a fuller understanding of the student's interests. Furthermore, personal attention and welcoming words should be given to the challenging child when coming into the classroom. If problems occur during the day, you could call the student at home in the evening to express concern and inquire about the problem.

Relating to the student as an individual is important. Take time to talk with the student or involve yourself with him or her in school activities. The individual attention of a caring adult can make a big difference. Visiting the student at home is another way of showing your concern.

■ CLASSROOM CASE STUDY   A Class with a History of Disruption

David DeFranco had some concerns when preparing his fifth-grade classroom for the new school year. This particular class of students had a reputation from their previous grades for teasing, arguing, insulting, and pushing each other to the limits. Mr. DeFranco followed the guidelines for effectively starting the school year by making management and instructional preparations, establishing rules and procedures, and so on.

Despite his preparation and guidance, within a couple weeks his students started to exhibit the same challenging behaviors he heard from the students' previous teachers. They argued with each other and just didn't seem to like or respect each other. This led to disturbances and conflicts during instructional time and also transition times. Three students, in particular, seemed to be the ones encouraging this disruptive behavior by needling others and provoking reactions. All of this led to a significant decrease in quality instructional time, and the classroom atmosphere always seemed tense since another disruption could occur at any moment.

Mr. DeFranco decided he couldn't continue with his typical instruction and his typical responses to student misbehavior any longer. The students just didn't appear to have the social and interpersonal skills to effectively deal with conflict. After assessing the situation, Mr. DeFranco decided to take a multipronged approach. First, he decided to meet individually with the three students who were the ring-leaders, and then set up behavioral contracts for each that included rewards and penalties. By checking the behavior of these students, he reasoned much provocation would be reduced.

Second, Mr. DeFranco decided the entire class would benefit from some training on social skills, conflict resolution, and self-management skills. He located some commercially prepared materials that included lesson plans and discussion guides to teach these skills. He planned to use regular class time to discuss the problems the class was experiencing and to have the students go through the training materials. Third, Mr. DeFranco talked with the principal and school counselor to inform them of the situation and to seek any advice and assistance they might offer.

Focus Questions

1. Do you agree or disagree with the three actions that Mr. DeFranco selected? Why?

2. What other approaches might you suggest to Mr. DeFranco to address the problem?

3. With an understanding of these incoming students, would you start the school year differently from what you typically might do?

Decrease Inappropriate Behavior

Your rules and consequences for the class should be used for all students, including challenging students. Since the consequences selected may not work for challenging students, you may need to select alternative consequences for these students only. Some discipline plans include the delivery of a series of consequences based on the number of rule infractions the student has made. Several consequences are discussed below:

1. **Loss of privileges.** A number of special privileges may be provided for students. Withdrawing privileges can be an effective consequence, but you need to determine which privileges will have the most influence on correcting the student's behavior if the privilege is withdrawn.

2. **Time-out.** Time-out involves removing the student from the instructional setting. Thus, the student is not given the opportunity to obtain reinforcement for the misbehavior. There are several types of time-out. One of the most effective approaches is to remove the student from the instructional situation to be seated apart from the rest of the class; however, the student is expected to continue to do the work or listen to the lesson. In this way, the disruption stops, the rest of the class gets back to work, and the disrupting student is given an opportunity to calm down and get back to the instructional activities. You may ask the student to complete an incident reaction sheet during the time-out.

3. **Time after class.** Keeping the student for about a minute after class can be an important consequence for students moving on to another classroom after your class. This separates the student from peers, which can be perceived as a big penalty, and provides you with an opportunity to speak to the student about his or her behavior and the better choices that could have been made. At this time, you could give the student an index card on which to write a brief description of what was done in class to warrant staying after class. He or she could then sign and date the card for you to use as documentation in the event that the principal, parents, or others need to be contacted.

4. **Detention.** Detention involves the loss of free time and the opportunity to socialize with other students. Loss of recess time and staying after school are two common types of detention. Students should understand the reasons for the detention, and the time should not be excessive. You may ask the student to complete an incident reaction sheet during detention.

5. **Student calls a family member.** Having the student call his or her family at home or at work in your presence can be a strong deterrent. The student is expected to explain the problem behavior and what will be done to improve. The call should be made as soon as possible after the incident when both you and the student can get to a phone in the building. This may take place at recess, at lunch, or at the end of the class period.

6. **Time-out in another classroom.** If a student is highly disruptive, it may be useful to send him or her to another classroom at the same or higher grade level for a specified amount of time. This approach is useful for students who seek attention, because they are removed from the peers whose attention they seek. It is important that participating teachers discuss and agree to arrangements for sending and receiving disruptive students for a time-out. If students disrupt the classroom where they are sent for the time-out, they should know that the next consequence will be delivered, which may be a trip to the principal's office.

Prepare a Behavioral Contract

A *behavioral contract* is a written agreement between you and the student that represents a commitment for the student to behave more appropriately. A contract commonly includes (a) a statement of the expected, appropriate behavior; (b) a specified time period during which the student

■ WHAT WOULD YOU DECIDE?   Preparing a Behavioral Contract

Students in your classroom are working in small groups when you notice that one student argues with others in the group, delays completing expected group work, and does the opposite of what is expected. This student consistently displays this behavior when there is small group work; it is a pattern with her behavior. She displays these actions even when there is whole-class instruction. You decide that something must be done to deal with this challenging student. You decide to prepare a behavior contract for her, and you consider the four parts that are in a typical contract:

1. What is the expected, appropriate behavior that you would include in the contract?

2. What rewards or positive support would you identify when she exhibits the appropriate behavior?

3. What penalties or corrective actions would you include?

4. Would you decide on all of these items yourself, or would you involve the student in the discussion? Why would you handle it yourself? Why would you involve the student?

is to exhibit such behavior; (c) rewards or positive support for exhibiting the appropriate behavior; and (d) penalties or corrective actions that will be taken if the student does not exhibit the appropriate behavior.

Behavioral contracts are not necessary for all challenging students. Some students may respond favorably to the approaches that have been discussed up to this point. A behavioral contract should be prepared for students who do not respond to the techniques previously described, or if you are delivering more and more consequences for a particular student or are getting frustrated or angry. A behavioral contract should then be drawn up.

Behavior contracting can be used at any grade level but is often more appropriate and effective with elementary and middle level students, as older students may resent obvious attempts to manipulate their behavior. This contract is also effective with special education students.

Know When to Involve Others

Consultations made earlier with the principal, school counselor, or psychologist were intended to provide information and advice as you deal with the challenging student. Sometimes, however, students do not respond to any of your strategies, and the misbehavior may continue to be chronic and serious. In such cases, it is necessary to involve others in helping the student. Deviant and disruptive behavior warrants referrals to outside help.

Prior informal contacts, telephone calls, and conferences with family members informed them of the student behaviors and your actions. Now, you need formal contact with the principal or counselors to solicit their assistance.

The principal can counsel or intervene in various ways when handling a challenging student. A referral to the school counselor or psychologist is warranted when you recognize that a developing problem is beyond your professional expertise. Remember that you have not been trained to be a psychologist, counselor, or social worker, and you should not view yourself as a failure when referring the student to receive help from someone with appropriate training. Some districts use an intervention assistance team approach. Many district and community agencies work with schools and families, and these agencies also might be contacted.

Be Ready for Urgent Action

It is important to have a thoughtful, deliberate plan to deal with challenging or violent students, as outlined earlier. However, unexpected, disturbing events may occur in your classroom that require immediate action. For example, students may become involved in a physical fight, have a tantrum, destroy property, exhibit bullying behavior, tease others in a mean way, show cruel behavior, or carry a weapon.

Give advance thought to how you would deal with disturbing events that might occur and decide on the general ways that you will respond to those events. For example, if there is a physical fight, you may tell students to stop, disperse the other students, do not physically intervene, and get help. You cannot foresee every type of incident, but your advance thought and decision making will enable you to be ready for urgent action if it is needed.

Seeking Outside Help

After deciding to seek outside help, you first need to gather all the documentation that you have prepared up to this time. You then need to select the most appropriate person to contact. When outside help is needed, it is common practice in many schools to first contact the principal, who may take some actions or recommend that you contact the counselor or psychologist. Family members may be involved at any point, depending on the recommendations of the principal, counselor, or psychologist.

Principal

When dealing with chronic or serious misbehavior, the principal has the authority to make certain decisions. The principal may counsel or intervene when dealing with challenging students, including rewarding positive behavior. In consultation with you, the principal may be helpful in giving words of praise or other rewards when the student's behavior has improved. The principal might counsel the student by talking with the student. This additional guidance about the consequences of the student's choices can make a difference in turning the behavior around.

The principal might contact the family. This keeps the family informed of actions taken up to that time and they can be asked to support those actions at home. The principal might recommend that the family members come to the school for a conference with the teacher or others. The principal might approve new placements, services, or suspensions. Depending on the circumstances, the principal may take several actions such as changing the classroom placement, arranging for in-school suspension in a separate room, or referring the student to a counselor or psychologist. In more serious cases, the principal has the authority to seek placement in specialized educational settings outside the school, arrange for long-term suspension, or contact the police or other appropriate community agencies.

Sometimes a student's problems are rooted in deeper and more pervasive personality disturbances or family problems. The school psychologist can provide more intensive evaluation and diagnostic study. The psychologist will use the anecdotal and other records that you have accumulated concerning the student and will supplement them with other tests, interviews, and observations. This analysis can lead to recommendations for actions to be taken by those at the school or may result in referrals to outside agencies or resources.

Counselors and Psychologists

Other than the principal, the school counselor is often one of the first people contacted when outside help is needed for dealing with challenging students. The counselor may explore the student's behavior, the classroom environment, your teaching style, the classroom management plan, or a variety of related issues. The counselor then tries to provide objective feedback and suggestions for new approaches to deal with the problems. By considering the viewpoints of both you and the student, the counselor can serve as an intermediary for any potential conflicts.

VOICES FROM THE CLASSROOM   A Meeting with the Family

Beth Schmar, sixth-grade teacher, Topeka, Kansas

In the middle of March, my principal and I realized that Brad had taken control of the classroom. The other students hung on his every word and followed each of his actions. Brad was constantly seeking the other students' attention by rotating between being the class clown and the class bully. Either way, he had their admiration or awe.

From the start of the school year, the principal and I tried many behavior-management approaches, from a contract to suspension. In an act of desperation, we requested a meeting with Brad and his family. We decided to include Brad for the entire meeting and to speak to him frankly. The principal and I shared our expectations for Brad's behavior and explained how his current behavior fell below these expectations. With the help of Brad and his family, we developed a behavior plan that we all could live with.

We expressed to Brad genuine caring and concern about his future, along with our own frustrations about his lack of success. Our honesty helped Brad react differently. He even commented to his family later, "At least now I know the principal and teacher don't hate me." The meeting was the beginning of a new understanding that made our time together more positive.

Problem-Solving Teams

Some schools have a committee that assists teachers in dealing with classroom problems. *Problem-solving teams* consist of groups of educational personnel, parents, and other involved parties that meet systematically to discuss problems referred to them by other educational personnel within their school. The teams provide collegial assistance for teachers with a minimum of bureaucracy. The teams also increase commitment, communication, and morale by involving teachers and families as expert resources and collaborators in problem solving.

The problem-solving team identifies the needs, receives referrals, and plans and coordinates interventions with teachers, family members, other educational personnel, and community agencies. Some teams become involved in preventive interventions, crisis intervention, and interagency coordination. Teams can provide (a) help for teachers in dealing with educational, behavioral, and discipline problems; (b) early identification and schoolwide prevention of the problems; (c) a means of in-school intervention for the problems; and (d) a mechanism for referral to appropriate educational resources.

Families

Many teachers, principals, counselors, and psychologists prefer that they be contacted before the families are contacted. In this way, those at the school can explore all appropriate interventions without prematurely involving the parents. If it becomes necessary to contact the family members, they are often more responsive when they learn that steps have been taken already. Family members may then visit with you or others in the school. This is a more formal meeting than previous informational contacts, and the principal or others at the school may participate.

The initial meeting with the family gives all parties the opportunity to share information about the student and formulate a common information base. Teachers and counselors, for example, may review the set of documentation about the series of incidents and actions that have taken place. Family members may share information about the child's attitudes and behaviors at home. Together, those present at the meeting can develop a plan of action. Depending on the nature of the problem, they may conclude that some outside agency should be consulted.

The student may be asked to attend this meeting or will be informed by the teacher, counselor, or principal about the results of this meeting shortly after the meeting occurs. The primary purposes of this meeting are to share information, develop a plan of action to help the child be successful, and gather the support of the family.

District or Community Agencies

Community agencies work with schools and families to help each child be successful. For example, Cities in Schools is a national nonprofit organization dedicated to decreasing the dropout rate. Its mission is to assist a targeted group of children to achieve academic and social success by coordinating existing community services to them and their families through the schools. That agency might be contacted to assist in some way.

Many districts or city governments have an office of substance abuse and violence prevention and intervention, and its resources may be useful. Social workers are available in various community agencies. Other types of offices and organizations within the district or community might also be contacted for help.

MAJOR CONCEPTS

1. Challenging students often have excessive noncompliant and aggressive behavior or behavioral deficits in self-management, social, and academic skills.

2. Underlying influences that may contribute to persistent misbehavior include emotional or physical abuse or neglect, organic conditions, drugs or alcohol, or gangs.

3. A commitment and a plan must be made to help each challenging student succeed.

4. Specific strategies can be used to help students manage their anger constructively, calm their anger, and deal with another person's anger.

5. Students can be taught new behavioral skills, such as social skills, conflict resolution skills, and self-management skills, as a means to help them seek alternatives to disruption and violence.

6. Documentation of the student's behavior and the teacher's actions is needed. This may include anecdotal records, incident reaction sheets, or records of meeting and contracts.

7. The plan of action for the classroom involves assessing the situation, meeting with the student, consulting and informing others, providing positive support for the student, taking steps to decrease inappropriate behavior, preparing a behavioral contract, and knowing when to involve others.

8. The principal, counselor, psychologist, problem-solving teams, or family members may be contacted if actions taken in the classroom are not successful.

DISCUSSION/REFLECTIVE QUESTIONS

1. Should teachers deal only with the student's problem classroom behavior or should they also try to address the underlying influences? What are your reasons?

2. Why might teachers sometimes have difficulty in making a commitment to help challenging kids?

3. How might your grade level and the characteristics of your particular students affect how you select and teach strategies to deal with anger, solve problems, and develop new behavioral skills?

4. From your experience as a K–12 student, how did other students express anger in the classroom? Did those episodes interrupt instruction? How did the teacher respond?

5. When you respond to disruptive or challenging behavior, why is the step on "assess the situation" important?

6. What are the reasons for meeting with the challenging student to address the problems? What can be gained from this meeting?

7. At what point would you go to the principal concerning challenging students in your classroom? What might the principal do to help out?

SUGGESTED ACTIVITIES

1. Ask several teachers about how they deal with challenging students in their classrooms. What are examples of troubling behavior? Do the teachers have any particular approaches or overall plan or strategy?

2. Reflect on what makes you upset and angry and also how you respond when you are upset. What guidelines can you establish for yourself when you might get upset about something that happens in your classroom?

3. Obtain and read resource material on teaching students new behavioral skills such as social skills, conflict resolution skills, and self-management skills. How might you apply those skills into your own classroom?

4. Talk to a school counselor, psychologist, or a member of a school problem-solving team about cases concerning challenging or violent students. What were the behaviors? What recommendations or actions were taken in working with these students?

FURTHER READING

Curwin, R. L., Mendler, A. N., & Mendler, B. D. (2018). *Discipline with dignity* (4th ed.). Alexandria, VA: Association for Supervision and Curriculum Development.
Is a solid source for ways to build responsibility, relationships, and respect in your classroom. Includes chapters on special challenges and students who chronically misbehave.

Kaiser, B., & Rasminsky, J. S. (2017). *Challenging behavior in elementary and middle school* (4th ed.). Boston, MA: Pearson.
Provides comprehensive discussion of risk factors, influences, relationships, culture, preventive strategies, guidance and other disciplinary strategies, bullying, and working with families.

Kapalka, G. (2009). *8 steps to classroom management success: A guide for teachers of challenging students*. Thousand Oaks, CA: Corwin Press.
Provides useful actions to address challenging students, such as giving effective warnings, handling flare-ups, constructing a behavioral contract, managing transitions, and discouraging disruptions.

Otten, K. L., & Tuttle, J. L. (2011). *How to reach and teach children with challenging behavior*. San Francisco, CA: Jossey-Bass.
Is a comprehensive resource that includes, practical, ready-to-use interventions. Has a K–8 focus. Includes sections on social skills instruction, preventing challenging behavior, reinforcing desired behavior, and using consequences.

chapter

11

© Michael Newman/PhotoEdit Inc.

Collaborating with Colleagues and Families

CHAPTER OUTLINE

CHAPTER OBJECTIVES

This chapter provides information that will help you:

- Collaborate with colleagues for assistance and professional development.

- Describe the reasons for contacting and interacting with families.

- Recognize the reasons some families resist involvement.

- Determine ways to work through cultural and language differences.

- Communicate with families through a variety of approaches.

- Prepare for and effectively conduct parent–teacher conferences.

Can you imagine how challenging it must have been to teach in a one-room school-house? There were so many responsibilities and challenges with the curriculum, instructional materials, and student behavior, and no one to turn to for help. Fortunately, teachers today have a number of colleagues to whom they can turn for assistance concerning a variety of issues.

Families can also be contacted for assistance when working with their children. In addition, teachers must take a variety of steps to contact and communicate with families about the school program and the progress of their children. This chapter addresses ways to work with both colleagues and families.

Working with Colleagues

Teachers don't teach in isolation. They need to interact with others in various ways to meet the needs of the students in their classroom. There has been increasing recognition of collaboration in the profession. For example, when the InTASC standards for teachers were revised in 2011, a new standard was included concerning leadership and collaboration (see those standards in this book on pages xv–xvi) (Council of Chief State School Officers [CCSSO], 2011). The number of professional education resource books on collaboration has also increased in recent years. This is happening because collaboration is needed in schools, and educators are looking for resources to be successful in their collaborative activities.

What Is Collaboration?

Collaboration is a style of interaction between individuals engaged in shared decision making as they work toward a common goal. People who collaborate have equally valued resources to contribute, and they share decision-making authority and accountability for outcomes (CCSSO, 2011, p. 20).

Teachers often need to turn to others for assistance when dealing with student behavior problems, reading or language problems, media and instructional technology, students with special needs, curricular issues, instructional strategies, and numerous other issues. Depending on the issue, teachers may turn to one or more of these colleagues and resource people: principals, counselors or psychologists, reading specialists, special education resource teachers, librarians, media specialists, curriculum specialists, school or district committees, or district or community agencies.

Sometimes, this interaction is only to obtain information from a colleague; at other times there is genuine interaction and shared decision making toward a common goal about an issue—this is collaboration. But collaboration is not only about addressing an issue concerning a certain student; there are several purposes of collaboration, as noted in the next section.

Why Collaborate?

There are several reasons for going out of your own classroom to interact and collaborate with others. You might be applying your school's Response to Intervention (RTI) plan when addressing the learning needs of several students in your class, and you need to arrange for intensive intervention by another educator. You might have three students with disabilities, and you need to interact with the special education teacher. You might have a student who is having trouble dealing with a family problem, and you need to contact the school psychologist or counselor. You might be seeking information on how to use formative assessment, and you choose to work with another teacher on this topic. You might be asked to serve on a schoolwide committee addressing student dropouts in high school.

Many more examples could be provided, but the reasons for collaborating fall into the following categories:

1. **To meet the needs of the students.** Let's say you are dealing with a student who has significant misbehavior problems. It is wise to consult with the principal, school counselor, and/or psychologist to obtain information and advice as you work with this challenging student. Sometimes, however, students do not respond to any of your strategies, and the misbehavior may continue to be chronic and serious. Deviant and disruptive behavior warrants referrals to outside help. In such cases, you may need to refer this student to the school counselor or psychologist when you recognize that a developing problem is beyond your professional expertise. Remember that you have not been trained to be a psychologist, counselor, or social worker, and you should not view yourself as a failure when referring the student for help from someone with appropriate training.

   Before students' problem behavior gets serious enough for these referrals, it is often helpful to have telephone calls and conferences with families to inform them of the student behaviors and your actions and to solicit their assistance. In addition, the principal can counsel or intervene in various ways when handling a challenging student.

   In serious cases, district and community agencies might need to be contacted to work with the school and the family. Many districts or city governments have an office of substance abuse and violence prevention and intervention, and its resources may be useful. Social workers are available in various community agencies. Other types of offices and organizations within the district or community might be contacted for help.

2. **To improve professional competence by engaging in professional development activities.** Ongoing professional development is crucial when trying to meet the needs of all students. Teachers need to learn about new aspects of the curriculum, how to apply new instructional techniques, how to effectively check for student understanding, how to integrate technology into their instruction, how to provide better guidance to read in the content area, and a host of other interests and needs. Therefore, teachers seek out collaborative opportunities to increase their knowledge and skills in any number of areas. Some of these collaborative approaches to professional development include mentoring programs, co-teaching, peer coaching, teacher support groups, and teacher centers.

3. **To provide leadership when addressing a school improvement issue.** Teachers can be agents for change and for school improvement by serving on schoolwide or districtwide committees or task forces. Many types of special task forces or ongoing committees exist in schools and districts. They deal with issues such as discipline, textbook adoptions, curriculum development and revisions, improving reading ability, professional development programs, assisting English language learners, and a variety of other topics. By working in a collaborative way on these committees, teachers can address important school issues and be advocates for the students.

■ **WHAT WOULD YOU DECIDE?** **Collaborating to Help a Student**

In your first year of teaching, you have a student who is particularly challenging. She is not performing well academically and does not appear to be concerned about this. The student might have a learning disability, but you are not certain since you were not trained as a special education teacher. She seems to have a quick temper when interacting with other students, and you get the impression that there also might be some situation in her home that is contributing to the student's behavior. You know that you need to collaborate with others to find out more information about the student and to determine ways to best address the student's needs.

1. Who would you go to for information about the student and to seek assistance in addressing her issues?

2. How might the student's former teachers help? School social workers? Special education teachers? What type of information or assistance might these people provide in this case?

3. How might you approach the student's family to seek information and help?

Collaborate with Whom?

To serve the three reasons for collaboration, teachers interact and collaborate with a variety of people. The particular need or circumstance will typically dictate whom the teacher may contact.

Other Teachers

When trying to meet the learning needs or the behavior of their students, teachers often turn to colleagues as a source of ideas and support. This may take place in an informal manner but also may occur in grade-level or subject-area teams in more formal structures.

When trying to improve professional competence or to address a school improvement issue, teachers work with other teachers in many different ways, such as mentoring teams, peer coaching, lesson study groups, professional learning communities, action research groups, and co-teaching arrangements. Many teachers co-plan and co-teach with other teachers (Bauml, 2016; Beninghof & Leensvaart, 2016). Resource books are available on these collaborative approaches, as illustrated by these examples:

- *Collaborate, Communicate, and Differentiate* (Murawski & Spencer, 2011)
- *A Guide to Co-Teaching* (Villa, Thousand, & Nevin, 2013)
- *The Practice of Authentic Professional Learning Communities* (Venables, 2011)
- *Teacher Collaboration for Professional Learning* (Lassonde & Israel, 2009)
- *Action Research* (Mertler, 2020)

Other School Professionals

Teachers collaborate with many other school professionals, including counselors or psychologists, reading specialists, special education resource teachers, librarians, media specialists, and curriculum specialists. Educators in these other roles have specialized training for their particular responsibilities. Thus, they are an important source of information and expertise as teachers collaborate with them.

Teachers often interact with other school professionals when they have questions or needs related to teaching and meeting the needs of their students. In addition to working with individual teachers concerning specific needs, these other school professionals may also be involved in professional development efforts for large groups of teachers and service on school-wide committees.

VOICES FROM THE CLASSROOM   Collaborating with Colleagues for Data-Driven Decision Making

Wendy Whitten-Lavery, third-grade teacher, Ocala, Florida

My third-grade team recently collaborated with our reading coach to develop a systematic approach to data-driven planning. First, our reading coach analyzes the data for the upcoming skill we are going to teach. She checks to see how our grade level did with the skill on assessments, reviews the types of questions that seemed to be a challenge for students, and then sends a list of the types of essential questions that we should have our students become familiar with.

Then our data groups meet. We divided our third-grade team into two data groups, which meet once per week. One group focuses on finding or developing skill-related activities, while the other group creates data-driven essential questions to go along with the reading materials for the skill. Finally, the information is shared through email so that all of the teachers in the grade level are given input and have access to a wide variety of materials and approaches to teach the skill. This approach divides a task among many people so that all students in the grade level can receive a well-formulated plan of instruction. This collaboration to inform our decision making has made a big difference.

School Administrators

Each school will have a school principal. Depending on the size of the school and the level of complexity, there may be additional school administrators such as an assistant principal or a director of the reading program. Teachers may need to consult and collaborate with one or more of these administrators concerning the students in their class, their professional development, or their involvement in school improvement opportunities.

Schoolwide Committees or Teams

There may be various types of schoolwide committees or task forces to deal with issues such as discipline, textbook adoptions, curriculum development and revisions, improving reading ability, professional development programs, assisting English language learners, and a variety of other topics. Teachers are often members of such committees. If not a member, teachers may need to consult or interact with the committees if they have a need to be addressed.

To address discipline problems, some schools have problem-solving teams composed of the school psychologist, special educators, administrators, and other colleagues (Minahan & Baker, 2015). The teams often examine the causes of the behavior, identify ways to address the causes, and take steps to support the classroom teacher in working with the student. One district in Wisconsin, for example, formed a district-wide behavior intervention committee to address challenges for students experiencing trauma (Platt, 2019).

Students

Although the degree of collaboration may not be the same as with other educators, teachers can collaborate with their students in various ways. If a teacher is conducting action research in her own classroom, for example, the students may be involved in the process. Collaboration can also occur with students as co-teachers in cooperative learning groups (Villa, Thousand, & Nevin, 2010).

Families

When considering the purposes of collaboration, teachers most often collaborate with families to support the learning of their children. There should be more than communication by the teacher to the families; there should be interaction and collaboration to promote the learning of the students. Parents can be partners in supporting the learning of their children.

Due to the nature of the condition and the learning needs, teachers may need to interact and collaborate more often with the parents of students with disabilities or special needs. Fortunately, there are some useful resources available to provide guidance (e.g., Cramer, 2006; Dardig, 2008). In addition, extra efforts need to be made to provide culturally responsive family involvement and collaboration (Grant & Ray, 2019).

School–Community Partnerships

Schools sometimes reach out to community agencies to capture support for student learning and to address certain problems. For example, it is becoming increasingly common for businesses to financially support certain school interests, needs, or programs. They might purchase necessary school equipment, such as computers, or support certain school programs, such as the theater department. Common community partnerships with schools include the following (Epstein & Associates, 2018): (a) businesses and corporations; (b) universities and other institutions of higher learning; (c) national and local volunteer organizations; and (d) social service agencies and health partners.

These partnerships are often coordinated by a school administrator, but teachers are typically involved in developing the school–community partnership proposals and in conducting the actions designated in the partnership. Roles, responsibilities, and relationships between the school professionals, community agencies, and service providers must be carefully defined if the partnerships are to succeed (Kochhar-Bryant & Heishman, 2010).

Collaboration Skills and Dispositions

Teachers need certain tools to effectively partner with others. Regardless of the purpose of the collaboration or the people with whom you collaborate, the following skills and dispositions can lead to more successful partnerships.

Skills

What skills are needed to effectively collaborate with others? InTASC Standard #10: Leadership and Collaboration provides a perspective on what teachers might be expected to do when providing leadership and collaborating with others (CCSSO, 2011). Clues about necessary collaboration skills can be inferred from those performance statements. Here are some representative performances from that standard requiring collaboration:

- Take an active role on the instructional team, give and receive feedback on practice, examine learner work, analyze data from multiple sources, and share responsibility for decision making and accountability for each student's learning.

- Work collaboratively with learners and their families to establish mutual expectations and ongoing communication to support learner development and achievement.

- Work with school colleagues to build ongoing connections with community resources to enhance student learning and well-being.

- Engage in professional learning, contribute to the knowledge and skill of others, and work collaboratively to advance professional practice.

When examining these representative performances, some broader skills necessary for effective collaboration become apparent. These collaboration skills include the following:

1. **Communication skills.** Effective verbal and nonverbal communication skills are needed. How a person uses these skills also makes a difference in collaboration. Active listening, providing information, and asking questions are part of good interpersonal relations that are based on communication skills.

2. **Problem-solving skills.** There are several steps in problem solving: identify the problem, generate potential solutions, evaluate potential solutions, select the solution, implement the solution, and evaluate the outcome. Collaboration often involves addressing problems, and problem-solving skills are needed for effective collaboration.

3. **Conflict resolution skills.** Collaboration with others may be needed to address a conflict situation with students or others. Also, conflicts might arise with your collaborative partners when addressing issues of attention or concern. Mediation and negotiations skills may be needed to resolve the conflict.

4. **Administrative and management skills.** Skills are needed to coordinate and implement the actions identified from the collaborative discussions. This might involve practical matters such as scheduling and coordinating services. When interacting with other school professionals on an ongoing basis, additional skills may be needed. When working with a paraprofessional, for example, a teacher will need skills related to training, planning, assigning responsibilities, communicating, supervising, and evaluating the work of the paraprofessional (Ashbaker & Morgan, 2013; Friend & Cook, 2017).

Dispositions

In addition to the skills just reviewed, certain dispositions are needed for effective collaboration. Here are some representative dispositions:

- Takes the initiative to grow and develop with colleagues through interactions that enhance practice and support student learning.

- Respects families' beliefs, norms, and expectations and seeks to work collaboratively with learners and families in setting and meeting challenging goals.

- Willing to be helpful in making necessary compromises to accomplish a common goal. Willing to assume shared responsibility for collaborate work.

- Willing to participate in respectful and reciprocal communication.

Many schools have various types of committees and task forces, and collaboration takes place in those venues. These groups may meet in an ongoing basis, and certain skills are needed to conduct these committees in an effective manner (Glaser, 2005). The responsibility for conducting these committees falls to the group leader. The skills of effective group processing are also needed for collaboration in this context.

Working with Families

Imagine that you are a parent and that you and your family just moved into a new community during the summer. You have one child in third grade and another in seventh grade. Because

■ CLASSROOM CASE STUDY   Working with Colleagues and Families

Hui Chen is an eighth-grade mathematics teacher at a middle school. At a grade-level team meeting about six months into the school year, Ms. Chen and her colleagues discussed issues of concern. They noted that one of their students, Miranda, had been struggling in all of her classes all year. Miranda was on the verge of failing three of these classes, and she would likely have to repeat the eighth grade unless her performance improved. Even when the teachers had discussed Miranda in previous team meetings, they had agreed that her poor organizational and study skills contributed to her current academic standing.

Ms. Chen and her colleagues scheduled a student–teacher meeting with Miranda where they discussed ways to improve her organizational and study skills. Miranda was given a booklet to record her homework assignments, and she was encouraged to attend after-school homework sessions. Despite these efforts, Miranda continued to struggle in all of her classes, and her grades worsened. After determining that Miranda was on the verge of being held back, Ms. Chen and her colleagues decided to contact Miranda's family.

When Ms. Chen telephoned Miranda's family, the conversation was tension-filled and awkward. Miranda's parents were frustrated that they had not been contacted sooner. They stated that Miranda had never performed at the top of her class but that she always earned passing marks. Even though Ms. Chen attempted to address the issues and schedule a meeting about the concerns, Miranda's parents refused and declared that they would go straight to the school administration to discuss their daughter's situation.

Focus Questions

1. What errors did the teachers make in handling the situation with Miranda?

2. How could the teachers have handled the situation differently to establish better communication and collaboration with Miranda's parents from the start?

you moved from another state, you are concerned that the curriculum might be quite different in this new district, and you wonder how your children will adjust to the new community and their new school and teacher. Wouldn't you want to talk to the teachers to share some of these issues? Wouldn't you like to hear about the curriculum and how the teachers will handle instruction? Wouldn't you like to maintain ongoing contact throughout the school year? Yes, of course!

Good communication with families should be a priority because it keeps teachers and families informed about what is happening. It also builds trust so that there can be a working partnership in the event there are difficulties with the students. Although a teacher's primary responsibility is to work with students, it is important to communicate and interact with the students' families throughout the school year. The reason for the communication will often determine the timing of the contact and the means by which the contact will be made.

At the start, we must recognize that children come from many types of family settings. While some students come from traditional or nuclear families (47%), others come from single-parent families (27%), blended families (16%), extended or multigenerational families (6%), or other types of families such as gay and lesbian families, families headed by grandparents, families with adopted or foster children, and even homeless families (Olsen & Fuller, 2012; Scully, Stites, Roberts-King, & Barbour, 2019). As a result of these various family settings, the term *parent* is used throughout this book to represent the adult or adults who have parental responsibility. Thus, this definition of a parent could include the biological parents, foster or stepparents, a grandparent, an aunt or uncle, an older sibling, or a guardian.

It is important to listen carefully to families to identify their concerns and suggestions. Trust is developed when they know that their ideas are recognized and understood. The full benefits of parent–school relationships are not realized without this interaction and collaboration. Fortunately, a number of useful resources provide guidance when working with families (e.g., Berger & Riojas-Cortez, 2019; L. Canter & Canter, 2001; R. LeBlanc-Esparza & LeBlanc-Esparza, 2013; Olender, Elias, & Mastroleo, 2010; Olsen & Fuller, 2012; Santana,

Rothstein, & Bain, 2016). In *Understanding Families*, Hanson and Lynch (2013) provide important foundational information about many types of families and ways to communicate and collaborate with them to benefit their children.

In a review of research literature on parental engagement, Walker and Hoover-Dempsey (2015) report that parental engagement has been positively related to achievement across grade levels and ethnic groups, and research demonstrates that when teachers and parents work together, student learning and engagement are enhanced. Thus, it is important to create and maintain open lines of communication between the school and the families to promote student learning and engagement. Many ways to provide that communication are described later in this chapter.

Reasons for Working with Families

Students ultimately benefit from good communication and effective working relationships between the school and home. Families' involvement in their children's schooling has been associated with better attendance, more positive student attitudes and behavior, greater willingness to do homework, and higher academic achievement. There are several reasons why you should communicate with parents:

1. **To create open, two-way communication and to establish friendly relations.** Positive contacts with families early in the year help establish positive, friendly relations. In this way, families see each other not as adversaries but as allies in helping the student be successful. Two-way communication can be fostered, and that will result in appropriate school–community relations that will benefit everyone involved.

2. **To understand the student's home condition.** Information about a student's home setting can help you decide on an appropriate course of action with the student. You may learn the parents are having marital problems, have limited ability to read or speak English, exert excessive pressure for the child to excel academically, or tend to be abusive to the student when there are problems at school. Such factors can be important as you decide how best to help each student academically and behaviorally.

3. **To inform families of academic expectations and events as well as student performance.** Families appreciate knowing your policy concerning homework, late papers, and grading guidelines. Informing parents at the start of the school year helps prevent misunderstandings about your expectations. They also like to know what content will be covered, when the quizzes or tests are scheduled, and what special events are scheduled. Introductory letters or a back-to-school night is helpful, as are newsletters devoted to special events, units to be covered, or the academic schedule. Finally, families want to know how their children are doing. Report cards and conferences provide information periodically, but families appreciate learning about early indications of academic difficulties.

4. **To enlist help from families about academic issues.** Teachers often seek help from families at the start of the year. They may send a list of needed classroom and instructional supplies home to the families to supplement purchases made by the school district. You may want to identify family members who might be available to serve as classroom aides or chaperones for regular or special events. This assistance may include preparing materials for bulletin boards, assisting during a field trip, and the like.

5. **To inform families of disciplinary expectations and actions.** At the start of the year, teachers often inform families of their disciplinary policy and their expectations for student conduct. As with the academic information at the start of the year, this communication is often

accomplished through an introductory letter or a newsletter, or at the back-to-school night. If students misbehave, you may need to inform the families of the situation.

6. **To enlist help from families about dealing with their children.** When a student has difficulties, the family should be contacted to identify ways they might help. When a student misbehaves, the family should be contacted so that you can work together to help the student stay on task and be successful. Families exert much influence on their children, and they can cooperate and support your actions. You and the families may agree on strategies to help the child and to build the child's cooperation and commitment to address any problems.

Why Some Families Resist Involvement

As much as you would like the cooperation and support of families when dealing with a student with academic or behavioral difficulties, you may find families apathetic or resistant to involvement. There also may be circumstances in the lives of the families that create barriers to good communication and involvement, such as work schedules or English language limitations. There are several possible barriers or reasons for family resistance to involvement (Appelbaum, 2009; McEwan-Adkins, 2019):

- **Use of coping mechanism.** Families of children who have a history of misbehavior may adopt coping mechanisms in an effort to deal emotionally with the problems (Shae & Bauer, 2012). Their responses may point to self-doubt, denial, withdrawal, hostility, and frustration. These families may resist involvement with all school personnel.

- **Deferring to the experts.** Some families view teachers, principals, counselors, and other school personnel as the experts in addressing issues such as misbehavior (Turnbull, Turnbull, Erwin, Soodak, & Shogren, 2015). Consequently, they may resist involvement because they do not want to interfere with the actions taken by the teacher or other officials.

- **Uncertainty about what is appropriate.** Diversity among the families, population, or a general sense of being different from school personnel may make families uncomfortable in seeking contact with teachers or administrators. For example, Asian immigrant parents may think that communication with teachers is considered to be "checking up on them" and an expression of disrespect. Members of other ethnic groups, likewise, may feel out of place.

- **Logistical challenges.** Some families don't become involved with the school for practical reasons. They may not speak English or may have limited competency in English. They may not drive a car, or they may have limited access to transportation. They may not have access to a babysitter or cannot afford one.

- **Personal problems.** Some families may have personal problems themselves, and these factors may interfere with good communication and involvement with the school. Perhaps they are tired after a long day at work. Maybe the parents are separated or divorced, or there are problems such as abuse, addiction, dysfunction, and mental illness in the home. Also, some people just like to complain.

Some parents may be more than resistant, they may be difficult to work with in various ways. In *Turning Tough Parents into Strong Partners*, Mendler and Mendler (2017) offer several suggestions to build and maintain positive relationships with parents (also discussed in Curwin, Mender, & Mendler, 2018). Their suggestions in working with parents include the following:

- Get on their side early. Make contact early in the school year.

- Form a team. Invite the parents to think of you and them as a team, working together for the benefit of their child.

- Ask, "What works at home?"

- Make at least two phone calls before problems occur.

- Send complimentary notes home occasionally.

- Solicit information from parents.

- Share and explain your goals.

- Tell parents when they can contact you.

Working Through Cultural and Language Differences

An increasing number of students are from culturally and linguistically diverse families. It is imperative that you make adjustments in how you approach and interact with the families to develop successful home–school communication and partnerships (Grant & Ray, 2019):

1. **Learn about the cultures of the families of students.** Information is available about families of different cultures. For example, Lynch and Hanson (2011) provide detailed cultural descriptions on families with Anglo-American, American Indian, African American, Latino, Asian, Filipino, and Middle Eastern roots. *Involving Latino Families in Schools* (Gaitan, 2005), *Teaching Hispanic Children* (Jones & Fuller, 2003), and *Educating Immigrant Students in the 21st Century* (Rong & Preissle, 2009) are examples of books addressing specialized cultures.

2. **Use school resources and interpreters to communicate with families who have limited English language proficiency.** With increasing student diversity, many schools have forms, letters, policies, and other types of communication translated into one or more languages beyond English to facilitate communication with families. In addition, schools sometimes have interpreters available for one or more other languages. Classroom teachers need to use these school resources to effectively communicate with the families of students in their classrooms.

3. **Acknowledge and adapt to cultural differences in social etiquette and ways of communicating and expressing respect.** If you do not speak the same language as the family, your nonverbal messages become more important. Use positive body language when you meet family members at an open house or other school event. Greeting families at the door, for example, expresses respect. Any notes, letters, or newsletters sent home should be translated into the home language.

■ WHAT WOULD YOU DECIDE?   **Families Not Attending**

Let's assume that you teach in a school that has much ethnic diversity and that some families do not attend the back-to-school night or the parent–teacher conferences at the end of the report card periods.

1. How can you find out why the families do not attend?

2. How can you communicate to those families that it is acceptable to attend such sessions and that their child will ultimately benefit from their attendance?

3. What are some alternative ways that you can communicate important information to the families who do not attend these events?

---

4. **Have early and frequent teacher–family contacts.** Initiate positive home–school contact and dialogue by chatting, making phone calls and home visits, talking with community workers, and arranging for afternoon homework help or tutoring to promote student success.

5. **Provide families with information about the school.** Keep families informed (in the home language, if possible) about important classroom, school, and community events; help available in the school or from community-based organizations; and sources of academic support. Communicate through student-produced newsletters, telephone calls, and other notices. Provide materials in the home language.

6. **Encourage family participation at the school and in the home.** Encourage and welcome families to come to school meetings and social events and even come to the classroom. Encourage family members to come to class to share skills or to discuss their culture. Provide suggestions for ways families can enable their students' learning by supporting homework and creating a positive learning environment at home.

7. **Adjust how you conduct family–teacher conferences.** Schedule time for the conference that is convenient for family members, and show them a portfolio of the student's successes. By also including the student, this three-way conference can promote a dialogue about schooling. The use of an interpreter is sometimes necessary, and this shows respect for the home language of the family. Watch for any facial expressions, voice intonations, and body movements to extend communication (Diaz-Rico, 2020).

Contacting and Communicating with Families

As discussed previously, there are several reasons for working with families. The timing of the contact will depend on the reason for it. There are three points to consider when contacting families:

1. **Initial contact with all families.** This contact should occur at the start of the year. It would be designed to inform families about the academic program, grading guidelines, the homework policy, rules and procedures, and other academic and behavioral expectations. Requests for additional classroom supplies and for volunteers for activities are generally made at this time. You can make these contacts through an introductory letter, a newsletter, a back-to-school night, or other means.

2. **Ongoing contact with all families.** This contact occurs throughout the year to provide information about content being covered in class, the schedule for tests or other evaluation requirements, field trips, the progress of the students, and so on. You may need additional volunteers throughout the year and may contact family members at various times as the need arises. These ongoing contacts could be made through a newsletter or information sheet, an open house, report cards, or other means.

3. **Contact with selected families.** This contact needs to occur to inform them about concerns unique to their child's progress. It could occur when there is both positive and negative news to report. You will often contact families when there is a problem, yet it is easy to overlook contacting them when there is good news to report. Families especially appreciate reports of good news; if a problem arises later, they are often more willing to support and cooperate with the teacher. Guidebooks are available for advice on working with parents of students with special needs (e.g., Dardig, 2008; Fialka, Feldman, & Mikus, 2012) and even for working with parents of bullies and victims (e.g., Roberts, 2008, 2016).

Ways to Communicate with Families

There are many ways to communicate with families, and the method may be affected by its purpose. To discuss a serious act of misbehavior, for example, you would probably not wait for a parent–teacher conference scheduled at the end of a report card period to contact the family but would likely call them immediately.

Much communication with families occurs at the start of the year in the form of an introductory letter, a letter about classroom management and discipline, a back-to-school night, and information sheets. Ongoing communication may be through an open house, newsletters, notes and letters, phone calls, special events and informal contacts, sending home student work, report cards, and parent–teacher conferences. To contact families about their child's academic work or behavior, you could call them or arrange for a special conference. In *Engage Every Family*, Constantino (2015) advocates reaching out to every family in a variety of ways.

Introductory Letter

Teachers sometimes send an *introductory letter* home with the students to give to their parents or guardians during the first week of school prior to the back-to-school night. This letter is intended to serve as a brief welcome to the new year, include some basic information about the class, and invite the family members to the back-to-school night that will soon follow.

The letter may include some information about classroom and school policies such as the schedule, homework, absences, and the curriculum. You may mention in the letter that more will be said about these and other issues at the back-to-school night. A sample introductory letter to families is displayed in Figure 11.1. You can adapt this letter for your particular situation.

Newsletters

At the start of the school year or a new course, teachers sometimes prepare a newsletter that will go to the families of all the students in the class. An initial newsletter may be sent instead of an introductory letter to the families. This newsletter often includes information about the course content, instructional activities, and grading procedures and student requirements. Of course, the

---

September 4

Dear Parents:

Now that the school year has begun, I'd like to introduce myself. I am Melissa Riley, and I am your child's ninth-grade algebra teacher this year. I have taught in this school district for 14 years and have taught pre-algebra, algebra, geometry, and trigonometry. I completed my undergraduate work at the University of Illinois and my master's degree at Kansas State University.

I want this to be a successful school year for you and your child. To ensure this success, it is important that we maintain open communication. Please do not hesitate to contact me if you have any questions or concerns. You could call me at school after dismissal between 3:30 and 4:30 p.m. at 555-7308. Or you could call anytime during the day and leave a message for me to call you back. My email address is mriley@centralschooldistrict.org.

At various times throughout the school year, I will be sending a newsletter home with your child to provide information about classroom activities and special events. On a regular basis, your child will bring home graded assignments for you to look at. I also look forward to seeing you at the conference session that we schedule at the end of each report card period.

The annual back-to-school night for this school is scheduled for next Thursday, September 12, from 7:30 to 9:15 p.m. On that evening, you will have the opportunity go through your child's schedule of classes in shortened 10-minute class periods. When you meet me during algebra class, I will share information about the curriculum, my approach to instruction, my academic expectations and procedures, my policy on discipline, and other issues. The books and materials that we will be using this year will also be on display. I encourage you to attend back-to-school night because it will give you an opportunity to understand the mathematics program and become better acquainted with me.

By working together and keeping in good contact, I'm confident that this will be an exciting and successful school year. I look forward to meeting you at back-to-school night.

Sincerely,

Melissa Riley

FIGURE 11.1   Sample introductory letter to families.

nature of the initial newsletter will vary with the grade level and the type of teaching assignment. As a guide, though, the initial newsletter may include a description of the following: (a) course title or subject area; (b) brief course or subject area description; (c) course objectives; (d) a brief content outline; (e) typical; (f) learning activities; (g) grading procedures; (h) materials that the student will need; (i) behavioral guidelines and expectations; and (j) the school telephone number and your district email address.

It is important that you convey this initial information to the students as well. Students especially need to know grading procedures and guidelines and also behavioral expectations. During the school year, additional newsletters might be sent to all families with information about special events, programs, content to be covered in the curriculum, tests or quizzes that are coming up, student projects, and other issues. Newsletters can be as brief as one page or longer, according to need. You can report accomplishments of the class and of individual students. Computers can be used to prepare the newsletters. Students can prepare the newsletter as a group or class project, under suitable circumstances.

Letter About Classroom Management and Discipline

You need to share your plan for classroom management and discipline with the families and the principal. If you expect them to be involved when you need them, they need to know that you have a plan and to be aware of your rationale for rules, positive recognition, and consequences.

At the start of the school year, you need to discuss rules, consequences, and other aspects of management with the students. A copy of this information sheet should be given to the students to take home to their parents. The letter should provide details of the classroom management and discipline plan and should explain why it is important. Ask the parents to discuss the plan with their children, sign the plan, and return the signature portion to you.

If the back-to-school night is scheduled early in the year, you may ask the families to return the signature portion at that time. Or you may prefer to wait and present the letter to the families at the back-to-school night and get the signatures at that time. Letters can then be sent home to families who did not attend that evening.

Back-to-School Night

Many schools schedule a *back-to-school night* or family night during the first or second week so families can receive information about the academic program, grading guidelines, homework policy, rules and procedures, and other expectations. Requests for additional classroom supplies and for volunteers for activities are generally made at this time.

Some schools do not schedule a back-to-school night or, if they do, it comes later than the first or second week of school. You may find other ways to communicate with families since it is important to establish contact as early as possible. For example, a letter about classroom management and discipline might be expanded to include information that is commonly covered at a back-to-school night.

The scheduling of the back-to-school night is handled in different ways. For middle, junior high, and senior high schools, families are often given their child's schedule, and they follow it just as the student would, but in shortened class sessions of 10–15 minutes. In this way, they see every teacher in the way that their child would during the school day. Teachers often use this time to present information to the families about academic and behavioral guidelines and expectations.

Preparing for Back-to-School Night

A back-to-school night is often your first contact with families, so thorough preparation is necessary. There are many ways to prepare for this evening:

- **Prepare your own introductory letter to families about the back-to-school night in your classroom.** See the sample introductory letter in Figure 11.1. Do not rely only on notices that the school sends home. Some teachers like to have their students prepare special invitations for their own families.

- **Make sure the classroom looks attractive and neat.** Post your name and room number prominently on the door and the front chalkboard. Display samples of work by all students. Display copies of the textbooks and other instructional materials.

- **Prepare a list of any instructional supplies or materials that families might be able to provide.** This list will vary, depending on the subject and grade level. It may include such items as rulers, buttons, a box of facial tissues, or other supplies. Have enough copies of the list to give to all families.

- **Prepare separate sign-up sheets for families.** These may concern the need for a private, follow-up conference about their child; volunteers to help at special events such as field trips; volunteers such as guest speakers in class; or volunteers to provide various instructional supplies requested by the teacher.

- **Plan a well-organized, succinct presentation.** Families want to hear about your background and experience, behavioral and academic expectations, procedures for issues such as homework and absences, and other policies. Be sure to plan for time at the end of the presentation for questions.

- **Prepare handouts for your presentation.** Families will receive the handouts at the back-to-school night. Have enough copies of this material to give to all of them. A sample content outline of the presentation is shown in Table 11.1; your handout should include details about issues such as those listed in that table, along with extra sheets that provide additional information on selected topics. To simplify distribution, staple all the handouts together as one set of materials sequenced in the order that you will cover the material during the presentation.

Conducting the Back-to-School Night

Take several guidelines into account when conducting the back-to-school night. Since your presentation is usually limited, possibly to only 10–15 minutes, it is important to plan how to conduct yourself. Greet families at the door, introduce yourself, and ask them to be seated. Begin your presentation using the handout that you previously prepared concerning your background, the daily and weekly schedule, the curriculum, academic goals and activities, academic expectations

■ TABLE 11.1   **Sample Content Outline for Your Back-to-School Night Presentation**

1. Background about yourself
   a. College training and degrees earned
   b. Professional experience, including length of teaching service, grade levels taught, where taught
   c. Personal information (e.g., family, hobbies, special interests, or experiences)
2. The curriculum, academic goals, and activities
   a. Overview of the curriculum and the topics to be covered (refer to the textbooks and related instructional materials on display in the room)
   b. Your approach to instruction
   c. Instructional activities and any special events such as field trips or unique programs
3. Academic expectations and procedures
   a. Grading guidelines and procedures (how grades are determined)
   b. Grading requirements (e.g., tests, quizzes, homework, and projects)
   c. Homework (purposes, how often, make-up policy, absences)
   d. When report cards are delivered
   e. Parent–teacher conferences
4. Discipline
   a. Classroom rules
   b. Positive rewards
   c. Consequences for breaking the rules
   d. Incremental steps taken when misbehavior continues
   e. When parents will be contacted
   f. Sheet concerning the classroom management and discipline policy that parents need to sign
5. Opportunities for parents to sign up for selected issues
   a. For a private, follow-up conference about their child
   b. For parent volunteers for providing instructional materials and supplies
   c. For parent volunteers to help at special events such as field trips
   d. For parent volunteers such as guest speakers in class
   e. Express an interest in hearing any ideas and concerns from families at any time
   f. Time for questions at the end of the session (save several minutes, if possible)

and procedures, discipline, and other issues. At the start, give a copy of the handout to each family member.

Have parents sign up for individual follow-up conferences if they want to talk with you at length about their child. Back-to-school night is not intended to deal with concerns about individual students. Allow time for family members to ask questions. This will be an opportunity for you to provide clarification about issues and to hear families' concerns.

Information Sheets

Not all schools schedule a back-to-school night, and not all families attend a scheduled night. As a result, you can prepare a packet to send home that provides information about the curriculum, grading expectations and requirements, rules and procedures, the discipline plan, and other matters. The sheets may be the same as those given to families who attend the back-to-school night, or a shortened version.

Open House

Once or twice a year, most schools schedule an open house for families to visit the classrooms during a particular evening to see their child's teacher, observe the classroom and samples of student work, and learn about books and materials being used. Some districts do not have a back to-school night but instead schedule the first open house in mid to late September. At open house, teachers may give a formal presentation about the program. Or schools may allow family members to drop in at any time during open house to discuss issues informally with the teacher.

Since open houses are conducted well into the school year, materials and projects that students have prepared can be displayed. Science fairs, for example, may be scheduled at the same time as an open house to provide an opportunity for families to see students' science displays. Since some of the families attending the open house may not have attended the back-to-school night, it is often useful to have extra copies of the handout provided at the back-to-school night to describe your policies.

Assignment Sheets

Another way to communicate with families is through an assignment sheet that describes the assignments for the next week or two. Students are asked to show it to their families. Some teachers prefer that parents sign the sheet and return it to school. The assignment sheet also helps students recognize the assignments that are due in the next week or two and enables the students to make plans to complete the assignments on time. Especially when students have many school-related activities or other outside-school activities, they can plan which day or days they will work on school-related assignments while still participating in their other activities.

Individual Notes and Letters

Notes and letters are written to individual parents to discuss some particular issue about their child. You can use them to request that a conference be arranged with you, to invite family members to class functions, to inform them about their child's work, or to offer suggestions. Notes should be carefully written. They should be free of errors in spelling, grammar, and sentence structure. Furthermore, they should be brief, clear, honest, and factual. Educational jargon should not be used. Notes and letters are especially useful for contacting family members who are hard to reach by telephone.

Be cautious about sending notes home to families only when there is bad news to deliver. Certainly, there are times when such notes need to be sent. You should also send notes home to families with good news about the child's academic work or behavior. Briefly, positive notes take only a few minutes to write to express pleasure about the child's performance. By systematically writing one or two notes to different parents each day, you will provide good news and help build positive relationships with them. Family members will usually talk with their child about the note, and the child may come to school the next day with a more positive attitude.

Phone Calls

Like notes and letters, telephone calls are made to families to discuss a particular issue. The phone call could request that a conference be arranged with you, invite the family to class functions, inform them about their child's work, or offer suggestions. As with notes and letters, be cautious about calling families only when you have bad news. Also call them when there is good news to report.

Phone calls can be quite brief because you only need to have two or three positive statements to share. They are not intended to be a lengthy discussion about the student. The parents should be asked to tell the child about the phone call.

There are times when you need to contact the family about the child's misbehavior. You need to plan ahead before making the call. The call should begin with a statement of concern, such as "Mrs. Erickson. I am Kristina's teacher, and I need your help. I care about Kristina, and I feel that her behavior in the classroom is not in her best interest." You then should describe the specific problem and present any pertinent documentation. You should go on to describe what you are doing and have done to deal with the misbehavior. At this point, it is helpful to invite the family's input by asking questions such as "Has Kristina had similar problems in the past? Why do you feel she is having these problems at school? Is there something going on at home that could be affecting her behavior?"

It is then useful to get input about how to solve the problem. State what you will do to help solve the problem and explain what you want the parent to do. Before ending the telephone conversation, you should let the family know that you are confident that the problems can be worked out and tell them that there will be follow-up contact from you. Then recap the conversation.

Websites and Email

Increasingly, schools are using the internet to make information available to parents, students, and the public. A school's website might include the school calendar; directories for teachers, administrators, and the staff; school policies; information about athletics and extracurricular activities; special events; and other information. Some school districts also communicate through Twitter, Facebook, and text messages directly to cell phones.

VOICES FROM THE CLASSROOM   Making "Good News" Phone Calls to Families

Bernadette Hampton, high school mathematics teacher, Beaufort, South Carolina

To build positive relationships with parents and students, I call home for the top three students after a quiz or a test. I do this to encourage and motivate the student to excel. You can also select other criteria for the phone calls, such as most improved, most creative, or others to include most students over time.

Parents are often surprised to receive this phone call, especially when they usually receive phone calls with negative news. Students return to school with much appreciation for the good news call. The student's self-esteem is increased, and support is gained from the parent. If I need to call the parent about difficult behavior or another troublesome issue, I then have the support of the parent. The "good news" phone calls help me develop a positive relationship with the parents as well as the students.

■ WHAT WOULD YOU DECIDE?   Creating Your Own Classroom Website

Many schools make provisions so that each teacher has a web-page for his or her classroom. Teachers may post their syllabi, rules and procedures, notices about special events, listing of assignments or homework, links to useful resources, and much more.

1. If you had a webpage available for your use for your classroom, how might you use it? What information might you post?

2. Would you want to only post information, or would you want the webpage to have interactive capability (like a blog)? What advantages or problems might there be with a classroom blog?

Some schools make provisions so that each teacher has a webpage for his or her classroom. In these cases, teachers can place information on their classroom website to communicate to students and families about their syllabus, rules and procedures, notices about special events, listing of assignments or homework, Web links to useful resources, and much more. These classroom websites can be prepared, developed, and tailored by each teacher, and they can be a fine source of information for the students and families. Since these classroom websites are on the district's website, they typically are not blocked by firewalls and thus are easily accessible for good communication.

Special Events and Informal Contacts

Throughout the year, teachers and families may attend many special events. These may include sporting events, concerts, plays, carnivals, craft displays, and others. Contacts with family members at these events may provide brief opportunities to share a few words about their child's work. These contacts are especially useful as progress reports and as a means of discussing a particular issue. You might say something about the student's interests, such as, "Josh's work during our unit on Australia focuses on the animal life. He is very interested in animal life in all of our studies."

Sending Home Student Work

You can inform families about their child's academic progress by sending home completed and graded student work. They can see what you have covered, the child's work, and any notes or remarks you have made.

It is useful to send home a variety of materials including worksheets, tests, quizzes, home-work, projects, lab reports, writing samples, artwork, or other types of student products. Be sensitive about notes or remarks you place on the papers. These notes are evaluative statements, but they should also include comments about good points and improvement, as well about areas still needing attention.

Recognize that papers sent home with students to show their parents may not even get home, and those that do get home may not be shown to the family members. To overcome these problems, you might devise various ways to have family members sign a sheet to indicate that they have seen the material. For example, a parent response sheet might list the material being sent home, with a blank space for parents to sign and date indicating that they discussed the piece with their child. The form could also include space for the family members to write any comments. The student then returns the response sheet to you.

Report Cards

Families are informed of their child's academic performance when report cards are distributed. Most report cards have an area where you can either write a statement or indicate a code for a statement concerning effort and citizenship. As with notes, letters, and phone calls, you should avoid making only negative notes on report cards. Deserving students should receive positive notes.

When warranted, include notes on the report card to indicate the need to improve and the actions needed to improve the situation. Families may call teachers shortly after report cards have been delivered if they have any questions about them. Have documentation ready to justify what you have noted.

Gradebook software often provides the capability to print out reports for individual students, which display each assessment measure, points earned, and point tallies. These individual student printouts can be useful if family members inquire about their child's grade. The printouts can also be generated for individual students for parent–teacher conferences, which are considered in the next section.

Parent–Teacher Conferences

Another important way of communicating with families is through *parent–teacher conferences* to report information about progress, academic performance, or behavior. Many school districts schedule a day or two at the end of each report card period for parent–teacher conferences so parents can meet individually with the teachers. Conference days are typically scheduled only for elementary grades; all parents are invited to attend these individually scheduled conferences.

Many middle schools, junior high schools, and high schools do not schedule parent–teacher conferences, but instead arrange for a block of time on one day at the end of the report card period for families to visit with each teacher on a drop-in basis. The ways to prepare for and conduct this session will be somewhat different from those used at the elementary level, but the general principles discussed here for preparing for this contact still apply.

In addition to the conferences conducted at the end of report card periods, parent–teacher conferences are held with particular parents as the need warrants. When a student persistently misbehaves or has academic problems, you may ask the family of that child to come to the school for a conference. Prior to having such a conference, you may want to meet with the student to work out a plan to address the problem. If this meeting with the student does not lead to resolution, then a meeting with the family is warranted, and the student may be asked to also attend.

Preparing for the Conference

Preparation for a drop-in conference with the family at the end of the report card period will be different from preparation for an individually scheduled parent–teacher conference. Administrators in middle schools, junior high schools, and high schools commonly take steps to inform families about the day and time for the drop-in conferences at the end of the report card periods. Since these teachers have responsibility for many students, it is usually not feasible to have sample materials available for all of them. Instead, teachers often have the gradebook on hand, along with sample tests, quizzes, homework, and projects that students completed throughout the marking period.

If an individual parent–teacher conference is needed, the teacher often calls the family to select a day and time. Before the conference, the teacher may gather pertinent materials about the student and the situation. If it is an academic issue, the teacher may collect the gradebook and a sample of work done by the student, including tests, projects, and homework to be shown to the family during the conference. If it is a behavioral issue, anecdotal record sheets and other documentation may be gathered.

Whether for a drop-in conference at the end of the report card period or for an individually scheduled conference, the physical environment needs to be prepared for the session. You can arrange for these materials: (a) a table for the conference; (b) three or four adult-sized chairs for the table; and (c) a clean, tidy room. Be sure to allow enough time for the conference, and do not overwhelm parents with the presence of other school personnel or irrelevant materials.

Conducting the Conference

Discussion and questions in the conference should be sequenced to develop rapport, obtain information from the family, provide information to them, and summarize and follow up. The following guidelines include a technique to "sandwich" your main messages between good news or positive statements at the start and at the end of the conference. The parents who hear good comments at the start will be in a comfortable frame of mind. As the conference comes to a close, it is useful to summarize your main points and then conclude with additional positive statements. Consider these guidelines:

1. **Begin the conference in a positive manner.** Walk up to the family members, introduce yourself, and welcome them into the room. Start the conference with a positive statement about the student, such as, "Emily really enjoys providing leadership for students in her small group when working on projects."

2. **Present the student's strong points before describing the matters needing improvement.** Highlight the student's strengths as you move into a discussion about his or her

performance. Show samples of the student's work to the family. Later, identify matters that need further improvement.

3. **Present documentation for the student's grades.** Review the assessments that were conducted and identify the student's grades for the assessments.

4. **Encourage the family to participate and share information.** Allow opportunities to ask questions and share information about the student. Pose questions to parents at various points of the conference to encourage their input.

5. **Plan a course of action cooperatively.** If the student needs to work on a particular issue, discuss the possible actions that you and the parents could take. Come to agreement about the course of action that each of you will take.

6. **End the conference with a positive comment.** Thank the family for coming and say something positive about the student at the end of the conference.

7. **Use good human relations skills during the conference.** To be effective, you should be friendly and informal, positive in your approach, willing to explain in understandable terms, willing to listen, willing to accept parents' feelings, and careful about giving advice. You should avoid the following: arguing and getting angry; asking embarrassing questions; talking about other students, teachers, or families; bluffing if you do not know an answer; rejecting parents' suggestions; and being a "know-it-all" with pat answers (Miller, Linn, & Gronlund, 2013).

Handling Conference Follow-Up

During the conferences, it is useful to make a list of follow-up actions. These actions may include providing more thorough feedback to the student during the next marking period, recommending additional readings to some students, providing certain families with periodic updates on their child's performance, or a host of other actions. It is important to follow up in the ways that were identified during the parent–teacher conference.

■ TABLE 11.2   Fourteen Ways to Communicate with Families

1. An introductory letter
2. Newsletters
3. A letter about classroom management and discipline
4. Back-to-school night
5. Information sheets
6. Open house
7. Assignment sheets
8. Individual notes and letters
9. Phone calls
10. Websites and email
11. Special events and informal contacts
12. Sending home student work
13. Report cards
14. Parent–teacher conferences

MAJOR CONCEPTS

1. Teachers often need to turn to others for assistance when dealing with student behavior problems, reading or language issues, media and instructional technology, special needs, curricular issues, instructional strategies, and numerous other issues.

2. Collaboration is a style of interaction between individuals engaged in shared decision-making as they work toward a common goal.

3. Teachers collaborate with others to: (a) meet the needs of their students; (b) improve professional competence by engaging in professional development activities; and (c) provide leadership when addressing a school improvement issue.

4. Teachers work with families to (a) understand the student's home setting; (b) inform parents of academic expectations and events as well as student performance; (c) enlist family members' help with academic issues; (d) inform them of disciplinary expectations and actions; and (e) enlist their help in dealing with their children.

5. Families' resistance may be due to (a) their unhappy experiences when they were students; (b) their coping mechanisms in dealing with ongoing problems with their children; (c) their view that educators are the experts; or (d) their perception of the intimidation and bureaucracy of the school.

6. To accommodate differences in culture and language, teachers must adjust how they approach and interact with families to develop successful home–school communication and partnerships.

7. The timing of the contact with the families will be determined by the reason for the contact. The three main times of family contact are (a) initial contacts with all families at the start of the school year; (b) ongoing contacts with all families throughout the school year; and (c) contact with selected families concerning their child's academic or behavioral progress.

8. Initial communication with the family occurs at the start of the school year in the form of an introductory letter, a letter about classroom management and discipline, a back-to-school night, and information sheets.

9. Ongoing communication throughout the school year may occur with an open house, newsletters, assignment sheets, notes and letters, phone calls, websites and email, special events, informal contacts, sending home student work, report cards, and parent–teacher conferences.

10. To contact individual families about their child's academic work or behavior, teachers often call the parents/guardians and sometimes arrange for a special parent–teacher conference to address issues.

DISCUSSION/REFLECTIVE QUESTIONS

1. If a student in your class has been causing serious disruptions, which colleagues in your school might you collaboration with for assistance? How might those colleagues help?

2. How might information about a student's home setting help you as a teacher decide on an appropriate course of action with the student? How might this information create some problems for you?

3. When is an appropriate point to contact families if a student is exhibiting mild misbehavior? Moderate misbehavior?

4. In what ways did your teachers in the middle and secondary grades contact and interact with your parents? When and how did this communication occur?

5. What advantages would there be if the teacher prepared and distributed a newsletter for families at the start of the school year concerning course content, learning activities, grading procedures, and student expectations? What might be some challenges in preparing and distributing the newsletter?

6. How can you communicate with families who do not show up for back-to-school night or parent–teacher conferences?

SUGGESTED ACTIVITIES

1. Talk to a school counselor or a school psychologist to find out what services they provide for students and teachers. Ask how they collaborate with teachers to address problems.

2. Talk with several teachers and ask who they turn to for assistance when dealing with instructional or disciplinary problems. Ask them to describe the type of assistance they provide.

3. Ask several teachers to describe the ways that they prepare for and conduct the back-to-school night. What recommendations do they have to aid your preparation?

4. Think about the reasons that families may not attend parent–teacher conferences. Identify ways that you might communicate to those particular families.

FURTHER READING

Canter, L., & Canter, M. (2001). *Parents on your side: A teacher's guide to creating positive relationships with parents* (2nd ed.). Bloomington, IN: Solution Tree.
Provides thorough, practical guidance about ways to communicate, to establish positive relationships, and to solve problems that may occur.

Friend, M. D., & Cook, L. (2017). *Interactions: Collaboration skills for school professionals* (8th ed.). Boston: Pearson.
Provides comprehensive discussion about many aspects of collaboration, such as interpersonal communication and problem solving, teams, meetings, consultations, co-teaching, paraeducators, and dealing with difficult interactions.

Grant, K. B., & Ray, J. A. (2019). *Home, school, and community collaboration: Culturally responsive family engagement* (4th ed.). Thousand Oaks, CA: Sage Publications.
Provides comprehensive information and guidance for understanding family engagement, appreciating today's diverse families, and putting knowledge and skills in action when working with families.

LeBlanc-Esparza, R., & LeBlanc-Esparza, K. (2013). *Strengthening the connection between school and home*. Bloomington, IN: Solution Tree.
Provides many ways to create and implement a family engagement plan, including ways to create a family-friendly school and classroom and to communicate with families.

McEwan-Adkins, E. K. (2019). *How to deal with parents who are angry, troubled, afraid, or just seem crazy*. Thousand Oaks, CA: Corwin Press.
Provides strategies to defuse angry parents and to work with parents to advance the success of their children. Includes guidelines when meeting with parents during annual reviews and IEP meetings.

References and Further Readings

Albert, L. (2003). *A teacher's guide to cooperative discipline: How to manage your classroom and promote self-esteem* (Rev. ed.). Circle Pines, MN: American Guidance Service Publishing.

Allington, R. L. (2009). *What really matters in response to intervention*. Boston, MA: Pearson.

Anderman, E. M., & Anderman, L. H. (2014). *Classroom motivation* (2nd ed.). Boston, MA: Pearson.

Anderson, M. (2016). *Learning to choose, choosing to learn: The key to student motivation and achievement.* Alexandria, VA: Association for Supervision and Curriculum Development.

Anderson, M. (2019). *What we say and how we say it matter*. Alexandria, VA: Association for Supervision and Curriculum Development.

Appelbaum, M. (2009). *How to handle the hard-to-handle parents*. Thousand Oaks, CA: Corwin Press.

Ashbaker, B. Y., & Morgan, J. (2013). *Paraprofessionals in the classroom* (2nd ed.). Boston, MA: Pearson.

Ashbaker, B. Y., & Morgan, J. (2015). *The paraprofessional's guide to effective behavioral interventions.* New York, NY: Routledge/Taylor & Francis.

Banks, J. A. (2016). *Cultural diversity and education: Foundations, curriculum, and teaching* (6th ed.). New York, NY: Routledge/Taylor & Francis.

Barr, R. D., & Parrett, W. H. (2007). *The kids left behind: Catching up the underachieving children of poverty.* Bloomington, IN: Solution Tree.

Bateman, D. F., & Cline, J. L. (2016). *A teacher's guide to special education*. Alexandria, VA: Association for Supervision and Curriculum Development.

Bauml, M. (2016). The promise of collaboration. *Educational Leadership, 74*(2), 58–62.

Bear, G. G. (2015). Preventive and classroom-based strategies. In E. T. Emmer & E. J. Sabornie (Eds.), *Handbook of classroom management* (2nd ed., pp. 15–39). New York, NY: Routledge/Taylor & Francis.

Bender, W. N. (2012). *Project-based learning: Differentiated instruction for the 21st century*. Thousand Oaks, CA: Corwin Press.

Beninghof, A., & Leensvaart, M. (2016). Co-teaching to support ELLs. *Educational Leadership, 73*(5), 70–73.

Berger, E. H., & Riojas-Cortez, M. R. (2019). *Families as partners in education: Families and schools working together* (10th ed.). Boston, MA: Pearson.

Berk, L. E. (2018). *Development through the lifespan* (7th ed.). Boston, MA: Pearson.

Berk, L. E. (2019). *Exploring child development*. Boston, MA: Pearson.

Berk, L. E., & Meyers, A. B. (2016). *Infants, children, and adolescents* (8th ed.). Boston, MA: Pearson.

Bluestein, J. (2010). *Becoming a win–win teacher: Survival strategies for the beginning teacher*. Thousand Oaks, CA: Corwin Press.

Bomer, R., Dworin, J. E., May, L., & Semingson, P. (2008). Miseducating teachers about the poor: A critical analysis of Ruby Payne's claims about poverty. *Teachers College Record, 110*(12), 2497–2531.

Bongolan, R., Moir, E., & Baron, W. (2010). *Keys to the secondary classroom: A teacher's guide to the first months of school*. Thousand Oaks, CA: Corwin Press.

Books, S. (2004). *Poverty and schooling in the U.S.: Contexts and consequences*. Mahwah, NJ: Lawrence Erlbaum Associates.

Bosch, K. A. (2007). *Planning classroom management* (2nd ed.). Thousand Oaks, CA: Corwin Press.

Bosch, K. A., & Bosch, M. E. (2015). *The first-year teacher: Be prepared for your classroom*. Thousand Oaks, CA: Corwin Press.

Boss, S., & Larmer, J. (2018). *Project-based teaching: How to create rigorous and engaging learning experiences*. Alexandria, VA: Association for Supervision and Curriculum Development.

Boykin, W., & Noguera, P. (2011). *Creating the opportunity to learn: Moving from research to practice to close the achievement gap*. Alexandria, VA: Association for Supervision and Curriculum Development.

Brady, K., Forton, M. B., & Porter, D. (2011). *Rules in school* (2nd ed.). Turners Falls, MA: Center for Responsive Schools.

Breakstone, S., Dreiblatt, M., & Dreiblatt, K. (2009). *How to stop bullying and social aggression*. Thousand Oaks, CA: Corwin Press.

Brown, E. L., Geor, P. C., & Lazaridis, G. (Eds.). (2014). *Poverty, class, and schooling*. Charlotte, NC: Information Age Publishing.

Brown, M. A. (2018). *Creating restorative schools: Setting schools up to succeed*. St. Paul, MN: Living Justice Press.

Brulles, D., & Brown, K. L. (2018). *A teacher's guide to flexible grouping and collaborative learning: Form, manage, assess, and differentiate in groups*. Minneapolis, MN: Free Spirit Publishing.

Bryant, D. P., Bryant, B. R., & Smith, D. D. (2016). *Teaching students with special needs in inclusive classrooms*. Thousand Oaks, CA: Sage.

Budge, K. M., & Parrett, W. H. (2018). *Disrupting poverty: Five powerful classroom practices*. Alexandria, VA: Association for Supervision and Curriculum Development.

Bullough, R. V., & Richardson, M. (2015). Teacher perspectives on classroom management: Rules, ethics, and "crime control." In E. T. Emmer & E. J. Sabornie (Eds.), *Handbook of classroom management* (2nd ed., pp. 283–300). New York, NY: Routledge/Taylor & Francis.

Burden, P. R., & Byrd, D. M. (2019). *Methods for effective teaching* (8th ed.). Boston, MA: Pearson.

Burke, K. (2008). *What to do with the kid who. . .: Developing cooperation, self-discipline, and responsibility in the classroom* (3rd ed.). Thousand Oaks, CA: Corwin Press.

Canter, L. (2010). *Assertive discipline: Positive behavior management for today's classroom* (4th ed.). Bloomington, IN: Solution Tree Press.

Canter, L. (2014). *Classroom management for academic success*. Bloomington, IN: Solution Tree Press.

Canter, L., & Canter, M. (2001). *Parents on your side: A teacher's guide to creating positive relationships with parents* (2nd ed.). Bloomington, IN: Solution Tree Press.

Canter, L., & Canter, M. (2008). *Succeeding with difficult students: New strategies for reaching your most challenging students*. Bloomington, IN: Solution Tree Press.

Cartledge, G., Lo, Y. Y., Vincent, C. G., & Robinson-Ervin, P. (2015). Culturally responsive classroom management.

In E. T. Emmer & E. J. Sabornie (Eds.), *Handbook of classroom management* (2nd ed., pp. 411–430). New York, NY: Routledge/Taylor & Francis.

Cash, R. M. (2017). *Advanced differentiation: Thinking and learning for the 21st century*. Minneapolis, MN: Free Spirit Publishing.

Cassetta, G., & Sawyer, B. (2015). *Classroom management matters: The socio-emotional learning approach children deserve*. Portsmouth, NH: Heinemann.

Causton-Theoharis, J. (2009). *The paraprofessional's handbook for effective support in inclusive classrooms*. Baltimore, MD: Paul H. Brookes Publishing.

Chapman, C., & King, R. S. (2012). *Differentiated assessment strategies: One tool doesn't fit all* (2nd ed.). Thousand Oaks, CA: Corwin Press.

Chapman, C., & King, R. S. (2014). *Planning and organizing standards-based differentiated instruction* (2nd ed.). Thousand Oaks, CA: Corwin Press.

Charles, C. M., & Cole, K. M. (2019). *Building classroom discipline* (12th ed.). Boston, MA: Pearson.

Charney, R. S. (2002). *Teaching children to care: Classroom management for ethical and academic growth, K–8* (Rev. ed.). Turners Falls, MA: Center for Responsive Schools.

Cleveland, K. P. (2011). *Teaching boys who struggle in school: Strategies that turn underachievers into successful learners*. Alexandria, VA: Association for Supervision and Curriculum Development.

Clewell, B. C., Campbell, P. B., & Perlman, L. (2007). *Good schools in poor neighborhoods: Defying demographics, achieving success*. Washington, DC: Urban Institute Press.

Cohen, E. G., & Lotan, R. A. (2014). *Designing groupwork: Strategies for the heterogeneous classroom* (3rd ed.). New York, NY: Teachers College Press.

Cole, A. J., & Shupp, A. M. (2012). *Recognize and respond to emotional behavioral issues in the classroom: A teacher's guide*. Baltimore, MD: Paul H. Brookes Publishing.

Cole, R. W. (Ed.). (2008). *Educating everybody's children: Diverse teaching strategies for diverse learners* (Rev. 2). Alexandria, VA: Association for Supervision and Curriculum Development.

Coloroso, B. (2002). *Kids are worth it! Giving your child the gift of inner discipline* (Rev. ed.). New York, NY: HarperCollins.

Coloroso, B. (2017). *The bully, the bullied, and the not-so-innocent bystander* (revised and updated). New York, NY: HarperCollins.

Colvin, G., & Scott, T. M. (2015). *Managing the cycle of acting-out behavior in the classroom* (2nd ed.). Thousand Oaks, CA: Corwin Press.

Conoley, J. C., & Goldstein, A. P. (2004). *School violence intervention: A practical handbook* (2nd ed.). New York, NY: Guilford Press.

Constantino, S. M. (2015). *Engage every family: Five simple principles*. Thousand Oaks, CA: Corwin Press.

Cornelius-White, J., & Harbaugh, A. (2010). *Learner-centered instruction: Building relationships for student success*. Thousand Oaks, CA: Sage.

Council of Chief State School Officers (CCSSO). (2011, April). *Interstate Teacher Assessment and Support Consortium (InTASC) model core teaching standards: A resource for state dialogue*. Washington, DC: Author. Retrieved from http://www.ccsso.org/Documents/2011/InTASC_Model_Core_Teaching_Standards_2011.pdf

Cramer, S. F. (2006). *The special educator's guide to collaboration: Improving relationships with co-teachers, teams, and families* (2nd ed.). Thousand Oaks, CA: Corwin Press.

Crowe, C. (2009). *Solving thorny behavior problems: How teachers and students can work together*. Turners Falls, MA: Center for Responsive Schools.

Crowe, C. (2012). *How to bullyproof your classroom*. Turners Falls, MA: Northeast Foundation for Children.

Curwin, R. L. (2010). *Meeting students where they live: Motivation in urban schools*. Alexandria, VA: Association for Supervision and Curriculum Development.

Curwin, R. L., & Mendler, A. N. (1997). *As tough as necessary: Countering violence, aggression, and hostility in our schools*. Alexandria, VA: Association for Supervision and Curriculum Development.

Curwin, R. L., Mendler, A. N., & Mendler, B. D. (2018). *Discipline with dignity* (4th ed.). Alexandria, VA: Association for Supervision and Curriculum Development.

Dabrowski, J., & Marshall, T. M. (2018). *Motivation and engagement in student assignments: The role of choice and relevancy*. Washington, DC: The Education Trust.

Danielson, C. (2007). Enhancing professional practice: A framework for teaching (2nd ed.). *Alexandria, VA: Association for Supervision and Curriculum Development*.

Dardig, J. C. (2008). *Involving parents of students with special needs*. Thousand Oaks, CA: Corwin Press.

Davis, B. M. (2012). *How to teach students who don't look like you: Culturally relevant teaching strategies* (2nd ed.). Thousand Oaks, CA: Corwin Press.

Davis, H. A. (2013). Teacher-student relationships. In J. Hattie & E. M. Anderman (Eds.), *International guide to student achievement* (pp. 221–223). New York, NY: Routledge.

Davis, H. A., Summers, J. J., & Miller, L. M. (2012). *An interpersonal approach to classroom management: Strategies for improving student engagement*. Thousand Oaks, CA: Corwin Press.

Dean, C. B., Hubbell, E. R., Pitler, H., & Stone, B. (2012). *Classroom instruction that works: Research-based strategies for increasing student achievement* (2nd ed.). Alexandria, VA: Association for Supervision and Curriculum Development.

Delpit, L. (1995). *Other people's children: Cultural conflict in the classroom*. New York, NY: New Press.

Denton, P. (2014). *The power of our words: Teacher language that helps children learn* (2nd ed.). Turners Falls, MA: Northeast Foundation for Children.

Denton, P., & Kriete, R. (2015). *The first six weeks of school* (2nd ed.). Turners Falls, MA: Northeast Foundation for Children.

Derman-Sparks, L., & Edwards, J. O. (2010). *Anti-bias education for young children and ourselves*. Washington, DC: National Association for the Education of Young Children.

Diaz-Rico, L. T. (2020). *A course for teaching English learners* (3rd ed.). Boston, MA: Pearson.

Diffily, D., & Sassman, C. (2006). *Positive teacher talk for better classroom management*. New York, NY: Scholastic.

Dillon, J. (2012). *No place for bullying: Leadership for schools that care for every student*. Thousand Oaks, CA: Corwin Press.

Dillon, J. (2015). *Reframing bullying prevention to build stronger school communities*. Thousand Oaks, CA: Corwin Press.

Dillon, R. (2018). Room for improvement. *Educational Leadership, 76*(1), 40–45.

Doyle, M. B. (2008). *The paraeducator's guide to the inclusive classroom* (3rd ed.). Baltimore, MD: Paul H. Brookes Publishing.

Dreikurs, R., Cassel, P., & Ferguson, E. D. (2004). *Discipline without tears: How to reduce conflict and establish cooperation in the classroom* (Rev. ed.). New York, NY: Wiley.

Dreikurs, R., Grunwald, B. B., & Pepper, F. C. (1998). *Maintaining sanity in the classroom: Classroom management techniques* (2nd ed.). Philadelphia, PA: Taylor & Francis.

Drew, N. (2017). *No kidding about bullying* (Updated ed.). Minneapolis, MN: Free Spirit Publishing.

Dwyer, K., & Osher, D. (2000). *Safeguarding our children: An action guide*. Washington, DC: U.S. Departments of Education and Justice, American Institute for Research. Retrieved from http://cecp.air.org/guide/actionguide.asp

Echevarria, J. J., Frey, N., & Fisher, D. (2016). *How to reach the hard to reach: Excellent instruction for those who need it most*. Alexandria, VA: Association for Supervision and Curriculum Development.

Edwards, C. H. (2012). *Classroom discipline and management* (5th ed.). Hoboken, NJ: Wiley.

Edwards, J. (2010). *Inviting students to learn: 100 tips for talking effectively with your students*. Alexandria, VA: Association for Supervision and Curriculum Development.

Emmer, E. T., & Evertson, C. M. (2017). *Classroom management for middle and high school teachers* (10th ed.). Boston, MA: Pearson.

Emmer, E. T., & Sabornie, E. J. (Eds.). (2015). *Handbook of classroom management* (2nd ed.). New York, NY: Routledge/Taylor & Francis.

Englander, E. (2013). *Bullying and cyberbullying: What every educator needs to know*. Cambridge, MA: Harvard Education Press.

Epstein, J. L., & Associates. (2018). *School, family, and community partnerships: Your handbook for action* (4th ed.). Thousand Oaks, CA: Corwin Press.

Espelage, D. L. (2015). Emerging issues in school bullying research and prevention. In E. T. Emmer & E. J. Sabornie (Eds.), *Handbook of classroom management* (2nd ed., pp. 76–93). New York, NY: Routledge/Taylor & Francis.

Evertson, C. M., & Emmer, E. T. (2017). *Classroom management for elementary teachers* (10th ed.). Boston, MA: Pearson.

Farrell, T. S. (2009). *Talking, listening and teaching: A guide to classroom communication*. Thousand Oaks, CA: Corwin Press.

Fay, J., & Funk, D. (1995). *Teaching with love and logic*. Golden, CO: The Love and Logic Press.

Fialka, J. M., Feldman, A. K., & Mikus, K. C. (2012). *Parents and professionals partnering for children with disabilities*. (Rev. ed.). Thousand Oaks, CA: Corwin Press.

Fisher, D., & Frey, N. (2010). *Enhancing RTI: How to ensure success with effective classroom instruction and intervention*. Alexandria, VA: Association for Supervision and Curriculum Development.

Fisher, D., Frey, N., & Savitz, R. S. (2020). *Teaching hope and resilience for students experiencing trauma: Creating safe and nurturing classrooms for learning*. New York, NY: Teachers College Press.

Foley, D. (2012). *Ultimate classroom management handbook* (2nd ed.). Indianapolis, IN: JIST Publishing.

Fredricks, J. A. (2014). *Eight myths of student disengagement: Creating classrooms of deep learning*. Thousand Oaks, CA: Corwin Press.

Friend, M. D., & Cook, L. (2017). *Interactions: Collaboration skills for school professionals* (8th ed.). Boston, MA: Pearson.

Gaitan, C. D. (2005). *Involving Latino families in schools: Raising student achievement through home–school partnerships*. Thousand Oaks, CA: Corwin Press.

Gaitan, C. D. (2006). *Building culturally responsive classrooms: A guide for K–6 teachers*. Thousand Oaks, CA: Corwin Press.

Gallavan, N. P. (2011a). *Navigating cultural competence in grades K-5*. Thousand Oaks, CA: Corwin Press.

Gallavan, N. P. (2011b). *Navigating cultural competence in grades 6-12*. Thousand Oaks, CA: Corwin Press.

Garcia-Reid, P., Reid, R. J., & Peterson, N. A. (2005). School engagement among Latino youth in an urban middle school context valuing the role of social support. *Education and Urban Society, 37*(3), 257–275.

Gay, G. (2005). Politics of multicultural teacher education. *Journal of Teacher Education, 56*(3), 221–228.

Gay, G. (2018). *Culturally responsive teaching: Theory, research, and practice* (3rd ed.). New York, NY: Teachers College Press.

Gillies, R. M. (2007). *Cooperative learning: Integrating theory into practice*. Thousand Oaks, CA: Sage.

Gillies, R. M. (2015). Small-group work: Developments in research. In E. T. Emmer & E. J. Sabornie (Eds.),

Handbook of classroom management (2nd ed., pp. 261–279). New York, NY: Routledge/Taylor & Francis.

Ginott, H. G. (1972). *Teacher and child.* New York, NY: Macmillan.

Ginott, H. G. (1988). *Between parent and teenager.* New York, NY: Avon Books.

Ginott, H. G. (2003). *Between parent and child* (revised and updated by A. Ginott & H. W. Goddard). New York, NY: Three Rivers Press.

Glaser, J. (2005). *Leading through collaboration: Guiding groups to productive solutions.* Thousand Oaks, CA: Corwin Press.

Glasser, W. (1965). *Reality therapy.* New York, NY: Harper & Row.

Glasser, W. (1969). *Schools without failure.* New York, NY: Harper & Row.

Glasser, W. (1985). *Control theory: A new explanation of how we control our lives.* New York, NY: Harper & Row.

Glasser, W. (1986). *Control theory in the classroom.* New York, NY: Harper & Row.

Glasser, W. (1998a). *The quality school: Managing students without coercion* (Rev. ed.). New York, NY: Harper Perennial.

Glasser, W. (1998b). *The quality school teacher* (Rev. ed.). New York, NY: Harper Perennial.

Glasser, W. (2000). *Every student can succeed.* Chatsworth, CA: Black Forest Press.

Glossary of Education Reform. (2016). *Student engagement.* Portland, ME: Author. Retrieved from http://edglossary.org/student-engageme

Gollnick, D. M., & Chinn, P. C. (2017). *Multicultural education in a pluralistic society* (10th ed.). Boston, MA: Pearson.

Gonzalez, N., Moll, L. C., & Amanti, C. (Eds.). (2005). *Funds of knowledge: Theorizing practices in households, communities, and classrooms.* New York, NY: Routledge.

Good, T. L., & Brophy, J. E. (2008). *Looking into classrooms* (10th ed.). Boston, MA: Pearson.

Gootman, M. E. (2008). *The caring teacher's guide to discipline: Helping young students learn self-control, responsibility, and respect* (3rd ed.). Thousand Oaks, CA: Corwin Press.

Gordon, T. (1991). *Discipline that works: Promoting self-discipline in children.* New York, NY: Plume (a division of Penguin).

Gordon, T. (2003). *Teacher effectiveness training.* New York, NY: Three Rivers Press.

Gorski, P. C. (2008). The myth of the "culture of poverty." *Educational Leadership, 65*(7), 32–36.

Gorski, P. C. (2018). *Reaching and teaching students in poverty: Strategies for erasing the opportunity gap* (2nd ed.). New York, NY: Teachers College Press.

Grant, K. B., & Ray, J. A. (2019). *Home, school, and community collaboration: Culturally responsive family engagement* (4th ed.). Thousand Oaks, CA: Sage Publications.

Gregory, G. H., & Kaufeldt, M. (2015). *The motivated brain: Improving student attention, engagement, and perseverance.* Alexandria, VA: Association for Supervision and Curriculum Development.

Gremmen, M. C., van den Berg, Y. H. M., Segers, E., & Cillessen, A. H. N. (2016). Considerations for classroom seating arrangements and the role of teacher characteristics and beliefs. *Social Psychology of Education, 19*(4), 749–774.

Gruman, D. H., Harachi, T. W., Abbott, R. D., Catalano, R. F., & Fleming, C. B. (2008). Longitudinal effects of student mobility on three dimensions of elementary school engagement. *Child Development, 79*(6), 1833–1852.

Guillaume, A. M. (2016). *K–12 classroom teaching: A primer for new professionals* (5th ed.). Boston, MA: Pearson.

Gurian, M., & Stevens, K. (2010). *Boys and girls learn differently: A guide for teachers and parents.* (Rev. ed.). San Francisco, CA: Jossey-Bass.

Gurian, M., & Stevens, K. (2007). *The minds of boys: Saving our sons from falling behind in school and life.* San Francisco, CA: Jossey-Bass.

Gurian, M., Stevens, K., & King, K. (2008). *Strategies for teaching boys and girls: Elementary level.* San Francisco, CA: Jossey-Bass.

Hall, T. E., Meyer, A., & Rose, D. H. (2012). *Universal design for learning: A guide for teachers and educational professionals.* Arlington, VA: Council for Exceptional Children.

Hammeken, P. A. (2008). *The paraprofessional's essential guide to inclusive education* (3rd ed.). Thousand Oaks, CA: Corwin Press.

Hanson, M. J., & Lynch, E. W. (2013). *Understanding families: Supportive approaches to diversity, disability, and risk* (2nd ed.). Baltimore, MD: Paul H. Brookes Publishing.

Hardin, C. J. (2012). *Effective classroom management: Models and strategies for today's classroom* (3rd ed.). Boston, MA: Pearson.

Hargis, C. H. (2006). *Teaching low achieving and disadvantaged students* (3rd ed.). Springfield, IL: Charles C Thomas Publishers.

Harlacher, J. E. (2015). *Designing effective classroom management*. Bloomington, IN: Marzano Research.

Hayward, J. (2016). Classrooms that put people first. *Educational Leadership, 74*(1), 70–74.

Heacox, D., & Cash, R. M. (2014). *Differentiation for gifted learners: Going beyond the basics*. Minneapolis, MN: Free Spirit Publishing.

Henley, M. (2003). *Teaching self-control: A curriculum for responsible behavior* (2nd ed.). Bloomington, IN: Solution Tree Press.

Higgs, C. (2014). *Connecting with students: Strategies for building rapport with urban learners*. Lanham, MD: Rowman & Littlefield.

Holloman, H., & Yates, P. H. (2010). *What do you say when. . .? Best practice language for improving student behavior*. Larchmont, NY: Eye on Education.

Holtham, J. (2009). *Taking restorative justice to schools: A doorway to discipline*. Allen, TX: Del Hayes Press.

Howard, G. R. (2016). *We can't teacher what we don't know: White teachers, multiracial schools* (3rd ed.). New York, NY: Teachers College Press.

Howard, M. (2009). *RTI from all sides: What every teacher needs to know*. Portsmouth, NH: Heinemann.

Howard, T. C. (2020). *Why race and culture matter in schools: Closing the achievement gap in America's classrooms* (2nd ed.). New York, NY: Teachers College Press.

Hunter, M. (1994). *Enhancing teaching*. New York, NY: Macmillan.

Hyman, I. A. (1997). *School discipline and school violence*. Boston, MA: Pearson.

Jackson, R. R., & Lambert, C. (2010). *How to support struggling students*. Alexandria, VA: Association for Supervision and Curriculum Development.

Jacobs, G. M., Power, M. P., & Inn, L. W. (2003). *The teacher's sourcebook for cooperative learning*. Thousand Oaks, CA: Corwin Press.

James, A. N. (2009). *Teaching the female brain: How girls learn math and science*. Thousand Oaks, CA: Corwin Press.

James, A. N. (2015). *Teaching the male brain: How boys, think, feel, and learn in school* (2nd ed.). Thousand Oaks, CA: Corwin Press.

Jennings, P. A. (2018). *The trauma-sensitive classroom: Building resilience with compassionate teaching*. New York, NY: W. W. Norton & Company.

Jensen, E. (2009). *Teaching with poverty in mind*. Alexandria, VA: Association for Supervision and Curriculum Development.

Jensen, E. (2013). *Engaging students with poverty in mind: Practical strategies for raising achievement*. Alexandria, VA: Association for Supervision and Curriculum Development.

Jenson, W. R., Rhode, G., & Reavis, H. K. (2020). *The tough kid tool box* (3rd ed.). Eugene, OR: Pacific Northwest Publishing.

Jimerson, S. R., Nickerson, A., Mayer, M. J., & Furlong, M. J. (2012). *Handbook of school violence and school safety* (2nd ed.). New York, NY: Routledge/Taylor & Francis.

Jimerson, S. R., Swearer, S. M., & Espelage, D. L. (Eds.). (2009). *Handbook of bullying in schools*. New York, NY: Routledge/Taylor & Francis.

Johnson, D. W., & Johnson, F. P. (2017). *Joining together: Group theory and group skills* (12th ed.). Boston, MA: Pearson.

Johnson, D. W., & Johnson, R. T. (2005). *Teaching students to be peacemakers* (4th ed.). Edina, MN: Interaction Book Company.

Johnson, D. W., Johnson, R. T., & Holubec, E. J. (2007). *The nuts and bolts of cooperative learning* (2nd ed.). Edina, MN: Interaction Book Company.

Johnson, D. W., Johnson, R. T., & Holubec, E. J. (2009). *Circles of learning: Cooperation in the classroom*. Edina, MN: Interaction Book Company.

Johnson, J. A., Musial, D., Hall, G. E., & Gollnick, D. M. (2018). *Foundations of American education* (17th ed.). Boston, MA: Pearson.

Jolliffe, W. (2007). *Cooperative learning in the classroom: Putting it into practice*. Thousand Oaks, CA: Sage Publications.

Jones, F. H. (1987). *Positive classroom discipline*. New York, NY: McGraw-Hill.

Jones, F. H. (2013). *Tools for teaching* (3rd ed.). Santa Cruz, CA: Frederic H. Jones & Associates.

Jones, T. G., & Fuller, M. L. (2003). *Teaching Hispanic children*. Boston, MA: Pearson.

Jones, V. F., & Jones, L. S. (2016). *Comprehensive classroom management: Creating communities of support and solving problems* (11th ed.). Boston, MA: Pearson.

Jonson, K. F. (2010). *The new elementary teacher's handbook: Flourishing in your first year* (3rd ed.). Thousand Oaks, CA: Corwin Press.

Kagan, S., Kyle, P., & Scott, S. (2004). *Win–win discipline*. San Clemente, CA: Kagan Publishing.

Kaiser, B., & Rasminsky, J. S. (2017). *Challenging behavior in young children: Understanding, preventing, and responding effectively* (4th ed.). Boston, MA: Pearson.

Kapalka, G. (2009). *8 steps to classroom management success: A guide for teachers of challenging students*. Thousand Oaks, CA: Corwin Press.

Kaplan, A., & Patrick, H. (2016). Learning environments and motivation. In K. R. Wentzel & D. B. Miele (Eds.), *Handbook of motivation at school* (2nd ed., pp. 251–274). New York, NY: Routledge/Taylor & Francis.

Kaufman, P., & Schipper, J. (2018). *Teaching with compassion; An educator's oath to teach from the heart*. Lanham, MD: Rowman & Littlefield.

Kelly, M. (2010). *The everything new teacher book* (2nd ed.). Avon, MA: Adams Media.

Kerr, M. M., & Nelson, C. M. (2010). *Strategies for addressing behavior problems in the classroom* (6th ed.). Boston, MA: Pearson.

Khalsa, S. S. (2007a). *Break the bully cycle: Intervention techniques and activities to create a respectful school community*. Tucson, AZ: Good Year Books.

Khalsa, S. S. (2007b). *Teaching discipline and self-respect*. Thousand Oaks, CA: Corwin Press.

Knapp, M. L., Hall, J. A., & Horgan, T. G. (2014). *Nonverbal communication in human interaction* (8th ed.). Boston, MA: Wadsworth, Cengage Learning.

Kochhar-Bryant, C. A., & Heishman, A. (2010). *Effective collaboration for educating the whole child*. Thousand Oaks, CA: Corwin Press.

Kohn, A. (1999). *Punished by rewards* (Rev. ed.). Boston, MA: Houghton Mifflin.

Kohn, A. (2006). *Beyond discipline: From compliance to community* (10th anniversary ed.). Alexandria, VA: Association for Supervision and Curriculum Development.

Korb, R. (2012). *Motivating defiant and disruptive students to learn: Positive classroom management strategies*. Thousand Oaks, CA: Corwin Press.

Kottler, E., Kottler, J. A., & Street, C. (2008). *English language learners in your classroom* (3rd ed.). Thousand Oaks, CA: Corwin Press.

Kottler, J. A., & Kottler, E. (2007). *Counseling skills for teachers* (2nd ed.). Thousand Oaks, CA: Corwin Press.

Kounin, J. S. (1970). *Discipline and group management in classrooms*. New York, NY: Holt, Rinehart & Winston.

Kronowitz, E. L. (2012). *The teacher's guide to success* (2nd ed.). Boston, MA: Pearson.

Ladson-Billings, G. (2009). *The dreamkeepers: Successful teachers of African American children* (2nd ed.). San Francisco, CA: Jossey-Bass.

Larrivee, B. (2009). *Authentic classroom management: Creating a learning community and building reflective practice* (3rd ed.). Boston, MA: Pearson.

Lassonde, C. A., & Israel, S. E. (2009). *Teacher collaboration for professional learning: Facilitating study, research, and inquiry communities*. San Francisco, CA: Jossey-Bass.

Leathers, D., & Eaves, M. H. (2008). *Successful nonverbal communication: Principles and applications* (4th ed.). Boston, MA: Pearson.

LeBlanc-Esparza, R., & LeBlanc-Esparza, K. (2013). *Strengthening the connection between school and home*. Bloomington, IN: Solution Tree.

Lee, J. S., & Bowen, N. K. (2006). Parent involvement, cultural capital, and the achievement gap among elementary school children. *American Educational Research Journal, 43*, 193–218.

Levin, J., & Nolan, J. F. (2014). *Principles of classroom management* (7th ed.). Boston, MA: Pearson.

Lopez, I. (2017). *Keeping it real and relevant: Building authentic relationships in your diverse classroom*. Alexandria, VA: Association for Supervision and Curriculum Development.

Love, A., & Roderick, J. (1971). Teacher non-verbal communication: The development and field testing of an awareness unit. *Theory into Practice, 10*, 295–299.

Lundy, K. G., & Swartz, L. (2011). *Creating caring classrooms: How to encourage students to communicate, create, and be compassionate of others.* Markham, Ontario, Canada: Pembroke Publishers. (Distributed in the U.S. by Stenhouse Publishers)

Lynch, E. W., & Hanson, M. J. (Eds.). (2011). *Developing cross-cultural competence: A guide for working with children and their families* (4th ed.). Baltimore, MD: Paul H. Brookes Publishing.

MacKenzie, R. J., & Stanzione, L. E. (2010). *Setting limits in the classroom: A complete guide to effective classroom management with a school-wide discipline plan* (3rd ed.). New York, NY: Three Rivers Press.

Manning, M. L., & Bucher, K. T. (2013). *Classroom management: Models, applications, and cases* (3rd ed.). Boston, MA: Pearson.

Marlowe, M. J., & Hayden, T. (2013). *Teaching children who are hard to reach: Relationship-driven classroom practice.* Thousand Oaks, CA: Corwin Press.

Marshall, M. L. (2012). *Discipline without stress, punishments, or rewards: How teachers and parents promote responsibility and learning* (Rev. 2). Los Alamitos, CA: Piper Press.

Martin, J. (2019). *Strategic classroom design: Creating an environment for flexible learning.* Portsmouth, NH: Heinemann.

Marzano, R. J. (2017). *The new art and science of teaching.* Bloomington, IN: Solution Tree Press. A joint publication with the Association for Supervision and Curriculum Development.

Marzano, R. J., Gaddy, B. B., Foseid, M. C., Foseid, M. P., & Marzano, J. S. (2009). *A handbook for classroom management that works.* Boston, MA: Pearson.

Marzano, R. J., Marzano, J. S., & Pickering, D. J. (2003). *Classroom management that works: Research-based strategies for every teacher.* Alexandria, VA: Association for Supervision and Curriculum Development.

Mastropieri, M. A., & Scruggs, T. E. (2018). *The inclusive classroom: Strategies for effective differentiated instruction* (6th ed.). Boston, MA: Pearson.

Mazur, A. J., & Doran, P. R. (2010). *Teaching diverse learners: Principles for best practice.* Thousand Oaks, CA: Corwin Press.

McEwan-Adkins, E. K. (2019). *How to deal with parents who are angry, troubled, afraid, or just seem crazy.* Thousand Oaks, CA: Corwin Press.

McKinley, J. (2010). *Raising black students' achievement through culturally responsive teaching.* Alexandria, VA: Association for Supervision and Curriculum Development.

Mendler, A. N., & Curwin, R. L. (2007). *Discipline with dignity for challenging youth* (Rev. ed.). Bloomington, IN: Solution Tree Press.

Mendler, A. N., & Mendler, B. D. (2017). *Turning tough parents into strong partners.* Rochester, NY: Teacher Learning Center.

Mertler, C. A. (2020). *Action research: Improving schools and empowering educators* (6th ed.). Thousand Oaks, CA: Sage.

Meyer, L. H., & Evans, I. M. (2012). *The teacher's guide to restorative classroom discipline.* Thousand Oaks, CA: Corwin Press.

Middleton, M., & Perks, K. (2014). *Motivation to learn: Transforming classroom culture to support student achievement.* Thousand Oaks, CA: Corwin Press.

Miller, M. D., Linn, R. L., & Gronlund, N. E. (2013). *Measurement and assessment in teaching* (11th ed.). Boston, MA: Pearson.

Miller, P. W. (2005). *Body language: An illustrated introduction for teachers.* Munster, IN: Patrick W. Miller & Associates.

Milner, H. R., IV (2015). Research on classroom management in urban schools. In E. T. Emmer & E. J. Sabornie (Eds.), *Handbook of classroom management* (2nd ed., pp. 167–185). New York, NY: Routledge/Taylor & Francis.

Miltenberger, R. G. (2016). *Behavior modification* (6th ed.). Belmont, CA: Wadsworth, Cengage Learning.

Minahan, J., & Baker, D. (2015). The skill-building lens: Helping students with behavioral challenges. *Educational Leadership, 73*(2), 68–72.

Montuoro, P., & Lewis, R. (2015). Student perceptions of misbehavior and classroom management. In E. T. Emmer & E. J. Sabornie (Eds.), *Handbook of classroom management* (2nd ed., pp. 344–362). New York, NY: Routledge/Taylor & Francis.

Mooney, C. G. (2005). *Use your words: How teacher talk helps children learn.* St. Paul, MN: Redleaf Press.

Moral, A., Wylie, K., & Abdus-Salaam, R. (2019). *Seeing the good in students: A guide to classroom discipline in middle school.* Turners Falls, MA: Northeast Foundation for Children.

Moran, C., Stobbe, J., Baron, W., Miller, J., & Moir, E. (2009). *Keys to the elementary classroom: A new teacher's guide to the first month of school* (3rd ed.). Thousand Oaks, CA: Corwin Press.

Morgan, D. P., Young, K. R., West, R. P., & Smith, D. J. (2012). *Teaching self-management strategies to adolescents* (2nd ed.). Frederick, CO: Cambium Learning Group/Sopris.

Muhammad, A. (2015). *Overcoming the achievement gap trap*. Bloomington, IN: Solution Tree.

Murawski, W. W., & Spencer, S. (2011). *Collaborate, communicate, and differentiate! How to increase student learning in today's diverse schools*. Thousand Oaks, CA: Corwin Press.

Murphy, A., & Van Brunt, B. (2018). Addressing dangerous behavior in the classroom. *Educational Leadership, 76*(1), 66–70.

National Center for Education Statistics (NCES). (2017a). *Digest of education statistics: 2017.* Table 204.30, Children 3 to 21 years old served under IDEA. Washington, DC: Author. Retrieved from https://nces.ed.gov/programs/digest/d17/tables/dt17_204.30.asp

National Center for Education Statistics (NCES). (2017b). *Digest of education statistics: 2017.* Table 204.90, Percentage of public school students enrolled in gifted and talented programs. Washington, DC: Author. Retrieved from https://nces.ed.gov/programs/digest/d17/tables/dt17_204.90.asp

National Center for Education Statistics (NCES). (2018). *Indicators of school crime and safety: 2018.* Washington, DC: Author. Retrieved from https://nces.ed.gov/programs/crimeindicators/index.asp

National Center for Education Statistics (NCES). (2019a). *Status and trends in the education of racial and ethnic groups in public schools*. Washington, DC: Author. Retrieved from https://nces.ed.gov/programs/raceindicators/indicator_rbb.asp

National Center for Education Statistics (NCES). (2019b). *Student reports of bullying: Results from the 2017 school crime supplement to the national crime victimization survey*. Washington, DC: Author. Retrieved from https://nces.ed.gov/pubs2019/2019054.pdf

National Center on Universal Design for Learning. (2011). *Universal design for learning guidelines version 2.0.* Retrieved from http://www.udlcenter.org/aboutudl/udlguidelines.

National Institute of Mental Health. (2017). *Attention deficit hyperactivity disorder*. Washington, DC: Author. Retrieved from https://www.nimh.nih.gov/health/statistics/attention-deficit-hyperactivity-disorder-adhd.shtml

Nelsen, J. (2006). *Positive discipline* (Rev. ed.). New York, NY: Ballantine Books.

Nelsen, J., Lott, L., & Glenn, H. S. (2013). *Positive discipline in the classroom: Developing mutual respect, cooperation, and responsibility in your classroom* (Rev. 4). New York, NY: Three Rivers Press/Crown Publishing Group.

Nelsen, J., & Gfroerer, K. (2017). *Positive discipline tools for teachers: Effective classroom management for social, emotional, and academic success*. New York, NY: Harmony Books.

Nevin, A. I., Villa, R. A., & Thousand, J. S. (2008). *A guide to co-teaching with paraeducators: Practical tips for K–12 educators*. Thousand Oaks, CA: Corwin Press.

Nieto, S. (2013). *Finding joy in teaching students of diverse backgrounds: Culturally responsive and socially just practices in U.S. classrooms*. Portsmouth, NH: Heinemann.

Nieto, S., & Bode, P. (2018). *Affirming diversity: The sociopolitical context of multicultural education* (7th ed.). Boston, MA: Pearson.

Nuri-Robins, K., Lindsey, D. B., Lindsey, R. B., & Terrell, R. D. (2011). *Culturally proficient instruction: A guide for people who teach* (3rd ed.). Thousand Oaks, CA: Corwin Press.

Oakes, J. (2005). *Keeping track: How schools structure inequality* (2nd ed.). New Haven, CT: Yale University Press.

Office of English Language Acquisition (OELA). (2018a). *Languages spoken by English learners*. Washington, DC: Author. Retrieved from https://www.ncela.ed.gov/files/fast_facts/FastFacts-Languages-Spoken-by-ELs-2018.pdf

Office of English Language Acquisition (OELA). (2018b). *Profiles of English learners*. Washington, DC: Author. https://www.ncela.ed.gov/files/fast_facts/Profiles_of_ELs_4.12.18_MM_Final_Edit.pdf

Olender, R. A., Elias, J., & Mastroleo, R. D. (2010). *The school-home connection: Forging positive relationships with parents*. Thousand Oaks, CA: Corwin Press.

Olsen, G. W., & Fuller, M. L. (2012). *Home and school relations: Teachers and parents working together* (4th ed.). Boston, MA: Pearson.

Ormrod, J. E., Anderman, E. M., & Anderman, L. H. (2020). *Educational psychology: Developing learners* (10th ed.). Boston, MA: Pearson.

Otten, K. L., & Tuttle, J. L. (2011). *How to reach and teach children with challenging behavior*. San Francisco, CA: Jossey-Bass.

Parrett, W. H., & Budge, K. M. (2012). *Turning high-poverty schools into high-performing schools*. Alexandria, VA: Association for Supervision and Curriculum Development.

Payne, R. K. (2005). *A framework for understanding poverty* (Rev. ed.). Highlands, TX: aha! Process, Inc.

Payne, R. K. (2008). Nine powerful practices. *Educational Leadership, 65*(7), 48–52.

Platt, R. (2019). What's love got to do with it? *Educational Leadership, 77*(2), 42–46.

Pollock, J. E., Ford, S. M., & Black, M. M. (2012). *Minding the achievement gap one classroom at a time*. Alexandria, VA: Association for Supervision and Curriculum Development.

Polloway, E. A., Patton, J. R., Serna, L., & Bailey, J. W. (2018). *Strategies for teaching students with special needs* (11th ed.). Boston, MA: Pearson.

Porton, H. D. (2013). *Helping struggling learners succeed in school*. Boston, MA: Pearson.

Powell, R. G., & Powell, D. L. (2015). *Classroom communication and diversity: Enhancing instructional practice* (3rd ed.). New York, NY: Routledge/Taylor & Francis.

Powell, S. D. (2010). *Wayside teaching: Connecting with students to support learning*. Thousand Oaks, CA: Corwin Press.

Protheroe, N., Shellard, E., & Turner, J. (2004). *Helping struggling learners in the elementary and middle grades*. Bethesda, MD: Educational Research Service.

Purkey, W. W., & Novak, J. M. (1996). *Inviting school success: A self-concept approach to teaching, learning, and democratic practice* (3rd ed.). Belmont, CA: Wadsworth.

Purkey, W. W., Novak, J. M., & Schoenlein, A. T. (2016). *Fundamentals of invitational education* (2nd ed.). Nicholasville, KY: International Alliance for Invitational Education.

Quate, S., & McDermott, J. (2009). *Clock watchers: Six steps to motivating and engaging disengaged students across content areas*. Portsmouth, NH: Heinemann.

Raczynski, K. A., & Horne, A. M. (2015). Communication and interpersonal skills in classroom management. In E. T. Emmer & E. J. Sabornie (Eds.), *Handbook of classroom management* (2nd ed., pp. 387–408). New York, NY: Routledge/Taylor & Francis.

Rajagopal, K. (2011). *Create success! Unlocking the potential of urban students*. Alexandria, VA: Association for Supervision and Curriculum Development.

Reeve, J. (2015). Rewards. In E. T. Emmer & E. J. Sabornie (Eds.), *Handbook of classroom management* (2nd ed., pp. 496–515). New York, NY: Routledge/Taylor & Francis.

Responsive Classroom. (2015). *First six weeks of school* (2nd ed.). Turners Falls, MA: Center for Responsive Schools.

Responsive Classroom. (2018a). *Building an academic community: The middle school teacher's guide to the first four weeks of the school year*. Turners Falls, MA: Center for Responsive Schools.

Responsive Classroom. (2018b). *Teaching self-discipline: The Responsive Classroom guide to helping students dream, behave, and achieve in elementary school*. Turners Falls, MA: Center for Responsive Schools.

Responsive Classroom. (2019). *Seeing the good in students: A guide to classroom discipline in middle school*. Turners Falls, MA: Center for Responsive Schools.

Rhode, G., Jenson, W. R., & Reavis, H. K. (2020). *The tough kid book: Practical classroom management strategies* (3rd ed.). Eugene, OR: Pacific Northwest Publishing.

Richmond, V. P., McCroskey, J. C., & Hickson, M. L. (2012). *Nonverbal behavior in interpersonal relations* (7th ed.). Boston, MA: Pearson.

Roberts, W. B. (2006). *Bullying from both sides*. Thousand Oaks, CA: Corwin Press.

Roberts, W. B. (2008). *Working with parents of bullies and victims*. Thousand Oaks, CA: Corwin Press.

Roberts, W. B. (2016). *Working with kids who bully: New perspectives on prevention and intervention*. Thousand Oaks, CA: Corwin Press.

Rong, S. L., & Preissle, J. (2009). *Educating immigrant students in the 21st century: What educators need to know* (2nd ed.). Thousand Oaks, CA: Corwin Press.

Rothstein-Fisch, C., & Trumbull, E. (2008). *Managing diverse classrooms: How to build on students' cultural strengths*. Alexandria, VA: Association for Supervision and Curriculum Development.

Rumberger, R. W. (2011). *Dropping out: Why students drop out of school and what can be done about it*. Cambridge, MA: Harvard University Press.

Sadker, D. M., & Silber, E. S. (Eds.). (2007). *Gender in the classroom: Foundations, skills, methods, and strategies across the curriculum.* New York, NY: Routledge/Taylor & Francis.

Salend, S. J. (2016). *Creating inclusive classrooms: Effective, differentiated, and reflective practices* (8th ed.). Boston, MA: Pearson.

Salend, S. J., & Whittaker, C. R. (2017). UDL: A blueprint for learning success. *Educational Leadership, 74*(7), 59–63.

Santana, L., Rothstein, K., & Bain, A. (2016). *Partnering with parents to ask the right questions.* Alexandria, VA: Association for Supervision and Curriculum Development.

Sapon-Shevin, M. (2007). *Widening the circle: The power of inclusive classrooms.* Boston, MA: Beacon Press.

Sapon-Shevin, M. (2010). *Because we can change the world: A practical guide to building cooperative, inclusive classroom communities* (2nd ed.). Thousand Oaks, CA: Corwin Press.

Schell, L. M., & Burden, P. R. (2006). *Countdown to the first day of school* (3rd ed.). Washington, DC: National Education Association.

Schunk, D. H., Meece, J. R., & Pintrich, P. R. (2014). *Motivation in education: Theory, research, and applications* (4th ed.). Boston, MA: Pearson.

Schwab, Y., & Elias, M. J. (2015). From compliance to responsibility: Social and emotional learning and classroom management. In E. T. Emmer & E. J. Sabornie (Eds.), *Handbook of classroom management* (2nd ed., pp. 94–115). New York, NY: Routledge/Taylor & Francis.

Scott, M. (2017). *Even on your worst day, you can be a student's best hope.* Alexandria, VA: Association for Supervision and Curriculum Development.

Scully, P., Stites, M. L., Roberts-King, H., & Barbour, C. H. (2019). *Families, schools, and communities: Building partnerships for educating children* (7th ed.). Boston, MA: Pearson.

Shae, T. M., & Bauer, A. (2012). *Behavior management: A practical approach for educators* (10th ed.). Boston, MA: Pearson.

Shostak, R. (2014). Involving students in learning. In J. M. Cooper (Ed.), *Classroom teaching skills* (10th ed., pp. 77–99). Belmont, CA: Wadsworth, Cengage Learning.

Simonds, C. J., & Cooper, P. J. (2011). *Communication for the classroom teacher* (9th ed.). Boston, MA: Pearson.

Skiba, R. J., & Rausch, M. K. (2015). Reconsidering exclusionary discipline: The efficacy and equity of out-of-school suspension and expulsion. In E. T. Emmer & E. J. Sabornie (Eds.), *Handbook of classroom management* (2nd ed., pp. 116–138). New York, NY: Routledge/Taylor & Francis.

Skinner, B. F. (1971). *Beyond freedom and dignity.* New York, NY: Knopf.

Slavin, R. E. (2018). *Educational psychology: Theory and practice* (12th ed.). Boston, MA: Pearson.

Smith, D., Fisher, D., & Frey, N. (2015). *Better than carrots or sticks: Restorative practices for positive classroom management.* Alexandria, VA: Association for Supervision and Curriculum Development.

Smutny, J. F., & von Fremd, S. (2011). *Teaching advanced learners in the general education classroom.* Thousand Oaks, CA: Corwin Press.

Snow, D. R. (2005). *Classroom strategies for helping at-risk students.* Alexandria, VA: Association for Supervision and Curriculum Development.

Souers, K. V. (with Hall, P.). (2019). *Relationship, responsibility, and regulation: Trauma-invested practices for fostering resilient learners.* Alexandria, VA: Association for Supervision and Curriculum Development.

Sprick, R. S. (2013). *Discipline in the secondary classroom: A positive approach to behavior management* (3rd ed.). San Francisco, CA: Jossey-Bass.

Stairs, A. J., Donnell, K. A., & Dunn, A. H. (2012). *Urban teaching in America: Theory, research, and practice in K-12 classrooms.* Thousand Oaks, CA: Sage.

Sullo, B. (2009). *The motivated student: Unlocking the enthusiasm for learning.* Alexandria, VA: Association for Supervision and Curriculum Development.

Swearer, S. M., Espelage, D. L., & Napolitano, S. A. (2009). *Bullying prevention and intervention: Realistic strategies for schools.* New York, NY: Guilford Press.

Thompson, G. L. (2007a). *Through ebony eyes: What teachers need to know but are afraid to ask about African American students.* San Francisco, CA: Jossey-Bass.

Thompson, G. L. (2007b). *Up where we belong: Helping African American and Latino students rise in school and life.* San Francisco, CA: Jossey-Bass.

Thompson, G. L., & Thompson, R. (2014). *Yes, you can! Advice for teachers who want a great start and a great finish with their students of color.* Thousand Oaks, CA: Corwin Press.

Thompson, J. G. (2011). *Discipline survival guide for the secondary teacher* (2nd ed.). San Francisco, CA: Jossey-Bass.

Thompson, J. G. (2018). *The first-year teacher's survival guide* (4th ed.). San Francisco, CA: Jossey-Bass.

Tileston, D. W., & Darling, S. K. (2008). *Why culture counts: Teaching children of poverty.* Bloomington, IN: Solution Tree Press.

Tomlinson, C. A. (2016). *The differentiated classroom: Responding to the needs of all learners* (2nd ed.). Boston, MA: Pearson.

Tomlinson, C. A. (2017). *How to differentiate instruction in academically diverse classrooms* (3rd ed.). Alexandria, VA: Association for Supervision and Curriculum Development.

Tucker, C. R. (2016). Don't waste the first week. *Educational Leadership, 74*(1), 87–88.

Turnbull, A. A., Turnbull, H. R., Erwin, E. J., Soodak, L. C., & Shogren, K. A. (2015). *Families, professionals, and exceptionality* (7th ed.). Boston, MA: Pearson.

Turnbull, A. A., Turnbull, H. R., Wehmeyer, M. L., & Shogren, K. A. (2020). *Exceptional lives: Practice, progress, and dignity in today's schools* (9th ed.). Boston, MA: Pearson.

U.S. Department of Education. (2015). *Performance on NAEP reading tests by grade and family income* (from NAEP Data Explorer). Washington, DC: Author.

U.S. Department of Education. (2019). *Stop bullying.* Retrieved from www.stopbullying.gov.

Udvari-Solner, A., & Kluth, P. (2018). *Joyful learning: Active and collaborative learning in inclusive classrooms* (2nd ed.). Thousand Oaks, CA: Corwin Press.

Vaughn, S. R., Bos, C. S., & Schumm, J. S. (2018). *Teaching students who are exceptional, diverse, and at-risk in the general education classroom* (7th ed.). Boston, MA: Pearson.

Venables, D. R. (2011). *The practice of authentic PLCs: A guide to effective teacher teams.* Thousand Oaks, CA: Corwin Press.

Villa, R. A., Thousand, J. S., & Nevin, A. I. (2010). *Collaborating with students in instruction and decision making.* Thousand Oaks, CA: Corwin Press.

Villa, R. A., Thousand, J. S., & Nevin, A. I. (2013). *A guide to co-teaching: New lessons and strategies to facilitating student learning* (3rd ed.). Thousand Oaks, CA: Corwin Press.

Walker, J. M. T., & Hoover-Dempsey, K. V. (2015). Parental engagement and classroom management. In E. T. Emmer & E. J. Sabornie (Eds.), *Handbook of classroom management* (2nd ed., pp. 459–478). New York, NY: Routledge/Taylor & Francis.

Weinstein, C. S., & Novodvorsky, I. (2015). *Middle and secondary classroom management: Lessons from research and practice* (5th ed.). New York, NY: McGraw-Hill.

Weinstein, C. S., & Romano, M. E. (2019). *Elementary classroom management: Lessons from research and practice* (7th ed.). New York, NY: McGraw-Hill.

Weinstein, R. S. (2002). *Reaching higher: The power of expectations in schooling.* Cambridge, MA: Harvard University Press.

Wentzel, K. R. (2016). Teacher-student relationships. In K. R. Wentzel & D. B. Miele (Eds.), *Handbook of motivation at school* (2nd ed., pp. 182–201). New York, NY: Routledge/Taylor & Francis.

Wentzel, K. R., & Brophy, J. E. (2014). *Motivating students to learn* (4th ed.). New York, NY: Routledge/Taylor & Francis.

Wentzel, K. R., & Miele, D. B. (Eds.). (2016). *Handbook of motivation at school* (2nd ed.). New York, NY: Routledge/Taylor & Francis.

Whitten, E., Esteves, K. J., & Woodrow, A. (2019). *RTI success: Proven tools and strategies for schools and classrooms* (revised and expanded ed.). Minneapolis, MN: Free Spirit Publishing.

Willard, N. (2006). *Cyberbullying and cyberthreats: Responding to the challenge of online social cruelty, threats, and distress.* Eugene, OR: Center for Safe and Responsible Internet Use.

Wilson, M. B. (2013). *Teasing, tattling, defiance and more: Positive approaches to 10 common classroom behaviors.* Turners Falls, MA: Northeast Foundation for Children.

Winebrenner, S., & Brulles, D. (2014). *Teaching gifted kids in today's classroom: Strategies and techniques every teacher can use.* Minneapolis, MN: Free Spirit Publishing.

Winslade, J., & Williams, M. (2011). *Safe and peaceful schools: Addressing conflict and eliminating violence.* Thousand Oaks, CA: Corwin Press.

Wolfgang, C. H. (2009). *Solving discipline and classroom management problems* (7th ed.). Hoboken, NJ: Wiley.

Wong, H. K., & Wong, R. T. (2018a). *The first days of school: How to be an effective teacher* (5th ed.). Mountain View, CA: Harry Wong Publications.

Wong, H. K., & Wong, R. T. (2018b). *The classroom management book* (2nd ed.). Mountain View, CA: Harry Wong Publications.

Wormeli, R. (2016). What to do in week one? *Educational Leadership*, *74*(1), 10–15.

Wray, S. (2017). Shaping effective learning through student engagement. In D. Schwarzer & J. Grinberg (Eds.), *Successful teaching: What every novice teacher needs to know* (pp. 127–141). Lanham, MD: Rowman & Littlefield.

Wubbels, T., Brekelmans, M., Den Brok, P., Wijsman, L., Mainhard, T., & Van Tartwijk, J. (2015). Teacher-student relationships and classroom management. In E. T. Emmer & E. J. Sabornie (Eds.), *Handbook of classroom management* (2nd ed., pp. 363–386). New York, NY: Routledge/Taylor & Francis.

Yazzie-Mintz, E. (2007). *Voices of students on engagement: A report on the 2006 high school survey of student engagement*. Bloomington, IN: Center for Evaluation and Educational Policy, Indiana University.

Zacarian, D., Alvarez-Ortiz, L., & Haynes, J. (2017). *Teaching to strengths: Supporting students living with trauma, violence, and chronic stress*. Alexandria, VA: Association for Supervision and Curriculum Development.

Name Index

Subject Index